Glass Cutters

With a Brief History of Flat Glass

By Charles Norton Williams

"Glass Cutters with a Brief History of Flat Glass," by Charles Norton Williams. ISBN 978-1-62137-052-9.

Published 2012 by Virtualbookworm.com Publishing Inc., P.O. Box 9949, College Station, TX 77842, US.

Manufactured in the United States of America.

Glass Cutters

With a Brief History of Flat Glass

By Charles Norton Williams

Table of Contents

About the Author

The author, now retired, was born and raised in central New York, and attended colleges in Michigan, New York and Illinois. He received a BS in liberal arts and a MS in ceramic engineering and is a US Army veteran. He has worked for the National Bureau of Standards, Boeing, Dow Chemical, and Howmet in the area of ceramic engineering. For seventeen years he was owner and operator of The Topical Review Book Company, formerly located in Auburn, NY. He is a past president of the Skaneateles Rotary Club, a charter member of the Skaneateles Antiques Club, and served as chair of the Skaneateles Historic Landmarks Preservation Commission for 25 years. He served six years on the board of directors of Westminster Manor, Auburn, NY, a home for the well elderly, and served six years on the board of directors of the Skaneateles Lake Transportation Project (a volunteer transport for senior citizens). He is a member of the Mid-West Tool Collectors Association, CRAFTS of New Jersey and Early American Industries Assoc., Inc. In 2002, he co-authored two history books with his son Paul through Arcadia Publishing titled "Owasco Lake" and "Skaneateles Lake."

Acknowledgements

This book has been many years being in progress and during those years many tool dealers and others have assisted me in my quest for glass cutters. Ones I would like to mention are Bill Curtis, Martin Donnelly, Gus Elzinga and George Lee. The staff personnel at the following libraries were most helpful: Alfred University(NYS College of Ceramics), Corning Glass, Francis DuPont Winterthur Museum, George Eastman House Museum, and the Seymour Library, Auburn, N.Y.

I would like to dedicate this book to my very patient son Paul who converted much of my handwritten and typed notes into a printable version and to my wife Nancy who tolerated my obsession for well over thirty years.

Preface

As one interested in antiques in general for years, coupled with an education as a ceramic engineer, collecting glass cutters might seem a natural. It was after I discovered four early cast iron combination tools in the bottom of a "dollar box" at auction that I thought that here is a tool that is easy to find, probably not too many varieties, is small and inexpensive. Well not exactly as we shall see.

At that time I found very little information readily available about glass cutters. Warman's of that time had a one line entry: "Glass cutter $1-6," with no picture. Antique dealers usually drew a blank when I asked about glass cutters or if they did know of them, their response was: "glass cutters eh?" Many dealers now know their value.

Some people yet say "seen one, you've seen them all," just like buttons, thimbles, stick pins, etc., but not so any more.

The collecting has gone on for over 35 years now with somewhere between 20 and 50 added each year. I have been pleasantly surprised by the variety that has appeared over the years. I have gotten these as gifts, at garage sales, flea markets, antique shows, dealers looking out for me, general auctions, but most recently through eBay auctions. With the advent of the eBay auctions the ones I "need" have shown up at the rate of 60 or so a year and I don't win all I want. Naturally the price is higher on average as well, but the "needle in the haystack" is easier to find.

Usually at a large antique show such as the August Madison-Bouckville in upstate New York where there are over 2000 dealers in the area, I will see maybe a dozen glass cutters and buy but six that are different for the collection.

I began the consideration of a book a number of years ago when the collection topped 500 different glass cutters and there were no reference books. Now that the number exceeds 1400, the time seems appropriate.

Scanning catalogs and communicating with other collectors one is led to believe that there are probably over 3,000 additional different ones "out there." This book is the culmination of over thirty-five years of collecting over 1,400 different glass cutters, about 500 US Patents, and other associated items. These 1,400 plus different glass cutters are representative of a number of different areas of tool collectors such as: bottle opener, combination tool, corkscrew, jackknife, kitchen novelty, knife and scissor sharpeners, pocket tool, and specific material such as brass, diamond, bone, or ivory. Through the years I've withstood the hassle from some that thought I, as a ceramic engineer, should have been collecting Carder – Steuben – Tiffany or exquisite pottery or the like.

What's a little common glass cutter tool got? Well it got me, and so in my defense let me quote from an article in a 1996 issue of *Forbes* magazine entitled "When Collections Become Obsessions:"

"Freud collected 2000 ancient Egyptian, Greek, and Roman statuettes and never thought it excessive. French furrier Pierre Bardinon once owned 50 Farraris: "Why not if you can afford it?" Leon Dixon's bike collection numbers about 1,000: "Now they say I'm a genius with vision." And Alastair Martin puts it: "No person can collect without a certain unsoundness of mind. Collectors are on the eccentric side." Doris Athineos; "If there weren't obsessive collectors, what would our museums be like?"[1]

And F. Neil Johnson writes, "Remarkably little has been written about the psychological basis of collecting, and the reason may be that given the great diversity of styles of collecting and things collected it is extraordinarily difficult to frame a single, comprehensive definition of what it is to be a collector and to engage in collecting activity. Nevertheless, many of those who possess collections must, at some time or another, have wondered about the forces which impel them to search out, acquire and keep new items, and about the often disturbingly strong emotions which are involved with the collecting urge...and of others whose collections have dominated the thoughts of their waking hours to the extent which has driven away all their friends and destroyed the foundations of family and social life."[2]

The internet provides one with an occasional insight about current glass cutter events. As a result of the increased airline security inspections after the terrorist attacks on September 11, 2001, confiscation of certain items attempted to be brought onboard aircraft was initiated. In December, 2004, a group of eight different glass cutters confiscated by airline security were being sold on the popular internet auction site eBay.[3] I bought those cutters. On April 16, 2003, a picture of Dr. Johnny George, General Director of Research Studies at the Iraq Museum in Baghdad is shown holding three diamond point glass cutters that were found on the museum floor following the massive looting of the museum.[4] As one can understand, letters to the Baghdad Museum inquiring about those glass cutters have not been answered.

And finally, however you look at collecting, it does a lot of different things for a lot of different people, be they buyers, sellers, researchers, or viewers. So with the above thoughts in mind and of the many other "collectors of whatever" enjoy this book and may you have good fortune in your personal quest for your "needle-in-the-haystack."

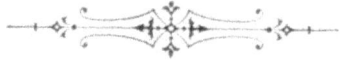

---

[1] Doris Athineos, "When Collections Become Obsessions," *Forbes*, December 16, 1996, pg. 406.
[2] F. Neil Johnson, "The Psychology of Collecting," *Christies*, December 1985-January 1986, pg. 4.
[3] The eight glass cutters were part of a one-ton lot of metal items being sold through Boulder City, Nevada.
[4] Matthew Schofield and Nancy A. Youssef, "Museum Looting Likely Well Executed Theft, Officials Say," Knight Ridder Newspapers, April 16, 2003.

List of Figures

List of Tables

Chapter One

A Brief History of Flat Glass and Manufacturing Methods

Ancient Egyptians and Assyrians produced glass items well before the advent of the Christian Era. However, this was ornamental in nature and always colored glass, with no "white," or transparent glass as we know it today. Glass blowers in front of a three foot high furnace are depicted in the tombs of Memphis and Beni Hassan (Egypt).[5]

The first Latin author to make reference to vitric art is Cicero(106-43 BC).[6] Some historians contend that Roman glass making began at least four centuries before Cicero. Under the Caesars the Romans spread glass making into Asia, Germany, France, and England. Window glass fragments were found in 1926 in Roman ruin excavations in England that dated from the period 75-130 AD.[7] No intact panes were recovered, and it is most likely that this glass was made by the casting process.[8] Many fragments of window glass have been in the ruins of a ninth-century monastery in Malise, Italy.[9]

The Fall of the Roman Empire put an end to the glass industry until the Middle Ages, in the 12th and 13th centuries, during which time small pieces of colored glass were incorporated as what we call "stained glass windows" in the Medieval churches.[10] It was expensive and probably identified with the church, thus not to be used in homes. A history of the medieval glazier has been summarized by Meridith P. Lillich.[11]

Popularity of transparent flat glass for domestic use began in the sixteenth century for several reasons.[12] The large stained and painted windows in cathedrals were in many instances considered expensive and heretical what with the Protestant Reformation. Merchants and artisans could now afford such luxuries.[13]

The Anglo-Saxon source of our word "window" was originally "winds eye." It let in the light, wind, cold and rain too. The word "pane" comes from the Latin word "pannus," which means cloth or rag. Actual usage through the years indicates use of oiled skins, horn,

---

[5] Editor, <u>Glass: History Manufacture And Its Universal Application</u>, Pittsburgh Plate Glass Co, 1923, p. 7.
[6] Ibid.
[7] George C. Boon, *Roman Window Glass From Wales*, Journal of Glass Studies, vol. 8, 1966, p. 41.
[8] Sarah Brown and David O'Connor, <u>Medieval Craftsman: Glass-Painters</u>, British Museum Press, 1991, p. 7.
[9] Francesca Dell'Acqua, "Ninth Century Window Glass From The Monastery of SanVincenzo al Volturno," *Journal of Glass Studies,* Vol. 39, 1997, pp. 33-49.
[10] Editor, <u>Glass: History Manufacture And Its Universal Application</u>, Pittsburgh Plate Glass Co., 1923, p. 9.
[11] Meridith P. Lillich, "Gothic Glaziers: Monks, Jews, Taxpayers, Bretons, Women," *Journal of Glass Studies*, Vol. 27, 1985, pp. 72-92
[12] Editor, Glass: History Manufacture And Its Universal Application.
[13] Brown and O'Connor, Medieval Craftsman: Glass-Painters. British Museum Press, 1991, pp. 68-69.

mica, alabaster, and shell. Of course house windows came first and if the house was sold, the seller took the glazed windows with him, or was listed in his will since they were such a valuable commodity. By the end of the 16th century the Italians were using glass windows in their carriages. The glazing of lanterns for ships was a special skill using the boudins (the bulls eye pontil area).[14] Window glass was considered a luxury in both England and America in the 1700s and as such it was taxed. [15]

The early 1600's saw a switch of furnace fuel from wood to coal in England. This made a change in furnace design a necessity as did the switch to natural gas in the late 1800s and early 1900s. This latter switch resulted in both improved product and economics of glassmaking.[16] Electric furnaces have been used for a number of years now which assists in reduction of pollution from stack gasses, and more recently oxygen enriched air or total replacement for combustion nearly eliminates the polluting nitrogen compounds.

Glass making in America began unsuccessfully in Jamestown in 1608-09 and was retried in 1621-24. Both of these ventures produced very small amounts of glass products which were sent back to England, but never profitably. Soon tobacco leaves supplants all other economic ventures. [17]

Several other attempts were made in the early 17th century which failed until Casper Wister and Henry William Stiegel, and later John Fredrick Amelung were successful for a time in the 18th century.[18] After the War of 1812, many glass plants were started with production focusing on bottles and glassware. Flat glass of this era was made by the crown and by the cylinder method. Discussed in later chapters, are the various vertical draw and plate methods which were essentially made obsolete by the "float glass" process.

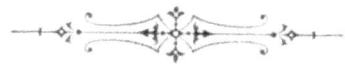

[14] Ada Polak, <u>Glass its tradition and its makers,</u> G. P. Putnam's Sons, New York, 1976, p. 122.
[15] Francis Buckly, <u>The Glass Trade in England in the Seventeenth Century</u>, London, 1914, and Anon., <u>Now Thus – Now Thus 1826 – 1926.</u>, Pilkington Bros., St. Helens, 1926, pg 74.
[16] Eleanor S. Godfrey, <u>The Development of English Glassmaking in 1560-1640</u>, Univ. of North. Carolina Press, Chapel Hill, 1975.
[17] J. Paul Hudson, Glassmaking at Jamestown, (1608-09 and 1621-24), reprint from: Iron Worker.
[18] Editor, <u>Discovering Antiques: The Story World of Antiques,</u> Greystone Press, New York- Tronto-London, 1972.

Glass Manufacturing Methods

For centuries glass was made by the batch process and melted in crucibles and/or clay pots. Some of these pots could be recharged a number of times prior to failure. Flat glass, via the crucible method, was made by casting on a table, and blown by the crown and cylinder technique until the early 20th century. Innovation throughout the 20th century saw the development of the continuous flow glass tank furnace resulting in the demise of the pot furnaces. A number of vertical draw systems for window glass and continuous casting for plate glass were developed. These were eventually replaced by the successful continuous float glass process, which made it possible to produce various thicknesses of parallel and a clean "fire polished finish" on both surfaces.

CROWN GLASS. So called because of the crown shape in the stage of processing between the gatherers molten mass on the blowpipe and the final disk or plate shape. Brown and O'Connor state that the blowpipe was invented about 40 BC in Syria or Israel.[19] A gatherer first collects a weight of molten glass, ranging from 20 to 40 pounds depending on the diameter and thickness required of the final disk, from a pot of molten refined glass. This molten glass is blown into a large bulb on the end of the blowpipe, then the glass gatherer attaches a punty opposite the blowpipe.

The blowpipe is severed from the glass bulb by touching the glass next to the blowpipe with a cold iron and with a quick tap it separates. Now the molten bulb is held by the punty and when reheated and spun rapidly it takes the shape of a crown, whence its name. With further heating and spinning, the crown opens up to a flat circular plate and as it cools to a rigid state it is broken from the punty, laid on a smooth sand bed, and annealed to eliminate stresses.[20]

The plate is thicker at the center even with every effort to maintain an even thickness. Concentric circular striations often appear on the surface of crown glass. A fire polished surface on both sides was produced by this method, especially after the introduction of gas-fired furnaces about 1880 in American glass factories.[21] Previous to that time coal and/or wood fired furnaces were used in both Europe and the United States and caused ash and combustion vapor surface defects.[22] The stages of a table of crown glass making are shown

---

[19] Brown and O'Connor, Medieval Craftsmen: Glass-Painters, p.6.

[20] Powell, "Technological Handbooks – The Principal of Glassmaking: Crown and Sheet Glass by Henry Chance; Together With treaties on Plate Glass by H.G. Harris," 1883, pp. 122-131.

[21] Editor, "The Manufacture of Window Glass With Natural Gas," *Scientific American*, vol. 54, No. 12., March 20, 1886.

[22] Sir Hugh Chance, "Records and the Nailsea Glassworks," *The Connoisseur*, vol. 163, 1967.

in Figure 1 and the layout for cutting various size panes from crown tables are shown in Figure 2.

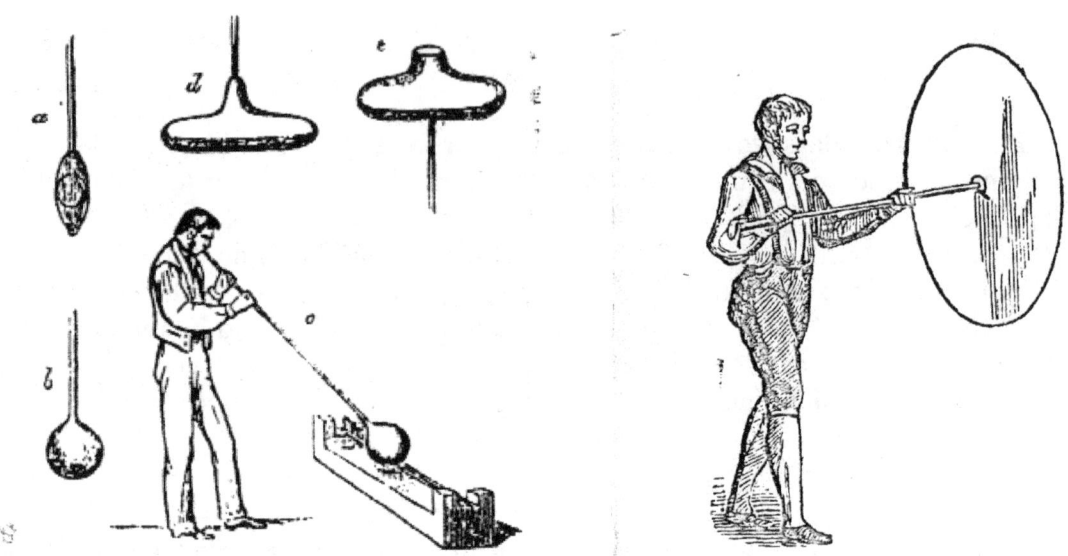

Figure 1. Progress of the Manufacture of a Table of Crown Glass and a glassblower with a completed crown or table of glass attached to the pontil rod.[23]

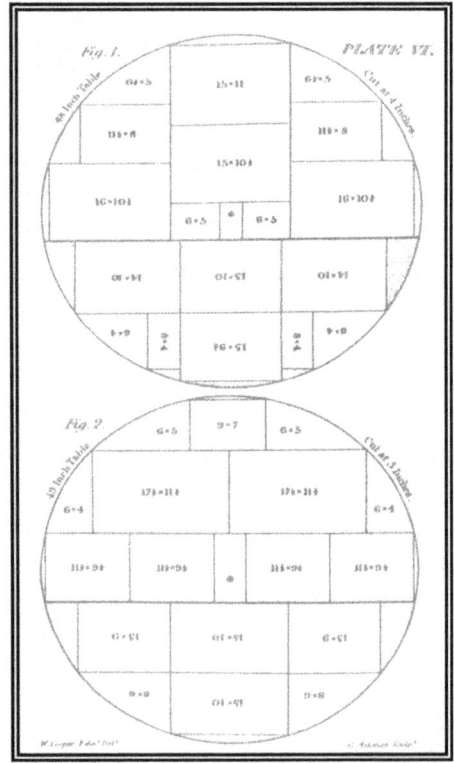

Figure 2. Layouts for Cutting up to 48 and 49 inch tables into standard size panes.[24]

---

[23] Progress illustration from Tomlinson, <u>Cyclopedia of Useful Arts and Manufactures</u>, London, c. 1851.
[24]Glassblower Illustration from Kenneth Wilson, "Window Glass in America," <u>Building Early America.</u>

The punty mark (bullion point, pontil, bulls eye) through its history has been utilized several ways. The first utilization was as scrap glass (cullet) for remelt as glass at this time was very expensive and from the seventeenth century some lanterns utilized the bulls eyes as lens.[25]

Secondly, as an example it was used as a semi-transparent small window unit in the Kreuzenstein Castle in Austria in about 1580-90 as shown in Figure 3. Later they were used as doorway sidelights or in the transoms of early houses. This would allow light in but would by-pass the 'window tax" assessed the transparent lights.

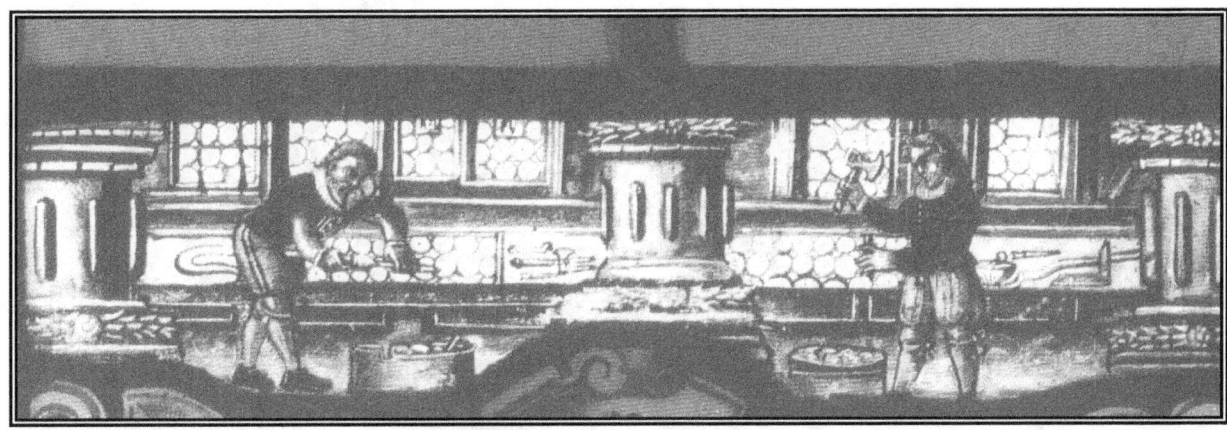

Figure 3. Detail from a Swiss domestic panel of ca 1580-90 from Kreuzenstein Castle in Austria. It shows the interior of a glaziers workshop where bulls eye windows are being leaded up and soldered. The workshop is lit by windows of this type.[26]

In 1696, a window tax was imposed in England by William III; it required the payment of four shillings per year on every house that had more than ten windows.[27] This was one of the many luxury taxes and glass windows were considered a luxury. The American colonies were subject to this English tax. The American Revolution ended the British taxes in the United States but the window tax persisted in England and was even increased several times before being repealed in 1845. From the seventeenth century some lanterns utilized the bulls eye lens. Lastly, from Victorian times (1851) to the present they are considered as functional decorative window units.

CYLINDER GLASS. The hand cylinder process (broad or muff) appears to have been used by the Romans in England around 300 AD and in the 9th century in Italy.[28] It was a product common to France and to the German states in the twelfth and thirteenth

---

[25] David Eveleigh, <u>Candle Lighting</u>, Thomas & Sons, England, 1985, p. 31.

[26] Brown and O'Connor, Medieval Craftsman: Glass-Painters, p. 48.

[27] Diamond, The Story of Glass, p. 114.

[28] Boon, "Roman Window Glass From Wales," and Francesca Dell'Acqua, "Ninth Century Window Glass From The Monastery of San Vincenzo Al Volturno (Molise, Italy)," *The Journal of Glass Studies*, vol. 39, 1997.

centuries.[29] It probably developed from the crown glass method where the gatherer blew the glass into the form of a cylinder instead of a spherical bulb. The gathering of glass weighed between 20 and 40 pounds according to the size of cylinder being made.[30] The cylinders varied from 12 to 20 inches in diameter and from 50 to 70 inches in length. The forming is done by swinging the cylinder of soft glass in a pit below the gaffers platform as shown in Figure 4.[31] The far end of the cylinder is removed by laying a hot ribbon of glass around the cooling but rigid cylinder. The hot ribbon softens that area of the cylinder sufficiently so it could be cut by shears; or the entire end of the cylinder was heated to where it could be blown open.[32] The end near the blowpipe was detached by use of the cold iron. The resulting rough end is taken off by the application of a hot thread of glass and the cold iron.

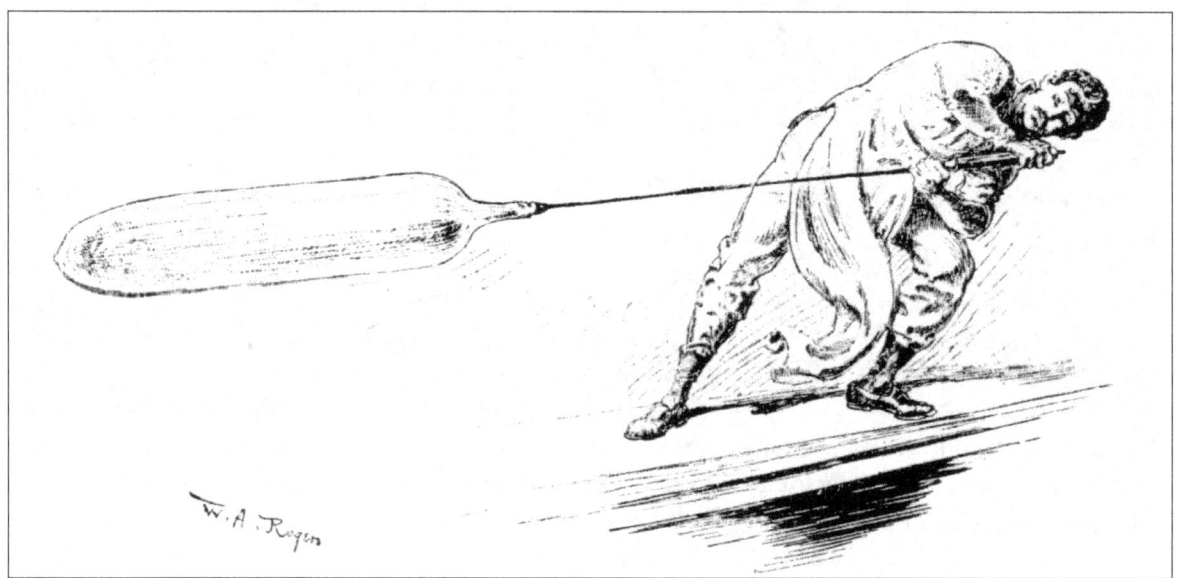

Figure 4. A Cylinder of glass - nearly done.[33]

The rough ended cylinders are annealed and stored awaiting further cutting. The ends are cut off to make a clean square end. The inside of the cylinder while laying on a clean soft cradle is scratched lengthwise by use of a diamond attached to a long handle as shown in Figure 5. This step is called shawling. The scratch line is then tapped and hopefully the cylinder cracks (cuts) neatly along the length of the scratch. Samples of these shawl cutters as they are called are shown as Nos. 26 through 29 in CATEGORY XXIII Miscellaneous.

---

[29] Diamond, *The Story of Glass,* p. 111.
[30] Walter Rosenhain, Glass Manufacture, Archibald Constable & Company, Ltd, United Kingdom, 1908.
[31] Antony Pacey, "A History of Window Glass Manufacture in Canada," *Association for Preservation Technology*, vol. 13, No. 3, 1981.
[32] Henry Chance, "Sheet Glass," The Principals of Glass-Making, Technological Handbooks, George Bell & Sons, London, 1883.
[33] Editor, "Great American Industries," *Harper's New Monthly Magazine*, vol. 79, No. 470, July 1889, p. 251.

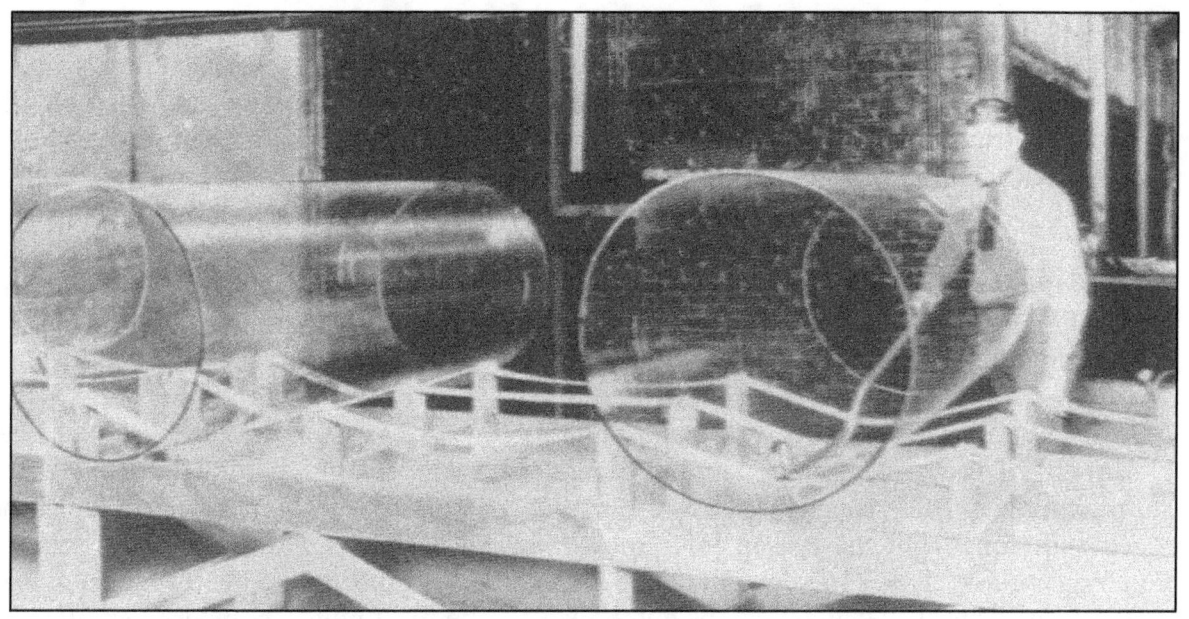

Figure 5. After the cylinder was cut into sections of desired length they were split lengthwise, a process known as shawling. The shawls were then reheated, flattened and annealed and ready for cutting into desired sizes.[34]

The use of the diamond in cutting plain surfaces of glass dates from at least the sixteenth century, but its application to the splitting of cylinders wasn't introduced until about 1835 by M. Claudet.[35] On the continent in the 1880's the cylinders were for the most part still being split with a red-hot iron with each blower splitting his own piece. The cylinder is rotated so when the split is uppermost, it is now ready for the flattener. The cylinder enters the reheat furnace on a bed of flat smooth sand. The heat soon softens the glass and the flattener opens the cylinder and the sides fall back into a wavy sheet on the flat sand bed. Now the flattener tries manually to smooth the sheet with a wood block on the end of a long iron rod. Straight wavy striations are evident on the finished sheet as well as some sand grains stuck to the lower surface.

Various defects in flat glass made by the hand-blown methods make cutting somewhat of a challenge. The hand-blown flat glass that was gathered from pot melts inherently had internal defects such as: stones, seeds, and blisters. Stones are small pieces of unmelted batch material or lining of the refractory melting pot or tank. Seeds and blisters are entrapped air or gas bubbles, either spherical or elongated, found in glass that was not adequately refined in the furnace. It also had surface defects called striations and attached sand grains from the flattening process. Striations on the surface can be caused by the shaping tools or by temperature or viscosity differences when the glass is being shaped or by layering of multiple gatherings for the larger sheets. The hand-blown sheet was seldom of uniform thickness and usually had some curvature as well, especially the cylinder. These defects combined to make the cutting difficult when the glass was new, but especially during recutting today after years of weathering on the surface.

---

[34] Editor, Glass: History Manufacture and its Universal Application, p. 177.
[35] Harry J. Powell, Technological Handbooks, pp 122-131.

Through the years there have been stories of how old glass has flowed or sagged in place in window installations. Glass is a super cooled liquid but its viscosity is so high it is considered a rigid solid. This story of glass flowing comes about from the observation of old glass, when removed from the sash, being thicker at the bottom edge. As mentioned previously, thickness variations were one of the properties of hand-blown glass. Now wouldn't it seem logical for a good glazier to install the pane of glass with the thick edge down for best support? End of story? Hardly! Even the "Ask Marilyn," column of *Parade Magazine* on November 19, 1995, adheres to the sagging of glass theory. She would not answer my refutations.

The author, during a recent major paint job on his 1891 former house in Skaneateles NY, found it was necessary to remove several panes of old glass from the two-over-two storm windows. The panes measured 13"x 30." The glass was striated and contained both seeds and stones, but the reason for removal was the curvature of the glass to reset and reputty the glass. The 3/16" bow on the 30" length made it difficult to keep adequate glazing on the sash. This curved glass can be cut, however, one must build up under the bow using a number of layers of heavy paper to support the glass in its curved shape. Figure 6 shows the Glass Factory at Clyde, New York about 1920, where both bottle and flat glass were made.

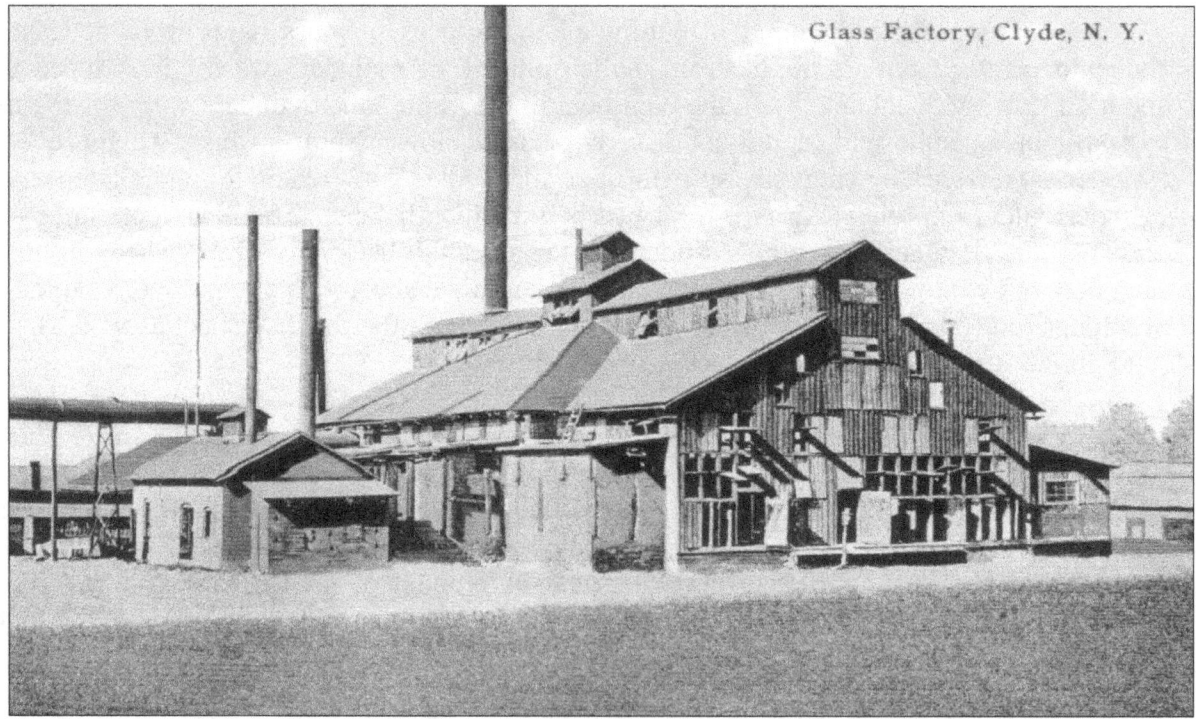

Figure 6. A postcard picture of the Glass Factory at Clyde New York, c. 1920, where both bottle and flat glass were made.[36]

---

[36] Postcard from author's collection.

THE CRYSTAL PALACE.   England dazzled the world, just six years after the window tax was repealed in 1845, in 1851 with the amazing Crystal Palace.[37]   The Chance Brothers were awarded the contract in 1850 for the glazing of the Crystal Palace in preparation for the Great International Exhibition of 1851.[38]   Joseph Paxton was knighted by Queen Victoria for his accomplishment in designing the building in nine days after more than two hundred designs had been rejected.   It was by far the largest building of any kind in the world.   It covered nearly eighteen acres and was high enough to house full grown trees, yet it was built in six months.[39]   The 300,000 sheets of glass measuring 10" X 49" were made by the cylinder process.   These cylinders were all hand blown.   Paxton perfected a method for sliding sheets of glass into wooden frames grooved to fit them.[40]   These were then attached to the iron girder frame of the building.   The building was moved in 1853 and burned in 1936.   A photograph of the original building is shown in Figure 7.

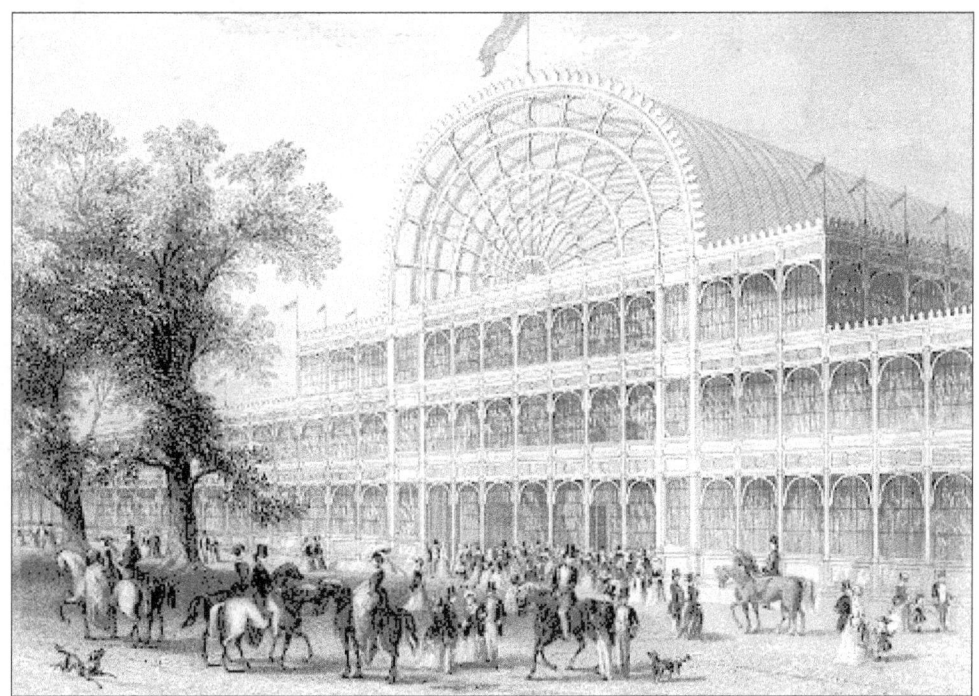

Figure 7. The Crystal Palace, built in 1851 in London, England.[41]

---

[37] Editor, <u>Glass: History Manufacture And Its Universal Application,</u> pg. 3, and Diamond, *The Story of Glass, p. 114.*
[38] Douglas and Frank, A History of Glassmaking.
[39] Diamond, The Story of Glass, p. 117.
[40] Diamond, The Story of Glass, p. 118.
[41] Illustration from Wikipedia.org (2007).

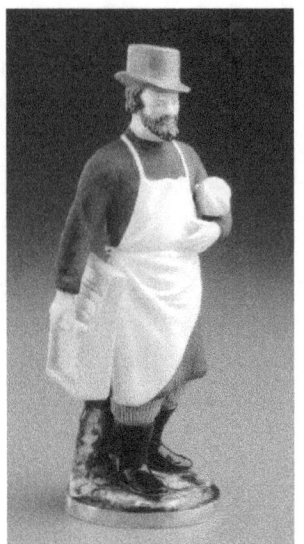

A glazier is one who selects, cuts, removes and installs commercial, industrial, and artistic glass. Pictures of glaziers at work down through the ages are shown in Figures 8 through 13.

Figure 8. An early 19th century porcelain figurine of a glazier 7 3/8" high made by the Gardner Factory, Moscow, Russia.[42]

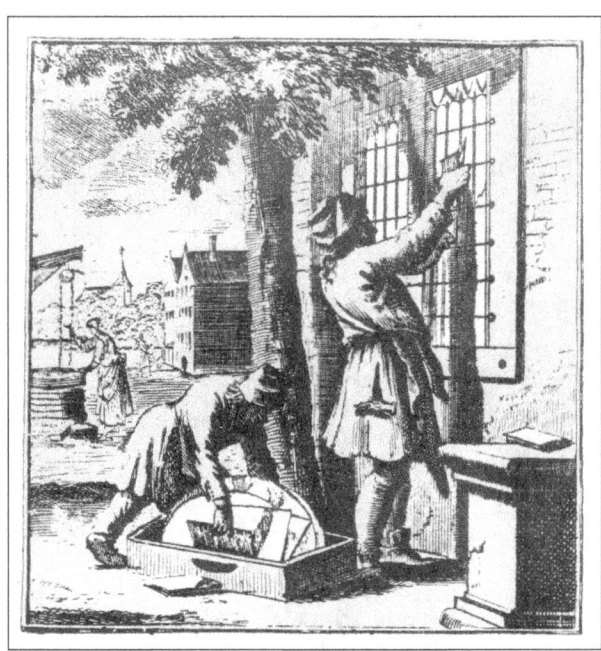

Figure 9. The Glazier, Chr. Weigels' artwork – 1699.[43]

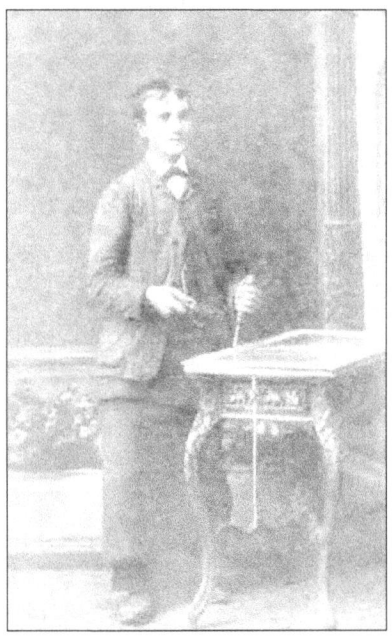

Figure 10. A young glazier (probably German) apparently reglazing what looks like a transom light using a rather ornate table as a work bench.[44]

---

[42] Illustration used by permission of the Hillwood Museum and Gardens, Washington, DC.
[43] A 1972 season's greeting card sent by the Bienenfeld Industries, Inc. Collection of the author.
[44] Illustration gleaned from a live auction on eBay.com.

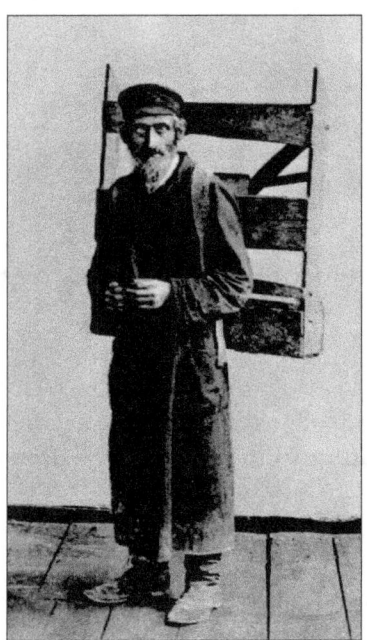

Figure 11. A picture postcard of an early 20th century wandering Eastern European glazier with a backpack type box of supplies.[45]

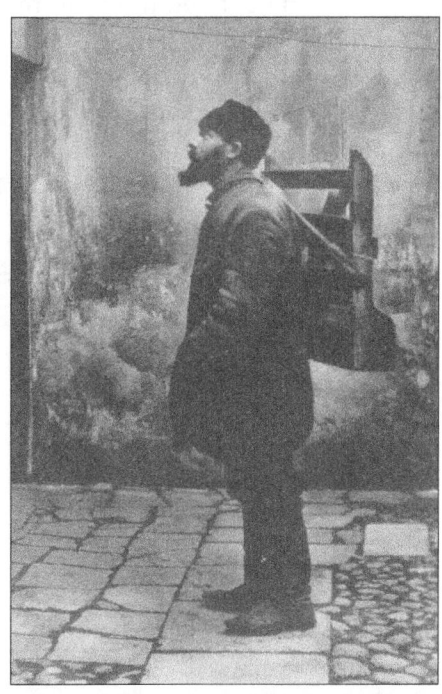

Figure 12. A postcard picture of a wandering Russian or Polish window glazier, with a backpack type box of supplies, postmarked 1917.[46]

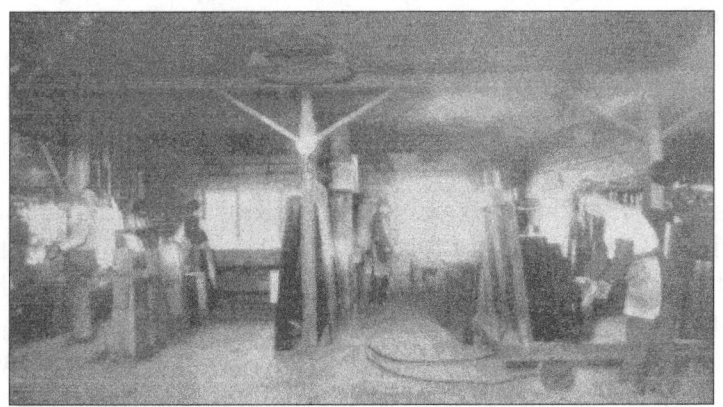

Figure 13. An early American postcard showing a cutting & sorting room with cutters at work, cutting & sorting the glass.[47]

---

[45] Postcard from the author's private collection.

[46] Ibid.

[47] Ibid.

MECHANIZATION OF THE
FLAT GLASS MANUFACTURING PROCESS

The beginning of the 20th century saw the introduction of mechanization of the window glass industry.[48] The data in Table 1 illustrates dramatically what took place.

Table 1. Evolution of the Flat Glass Process in the United States.[49] Most all of these as well as the plate glass processes were made obsolete with the introduction of the *float glass* process in the 1960's.

YEAR	HAND POTS*	CYLINDER MACHINES**	SHEET MACHINES***
1905	2,341	124	0
1910	2,315	116	0
1915	1,625	284	0
1920	1,183	329	6
1925	444	264	84
1929	-	60	117

*   Hand blown manufacturing process of window glass by both crown and cylinder process.
** Lubbers vertical cylinder draw process caught on quickly since its introduction in 1903, then by the mid 20's the drawing of sheets vertically put the cylinder process out to pasture.
*** Vertically drawn sheets by the Colburn (1916), Fourcault (1923), and Pennvernon (1926) processes.

The cylinder process of making sheet glass moved ahead rapidly after the introduction of the Lubbers process in 1903. This operation was introduced by the American Window Glass Co. and made possible the production of cylinders 40 feet long and two feet in diameter. This was accomplished by mechanically raising a 'bait ring" from the glass while simultaneously blowing compressed air into the pipe and glass until the desired diameter was attained.[50] Cylinder glass is being made in Europe at the present time for those desiring historically accurate replacement of sheet glass made by this process.[51] A picture of a four cylinder Lubbers process machine is shown in Figure 14. Note the four cradles in a horizontal position ready to be raised to receive the four cylinders already blown. This operation is somewhat like the reverse operation of launching a rocket today.

---

[48] Douglas and Frank, A History of Glassmaking.
[49] Angus-Butterworth, L. M. The Manufacture of Glass.
[50] Scoville, Revolution in Glassmaking – 1880-1920.
[51] Bock, *Old House Journal*, August 1998 and www.LondonCrownGlassCo.uk/History.html and Marinelli, "Architectural Glass and the evolution of the Storefront," *Old House Journal*, July/August 1988.

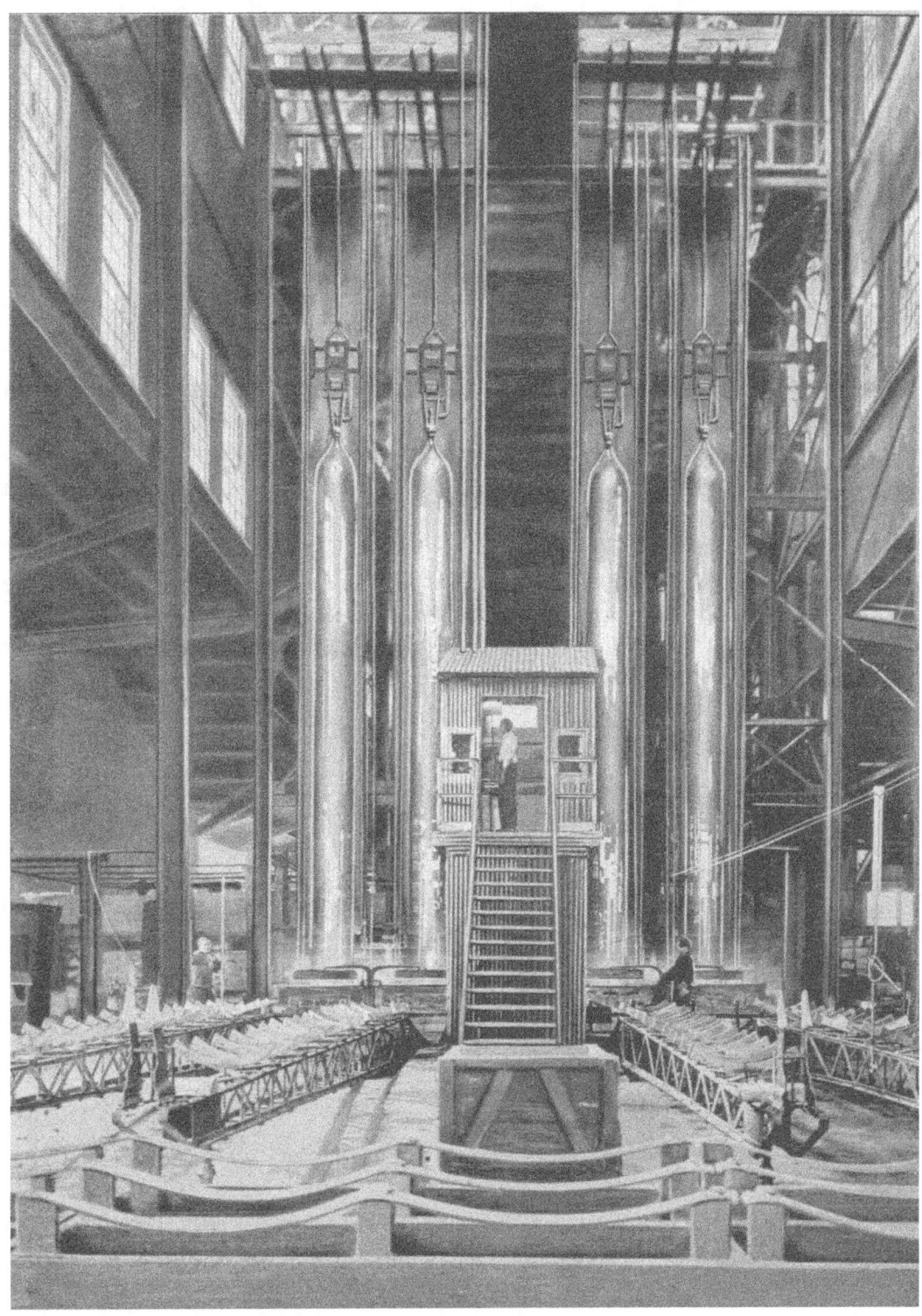

Figure 14. Illustration of a four cylinder Lubbers Process machine.[52]

[52] Illustration from John K. Lawo, Jr., "Fourth Time Proves to Be a Charm," *U.S. Glass, Metal & Glazing*, November/December 1983, p. 44.

Continuous Draw Flat Glass Sheet

An obvious development in sheet glass manufacture soon took place in the United States between 1903 and 1926. This was the drawing upward of a continuous flat sheet instead of the long cylinder which was a semi-continuous process. A very good summary of window glass production in Canada in the 19th and 20th centuries is included in Antony Pacey article entitled "A History of Window Glass Manufacture in Canada."[53]

On May 7, 1871 a French patent (No. 91,787) on the mechanical drawing of glass in a continuous manner was issued to Monsieur F. Vallin of Givors, resident of Me Cussac, Rue Neuve. St. Etienne, Loire, France[54] (see diamond point cutter No. 43 in Category IV). The melting process used a series of pots arranged so that there was continuous downward flow until the refined glass was drawn upward by use of guides, bent over a roll as the cooler sheet was pulled along by another series of rollers. Whence off to the cutting area. Again, a glass cutting tool is not mentioned, only: "To cut the horizontal panes, I make them slide over a table covered with asbestos." See Figure 15. All the details of this patent process of 1871 are to be found in the several different processes that were invented in 1907 and after (Fourcault, Colburn, and Pennvernon).

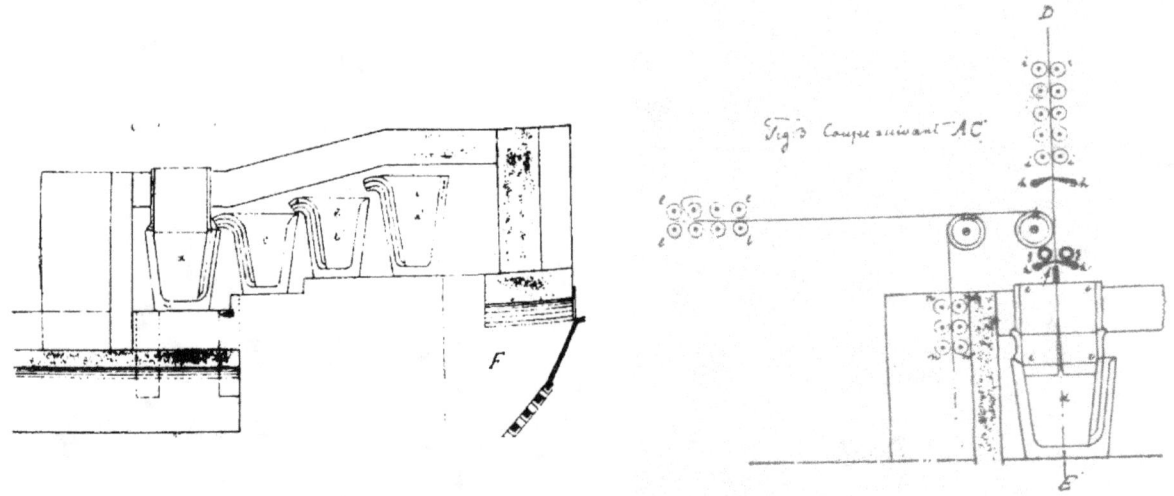

Figure 15. A sectional view of two patent diagrams to show the arrangement of the pots in the furnace and the vertical draw with bending roll as well as the series of pulling rollers.[55]

---

[53] Pacey, "A History of Window Glass Manufacture in Canada."
[54] Edward Borel (translated by S.R. Scholes), "A Drawn Sheet Glass Process of 1871," *The Glass Industry*, vol. 39, no. 9, September 1958.
[55] Borel, "A Drawn Sheet Glass Process of 1871."

THE FOURCAULT PROCESS [56]

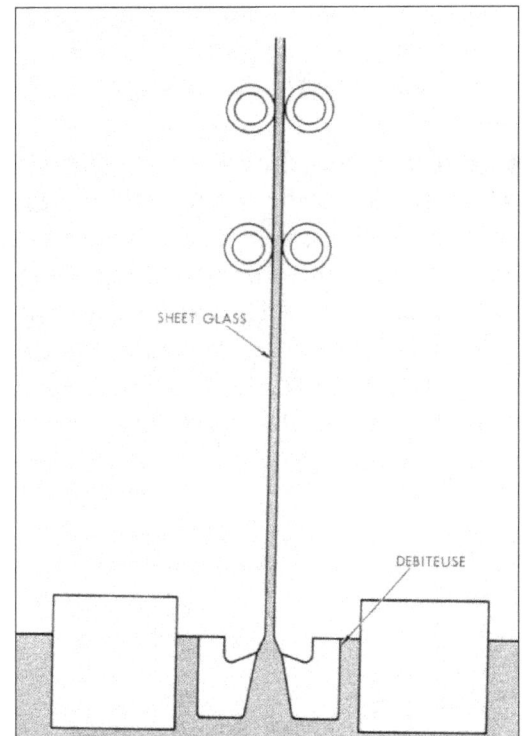

This process was developed in Belgium and Czechoslovakia in 1902 by Emile Fourcault, a Belgian.[57] Soon after the First World War it was introduced into the United States (1923) by The Blackford Window Glass Co. which later became The American St. Gobain Co. The glass sheet is drawn upward with the aid of asbestos covered rolls that contact both surfaces after the glass has become sufficiently rigid so that the surface is not marred. A sketch of this process is shown in Figure 16. The glass sheet rose upward for five or six stories at which time it was "cut."

Figure 16.
The Fourcault Process.

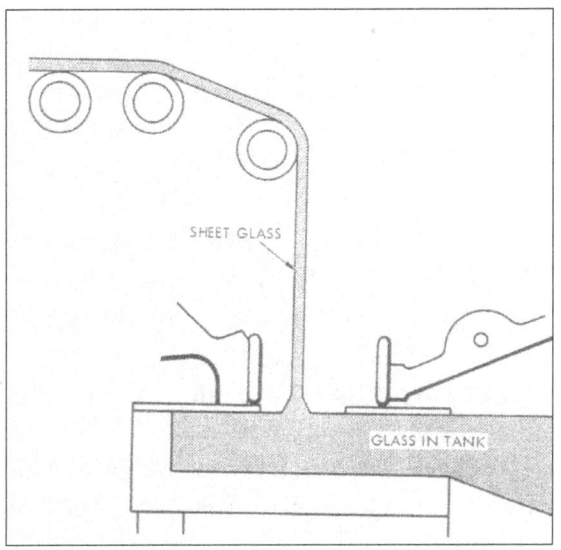

Figure 17. The Colburn Process.

THE COLBURN PROCESS [58]

In 1912, Irving W. Colburn, an American, invented his continuous draw glass process after watching a papermaking machine. In 1916 the first commercial Colburn machines were installed in Charleston WV in what was The Toledo Glass Company later to become Libbey-Owens-Ford Glass Co.[59] The process draws a width of glass vertically about two feet at which time it passes over a bending roll whence it moves horizontally through an annealing furnace. The top side of the drawn sheet is untouched while the bottom surface has been in contact with both the bending rolls and the rolls in the lehr, thus, the bottom surface will show some defects. See Figure 17 for details.

[56] Illustration from Schuler, Glassforming: Glassmaking for the Craftsman.
[57] Frederic and Lilli Schuler, <u>Glassforming: Glassmaking for the Craftsman</u>, Chilton Book Company, Philadelphia, 1970, and L.M. Angus-Butterworth, <u>The Manufacture of Glass</u>, Pitman Publishing, New York, 1948.
[58] Illustration from Schuler, Glassforming: Glassmaking for the Craftsman.
[59] Pacey, "A History of Window Glass Manufacture in Canada, " Schuler, <u>Glassforming: Glassmaking for the Craftsman</u>, Angus-Butterworth, <u>The Manufacture of Glass</u>, and Warren C. Scoville, <u>Revolution in Glassmaking</u>, Harvard University Press, 1948.

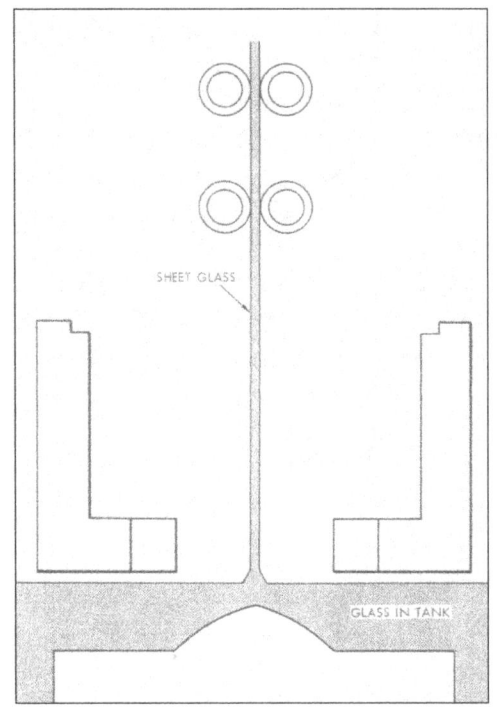

THE PENNVERNON PROCESS [60]

This process developed by the PPG Industries in 1926 is very similar to the Fourcault process.[61] The ceramic blocks at the glass melt surface where the sheet is drawn from is the basic difference.[62] See Figure 18 for comparison. The vertically drawn Fourcault and Pennvernon processes require buildings five to six stories high to allow the glass time to cool before it can be cut from the continuous vertical ribbon.[63]

Figure 18.
The Pennvernon Process.

PLATE GLASS – SEMICONTINUOUS PROCESS.

Until about 1913, in both the U. S. and Europe, plate glass was made by the batch casting process.[64] (8) Molten glass from a melting pot or small tank was poured on a cast-iron table about 16 feet wide and 30 feet long. This casting table was covered with a thin layer of sand to keep the molten glass from sticking and cooling to fast. A water cooled roller was passed over the glass to flatten it, then power knives trimmed and bisected the viscous slab into two blanks.[65] A picture of a smaller plate glass blank is shown in Figure 19. These large blanks were annealed and later ground and polished on both surfaces. In the third century the Romans cast small window pieces by pouring molten glass into a mold lined with sand.

---

[60] Illustration from Schuler, Glassforming: Glassmaking for the Craftsman

[61] Schuler, Glassforming: Glassmaking for the Craftsman.

[62] Josephine Perry, <u>America at Work: The Glass Industry</u>, Longmans, Green & Company, 1945.

[63] Schuler, Glassforming: Glassmaking for the Craftsman.

[64] Editor, "Great American Industries," Perry, <u>America at Work: The Glass Industry</u>, and

[65] Editor, Glass: History Manufacture and its Universal Application.

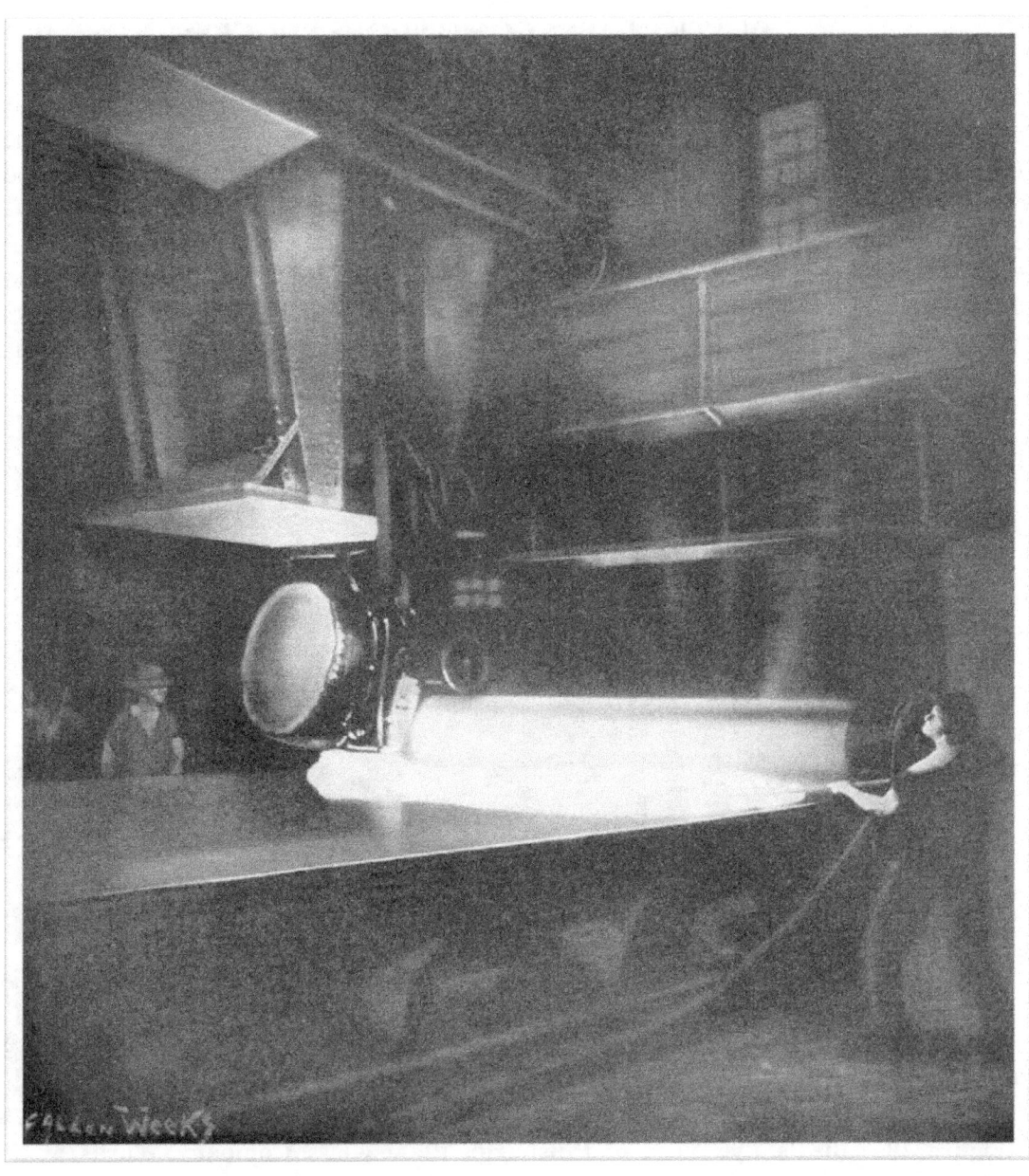

Figure 19. Making Plate Glass.[66]

---

[66] Editor, <u>Glass: History Manufacture And Its Universal Application</u>, Pittsburgh Plate Glass Company, 1923, p. 20.

PLATE GLASS - CONTINUOUS PROCESS.

Between 1922 and 1924 both the Pittsburgh Plate Glass Company and the Ford Motor Company introduced the continuous plate glass casting process.[67] This process required a furnace capable of producing a wide ribbon of molten glass flowing continuously out between water cooled rolls as previously noted for the semi-continuous process. For many years the glass blanks cut from this continuous ribbon were ground and polished on one side, turned over and the process repeated. Later at its most advanced state, plate glass technology incorporated twin grinding, which allowed both sides to be ground simultaneously. A postcard of the Pittsburgh Plate Glass Company Works at Ford City, Pennsylvania is shown in Figure 20.

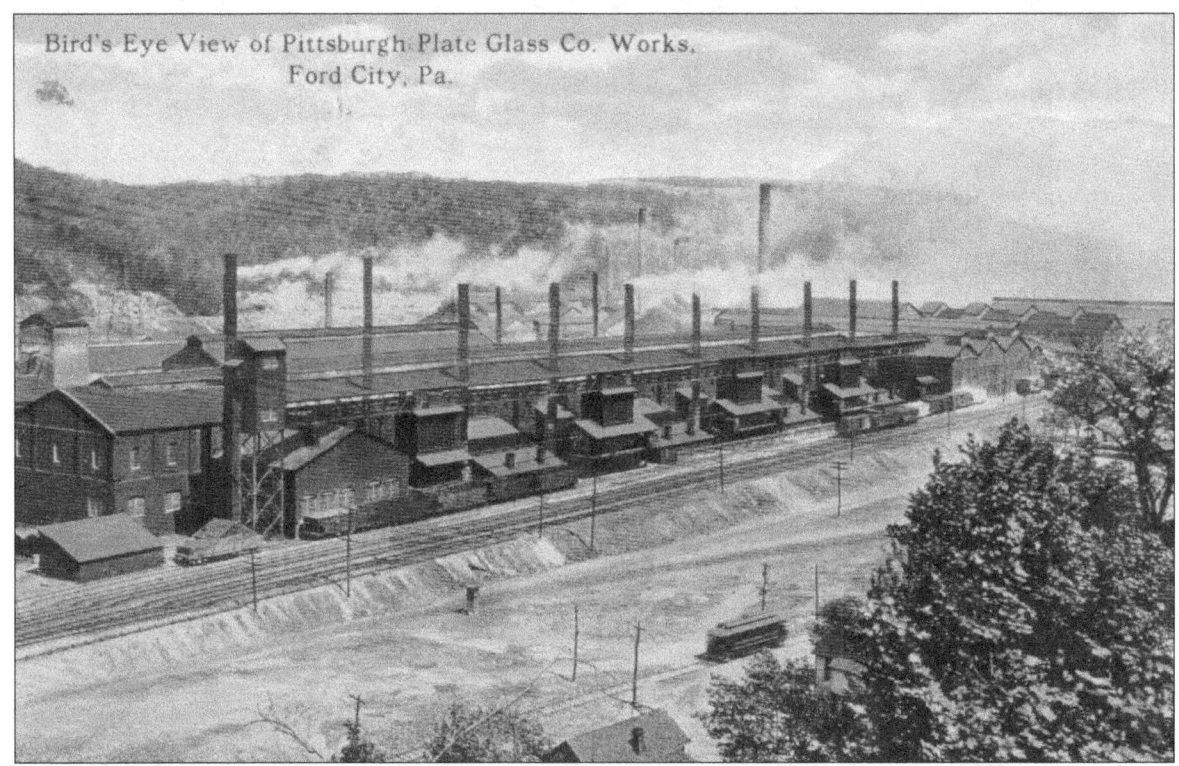

Figure 20. Bird's Eye View of Pittsburgh Plate Glass Company Works at Ford City, Pennsylvania about 1915.[68]

THE FLOAT PROCESS. A U.S. patent granted in 1902 to William Heal described the desirability of continuously melting and delivering molten glass onto a thin layer of molten tin in a controlled atmosphere chamber and then drawing the sheet of glass along the surface of the tin and into an annealing lehr. He also described how to control the thickness by the application of "drawing forces" applied to the cooling glass. William Heal never reduced his patent to commercial practice.[69]

---

[67] Perry, America at Work: The Glass Industry.
[68] Postcard from the private collection of the author.
[69] Robert C. Perry, "The Float Process for Manufacturing Flat Glass," *Glastechnische Berichte*, (13th International Congress of Glass Proceedings), Hamburg, Germany, July 1983.

The Pilkington name has been associated with the window glass industry since 1826. They initially made window glass only by the crown method until 1841 when they added the cylinder glass process having gotten the technology from France and Germany.

The float process was developed into a commercial success by the Pilkington Brothers, Ltd. of England in the late 1950's and is now licensed around the world by many companies. It was in 1952 that Pilkington began experimenting with the concept of floating the hot molten glass on a bath of molten tin. The development took seven years.[70] They announced the process in 1959, but further perfecting work was required and the first license agreement was made in 1962 to PPG. This process made the casting of plate glass and most window glass operations obsolete. The glass surfaces produced are very flat, fire polished, and parallel. For these reasons the float glass process has replaced both plate and sheet glass operations because of these superior qualities and further because now a great range of thicknesses can be obtained. A typical float glass furnace will produce about 400 tons of ten foot wide ribbon in 24 hours.

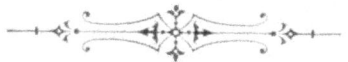

---

[70] Schuler, <u>Glassforming: Glassmaking for the Craftsman</u>, and Perry, "The Float Process for Manufacturing Flat Glass."

Chapter Two

History of Flat Glass Cutting Tools

The glass cutter has been one of the most overlooked tools based on its importance to our modern living standards. A treatise on a collection of glass cutters of many different styles must reflect on the imagination of the inventor as well as the utility of the user and the product being cut. Many early articles on window glass refer to its being "cut" to various sizes, but not by what method or tool. The word "cut" is really a misnomer, for the most part, as the glass is only scratched or heated and then cracked along the mark.[71] Cutting methods noted briefly but without detail were: shears (for hot glass); pieces of flint; grozing irons (yrnes), hot wire or rod with cold water; a hot glass ribbon with cold iron; diamond; hardened steel wheel; carbide wheel.[72] Grozing iron (in French: *gresoir* or *grugeoir*) (in German: *Kretzler*) is described by Theophelus in the 12th century.[73]

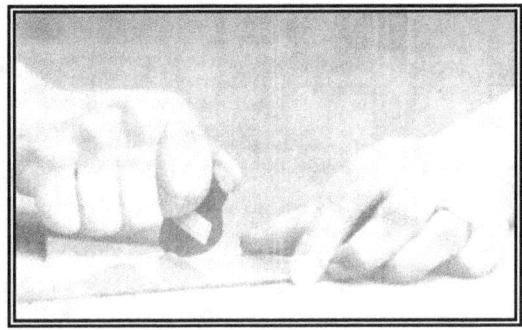

Figure 21. Cutting glass with a flint tool.

A short treatise published in the Journal of the British Society of Master Glass Painters in 1924 puts forth a strong case for "cutting" glass by use of a sharpened piece of flint. This material was not native to the areas where several glass houses were located at Chiddingfold in Surry, England south of London. Glass fragments cut by these flint tools were dated to the 4th, 12th, 14th, and 15th centuries. Mrs. Halahan states that these flint tools are quite easy to use. There is a depression on one side to fit the thumb and a smooth resting place on the other for the second joint of the first finger. Thus held, the knife edge of the flint rests on the glass almost at the right angle required for making a cut. See Figure 21.[74]

The use of flat glass for domestic windows dates from the Roman times, but was very limited in use as only very few specimens have survived the ages.[75] A glazier's guild is first mentioned in London in 1328, in Paris in 1467, Antwerp in 1470, and in Tournai in 1480.[76] The popularity of flat glass for domestic use began in the sixteenth century for several

---

[71] Polak, Glass: Its Tradition and Its Makers, p. 119.
[72] Brown and O'Connor, Medieval Craftsman: Glass-Painters.
[73] Ada Polak, Glass: Its Tradition and Its Makers, G.P. Putnam's Sons, New York, 1975.
[74] Halahan, "On the Association of Flint Chippings with Fragments of Old Glass Found in Medieval Glasshouses at Chiddingfold in Surry."
[75] Brown and O'Connor, Medieval Craftsman: Glass-Painters, and Boon, *Roman Window Glass From Wales*.
[76] Polak, Glass: Its Tradition and Its Makers, p. 118.

reasons. Merchants and artisans could then afford such luxuries.[77] The large stained and painted glass windows in cathedrals were in many instances considered both too expensive and heretical with the Protestant Reformation.[78] Thus the glaziers had to look for other markets, the literature mentions glazed windows as a great luxury brought from Italy to England in 1180.[79] There appears to be reason to doubt whether the "French masons" possessed the art of making glass notwithstanding that they knew how to make windows.

Documents mention grozing irons as early as 1351 where a Simon le Smyth was paid 1d. each for twelve grozing irons. Grozing irons were pencil size pieces of flat iron with notches near either end not unlike the notches on present day glass cutters [80] A York, England glass painter left a number of grozing yrne's to Thomas English in 1503. The shield in the coat of arms of the local Guild of Glaziers in York depicts two grozing irons crossed in saltire. It is concluded that the glaziers of the fourteenth century were quite adept at the use of the grozing iron to trim or chip and possibly feather the edges of the stained glass pieces that made up the large cathedral windows. The restoration artists have noted the old technique.

Diamonds as a "cutting" tool are noted as being used in Italy in the fourteenth century in a treatise by Antonio da Pisa. It is also documented that diamonds were attached to the ends of sticks in the mid 1800's.[81] The following by William Cooper, written in 1835, is an excellent description of the history of the diamond as a glass cutting tool: [82]

> "The 'ancients' were ignorant of the art of cutting the diamond, and therefore used it in its natural state. It was in 1456 that Robert de Berghen, a native of the Austrian Netherlands, discovered that a diamond might be cut and polished by a powder of diamond dust. The earliest mention of a diamond being used for writing on glass occurs in France in the 16th century. It was used in etching or engraving on glass vessels as early as 1562 in Venice, Italy. The art of cutting glass with a wheel used on crystal ware only was invented in the early 17th century by Caspar Lehmann, lapidary and glasscutter to The Holy Roman Emperor Rudolf II in Prague. It was not until early in the 18th century that the artificially cut diamond was discovered for use in cutting glass.
>
> In considering the diamond in its relations to the purposes of the window-glass cutter, there occur some circumstances worthy of remark. The cutting point of the diamond must be a natural one, an artificial point however formed, will only scratch the glass, not cut it. The diamond of a ring, for instance, will not cut a pane, but merely mark it with rough superficial lines, which penetrate very little inwards. Artificial points, corners, or angles, therefore, produced by cutting the diamond are adapted only for writing or for drawing figures on glass, and such

---

[77] Editor, Glass: History Manufacture And Its Universal Application.

[78] Diamond, The Story of Glass.

[79] Polak, Glass: Its Tradition and Its Makers.

[80] Brown and O'Connor, Medieval Craftsman: Glass-Painters, p. 36.

[81] Ronald S. Barlow, The Antique Tool Collectors Guide to Value, pg. 69.

[82] William Cooper, The Crown Glass Cutter and Glazier's Manual, Oliver and Boyd, Edinburgh, and Simkin, Marshall & Co, London, 1835, pg 84, 98, and Plate XIX.

were those used by the artists who ornamented glass vessels before alluded to. The cutting diamond does not write so well on glass, from the circumstances of its being apt to enter too deeply, and take too firm a hold of the surface, and thus become intractable. An accidental point, produced by fracturing the diamond, is as unfit for cutting as an artificial one. Such a point will also merely scratch the glass. No point, in short, that is not given by the natural formation of the mineral, will answer the purposes of the window-glass cutter.

The large sparks, as the diamonds used for cutting glass are called, are generally preferred to the small ones because of their being likely to possess a number of cutting points; while the very small sparks, are not always found to have more than one. Thus, if the point of the latter is worn, or broken off, although the spark be turned, and reset in its socket, it will still be without the power of cutting, and consequently useless, while the former, on undergoing the same operation, will present a new and effective point.

The large sparks are called *mother sparks*, and are sometimes cut down into as many smaller fragments bearing the same name, as there are natural points in the former. Each of these can have only one cutting point, and are consequently only proportionally valuable to the glazier, since they cannot be restored by resetting. The diamonds employed in glass-cutting, are classified as "bort", a classification which includes pieces that are too small to be cut, or are of a bad color, and thus unfit for ornamental use.

The next step is to temporarily secure the spark in a hollowed out end of a copper or brass wire. Then the setter proceeds to determine the cutting point direction by trying it on a piece of glass. Upon determination of point direction, make a slight notch on the wire exactly opposite to the cutting point as an alignment guide when fixing it permanently by soldering the copper or brass in the socket head on the handle.

SETTING THE DIAMOND. After selecting a stone, or spark, one must ascertain which is its best cutting point which has the cutting edges of the crystal placed exactly at right angles to each other, and passing precisely through a point of intersection made by the crossings of the edges. This is shown and described in Figure 22.

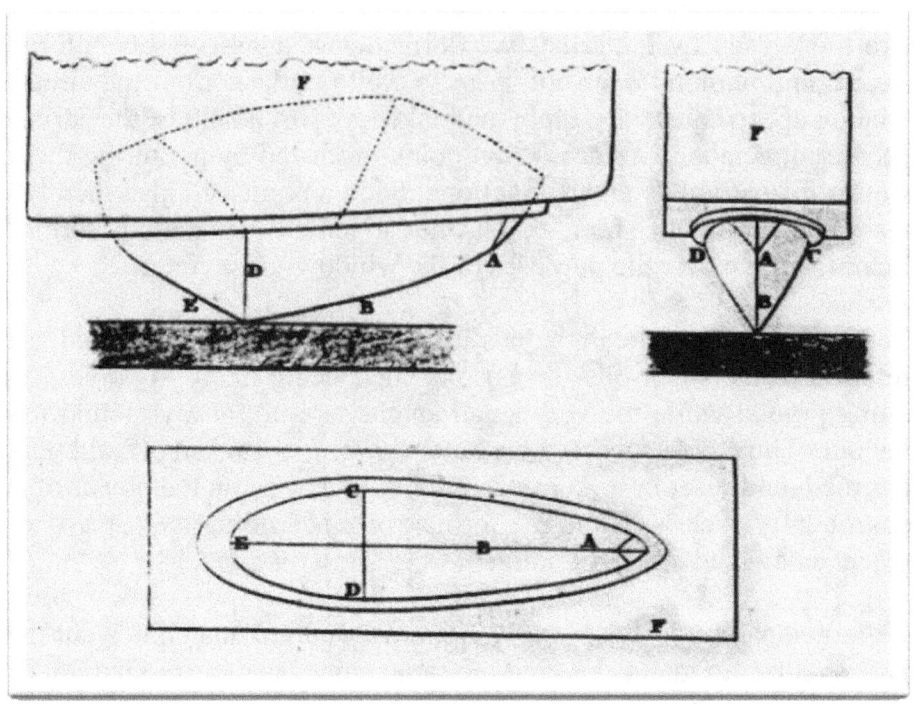

Figure 22. Showing the side and end elevations and the plan view of the diamond mount. (diagram by William Cooper, Plate XIX).

The art of managing the diamond in glass-cutting, so as to produce effective results, can only be attained by considerable experience. The diamond must be held in a particular position, and with a particular inclination, otherwise it will not cut. In the hands of an inexperienced person, it merely scratches the glass, leaving a long rough furrow, but no fissure. When the cut is a clean and effective one, the diamond produces a sharp, keen, and equal sound. When the cut is not a good one, the sound is harsh, grating, and irregular. Note the style of the glass cutter illustrated in Figure 23 which at present writing is the earliest depiction, 1835, discovered by the author for this design.

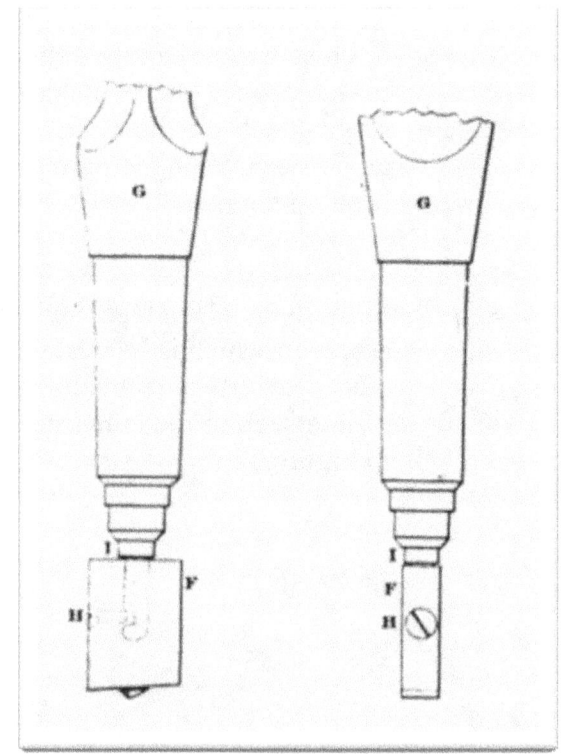

Figure 23. Views of a glazier's patent diamond mounted with a swivel adjustment (diagram by William Cooper, Plate XIX).

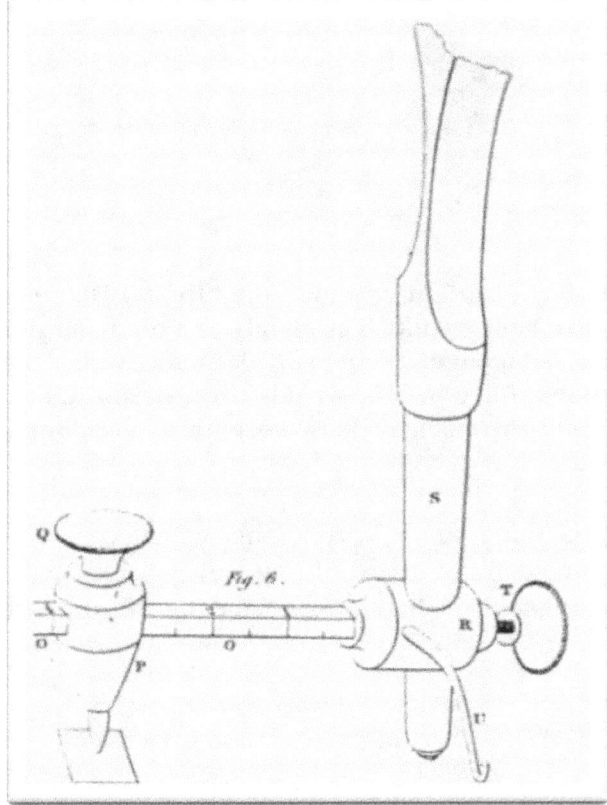

Figure 24. Luken's improved beam compass for cutting circles (diagram by William Cooper, Plate XIX).

Cooper also illustrated in Figure 24 "Luken's Improved Beam Compass for Cutting Circles." The tapering ferrule of a "pencil diamond" is set loosely into a conical hole in rigidly fixed cylinder R so as to rotate to determine the best cutting edge alignment of the diamond, then locked in place by turning knurled knob T. Cooper's description indicates a brass ball (not shown) at the left end of shaft O-O. Guide wire U is adjusted to just touch the glass during testing for best angle of inclination and then later during cutting it is used to guide the diamond pencil as the unit rotates. This is possible only by tilting the entire unit at pivot point P which is set into a small conical hole in a small metal plate adhered to the glass by a thin layer of beeswax, keeping in mind that this was 1835.

The industrial revolution and the Victorian period introduced a vast array of glass cutter designs especially for the diamond point cutters. With the invention of the revolving wheel cutter in 1869, inexpensive glass cutters were soon to be available. [83] Another major cost reducing item was the introduction of wood framing to replace the leaded windows. [84]

Controversy over who actually invented the wheel as a cutting tool for glass resulted in one of the most extensive patent legal cases up to that time. In any event, it is established that in 1868 a Mr. O. M. Pike, a jeweler, discovered that a hardened steel rod held at an angle to the glass surface and rotated with pressure would produce a scratch line like that of a diamond. He took his idea to the R. J. Ives Machine Shop in Bristol, Connecticut. Pike received patent No. 85,396 in 1868. At the Ives Machine Shop a man named Sam Monce was employed. He was intrigued with the steel rod tool and in June 1869 received patent No. 91,150 for the wheel cutter shown in the photograph in Figure 25. [85]

[83] H. Webster Wilson, "Old Glass - New Business," *Glass Studio*, vol. 34, 1982.
[84] Polak, Glass: Its Tradition and Its Makers.
[85] Picture courtesy of Fletcher Glass Company.

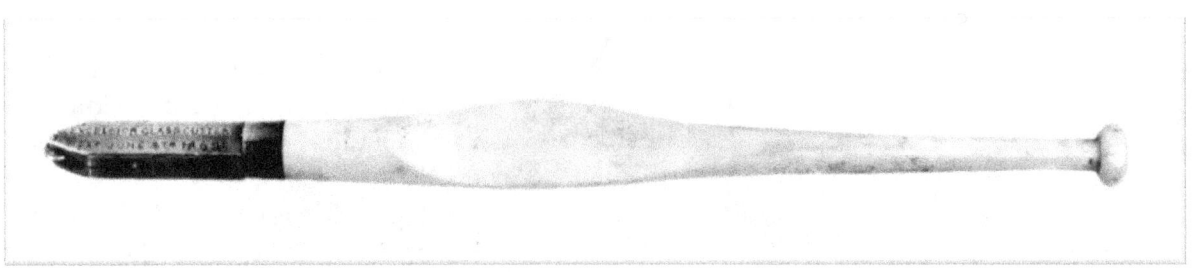

Figure 25. A photograph of the "revolving wheel" glass cutter called the "Bristol Diamond" patented by Samuel Monce in 1869.[86] **The slender bone handle is probably of a diamond point cutter of that time. Mr. Ives and Sam Monce formed a partnership in 1870. In a year or so Mr. Monce bought out Mr. Ives and went into business for himself. At this time, Bristol CT had become a leading clock manufacturing center and the clock makers were quick to adopt the new tool to the job of cutting dials and clock panels.**

Lovejoy's combination glass cutter and putty knife was an instant success when introduced in 1870.[87] To date the author has not seen nor heard of any Lovejoy glass cutter (There are early glass cutters with putty knives listed in Chapter Six, Category VI, pp 108 - 110).

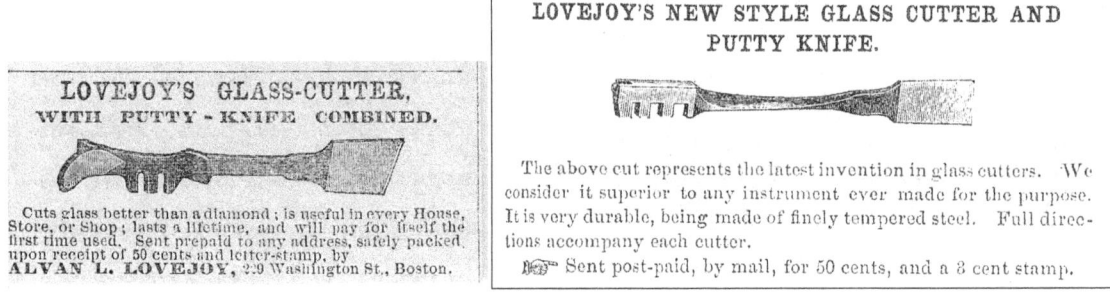

Figure 26. Two Lovejoy glass cutter advertisements [88]

In 1893 Mr. Monces' nephew, Fred S. Fletcher, moved east from Nebraska and went to work in the shop He improved the cutter by introducing interchangeable wheels, but Monce declined to manufacture it. In 1896 fire destroyed the plant. Mr. Monce rebuilt it in Unionville, CT and operated there until it was acquired in 1935 by the Fletcher-Terry Co. Fred Fletcher remained in Bristol and worked at the Sessions Clock Co. where he made the interchangeable wheel cutter. Fred Fletchers' two brothers and father-in-law, Franklin Terry, helped out and together formed a new company in 1903. Eight years later it was incorporated under the name it carries today: THE FLETCHER-TERRY CO. In 1969 the company moved into its current plant in Farmington, CT. The company is still family owned, however, in 1993 an employee stock ownership (ESOP) was created. A family corporate tree is outlined on the following page in Table 2.

---

[86] Philip E. Richardson, "A Phenomenal Impact," *Glass Digest*, April 1971.
[87] Ronald S. Barlow, The Antique Tool Collectors Guide to Value, 1985, pg. 69.
[88] American Agriculturalist Magazine, November 1873 (left); Wilson, Hood & Co's Annual Illustrated Catalog, October 1873 (right).

TABLE 2. The Fletcher-Terry Company Corporate family tree (as of 1993). [89]

Fletcher – Terry Company Family Tree

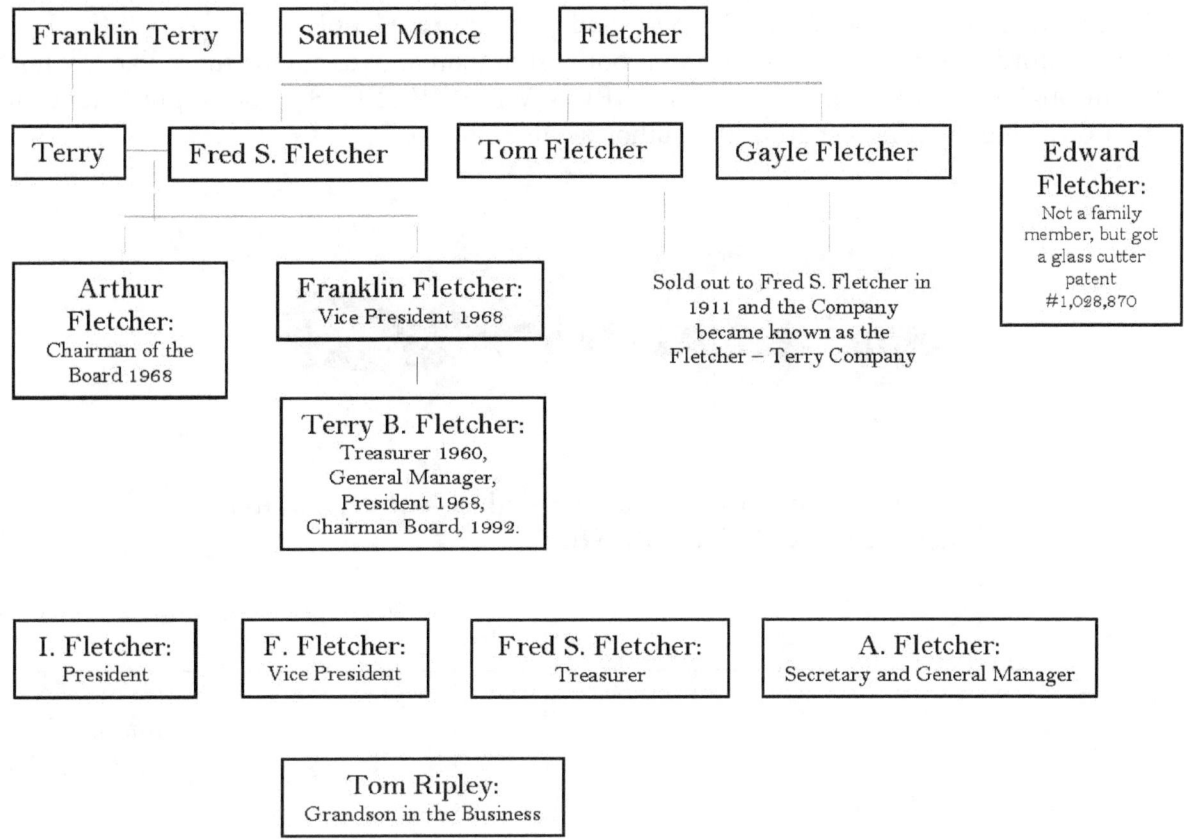

[89] The Fletcher – Terry Company is a family business and has not responded to several inquiries as to the accuracy of family names and dates included in the flow chart in Table 2.

The following letter written Jan 24, 1874 to F. R. Woodward of Hill, NH by a James B. Sanford of Buffalo, New York, an apparent sharp businessman not only recommends but practically writes the details of what a printed sales circular should be for the then current Woodward glass cutter. It is to be noted that the date of this letter predates the Woodward patent 166,954 on August 24, 1875 entitled "Rotary Paper Cutter" by seventeen months. This patent date is cast into a combination tool "The Woodward Tool" that contains a corkscrew and a knife sharpener, neither of which Mr. Sanford refers to. This particular glass cutter tool design was used by others: Monce patent June 8, 1869; W. L. Barrett patent 1873; The Artisans Tool July 22, 1874; and The Andress Tool August 24, 1875. I believe Mr. Sanford was purchasing a different tool design than above, maybe more like my numbers 44 through 49 in Category VI EARLY IRON WITH WHEELS. The original; letter in Mr. Sanford's handwriting is part of the author's collection.

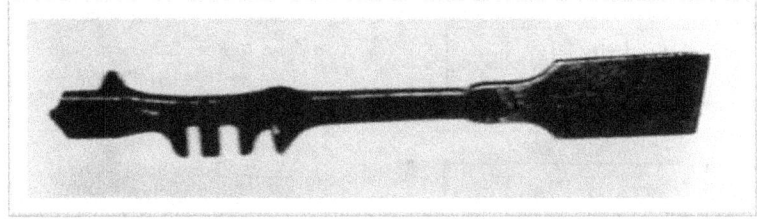

Figure 27. Possible Woodward glass cutter, painted black, imprinted: PAT. PEND.

Buffalo NY
Jan 24ᵗʰ 1874

F. R. Woodward

Dear Sir:

The cutters were received today and promptly accepted. I was disappointed not receiving 500 instead of 350. I have good prospect here so I send you enclosed $5.00 to secure you in sending me 500 more. Please send full count 500 cutters COD $30.00 which will make the total $35.00 for the 500. I will give your address to anyone asking, and wholesale them to myself at $12.50 per 100 cutters, and parties wishing to take hold of them can write to you for your terms. But money is scarce and "cutters" are a hard thing to sell unless one has experience. I have often sold 2 and 3 dozen to parties who couldn't sell them and then bring them back at their request
However I do wish I had some circulars to distribute, and your small circular does very well except the sentence "to sharpen the wheel rub it a few times in the same cut". In selling the cutters I do that occasionally but I call it a "test" to show that it is more durable than a diamond and offer $10.00 to any one who will put the diamond point to the same test and not spoil it. However your other

circular with the print of a cutter upon it I would distribute if you desire, but if you will have some circulars printed after this fashion I will be only too glad to distribute them for I know they would materially help me sell them as people are more convinced by seeing anything in print. I am now selling the cutters at 25ct but would prefer to have the retail price marked 50cts, so persons would suppose I was selling them at wholesale price.

> The Family Favorite Glass Cutter
> F. R. Woodward - Manufacturer
> Hill, NH
> Retail Price 50cts per dozen $3.00

This invention supplies a need long felt in every house. It cuts glass better than a diamond and a child can use it. The wheels of the cutters are sharp enough to cut paper and are hardened by a secret process so hard as to be about indestructible upon glass. It presents to the glass a thousand times the surface of the point of a diamond and its revolving freely prevents friction and its wearing out. Each and every cutter is guaranteed to cut 5000 panes of glass, but by keeping the pivot oiled it should last a glazier a life time. If a wheel is spoiled by ill use or abuse, enclose the wheel in an envelope with 10 cents and a new wheel and pivot will be returned. The cutter is a combination tool. The handle can be used as a putty knife, the "breakers" as a saw set, the wheel for cutting glass or paper patterns. Lay the paper on a pane of glass and you can cut it in any shape.

> Agents wanted to whom special inducements are offered
> Address: F. R. Woodward
> Hill, NH

Now if you have them printed, I will give one to every man that buys a cutter and trust you will increase your business considerable. I have been selling cutters the past ten months and I have great experience. I will stick by you if you will keep me supplied. Please send the 500 Immediately if possible send that style with one side near the wheel ground bright and blackened just near the putty knife if you have them on hand, if not send the plain kind. They are pretty and take a little better than the plain ones. I hope to send an order for 1000 before two weeks. There are no more holidays for awhile so I am going to stick close to business.

> Yours Very Truly,

Yours Very Truly,
James B. Sanford

James B Sanford
Send by American Express
Buffalo NY

There were hundreds of various large and small machine shops throughout the northeast in the last half of the 19th and the first half of the 20th centuries. . These shops suffered through disastrous fires, financial failures, deaths, and being acquired by others. Two additional glass cutter firms resulted; Millers Falls Co. and Red Devil Co., Inc.

The historical development of the Millers Falls Company is shown in a chart in Table 3. [90] An image of the plant in 1912 is shown in Figure 28.

TABLE 3. Historical Development of the Millers Falls Company.

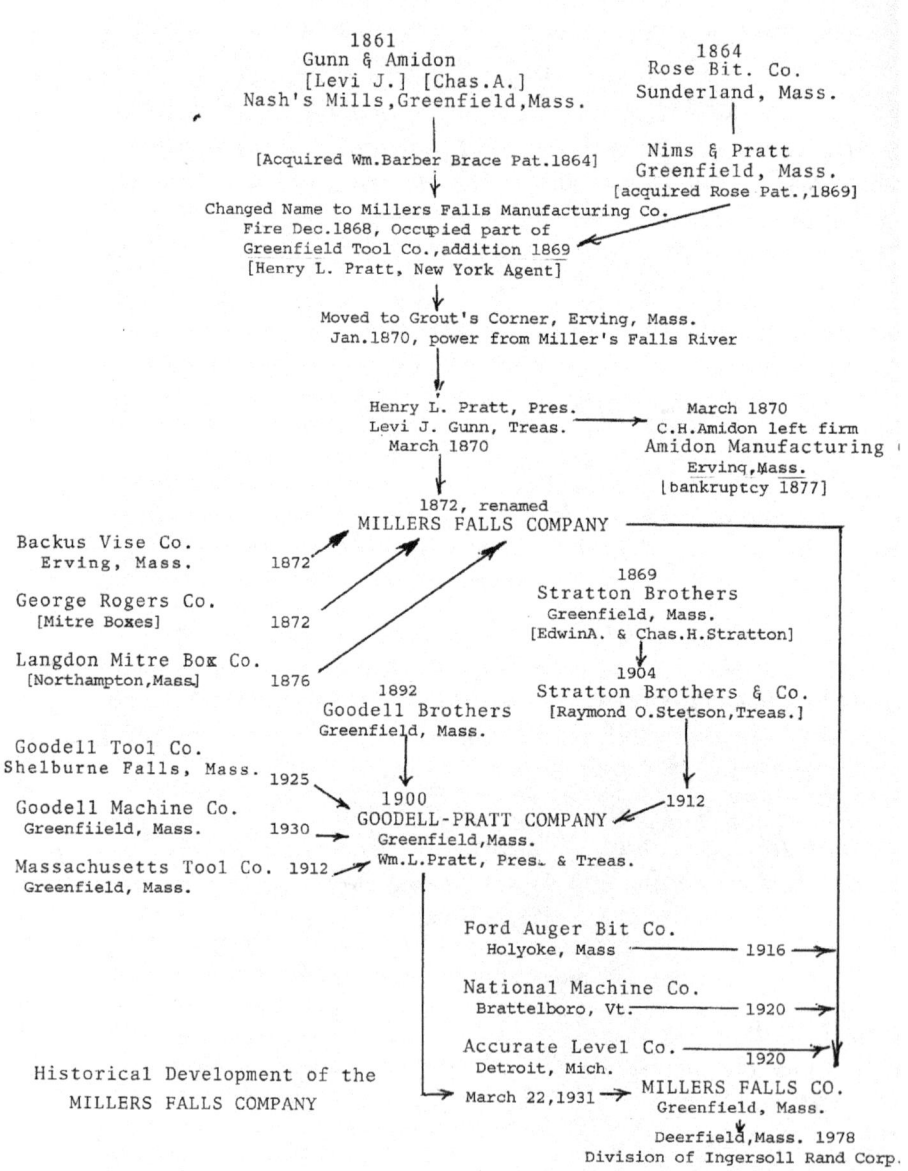

---

[90] Millers Falls Co. 1887 Catalog (Reprint by Ken Roberts Publishing, Fitzwilliam, New Hampshire.

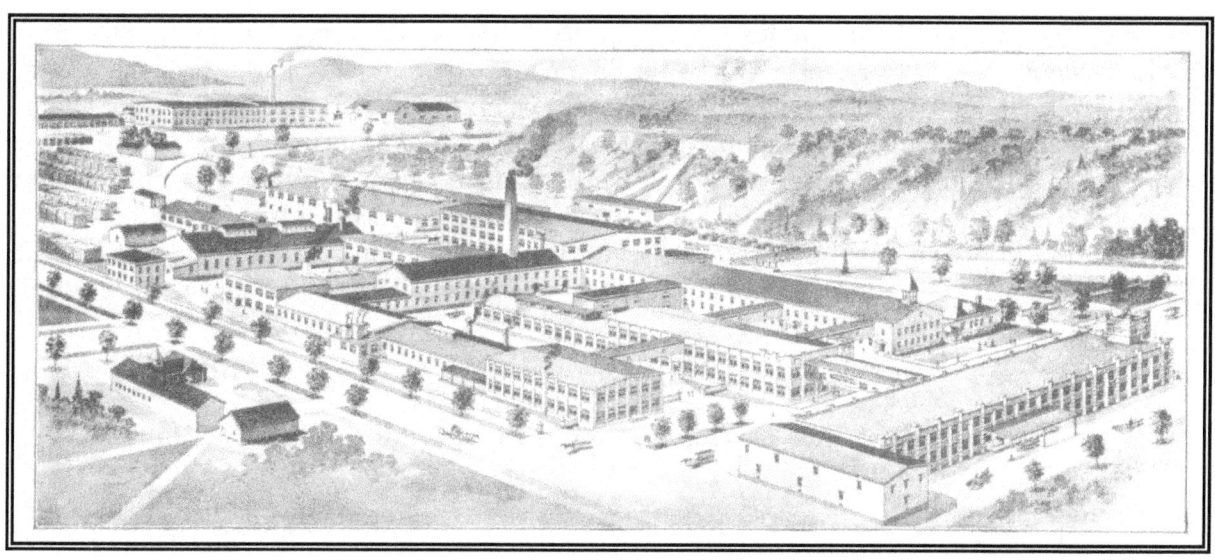

Figure 28. 1912 image of the Millers Falls Company at Millers Falls, Massachusetts. [91]

The 1887 Millers Falls Company catalogue contains two pages illustrating fourteen different glass cutters. The Goodall Tool Company (a maker of glass cutters) merged into the Goodall-Pratt Tool Company (also a glass cutter maker) in 1925 in Greenfield MA, which in turn was acquired by the Millers Falls Company in 1931.[92] The M-S (Mohawk-Shelburne) line of tools introduced in 1935 ended by 1949. In the ten year period, mid 50's to the mid 60's, the Millers Falls Company manufactured products for the Sears Craftsman line. In 1978 the Millers Falls Company became a subsidiary division of the Ingersall-Rand Corporation. The Greenfield plant was abandoned and four years later the Millers Falls Company trademark was sold to an employee.

How important is a glass cutter to the craftsman? A paragraph from the 1916 Millers Falls Company's *Handbook for Mechanics* tells how much: "To the glazier a good glass cutter is an absolutely indispensable tool, but the carpenter and the ordinary man-about-the-house as well finds a good glass cutter very convenient, despite the comparatively few times its use may be necessary. It is one of those tools that when you need it you want it badly, and nothing else will take its place." [93]

Red Devil, Inc. was founded as the Smith & Hemenway Company, Inc. in 1872, in Hill, New Hampshire. The company's founder, Landon P. Smith, adopted the "Red Devil" as his product line name after a visit to Sweden where he heard a blacksmith's remarks referring to the sparks from his forge as "the little red devils."

Prior to WWI several companies were acquired to expand the product line. The company name was changed to Landon P. Smith Company and relocated to Irvington, New

---

[91] Editor, Miller Falls Company, Catalogue No. 35, 1915 (reprinted 1981).
[92] Editor, The Antique Tool Collectors Guide to Value.
[93] Millers Falls promotional booklet, 1916.

Jersey. More than 30 companies were acquired within a 40 year period. In 1944 with the wide acceptance of the Red Devil product line name, the company name was changed again to: Red Devil Tools. With further acquisitions which broadened the product line again, the current name Red Devil, Inc., adopted in 1966 was more appropriate as they were now a lot more than just tools. Later, the hand tool facility was moved to Union New Jersey where the corporate headquarters was also located, then in 2005 moved to Tulsa, OK. Red Devil Inc. also produces private label products for a number of the country's retail chains. Some of the development of the Red Devil Inc. in regard to glass cutters and associated items is shown in Table 4.

TABLE 4. Historical Development of the Red Devil Incorporated Company.

Founded in Hill, NH in 1872 as
Smith and Hemenway, Co., Inc.

↓

Landon P. Smith, Inc.
101 Coit Street, Irvington, NJ
↓
Bought and/or merged with

↓

Hubbard & McClay Mfg. Co. in 1938, mfgr. glazier points
William L. Barnett, Bristol, CT (1890-1945) in 1950
(Made glass cutters for MONCE 1880-1893)
Glaziers Tool Manufacturing Co. (Trojan Brand), in 1944
Jak-Nife brand from Novelty Manufacturing Co., in 1944
(established in 1872 at Hill, New Hampshire)

↓

1944 Name Change to Red Devil Tools

↓

1966 Name Change to Red Devil, Inc. Union, NJ

↓

As of 2005, moved from Union, NJ to Tulsa, OK, and no longer makes
glass cutters.

A copy of an undated (prior to WWI) two – year BOND which is not a financial bond but is an assurance bond of tool performance is shown in Figure 29 below, and an early home of the Red Devil glass cutter is shown in Figure 30 below.

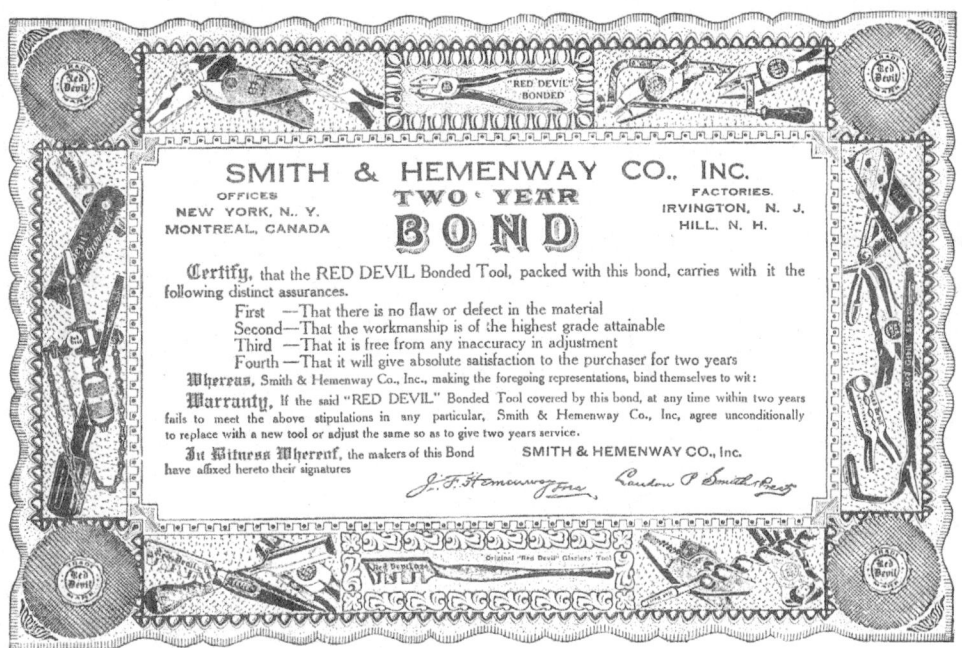

Figure 29. A Two-Year Bond for Assurance for unconditional replacement or adjustment to give two years service.

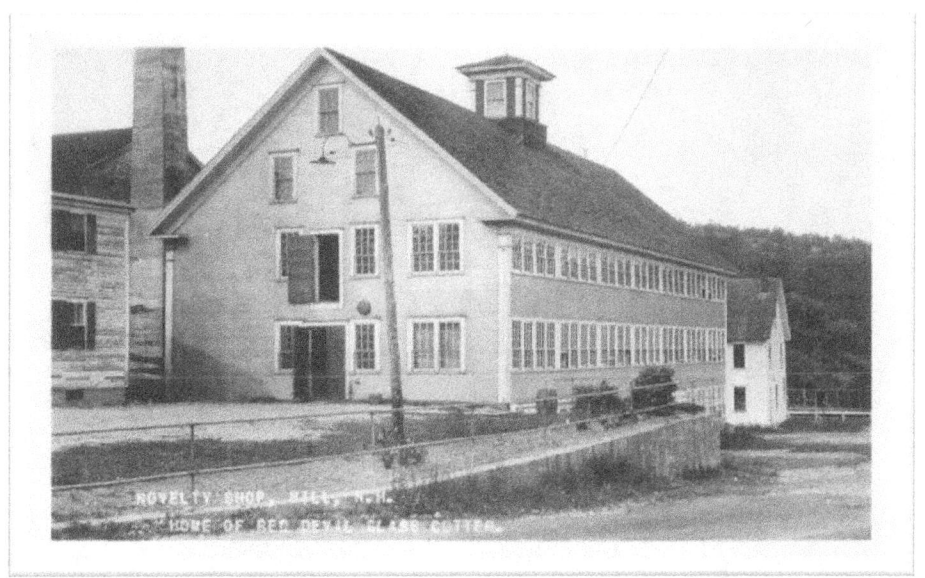

Figure 30. Home of the Red Devil glass cutter, illustrated in a real picture postcard by Putnam (undated). Author's collection

Chapter Three

Techniques For Cutting Flat Glass

Just about every company that sells glass cutters includes their suggestions as how to cut glass. Of course the first step is to obtain the proper diamond point or wheel for the particular type of glass to be cut. The larger supply houses have a multitude of different cutter designs and the accompanying wheels. An article by Bob Roger, "Tool Anatomy" in the December 2009 The Gristmill, brings to our attention in detail the different shapes of the glass cutter wheel used by the several early glass cutter producers. [94] It is advised to use eye protection and gloves while cleaning and cutting pieces of glass.

Clean the glass, as well as the flat surfaces of the workbench, board, or triangular wall mount unit. An exception to the flat surface will be when one cuts old glass that has a radius of curvature. In that case the under surface must be built up so that the pressure applied during cutting does not tend to flatten that curvature causing undue stress on typically brittle old glass. Try never to cut through seeds or stones in the glass. [95]

Make the cut: Use a straightedge to guide the cutter. Be sure the straightedge is firmly fixed, thick enough to guide the cutter, and allowance is made for the distance the wheel or diamond is offset from the straightedge. Start your cut as near to the far edge as possible, draw a firm steady continuous line only once, allowing the cutter to drop off the near edge onto a padded surface. Never repeat the cut.

Break the cut: Break (snap) the glass immediately after the cut. For narrow strip removal use the breaker notches (grozier) on the glass cutter or use special glass pliers. An excellent reference book for cutting techniques and glass cutters is How to Work in Stained Glass by Anita and Seymour Isenberg, chapters 4 & 6. [96]

The following Table 5. "WHEEL ANGLES" is a section taken from The Fletcher-Terry Company web site entitled *Glass Production & Fabrication; Fletcher Academy*.[97]

---

[94] Pp. 14-16.

[95] Three "How to" articles on cutting glass include Thomas J. Jaskowiak, "How to Cut Glass Correctly," *Glass Digest*, July 15, 1972, *How to Cut Glass* on gardendistrictglass.com (2000), and *How to Cut Without A Glass Cutter* on allislands.com/howto/howtocutglass_tpg_gn.htm (2001).

[96] Published by the Chilton Book Company, Radnor, Pennsylvania, 1972 (Reprinted 1983).

[97] www.fletcher-terry.com (2007)

TABLE 5. WHEEL ANGLES AND DIAMETERS

How does the wheel angle affect glass cutting? First let's consider what we are trying to do with a glass cutter. Actually, we do not "cut" glass with a glass cutter. The objective is to create a crack or "fissure" along which we expect the glass to break when we bend it. The idea is to produce a fissure which is continuous, and of uniform depth, without creating a flaky score line full of loose glass chips.

While the wheel angle is only one of several variables which influence the quality of the fissure, it is the best place to start. The other main variables are wheel diameter and cutting pressure.

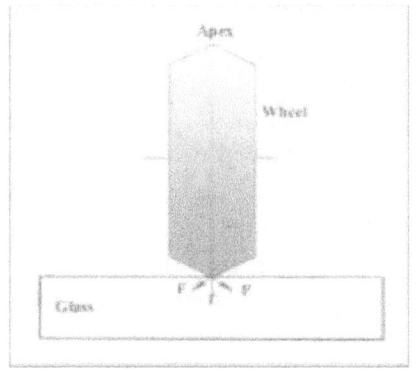

The sketch to the right shows a typical wheel used on single strength (.062" thick) and double strength (.122" thick) glass. The angle is identified as the included angle to which the apex is honed. When downward pressure is exerted on the wheel rolling along the glass, forces are created (F) which radiate down and to the side trying to shear or separate the glass along the surface. These forces are shown with arrows to indicate their direction. If these forces are great enough to overcome the inherent compressive conditions near the surface, a crack (fissure f) will be generated along the path of the wheel.

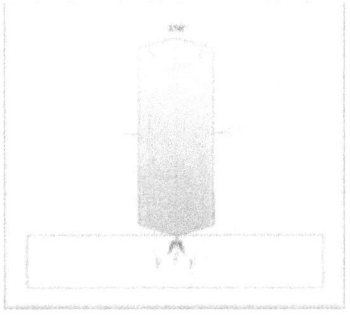

The direction of these shearing forces is determined by the wheel angle. The illustration on the left shows a wheel with a large or blunt angle. Notice the direction of the shearing forces. They tend to be directed downward more than to the side. As you can see, it would require a great deal more cutter pressure to create enough lateral force to overcome the compression in the glass. This explains why a cutter requires more pressure as it gets older. The apex tends to flatten so its effective angle becomes greater.

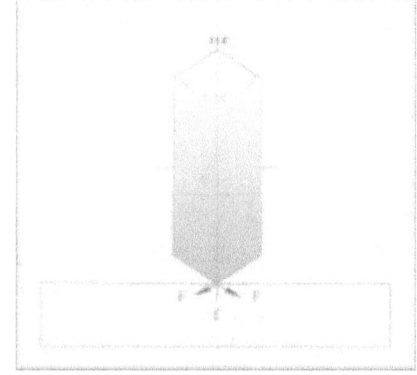

The illustration to the right shows a very sharp wheel angle. The shear forces are directed more parallel to the surface of the glass. This suggests it is easier to produce a fissure with a sharp wheel than a dull one. The shear forces are directly opposing the compressive condition near the surface of the glass therefore, requiring less downward pressure to make a crack. A sharp wheel tends to cause chips and a flaky score. If the shear forces (F) run close to the surface of the glass they are more likely to cause a lateral crack which then breaks out to the surface, creating a chip. You can see these chips leap out of the glass a minute or so after scoring. Again, the compressive condition of glass near the surface literally squeezes the fissure closed, spitting out loose chips. They can be seen lying on top of the glass.

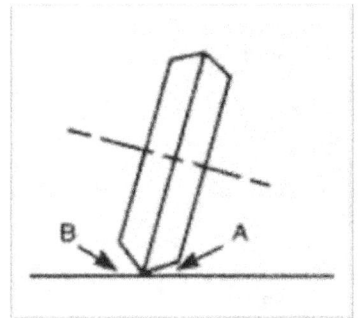

The illustration at the left shows what happens when you tilt the cutter to one side. It is as though two wheels were used simultaneously. The "B" side presents a much sharper angle to the glass and produces chips. The "A" side is much blunter and creates high stress. Another factor to consider in selecting the proper wheel angle is the "edge." The objective of good glass cutting is to produce an edge which is flat and relatively free of irregularities such as "shark teeth." Shark teeth are the occasional flakes on, and results in deep spikes in the edge of the glass.

What is the effect of glass thickness? Most of the glass being used today is produced by the "float method. In this process the glass travels horizontally from the furnace, on top of a thin molten tin bath which floats on a graphite bed, then through annealing lehrs, then continues on rollers where it is inspected, scored (cut) and snapped into the sizes required.

The key to subsequent cutting is the annealing cycle. Thicker glass tends to have less compression at the surface and tension in the interior. As a result, the glass cutting wheel encounters less resistance to producing a fissure which means the glass surface will chip more readily. Therefore, a larger wheel angle is required to prevent chipping. It is also common practice to use a larger diameter wheel and larger angle so the fissure can be driven deeper without chipping.

A typical general purpose cutter such as the steel wheel Fletcher die cast or traditional cast gradually wears the apex with extended use. What started out as an angle of 120 degrees becomes rounded and probably approaches 140 degrees or more. The professional glazier frequently uses this cutter on thicker glass.

What is a "hot" cutter? Professional glaziers consider a new cutter to be "hot" when it produces a flaky score even on single strength glass. They go through a period of breaking in the cutter. This breaking actually wears off the tiny points on the apex caused by intersecting lines produced by the grit of the grinding wheel. Each point acts like a very sharp spike, causing a chip. When broken-in, the apex is a uniform line where the two honed bevel surfaces of the wheel intersect and chipping no longer occurs.

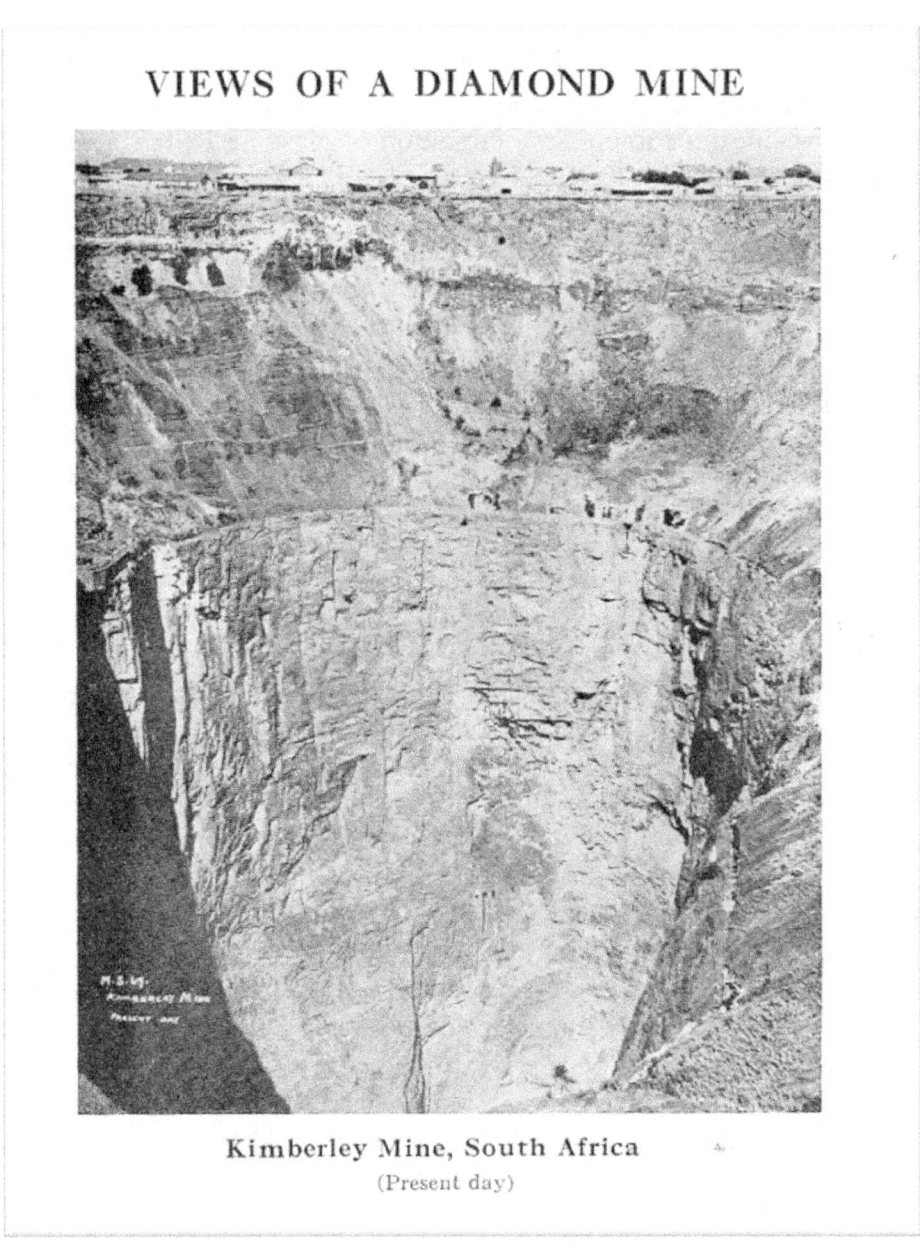

VIEWS OF A DIAMOND MINE

Kimberley Mine, South Africa
(Present day)

Figure 31. The open pit, Kimberly Diamond Mine in South Africa. [98] The author visited this site in 1999.

---

[98] *Diamonds Used in Tools*, Arthur A. Crafts & Co Catalog, 1921, pg. 3.

Chapter Four

U. S. Glass Cutter Patents and Design Patents

The evolution of glass cutter technology is portrayed in the patents. A listing of the lowest patent number of a particular year is given in Table 6. Four hundred ninety six U.S. Patents and twenty eight Design Patents are listed in Tables 7 and 8 respectively. These three tables will assist one in dating a particular item. It is not precise because the item could have been on the market several years prior to the patent issue date (Pat. Pending). There would be no limit as to the length of time a manufacturer would keep advertising the patent date and/or number unless it was superseded by an improvement. A number of these improvements pertain to the method of mounting the cutting wheel and/or the axle and for providing easier replacement of worn wheels.

It is to be noted that the "Knife Sharpener" patent by F. Pass (No. 1749442) does not indicate a glass cutter in the patent. A picture of this particular item is shown in: Category XVIII - 25 page 193 (Novelty-Kitchen) as well as several variations with wheels attached and imprinted with the same patent number.

After the Pilkington Bros. in England perfected the float glass process of continuous casting, there has been a profusion of patents on methods and or apparatus for scoring, cutting, and breaking the glass sheet. As I understand it, at one time the license agreements, all associated float glass operation patents were available to all licensees. Many of these patents are for use during the cutting of the continuously moving glass ribbon, and a few are included in the patent list in Table 8.

Many of these patented glass cutters probably will not be seen by the tool collector since they never made it commercially because of bad timing, were too expensive, under funded advertizing and distribution channels, or because some cutters were for in-house use only by large corporations. Where applicable, the patents in the master list have also been listed with the author's designation of various categories of glass cutters in Chapter 6.

Table 6. Lowest Patent No. of The Year

Year	Pat No.	Year	Pat No.	Year	Pat No.
1836	1	1896	552,502	1956	2,728,913
1837	110	1897	574,369	1957	2,775,762
1838	546	1898	596,467	1958	2,818,567
1839	1,001	1899	616,871	1959	2,866,973
1840	1,465	1900	640,167	1960	2,919,443
1841	1,923	1901	664,827	1961	2,966,681
1842	2,413	1902	690,385	1962	3,015,103
1843	2,901	1903	717,521	1963	3,070,801
1844	3,395	1904	748,567	1964	3,116,487
1845	3,875	1905	778,834	1965	3,165,865
1846	4,348	1906	808,618	1966	3,226,729
1847	4,914	1907	839,799	1967	3,295,143
1848	5,409	1908	875,679	1968	3,360,800
1849	5,993	1909	908,436	1969	3,419,907
1850	6,981	1910	945,010	1970	3,487,470
1851	7,865	1911	980,178	1971	3,551,909
1852	8,622	1912	1,013,095	1972	3,631,539
1853	9,512	1913	1,049,326	1973	3,707,729
1854	10,358	1914	1,083,267	1974	3,781,914
1855	12,117	1915	1,123,212	1975	3,858,241
1856	14,009	1916	1,166,419	1976	3,930,271
1857	16,324	1917	1,210,389	1977	4,000,520
1858	19,010	1918	1,251,458	1978	4,065,812
1859	22,477	1919	1,290,027	1979	4,131,952
1860	26,642	1920	1,326,899	1980	4,180,867
1861	31,005	1921	1,364,063	1981	4,242,757
1862	34,005	1922	1,401,948	1982	4,308,622
1863	37,266	1923	1,440,362	1983	4,366,579
1864	41,047	1924	1,478,996	1984	4,423,523
1865	45,685	1925	1,521,590	1985	4,490,855
1866	51,784	1926	1,568,040	1986	4,562,596
1867	60,658	1927	1,612,700	1987	4,633,526
1868	72,959	1928	1,654,521	1988	4,716,594
1869	85,503	1929	1,696,897	1989	4,794,652
1870	98,460	1930	1,742,181	1990	4,890,335
1871	110,617	1931	1,787,424	1991	4,980,927
1872	122,304	1932	1,839,190	1992	5,077,836
1873	134,504	1933	1,892,663	1993	5,175,886
1874	146,120	1934	1,941,449	1994	5,274,846
1875	158,350	1935	1,985,878	1995	5,377,359
1876	171,641	1936	2,026,516	1996	5,479,658
1877	185,813	1937	2,006,309	1997	5,590,420
1878	198,733	1938	2,104,004	1998	5.704,062
1879	211,078	1939	2,142,080	1999	5,855,021
1880	223,211	1940	2,185,170	2000	6,009,555
1881	236,137	1941	2,227,418	2001	6,167,569
1882	251,685	1942	2,268,510	2002	6,334,220
1883	269,820	1943	2,307,007	2003	6,502,244
1884	291,016	1944	2,338,081	2004	6,671,884
1885	310,163	1945	2,366,154	2005	6,836,899
1886	333,494	1946	2,391,856	2006	6,981,282
1887	355,291	1947	2,413,675	2007	7,155,746
1888	375,720	1948	2,433,824	2008	7,313,829
1889	395,305	1949	2,457,797	2009	7,472,428
1890	418,665	1950	2,492,044	2010	7,640,598
1891	443,987	1951	2,536,016	2011	7,861,317
1892	466,315	1952	2,580,379		
1893	488,976	1953	2,624,046	2012	8,087,094
1894	511,744	1954	2,664,562		
1895	531,619	1955	2,698,434		

TABLE 7. U.S. Glass Cutter Patents

Pat. #	Date	Inventor	Title	Pat. #	Date	Inventor	Title
30,722	11-27-1860	J .Collmann & Feenders	Glass cutter	526,444	09-25-1894	J. W. Heysinger	Holder for glass cutter
30,973	12-18-1860	M. Kleeman	Glass cutter	529,957	11-27-1894	G. A. Rogers	Glazier's tool
33,188	09-03-1861	J. Dickinson	Glass cutter	535,222	03-05-1895	G. A. Rogers	Glazier's tool
33,380	10-01-1861	J. Dichinson	Cutting glass	539,130	05-14-1895	H. T. Haynes	Combination tool
44,331	09-20-1864	A. S. McClure	Glass cutter	546,669	09-24-1895	J. Kohler	Compass & glass cutter
47,645	05-09-1865	M. Kleeman	Glass cutter	557,200	03-31-1996	A. D. Goodell	Glass cutter
56,231	07-10-1866	J. E. Karelsen	Glass cutter	565,493	08-11-1896	W. J. Miller	Glass Cutter
64,157	04-23-1867	P. Sinsz	Glass cutter	574,178	12-20-1896	N. M. Stebbins	Combination tool
85,396	12-29-1868	O. M. Pike	Glass-cutting mach.	596,205	12-28-1897	C. W. Garis	Non-refillable bottle
87,626	03-09-1869	F. Bowly	Glass board	599,620	02-22-1898	C. J. Meissner & Koenig	Window glass cutter
91,150	06-08-1869	S. G. Monce	Tool, cutting glass	601,737	04-05-1898	A. B. Smith	Combination tool
101,111	03-22-1870	G. D. Dunham	Holder, diamonds	607,009	07-12-1898	J. J. Bausch	Lens cutting machine
102,727	05-03-1870	S. C. Stokes	Sharpening mach.	616,825	12-27-1898	C. H. Churchill	Cutter
111,269	01-24-1891	T. Spenard	Glass cutter	630,100	08-01-1899	J. F. O'Neil	Combination rule
126,302	04-30-1872	P. Jennet	Glass cutter	634,336	10-03-1899	W. N. Greer	Compound tool
132,219	10-15-1872	S. C. Stokes	Imp w/ Glass cutter	635,265	10-17-1899	C. E Manning	Glass cutting machine
140,426	07-01-1873	S. G. Monce	Glaziers' tools	618,426	01-31-1899	E. D. Middlekauff	Can Opener
150,225	04-28-1874	H. P. Brooks	Knife sharpeners	655,007	07-31-1900	W. K. Rairigh	Combination tool
166,684	08-17-1875	H. H. Clark	Steel glass-cutters	667,914	02-12-1901	F. W. Klever, Jr.	Tool Scissors
166,954	08-24-1875	F. R. Woodward	Rotary paper cutters	672,312	04-16-1901	H. Cook	Glass tube cutter
167,575	09-07-1875	P. Sinsz	Glaziers' diamonds	673,988	05-14-1901	L. O. Linville	Lens cutting machine
188,058	03-06-1877	J. E. Karelsen	Glazier's diam-holder	674,735	05-21-1901	S. J. Johnston	Combination tool
207,809	09-10-1878	W. Heyn	Glass tube cutter	682,966	09-17-1901	J. W. Tester	Glass cutter
219,313	09-02-1879	B. N. Shelley	Combination tool	683,023	09-24-1901	T. J. Donovan	Glass cutting apparatus
229,228	06-29-1880	B. F. Adams	Revolving glass cutter	696,168	03-25-1902	G. W. Fowle	Lens cutting machine
231,225	08-17-1880	I. W. Heysinger	Glaziers tool	702,732	06-17-1902	D. B. Johnson	Circular glass cutter
246,419	08-30-1881	O. G. Rombotis	Combination tool	702,277	06-10-1902	W. L. Barrett	Glass cutter
266,193	10-17-1882	E. A. Parks	Combination tool	706,196	08-05-1902	W. Offutt	Compound tool
271,868	02-06-1883	H. U. Kistner	Combination tool	717,259	12-30-1902	H. L. Notter	Glass cutter & marker
295,603	03-25-1884	W. H. Walker	Glass cutting Apparat	728,417	05-19-1903	H. J. Sage	Glass cutting apparatus
308,709	12–02-1884	P. Sinsz	Glass cutter guide	742,179	10-27-1903	F. S. Fletcher	Glass cutter
310,914	01-20-1885	E. E. Rollins	Cutter for glass tubes	751,594	02-09-1904	W. L. Williams	Plier type tool
316,430	04-21-1885	J. C. Derby	Tool cut & trim glass	752,017	02-09-1904	W. Pannkoke	Apparatus cutting glass
333,235	12-29-1885	S. G. Lawson	Glass tube cutter	766,827	08-09-1904	H. F. Hughes	Glass cutter
363,563	05-24-1887	E. B. Toedt & Burnham	Glass tube cutter	772,783	10-18-1904	E. Clarke	Lens cutting machine
365,057	06-21-1887	A. T. Duncan	Glazier's diamond tool	778,023	12-20-1904	N. Fells	Glass cutter
365,190	06-21-1887	L. P. Lindgren	Glass tube cutter	781,211	01-31-1905	T. Kinkade	Glass cutter
376,825	01-24-1888	L. Kent	Combination. Pot hook	789,103	05-02-1905	A. M. Parker	Combination tool
395,704	01-08-1889	L. Kent	Combination hook	805,309	11-21-1905	J. Maloy & J. Abraham	Carbon & glass cutter
396,600	01-22-1889	A. McL. Rowland	Glass cutter	813,459	02-27-1906	W. W. Slade & H. Bower	Lens cutting machine
408,055	07-30-1889	J. Urbanek	Glazier's diamond	820,092	05-08-1906	B. A. Brown	Glazier's tool
433,537	08-05-1890	F. McGar	Glass tube cutter	847,633	03-10-1907	R. Anderson	Glass cutter
442,062	12-02-1890	J. E. Lloyd	Glazier's diamond	849,149	04-02-1907	N. A. Lybeck	Glass cutting device
427,002	04-29-1890	O. J. Michaels & Baeder	Glass cutting machine	858,532	07-02-1907	A. M. Parker	Sharpener tool
453,867	06-09-1891	S. G. Monce	Apparatus cutting glass	862,049	07-30-1907	W. Booth	Combination tool
454,322	06-16-1891	P. Smith	Glass tube cutter	863,316	08-13-1907	V. F. Reich	Glass cutter
457,732	08-11-1891	W. T. Levi	Glass tube cutter	887,604	05-12-1908	C. Dorn	Glass tube cutter
464,997	12-15-1891	G. Sandtman	Glazier's diamond	910,129	01-19-1908	W. H. Hanson	Glass cutting machine
467,500	01-26-1892	R. W. Fenwick	Glass tube cutter	911,342	02-02-1909	W. G. Stebbins	Glass cutter
476,626	06-07-1892	J. G. Fowler, Jr.	Glass tube cutter	915,447	03-16-1909	N. B. Keys	Glass cutter
482,256	09-06-1892	A. Landon & M. Mattel	Tool handle	915,818	03-23-1909	B. F. Baldwin	Glass cutter
482,601	09-13-1892	J. Urbanek	Imp. for cutting glass	922,361	05-18-1909	J. W. Tucker	Glazier's instrument
483,778	10-04-1892	A. W. Chesterton	Tool cutting glass tube	934,487	09-21-1909	E. N. Ward & C. Guffey	Glass tube cutter
494,921	04-04-1893	E. F. Hayward	Combo. Glazier's tool	936,674	10-12-1909	C. E. Skinner	Glass tube cutter
505,211	09-10-1893	A. Adams, Jr.	Glass tube cutter	939,843	11-09-1909	J. Lams	Glass cutting tool
506,466	10-10-1893	S. Bray	Glass cutter	942,152	12-07-1909	J. W. Tucker	Glass cutter
507,395	10-24-1893	E. Walsh, Jr.	Glass cutter & guide	950,273	02-22-1910	F. Blodgett	Water glass gage cutter
513,965	01-30-1894	R. W. Fenwick	Hand glass tube cutter	953,806	04-05-1910	T. F. Tivy	Combination tool
515,973	03-06-1894	J. C. Schlarbaum	Compound pocket imp.	958,941	05-24-1910	J. A. Rose	Washer & gasket cutter
515,298	02-20-1894	W. J. Miller	Glass cutter	959,311	05-24-1910	W. Chase, Jr.	Circular glass cutter
520,247	05-22-1894	P. Sinsz	Glazier's diamond				

Pat. #	Date	Inventor	Title	Pat. #	Date	Inventor	Title
983,173	01-31-1911	J. B. Suttleworth	Circular glass cutter	1,495,523	05-27-1924	C. R. MacLean	Cutting device glass etc.
989,603	04-18-1911	A. W. Hornig	Hand oper.glass cutter	1,504,696	08-12-1924	C. R. MacLean	Cutting device glass etc.
992,819	05-23-1911	D. E. Springer	Glass cutter	1,511,016	10-07-1924	A. P. Barker	Glass cutting mechanism
996,385	06-27-1911	G. H. Wilkins	Glass tube cutter	1,515,129	11-11-1924	A. L. Mayer	Glass cutting machine
997,310	07-11-1911	E. Mehlem	Guided glass cutter	1,538,903	05-26-1925	A. Ogint	Glass tube cutter
999,668	08-01-1911	T. A. Montaperto	Cutting bottles etc.	1,547,451	07-28-1925	G. T. Scott	Glass cutter
1,005,637	10-10-1911	R. Friebertshauser	Glass cutter	1,574,989	03-02-1926	A. E. Maynard	Lens cutter
1,024,120	04-23-1912	J. W. Crossley	Tool	1,579,980	04-06-1926	Le Roy A. Walters	Glass cutter
1,024,983	04-30-1912	R. L. Frink	Severing glass cylinders	1,581,883	04-20-1926	A. Steinle	Cut noncircular glasses
1,028,870	06-11-1912	E. F. Fletcher	Glass gage cutter	1,584,572	05-11-1926	F. Foz Bello	Cut tubes, decanters, etc.
1,056,353	03-18-1913	L. C. Moore	Circular glass cutter	1,589,536	06-22-1926	N. Luisi	Glass cutting implement
1,096,782	05-12-1914	P. F. Freytag	Combination tool	1,589,910	06-22-1926	J. Waterloo	Glass cutting apparatus
1,100,878	06-23-1914	G. W. Higgins & J. Ungar	Glass cutter's board	1,606,802	11-16-1926	C. W. Kurtz et al	Glass cutter
1,101,032	06-23-1914	C. T. Moore	Glass cutter	1,610,547	12-14-1926	J. Burda	Glass cutting device
1,101,604	06-30-1914	H. J. Wly	Glass cutter	1,634,323	07-05-1927	A. T. Fletcher	Glass cutter
1,102,843	07-07-1914	F. R. Woodward	Glass cutter	1,638,063	08-09-1927	W. Schluter	Lens cutting machine
1,109,274	09-01-1914	B. L. Altig	Glass cutter	1,649,282	11-15-1927	C. J. Bishop	Glass cutting holder
1,115,333	10-27-1914	H. O. Pease	Glass cutting tool	1,691,530	11-13-1928	F. A. Slayton	Glass tube cutter
1,117,736	11-17-1914	A. P. Whitmore	Sheet glass cut machine	1,697,044	01-01-1929	J. Burda	Glass cutting device
1,122,247	12-29-1914	A. G. Biegel	Lens cutting instrument	1,710,898	04-30-1929	C. A. Rowley	Sheet glass cutting app.
1,123,336	01-05-1915	H. D. Madden	Glass cutting machine	1,720,883	07-16-1929	F. N. Campbell et al	App for severing glass
1,124,784	01-12-1915	W. L. Monro	Glass cutter	1,721,361	07-16-1929	A. Vollm	Glass cutter
1,129,374	02-23-1915	F. R. Woodward	Glass cutter	1,731,257	10-15-1929	J. H. Moller	Glass cutting apparatus
1,134,292	04-06-1915	L. P. Smith	Glass cutter	1,749,442	03-04-1930	F. Pass	Knife sharpener
1,134,307	04-06-1915	F. R. Woodward	Magazine glass cutter	1,750,913	03-18-1930	A. Vollm	Glass cutter
1,135,507	04-13-1915	W. S. Essick	Lens cutting machine	1,753,191	04-08-1930	T. L. B. Armstrong	Combination rule gauge
1,140,143	05-18-1915	H. Falvey	Glass cutting machine	1,755,946	04-22-1930	O. Altenbach	Knife handle
1,141,192	06-01-1915	F. Klensk	Glass cutter	1,770,418	07-15-1930	G. C. McCaskill	Seven-tool combination
1,146,176	07-13-1915	J. Lambert	Glass cutter	1,807,619	06-02-1931	J. A. Boush	Bulb edge glass trimmer
1,153,092	09-07-1915	F. W. McDermott	Glazier's tool	1,865,242	06-28-1932	M. C. Eldredge	Cutting or marking tool
1,161,889	11-30-1915	L. Rothholz	Glass cutting tool	1,870,585	08-09-1932	R. C. Parks et al	Cutting or marking tool
1,167,254	01-04-1916	O. Benson	Glass cutting machine	1,884,635	10-25-1932	C. J. Fancher	Glass cutter
1,169,579	01-25-1916	F. M. Strauss	Glass tube cutter	1,904,568	04-18-1933	G. F. Taylor	Disk like cutting tool
1,169,714	01-25-1916	S. L. Braun	Glass cutter	1,907,297	05-02-1933	C. F. Klanges et al	Multiple glass cutting
1,170,588	02-08-1916	H. J. Wells	Glass tube cutter	1,932,659	10-31-1933	S. I. Granite	Tile cutting machine
1,176,707	03-21-1916	G. A Bader	Glass cutter	1,941,221	12-26-1933	E. B. Odgers	Glass cutter
1,179,706	04-18-1916	C. F. Doerr	Circular glass cutter	1,951,140	03-13-1934	E. H. Fahrney	Glass tube cutter
1,183,144	05-16-1916	J. Wagner	Glass cutting machine	1,962,238	06-12-1934	A. T. Fletcher	Glass cutter
1,186,254	06-06-1916	L. Wilhelm	Lens cutting machine	1,972,210	09-04-1934	F. B. Waldron	Score & snap flat glass
1,188,931	06-27-1916	G. E. Gray	Combination tool	1,988,565	01-22-1935	W. Owen	Glass cutting apparatus
1,201,515	10-17-1916	M. Sidon	Glass cutter	1,996,386	04-02-1935	W. Owen	Glass cutting apparatus
1,219,461	03-20-1917	A. F. Johnston	Circular glass cutter	1,997,561	04-09-1935	W. A. Lockhart	Lens cutting machine
1,221,076	04-03-1917	S. G. Monce	Mounting glass cutter	1,999,594	04-30-1935	W. Owen	Apparatus glass cutting
1,248,145	11-27-1917	A. E. Maynard	Cutting/marking machine	2,013,216	09-03-1935	C. M. McCarthy	Glass holding & breaking
1,263,129	04-16-1918	A. E. Schroeder	Glazier's tool	2,044,577	06-16-1936	N. H. Klages	Glass cutting machine
1,264,430	04-30-1918	M. J. Ossman	Combin. glazier's tool	2,058,091	10-20-1936	P. F. Marsella et al	Glass cutting appliance
1,301,950	04-29-1919	G. W. Klages	Sheet glass cutter holder	2,058,092	10-23-1936	P. F. Marsella et al	Glass cutting appliance
1,307,844	06-24-1919	F. C. Bennett	Cutting board	2,078,386	04-27-1937	M. B. Kendis	Glass cutting mechanism
1,308,260	07-01-1919	M. J. Scullin	Glass cutter	2,091,332	08-31-1937	W. Owen	Glass cutting apparatus
1,344,264	06-22-1920	W. H. Crummey	Compound tool	2,096,284	10-19-1937	G. L. Lee	Glass cutting apparatus
1,347,972	07-27-1920	V. F. Reich	Hand tool	2,122,258	06-28-1938	L. I. Louviaux	Cutting table
1,359,751	11-23-1920	J. R. Scohy	Glass cutter	2,125,864	08-09-1938	W. Auckland	Glass tube cutter
1,375,958	04-26-1921	O B. Gerdin	Glass cutter	2,155,802	04-25-1939	D. Resh	Glass cutter
1,385,732	07-26-1921	W. Taylor	Glass cutter apparatus	2,155,885	04-25-1939	W. E. Baxter	Glass cutter
1,402,961	01-10-1922	W. W. Ratcliff	Glass cutter	2,156,249	04-25-1939	G. C. Wyman	Glass cutter
1,411,524	04-04-1922	J. R. Scohy	Glass cutter	2,174,183	09-26-1939	A. L. Shaw	Glass cutting machine
1,419,310	06-13-1922	H. A. Ryther	Glass cutter	2,174,469	09-26-1939	J. Levin	Glass cutting guide
1,420,867	06-27-1922	J. R. Scohy	Glass cylinder cutter	2,184,126	12-19-1939	G. A. Phillippe	Glass cutting machine
1,421,921	07=04-1922	C. F. Doerr	Rotary glass cutter	2,199,807	05-07-1940	F. E. de G. Moreira	Glass tube cutter
1,423,127	07-18-1922	E. Levy	Scissors	2,205,717	06-25-1940	F. A. Fedon	Tile scoring & breaking
1,424,625	08-01-1922	C. F. Doerr	Rotary glass cutter	2,209,701	07-30-1940	A. J. McGann	Cut & score bottle necks
1,427,052	08-22-1922	A. A. Arnold	Glass cutter	2,210,193	08-06-1940	L. A. Aillaud	Glass cutter
1,435,985	11-21-1922	J. R. Scohy	Glass cutter	2,212,599	08-27-1940	R. F. Hall	Glass cutting appliance
1,442,926	01-23-1923	J. E. Dezell	Circular glass cutter	2,219,698	10-29-1940	W. Owen	App. severing gls.sheets
1,456,672	05-29-1923	O. Degrenier	Cutter	2,243,778	05-27-1941	T. J. Stansel	Glass cutter
1,459,369	06-19-1923	H. W. Hill	Glass cutter	2,254,162	08-26-1941	G. C. Wyman	Glass cutting device
1,462,030	07-17-1923	H. B. Davis	Glass cutting machine	2,246,055	06-17-1941	A. E. Maynard	Lens cutting machine
1,463,374	07-31-1923	H. Schuetz	Combination tool	2,250,159	07-22-1941	R. S. Grube	Glass cutter
1,465,366	08-21-1923	R. Schumann	Cutting spectacle glasses	2,254,541	09-02-1941	E. E. Nordgren	Sheet glass trim device
1,482,206	01-29-1924	L. L. Tuley	Glass tube cutter				
1,487,360	03-18-1924	S. J. Phillips	Combination tool				

Pat. #	Date	Inventor	Title
2,260,706	10-28-1941	M. C. Eldredge	Glass cutter
2,261,214	11-04-1941	W. Bierman	Glass cutter
2,265,955	12-09-1941	W. Roberts et al	Double glass cutter
2,268,257	12-30-1941	A. W. Kobylinski	Glass cutting tool
2,283,134	05-12-1942	R. C. Barrett	Glass cutter
2,289,718	07-14-1942	A. W. Moore	Glass cutter
2,302,174	11-17-1942	J. H. Boicey et al	Glass cutting method
2,312,635	03-02-1943	A. T. Fletcher	Glass cutter
2,314,327	03-23-1943	J. L. Drake	Glass cutting apparatus
2,341,030	02-08-1944	A. T. Fletcher	Glass cutter
2,341,201	02-08-1944	N. S. Ballard, Sr.	Contour cutting machine
2,361,049	10-24-1944	A. C. Oakes	Glass cutter
2,375,378	05-08-1945	J. R. Morris	Cutting machine
2,394,138	02-05-1946	F. C. Barrett	Glass cutter
2,425,093	08-05-1947	D. W. Fosler	Ampule cutter
2,430,349	11-04-1947	L. Lefebvre	Glass cutter
2,447.988	08-24-1948	L. A. Pierson	Ampule neck cutter
2,470,444	05-17-1949	G. A. Phillippe	Glass cutter
2,473,189	06-14-1949	W. M. Baker	Glass cutter
2,476,680	07-19-1949	W. D. Norgard	Elec. Glass tube cutter
2,503,517	04-11-1950	J. D. Sirica	Ampule neck cutter
2,504,655	04-18-1950	J. Dallas	Cutting sheet glass
2,507,779	05-16-1950	M. A. J. L. Gault	Glass cutting device
2,507,841	05-16-1950	R. P. Upton	Cutting glass means
2,513,876	07-04-1950	C. K. Judd, Jr.	Glass cutter
2,515,445	07-18-1950	V. M. Gilstrap	Glass cutting machine
2,516,668	07-25-1950	R. C. Barrett	Glass cutter
2,522,818	09-19-1950	J. H. Geula	Optical lens cutter
2,529,735	11-14-1950	H. Martin	Glass cutter
2,534,775	12-19-1950	C. K. Judd, Jr.	Glass cutting board
2,539,601	01-31-1951	O. F. Walker	Glass cutting tool
2,556,757	06-12-1951	L. V. Guild	Glass cutting apparatus
2,566,434	09-04-1951	J. J. Toth et al	Tube, ampule cutter
2,566,544	09-04-1951	G. C. Wyman	Glass cutter wheel, head
2,576,291	11-21-1951	A. T. Fletcher	Cutting glass discs
2,577,486	12-04-1951	F. G. Schwalbe	Glass cutting machine
2,573,919	12-18-1951	R. C. Bowers	Glass cutting table
2,582,078	01-08-1952	T. Solum et al	Glass cutting apparatus
2,591,828	04-08-1952	C. K. Judd, Jr.	Glass cutting device
2,595,862	05-06-1952	E. J. Lavander	Glass cutting device
2,603,873	07-22-1952	A. L. Shaw	Glass cutting gauge
2,612,001	09-30-1952	O. Denlinger	Cutting brittle tubing
2,612,689	10-07-1952	W. Kirkman et al	Template cut machine
2,619,775	12-02-1952	C. K. Judd, Jr.	Glass cutting board
2,629,173	02-24-1953	F. M. Mottet	Diamond holder attchmt
2,629,174	02-24-1953	D. R. Corrado	Glass cutting gauge
2,631,411	03-17-1953	L. A. Pierson	Glass tube cutter
2,652,659	09-22-1953	A. T. Fletcher	Glass cutter
2,674,066	04-06-1954	H. Pederson	Cutting glass tubing
2,685,764	08-10-1954	H. B. Hatfield, Jr.	Glass cutter
2,707,849	05-10-1955	G. C. De Vore	Pillow post
2,732,623	01-31-1956	W. Vaughan	Glass cutting machine
2,735,228	02-21-1956	W. H. Shortell	Glass cutting tool
2,750,674	06-19-1956	J. W. Lee	Glass cutter
2,756,545	07-31-1956	F. V. Atkeson	Glass cutting machine
2,763,929	09-25-1956	R. S. Metcalf	Glass Cutting gauge
2,774,188	12-18-1956	C. M. Jordan, Jr.	Lens cutting machine
2,778,115	01-22-1957	O. W. Dillon	Lens cutting machine
2,812,579	11-12-1957	W. M. Arck	Glass cutting tool head
2,814,163	11-26-1957	L. S. Krulwich	Glass cutting apparatus
2,818,651	01-07-1958	H. M. Polley	Cutting machine
2,839,871	06-24-1958	L. M. Austin	Glass rod & tube Cutter
2,892,291	06-30-1959	C. C. Coleman	Glass cutter holder
2,943,392	07-05-1960	R. B. Attridge	Beam compass tool
3,026,153	03-20-1962	C. K. Judd, Jr.	Ball axle assembly
3,058,220	10-16-1962	R. H. Eary	Glass scoring machine
3,084,431	04-09-1963	B. L. steirman	Glass rod & tube cutter
3,106,018	10-08-1963	C. K. Rudd, Jr.	Axle for glass cutters
3,122,953	03-03-1964	F. V. Atkeson	Glass cutting apparatus
3,126,636	03-31-1964	J. J. Brand	Glass cutter assembly
3,127,680	04-07-1964	E. Brichard et al	Cutting sheet glass
3,130,499	04-28-1964	H. P. Hanneken	Glass cutting apparatus
3,136,191	06-09-1964	J. G. Madge	Glass cutting head
3,138,868	06-30-1964	H. Kuthroff	Plate glass cutter
3,160,043	12-08-1964	C. K. Judd, Jr.	Pillar post for glass cut
3,165,017	01-12-1965	P. Galabert	Cutting strip of glass
3,169,683	02-16-1965	B. H. Pierce	Meth of breaking glass
3,175,745	03-30-1965	T. A. Insolio	Glass breaker
3,196,722	07-27-1965	H. V. Lewis et al	Pipe cutter
3,198,044	08-03-1965	B. Clin	Glass cutting apparatus
3,216,635	11-09-1965	M. Lefevre	Apr. break glass sheets
3,221,405	12-07-1965	A. Bohle	Glass cutter
3,224,098	12-21-1965	J. D. Terrell	Ellipse scriber
3,227,016	01-04-1966	C. H. Moeller	Glass cutting tool
3,253,756	05-31-1966	R. L. Haley et al	Apr. cutting glass sheets
3,274,390	09-20-1966	F. K. Umbel	Glass cutting apparatus
3,276,302	10-04-1966	T. A. Insolio	Glass cutter
3,280,676	10-25-1966	B. Grzymislanwski	Glass cutting apparatus
3,318,500	05-09-1967	D. L. Swanson	Cutting rigid tubing
3,392,445	07-16-1968	J. Koran et al	Combination glass cutter
3,373,488	03-19-1968	A. T. Fletcher	Glass cutting apparatus
3,395,493	08-06-1968	G. E. Bonin	Cutter for glass pipe
3,399,586	09-03-1968	T. A. Insolio et al	Glass cutting head
3,403,442	10-01-1968	R. C. Reese et al	Scoring glass articles
3,406,886	10-22-1968	P. E. Wesel et al	Cutting glass tubing
3,439,426	04-22-1969	R. D. Wilson	Glass cutting tool
3,461,755	08-19-1969	J. T. Gerew et al	Glasscutter
3,462,835	08-26-1969	L. J. Fancher	Glasscutter/plastic insert
3,518,907	07-07-1970	F. Pinel	Glass-cutting machine
3,537,344	11-03-1970	A. W. Nixon et al	Cutting glass
3,537,345	11-03-1970	A. Luppino	Glass cutting apparatus
3,550,273	12-29-1970	T. A. Insolio	Long reach glass cut tool
3,555,944	01-19-1971	K. Imamura	Scoring glass sheets
3,570,336	10-23-1971	K. G. Galla	Holder glass cutter wheel
3,572,564	10-23-1971	F. L. Fleming	Glass bottle & jug cutter
3,577,636	05-04-1971	R. P. Detorre	Resilient cutter
3,593,899	10-02-1971	R. P. Detorre	Glass scoring process
3,600,992	08-24-1971	J. M. Dryoon	Scoring of glass sheet
3,682,027	08-08-1972	T. A. Insolio	Glass cutter
3,699,829	10-24-1972	E. J. Gelfman	Cutting glass bottles
3,703,115	11-21-1972	Y. Nagae et al	Glass ribbon cutting
3,742,793	07-03-1973	J. M. Grey et al	Scoring sheet material
3,742,794	07-03-1973	C. F. Rupprecht et al	Glass cutting system
3,744,359	07-10-1973	E. J. Gelfman	Glass bottle cutter
3,744,692	07-10-1973	J. S. Doyel	Bottle cutter
3,756,104	09-04-1973	D. A. Bier et al	Cutting of glass
3,787,040	01-22-1974	B. W. Allen	Tiltable cutters table
3,797,339	03-19-1974	H. Pape et al	Glass cutting apparatus
3,797,340	03-19-1974	G. F. Pereman	Glass cutting device
3,800,639	04-02-1974	M. F. Restel	Glass cutter
3,812,748	05-28-1974	I. Nausbaum	Glass cutting device
3,821,910	07-02 1974	J. S. Tjaden	Glass cutting mechanism
3,839,006	10-01-1974	J. W. Pikor	Cutting notch sens mat'l
3,845,555	11-05-1974	J. E. Hanson	Bottle cutter
3,850,062	11-26-1974	T. A. Insolio	Glass cutter
3,850,063	11-26-1974	E. J. Witkoski	Pillar post glass cutter
3,865,673	02-11-1975	R. P. Detorre	Scoring glass sheets
3,880,028	04-29-1975	W. Frederick, Jr.	Control glass cutting
3,880,029	04-29-1975	R. M. Bonaddin et al	Ganged scoring of glass
3,902,643	09-02-1975	E. J. Gelfman	Cutting glass bottles
3,903,767	09-09-1975	S. Kupersmith	Glass cutting apparatus
3,908,878	09-09-1975	J. Blum	Glass knife mkg appratus
3,945,278	03-23-1976	G. Strauss et al	Making relief cuts
4,018,372	04-19-1977	T. A. Insolio	Glass cutting apparatus
4,028,801	06-14-1977	E. J. Gelfman	Hand-hed glass cutter
4,030,195	06-21-1977	T. A. Insolio	Scoring with edge guide

Pat. #	Date	Inventor	Title	Pat.#	Date	Inventor	Title
4,040,182	08-09-1977	D. R. O'Dell	Holder for glass cutter	4,446,768	05-08-1984	J. J. Sirmans	Glass cutter device
4,044,464	08-30-1977	G. Schless	Circular cutting device	4,451,981	06-05-1984	A. Kanfarz	Glass cutter
4,046,299	09-06-1977	J. G. Swartzfageer	Glass cutting method	4,494,444	01-22-1985	J. H. Masse	Glass cutting app
4,057,184	11-08-1977	E. R. Michalik	Arcurate scoring wheel	4,495,845	01-29-1985	J. E. Sherby	Pattern cutter
4,083,274	04-11-1978	T. A. Insolio	Glass cutter	4,528,752	07-16-1985	M-T Benedict	Glass cutter
4,098,155	07-04-1978	T. A. Insolio	Self-comp. Score head	4,541,176	09-17-1985	C. L. Croce	Glass cutter & accessory
4,098,156	07-04-1978	T. A. Insolio	Long axle & retainer hldr	4,571,828	02-25-1986	R. G. Miffitt	Lubricated glass cutter
4,110,907	09-05-1978	R.Einhorn et al	Glass cutter	4,576,079	03-18-1986	P. Donofrio	Glass scriber assembly
4,112,793	09-11-1978	D. C. Pierce	Oval cutter device	4,628,784	12-16-1986	P. Gach	Glass scoring assembly
4,120,220	10-17-1978	W. C. Mullen	Glass cutter apparatus	4,667,555	05-26-1987	P. Lisec	Glass cutting table
4,137,803	02-06-1979	J. A. Goldinger	Glass scoring device	4,672,874	06-16-1987	P. Gach	Glass scoring assembly
4,155,495	05-22-1979	W. P. Cathers	Sheet glass cutter	4,679,476	07-14-1987	E. Abreu	Guide & glass cutter system
4,161,819	07-24-1979	F. Pietrantonio	Glass cutter	4,691,438	09-08-1987	T. A. Insolio	Constant force glass cutter
4,171,657	10-23-1979	F. Halberschmidt et al	Numerical ctrl machine	4,709,483	12-01-1987	C. B. Hembree et al	Glass cutting device
4,175,684	11-27-1979	J. K. Butler	Mechanical glass scorer	4,726,500	02-23-1988	R. E. Rock	Glass scoring machines
4,183,274	01-15-1980	J. T. Kingsley	Roller scriber for glass	4,739,555	04-26-1988	W. Jurgens	Laminated glass cutter
4,187,755	02012-1980	K. Shiral	Sheet gls cutting apparatus	4,819,535	04-11-1989	C. M. Thomas	Glass cutting apparatus
4,197,639	04-15-1980	U. Bohle	Glass cutter	4,871,104	10-03-1989	A. Cassese	Auto. Vert. Glass cutting
4,201,104	05-06-1980	T. A. Insolio	Glass cutter	4,872,289	10-10-1989	I. Yukawa et al	Cutter
4,203,209	05-20-1980	T. A. Insolio	Glass cutter attachment	4,878,260	11-07-1989	W. A. Tunningley	Combination tool
4,205,438	06-03-1980	R. D. Sikorski	Scoring tool	4,881,439	11-21-1989	R. E. Biedermann	Cutting appar. Sheet mat'l
4,209,272	06-24-1980	M. Miyanaga	Holes in plate gless	4,890,526	01-02-1990	K. J. Slodic	Glass score- cutting appar.
4,210,052	07-01-1980	A. R. Fisfer	Scoring mechanism	4,916,820	04-17-1990	V. T. Kozyrski etal	Circle & strip cutting sys.
4,220,066	09-02-1980	B. Hargreaves et al	Cutting sheet apparatus	4,939,968	07-10-1990	R. E. Stoof	Glass cutting apparatus
4,221,150	09-09-1980	N. H. Bergfelt	Glass scribing apparatus	4,987,814	01-29-1991	V. T. Kozyrski etal	Turret for cutting head
4,222,300	09-16-1980	M. E. El-Habr	Glass Scoring apparatus	5,005,318	04-09-1991	A. Shafir	Appr. Cutting glass blanks
4,224,738	09-30-1980	A. F. Megawick	Precision glass cutter	5,012,393	04-30-1991	E. A. Knipe et al	Base for bottle lamp
4,225,072	09-30-1980	M. D. Reeves	Fracturing prescored glass	5,014,436	05-14-1991	V. T. Kozyrski	Circle cutting system
4,226,153	10-07-1980	T. A. Insolio	Comp. Glass score head	5,040,445	08-20-1991	U-F. Liou et al	Glass tile cutter
4,228,711	10-21-1980	T. A. Insolio	Self-castering glass cutter	5,044,245	09-03-1991	D. Molleker et al	Rotary circle cutter
4,275,633	06-30-1981	J. J. Littlehorn, Jr.	Pattern following free arm	5,070,563	12-10-1991	P. J. Tervola	Tool bearing rings
4,277,889	07-14-1981	E. T. Oberg	Glass cutting means	5,165,585	11-24-1992	P. Lisec	Appar. break glass sheets
4,283,852	08-18-1981	O. D. Hooper	Glass cutter attachment	5,168,788	12-08-1992	V. T. Kozyrski	Cutting head turret assy.
4,287,669	09-08-1981	T. Arai	Glass cutter	5,169,045	12-08-1992	W-H liu et al	Man-operated tile cutter
4,291,824	09-29-1981	R. P. DeTorre	Self-aligning method	5,337,483	08-16-1994	M. Jacobs	Glass cutter
4,296,662	10-27-1981	R. R. Reed et al	Sheet gls cutting apparatus	5,361,498	11-08-1994	B. Siebenlist	Cutting nippers
4,297,059	10-27-1981	M. Miyanaga	Holes in plate glass	5,381,713	01-17-1995	Q. C. Smith	Glass scoring mechanism
4,307,643	12-29-1981	H. F. Diegel	Multi head cutter machine	5,394,505	02-28-1995	S. R. Bidare	Thermal jet glass cutter
4,327,488	05-04-1982	P. Connolly	Hand held glass cutter	5,398,579	03-21-1995	S. Bando	Glass plate cutting device
4,339,877	07-20-1982	D. C. Pierce	Hand-held cutter	5,438,757	08-08-1995	S. Weschenfelder	Multifunction cutting tool
4,347,958	09-07-1982	D. C. Wood	Glass cutting apparatus	5,480,082	01-02-1996	M. Yasuga	Tile cutter
4,351,459	09-28-1982	P. Huey-Miin	Automatic glass tube cutter	5,507,212	04-16-1996	G. Morrison	Radial arm saw glass cutter
4,361,130	11-30-1982	A. R. Maglia	Glass grozing tool	5,535,933	07-16-1996	R. L. Dickerson	Glass scoring machine
4,372,471	02-08-1983	L.Galindez	Glass cutting system	5,558,565	09-24-1996	V. Dedonato	Glass patter cutting device
4,383,460	05-17-1983	R. D. Schotter	Pillar post for glass cutters	5,836,229	11-17-1998	H. Wakayama et al	Glass scribing disc
4,385,540	05-31-1983	W. J. Dieter	Scoring of glass sheets	5,924,618	07-20-1999	D. A. Doak	Magnet device scoring glass
4,392,404	07-12-1983	N. Schwarzenberg	Cutting head gls machine	6,065,215	05-23-2000	A. Arai	Cutter wheel
4,434,582	03-06-1984	G. Strauss et al	Glass trimming cutter	6,202,530	03-20-2001	R. Cawley	Glass cutting device
4,437,376	03-20-1984	D. L. Flint	Cntl pressure tool on glass	6,405,440	06-18-2002	R. G. Clark	Glass tap & cutting head
				6,818,477	11-02-2004	M. Funakubo	Handsaw for cutting glass

TABLE 8. U. S. Glass Cutter Design Patents

Pat. No.	Date	Issued To:	Title
34,761	07-09-1901	F. G. Reynolds	Frame for knife sharpeners & glass cutters
93,639	10-16-1934	W. H. Shortell	Design for glass cutter
107,180	11-23-1937	G. C Wyman	Glass cutter
120,613	05-21-1940	A. Deerf	Combination kitchen tool
199,132	09-15-1964	R. S. W. Lindsey	Combined blade tool & glass cutter
220,745	05-18-1971	S. J. Kovacik	Glass cutting tool
225,607	12-26-1972	T. A. Insolio	Handle for glass cutter or similar
230,130	01-29-1974	F. Greaves	Freehand glass cutter
233,308	10-22-1974	J. E. Hansen	Bottle cutter
252,131	06-19-1979	R. Einhorn, et al	Glass cutter
261,982	11-24-1981	T. Arai	Glass cutter
262,435	12-29-1981	T. Arai	Glass cutter
265,543	07-27-1982	P. Connolly	Glass cutting tool
267,853	02-08-1983	T. Arai	Glass cutter
268,392	03-29-1983	T. A. Insolio	Glass cutter attachment
273,082	03-20-1984	M-T. Benedict	Glass cutter
274,598	07-10-1984	M-T. Benedict	Glass cutter
275,071	08-14-1984	M-T. Benedict	Glass cutter
275,171	08-21-1984	M-T. Benedict	Glass cutter
275,260	08-28-1984	M.C. Williams etal	Glass cutter handle
276,694	12-11-1984	M-T. Benedict	Handle for glass cutter or the like
278,969	05-28-1985	C. E. Johnson	Glass cutter
285,285	08-26-1986	H. Soyama	Glass cutter
286,853	11-25-1986	C. E. Johnson	Pattern glass cutter
306,686	03-20-1990	H. R. Walden	Glass cutter
344,005	02-08-1994	T. Arai	Glass cutter
589,774	04-07-2009	Haraguchi & Mackawa	Glass cutter
589,775	04-07-2009	Haraguchi et al	Glass cutter

Chapter Five

Introduction to the Glass Cutter Collection

The small red or green metal glass cutter with the small wheel is likely to be found in many home tool kits. Whether it is ever used successfully or not is another matter. It is rather easy nowadays to go to the hardware store with your frame and say "do it". However, if one were to "do it" at home, one must first have a spare piece of glass large enough to "do it". How many keep piles of replacement glass around the house? Then, how many have luck cutting the nice straight line in exactly the right place, and at that without breaking while either cutting or installing? Most of the time I have good luck both with new and old glass, yes, I keep a quantity of old pre-1920 glass around.

This little tool to work properly must be taken care of, because if the diamond is out of alignment, the wheel loses its edge, or the axle seizes so the wheel does not rotate easily – forget it! The advent of the harder carbide wheel obviated part of the problem. A well mounted diamond cutter used properly does very nice.

With all the problems keeping and using a glass cutter, why if they don't work are they kept around? A non-working glass cutter has how many other uses? Maybe the combination tools are saved for their corkscrews, knife sharpeners, knife blades, bottle openers, etc., but most likely worked their way to the bottom of the tool box and forgotten.

Why are there knobs (or balls) on a number of the glass cutters and other tools as well? The debate continues: decoration, safety, functional, balance, etc. Old tool buffs are not of one accord and evidently the manufacturers don't elaborate. As far as glass cutters are concerned, one must concur that safety, balance and functionality are of uppermost consideration, but then why don't all have a knob end?[99]

The collection now numbers more than 1,400 "different" glass cutters and the author knows of 425 different ones in other collections, and hundreds more shown in catalogs that might still be "out there." Some things that make one glass cutter different from another, in my mind, may differ from someone else's idea. For example: Many of the diamond point cutters will look very much alike, but have a different wood in the handle or different inscriptions on the ferrule and/or steel head. The "French" brass crescent head is made in several countries with slightly different head and/or handle designs. Likewise the basic Red Devil or Fletcher and the myriad of look alikes from around the world

No attempt to define how rare any of the glass cutters are has been made. A number of them have only been seen once, others two or three times, yet others are common enough to have been seen ten or even hundreds of times in the last 35 plus years. A general price

---

[99] Ken Turner, "Questions Recently Raised & Discussed Among Three Tool Buffs," *The Gristmill*, No. 73, December 1993 and Watson Cutter, (Letter to the Editor), *The Fine Tool Journal*, Vol. 44, No. 2, Summer 1994.

range by group style has been given within each of the twenty three classification categories. Like most collectors, we get some free, some we get as very good deals, while others we pay too much for, but overall try to average out. Of course condition counts.

The names that appear on the various glass cutters are of several origins: The manufacturer; a secondary wholesaler or retailer; a trade name; or a trademark. A number of them, of course, are unmarked in any manner. The country or city of origin is marked on many. Some have been made when country of origin was not a requirement or were never intended to be used outside the country where they were made.

Many companies or wholesalers produced a variety of styles or categories. There are 400 different names indicated in this collection and there are many more different names in other collections and in old catalogs, etc. In Table 9, "Glass Cutter Names," an alphabetical listing of the glass cutter ID by name, manufacture, or retail/wholesale outlet company is given only for the cutters in this collection. Also included is country of origin, if known, and my classification type. Many glass cutters have no ID at all.

TABLE 9. Glass Cutter Company, Distributor, and / or Product Names

NAME	DESCRIPTION	ORIGIN	PAGE
ABBOTT	diamond	London..................69	
ACME	novelty	Toronto, Canada.....194	
ADAMS, J.	diamond	New York..............77	
ADAMS, J.H.	diamond	New York..............69, 77	
ADEPTO TOOL	misc. - table	USA...................190	
AFFUTTEUR	novelty	.........................195, 196	
A G & J	jackknife	Germany.............204	
ALL BEST BRITISH TOOL Co.	turret	Sheffield.............153	
AMERICAN HANDICRAFTS	bottle	Texas.................165	
ANDRESS TOOL	early cast iron	.........................105, 106	
ANTILL, T. E.	diamond	England...............69, 94	
APEX	standard - bottle opener – novelty	.... 191, 192, 194, 195, 209	
ARA	crescent	130	
ARTISANS TOOL	early iron	106	
ASHCROFT MFG. Co.	tube cutter	NY...................162	
3 – ATMUM	beaver tail	Russia or Bulgaria....89	
B & C	diamond	London................93	
BARRETT	standard - tubing – turret	USA.................110, 143, 145, 163, 209	
BARRETT,W.L.	early cast iron	USA.................106, 109	
BARTHELMES & SALCHOW	crescent	135	
BEANCO	diamond	England..............69	
BELFOR	novelty - 6 wheel turret	England..............201	
BELFOR SENIOR	turret	British made.........155	
BENRATH	diamond-circle	167	
BENSON BRADFORD	diamond	69	
BERK CUTLERY	jack knife	Germany.............204	
BEST	standard	USA...................216	
BICHON SODCE(FORGE)	jackknife	204	
BIDDLE & KING	diamond	London................69, 73, 77	
BINSWANGER	standard	USA...................210	
BLACK PANTHER	standard	USA...................210	
BOKER, HENRY	diamond / turret	Germany..............79, 145	
BORTON, H. & Co	diamond	London...............69	
BOWDEN	diamond	London................73	
BREVETE	misc. - hefty	.........................124, 240.	
BRITISH & FOREIGN GLASS	diamond	Glasgow.............101	
BROOK PHILLIPS & Co.	diamond	London................69	
BROOKS, H.P.	early cast iron	USA....................110	
BROOKSTONE	diamond	Japan...................69	
BROWNIE	standard	USA...................210	
B. S. G. D. G.	crescent - hefty	French............... 132, 134	
BTE SGDG	hefty - novelty	.........................117, 122, 200	
BUCK & HICKMAN	diamond	England..............69	
BUCK & RYAN	diamond	London................69	
BUCK, G.	diamond	London................69	
BULL DOG	standard	USA...................210	
BURGON	diamond	London................69	
BUSH & CHIPPER	diamond	England...............69, 77	
CAL-HAWK	standard	Taiwan...............210	
CAMP "BELL"	standard – turret – wheel	.....................142, 152, 210.	
CELEBRATE	diamond point – jackknife	Germany.............203	
CEMEHBb	crescent	Russian...............98	
CENTRAL SCIENTIFIC	tubing	Germany.............164	
CHANDOS	turret	England.............145	
CHESTERTON'S	tube cutter	USA................. 161, 162	
CHICAGO SPECIALTY MFG	tubing	Illinois.................163	
CITY GLASS Co.	diamond	Glasgow.............101	
C. K.	turret	W. Germany.........151	
CLARK BROS.	jack knife	Germany.............203	
CLEAN-CUT BOTTLE	bottle	Texas.................165	

NAME	DESCRIPTION	ORIGIN	PAGE
CLEARVIEW	misc	USA.....................238	
CLEMAC	novelty	England...................198	
COLLIN & Co.	crescent	134	
CORBETT	diamond	London – Birmingham.....69	
COSMO MFG Co.	jack knife	Germany...................205	
CRAFTS, ARTHUR A.	circle	USA.....................186	
CRAFTSMAN	standard – turret	USA...................145, 210, 219	
CRAWFORD & Co.	diamond	England.....................69	
CRESCENT	turret	145	
CRESSWELL, C.	diamond	London.....................100	
CRL	standard - single wheel	Germany.................143, 210	
CROWDEN & GARROD	diamond - single wheel	London 69, 138	
CROWNSHEET	diamond	70	
C. S. , PARIS	crescent head	Paris.....................130	
CUCUMBER	diamond	London.....................70	
CURRIE, A. P.	diamond	Glasgow.....................70	
D.F.&T. Co.	plier	Utica.....................113	
DANDY-GOLD MEDAL	can opener	196	
DE	diamond – standard	.........................100, 220.	
DELBRUECK, W. C.& SON	jackknife	Germany...................206	
DEPOSE(many others)	penta-head	France.....................94, 95, 116, 122, 123, 126, 132, 155, 196, 197	
DEPULLEY DIAMOND TOOL	diamond	London.....................70	
DEVOE, F. & RAYNOLDS, C.	diamond	New York...................77	
DBGM	misc.	Germany...................240	
DIACARBIDE PRODUCTS INC.	diamond	98	
DIAGLASS SPECIAL	hefty	Belgium....................118.	
DIAMANTOR	standard-wood handle-turret	Germany.................139, 143, 145, 210	
DIAMOND BRAND	diamond	China.....................77	
DIAMOND TOOL Co.	diamond	Chicago, USA.............79, 99	
DIAMOND TOOLS Ltd.	diamond	Birmingham, England.....70	
DIAMOVI S.G.D.C.	hefty	Paris.....................124	
DICKINSON, J.	diamond	New York...................80	
DICKINSON (SHAW)	diamond-ivory - circle	NYC & Phila.............79, 168	
DICKINSON, THOS L.	diamond	NY.....................73, 77	
DIXON, J CUTLERY	jackknife	Germany...................203	
DOMINION	diamond	India.....................73, 80	
DRAPER	turret	W. Germany...............146	
D-Tec	carbide "diamond"	73	
DUNHAM, G.D.	diamond	Chicago, USA.............77, 80, 99	
DUNLAP	turret	146	
DURANDAL	crescent	129	
EARL, D. & Co.	diamond	Chicago.....................77, 99	
ECLIPSE	standard	USA.....................210, 211	
EFTECO	standard	USA.....................211	
ELECTRA VOICE CORP	novelty	Chicago.....................197	
ELITE	circle	170	
ELLIOTT CUTLERY	jackknife	Germany...................203	
ELLIS	diamond	London.....................70	
EMBEE CORP.	standard	USA.....................211	
EMPIRE	standard	Taiwan.....................211	
ENDIA	diamond	England.....................70, 73	
ERIE	single wheel wood	138	
ERNST WATER COL. & GAGE Co.	tubing	Livingston, NJ............163	
ERSATZ – RAD	crescent	135	
ETALI	hefty	Frence.....................119	
ETIENNE	diamond – crescent	95	
EUREKA	circle	Chicago.....................184	
EURO - PRADEL	novelty	196	
EVERCUT	turret	Belgium.....................146	
EXAKT	crescent	136	
EXCELSIOR	diamond - wheel	USA.....................73, 137	

NAME	DESCRIPTION	ORIGIN	PAGE
FALLEUR & ORBAN	hefty	Gilly	118
FAR EAST	diamond	Korea	81
FARIS	misc		237
FARMILOE, T. & W.	diamond	Westminster	70
FIL D'ARGENT	turret		155
FIX "N" SAVE	wood handle turret	West Germany	146
FLASH	standard	USA	211
FLEMING BOTTLE & JUG	bottle	Seattle, WA	165, 166
FLETCHER	standard – turret - circle	USA	171, 176, 189, 190, 231, 232, 233
FLETCHER - TERRY	turret – tubing – circle - wall	USA	162, 178, 190, 233
FOREST CITY	standard		211
FRW	standard		211
F. T. Co.	standard	USA	231
GARANTIE STAHL	jackknife	Austria	207
GERLING CUTLERY	jackknife	Germany	203
GILKIN	standard		221
GLASTAR	circle		185
GLAZIER'S I. M. CO.	circle		179
GOODELL-PRATT	wood handle -standard –tube - turret	Greenfield, MA	139, 146, 147, 152, 163, 179, 211
GOODELL TOOL Co.	wood handle - tubing – misc	Shelburne Falls, MA	109, 139, 147, 148, 154, 163, 179, 211, 236
G-P Co.	standard - circle	USA	179, 211
GOVERNOR	turret	England	152
"GOVERNOR"	turret	USA	148
GRAFTON	novelty	England	198
GRANT TOOL MFGRS.	diamond – novelty	Cleveland, OH	81, 99, 194
GREAT NECK	standard	USA	211
GRENADE	diamond crescent	St. Eteinne	92
GRIFFIN	tube cutter	New Jersey, USA	164
G - T – L	turret	Sheffield	153
GUIDE	diamond crescent	French	94
GUTALSKY	jack knife	Germany	205
GUY'S HANDTOOL'S LTD	turret		148
H & B SERIES	turret	England	148
HAAKE, CHAS. , DICKINSON	diamond	New York	77
HAGA	turret		148
HALL	diamond	Bristol	74
HALL & SONS	diamond	Bristol	70
HANLINE BROS.	block	Baltimore, USA	99
HEWITT, J. & Co.	wood handle	Sheffield	142
HIBLENTS	misc.		236
HOLTHAUS & SON	diamond	Baltimore	70
HORLAVILLE	diamond	Rouen	93
HOWARD	standard	England	212
HOYNE	standard	USA	212
HUNT, A. L.	tubing	USA	162
HUNT, Jeff'N L.	diamond	Boston, USA	70
H. W. V. & Co. Ltd	turret	England	148
HYCO	standard	USA	216
HYDE	standard	USA	212, 216
IDEAL	standard/novelty		192, 196, 212
IMCO	turret – circle		148, 176
IMPERIAL	jack knife	USA	205, 208
INDIAN	standard	USA	212
INDUSTRIAL DIAMOND TOOLS	circle	New York	170
INDUSTRIAL TOOLS "STAR"	diamond	Birmingham, England	70
INNES-WELD GLASS CO	diamond	Chicago	101
IVY CLASSIC	standard	Taiwan	212
JACCARD	crescent	Swiss	119, 121
JANOS, Mester	novelty		198
JDEAL	novelty		201

NAME	DESCRIPTION	ORIGIN	PAGE
J. H. & Co	single wheel wood handle	138
J.K.O. Co.	diamond	70
JAMES, A.	diamond	London.....................70, 77
JENNINGS	standard	USA...........................212
JOBO	turret	Germany....................148
JOHNSON, R. W.	diamond	London....................70
JORDAN	turret	Germany...................148
"J.W."	standard	212
J.W.C.	standard	212
KARELSEN	diamond	New York................70, 74, 77, 78, 81, 82, 102
KEEN KUTTER	diamond -st'd. -single wheel	USA........................140, 212
KING, E. & F. & Co	diamond	Boston.......................70
KLAGES, G. W.	circle	Pittsburgh..................171, 175
KOBALT	turret	China..........................157
KRISTEE PRODUCTS CO.	novelty	Akron, OH..............191
LANDAU, A. & Co.	diamond	Phila.........................78, 83
LEE MASTER	novelty	197
LE DURABLE	crescent	Pont Arlier..............130
LENOX	standard	212
LE RESCHE	crescent head	French......................134
L'IDEAL	block	French......................103
LIZ-PAC	novelty	195
LLOYD	diamond	Brooklyn , NY...........74, 78, 83, 99
LOCKETT, CHUCK , & Co.	diamond	London.....................70
LORING	diamond	Boston, USA.............70
MacHOB, C. F.	beaver tail	USA............................89
MACINNES	standard	USA...........................220
MACLEOD, P & T	diamond	PERTH.....................101
MAGEWICK	standard	USA........ 219
MAGIC DIAMOND	block	USA...........................104
MAJESTIC CUTLERY	jackknife	Germany................204
MANOS CUTLERY	jack knife	Germany................203
MARPLES, Wm & SONS	diamond	London.....................70
MARSWELLS	block	London....................100
MARVEL RACK	wall unit	USA...........................189
MATHIESON, A., & SONS	diamond	Glasgow....................70
McREA & ROBERTS Co.	tube	160
MELHUISH, R. Ltd.	diamond	78
MENIDIAM	hefty	120
MENTONE	novelty	192
MEPHISTO	standard	212
MEYER	sheet metal novelty	France...................200
M. F. Co.	standard – turret – single wheel	USA........ ....142, 149, 152, 179, 213
M. H. Co.	wood handle	NY............................139
MILLERS FALLS Co.	standard - turret – tubing	M. Falls, MA..........137, 141, 142, 149, 152, 153, 163, 212, 213, 219, 220
MIRCLE GLASS & TILE	circle	China.....................185
M-S (Mohawk-Shelburne)	standard	USA...........................213
MOLETTE, RABOT	wheel, heavy	126
MONARCH	standard	USA...........................215
MONCE, S.G.	standard	Bristol, CT..............213, 220
MONCE	early cast iron	USA......................105, 106, 108, 109, 110, 213
MONCRIEFF'S, USL	tubing	161
\MONITOR	multi head	Millers Falls, MA.....152
MONTGOMERY & Co.	diamond	NYC........................74
MORETON, J., & Cº	diamond	London....................70
MULLI	novelty	198
NASHUA LOCK	early iron	106
N E	standard	213
NETTLEFORD & MOSER	diamond	70
NEW ERA	novelty	197
NICHOLS & CLARKE	diamond	England....................71
NICHOLSON, J. A, & C.	diamond	London....................70
NIPPON DIAMOND Co.	diamond	Japan.........................70
ηOΛTABA	diamond crescent – beaver tail	Russian...................89, 98
NURSE & Cº.	diamond	London...................70

NAME	DESCRIPTION	ORIGIN	PAGE
SHARRETT & NEWTH	diamond - circle - crescent	London 71, 74, 75, 78, 83, 84, 94, 98, 100, 102, 168, 170	
AINSWORTH, J.		71	
BAXENDALE		Manchester.....................71	
BROOKS and THOMAS & Co.		Dublin.......................71	
BROOKS, HENRY, & Co		71	
FLEMING , W.		72	
MARSWELLS		England...................100	
NICHOLS & CLARKE, Ltd.		71	
WHITTIER FULLER & CO		San Francisco.................78	
WILLIAMS & WATSON Ltd.		Liverpool....................71	
WINDER & HARROP		Beedles.......................75	
YOUNG, J. & Co.		Kennington....................71	
SHAW, A. & SON	diamond – turret – single wheel	London.......................72, 78, 101, 138	
SHAW, JOHN & SONS Ltd.	diamond	Wolverhampton.................72	
SHAW	diamond – standard –turret - circle	England........................72, 101, 138, 149, 151, 157, 169, 214, 215	
SHAW PATENT – KOMMEL	diamond	London.......................78	
SHEFFIELD	wood handle -jackknife – single- turret	England.......................138, 142, 153, 208	
SHOEMAKER	diamond	Phila., PA.....................78	
SHURON OPTICAL CO.	optical/circle	USA.......................188	
SILBERSCHNITT	circle – crescent -single wheel - turret	Germany.......................135, 143, 151, 157, 173, 182	
SINGER	standard - circle – turret	USA.......................156, 175, 215, 217	
SINSZ, P.H.	diamond	Baltimore.......................75, 79, 99, 100, 103, 125, 186	
SIXTY	standard	215	
SMIT, J. K. & SONS	diamond(beaver tail)	England.......................88	
SOLINGEN	jack knife	Germany.......................205, 206, 208	
SOLOMON, L. & SON	diamond	NY (made in England)........79	
SOMACA	single wheel wood	Germany.......................143	
SOMACA	standard	USA.......................215	
SOMMER & MACA	circle cutter- standard	Chicago, USA.................173, 184	
SPADICK	jackknife	Chicago.......................204	
SPARDIA	turret	149	
SPEEDY	tube	USA.......................163	
SPIRALUX	turret	England.......................149	
STAG BRAND	jackknife	Sheffield.......................206	
STANDARD	wood handle – turret	USA.......................149	
STANFORD STUDIO ENG.	misc.	USA.......................241	
STANLEY	standard - turret	USA.......................151, 215	
"STAR" INDUSTRIAL TOOL	diamond	Birmingham...................70	
STAR SHEET	diamond	72	
STAR WARRANTED	diamond	72	
STEELCRAFT	wood handle – turret	West Germany.................149, 150	
STOCK, SONS & TAYLORS	diamond	Birmingham...................72	
STOCK, W. & Cº	diamond	Manchester....................72	
STOKES, S. C. (Patent date of)	early iron(Lady legs)	111	
STRONG GUY	standard	Taiwan.......................215	
SUISSE(Rabot)	hefty	121	
SUPERCRAFT	diamond	China.......................79	
SUPREME	wood handle – turret	West Germany.................150	
SWAN WORKS CUTLERY	jackknife	Germany.......................203, 206	
SWEET, L. J.	Jackknife	England.......................206	
SYRONE	novelty	England.......................198	
TAN	misc.	China.......................236	
TARSA, ES	novelty	BPEST.......................198	
TASK FORCE	turret	158	
TECHNICAL DIAMONDS Ltd.	diamond	England.......................75	
TERTROP	hefty – circle	.....................120, 185	
TOMAHAWK BRAND	novelty	Taiwan.......................198	
TOTTENHAM	diamond	84	
TOUR EIFFEL	novelty	208	
TOYO	standard	Japan.......................221	
TREMONT TOOL	early cast iron	USA.......................106	
TROJAN	standard	Chicago, USA.................215	
TRU-CUT	circle	Brocton, MA.................173	
TYZAK, S. & SON	diamond	London.......................72	

NAME	DESCRIPTION	ORIGIN	PAGE
ULTIMATE	misc. - novelty	...................................202, 240	
U M C°	early cast iron	London.......................108	
UNI CORP	turret	Germany.......................150	
UNIPRISE	turret	150	
UNITED CUTLERY	misc	198	
UNIVEBEL	turret	156	
UNIVERSAL	turret-misc-beaver tail-turret	Germany , Austria............ 86, 150, 202	
URBANCK, JOH & Co	diamond	79	
USL MONCRIEFF'S GAGE	tubing	161	
UTENSILI A-B-C	circle	185	
UTICA	standard – turret - pliers	USA.......................113, 156, 216	
VERIBOR	turret - bottle	Germany.......................150, 158, 165, 166, 173	
VERY BEST	crescent head	 130	
VEST POCKET	misc.	236	
VITREX	standard - turret	England.......................158, 184, 185, 221	
VITREX	circle - standard	Swiss.......................184, 185, 216	
VITRUM	hefty	 125	
W. & G. GAGE	tube	161	
WADSWORTH, A.W., & SON	jack knife	Germany.......................203	
WAL – RICH CORP.	tubing	USA.......................164	
WARNER	standard	USA.......................216	
WATSON & C.	diamond	London.......................72	
WDK	single wheel	139	
W.G.C.L. of A.	diamond shawl cutter(misc)	...................................244, 245	
WHITTIER FULLER & C°	diamond	England/USA.................78	
WILKINS PATENT	tube	162	
WILSON	diamond	72	
WINDER & HARRUP	diamond	London.......................75	
WIZARD	standard	USA.......................216	
WOODWARD TOOL Co.	early cast iron - misc.	USA.......................106, 108, 237	
WOOLWORTH	standard	USA.......................216	
YOUNG & MARTEN	diamond	Stratford.......................72	
ZANDVOORT - GOUDA	single wheel wood	140	

We collectors thank those who have used and owned these tools in the past and now make them available to others.

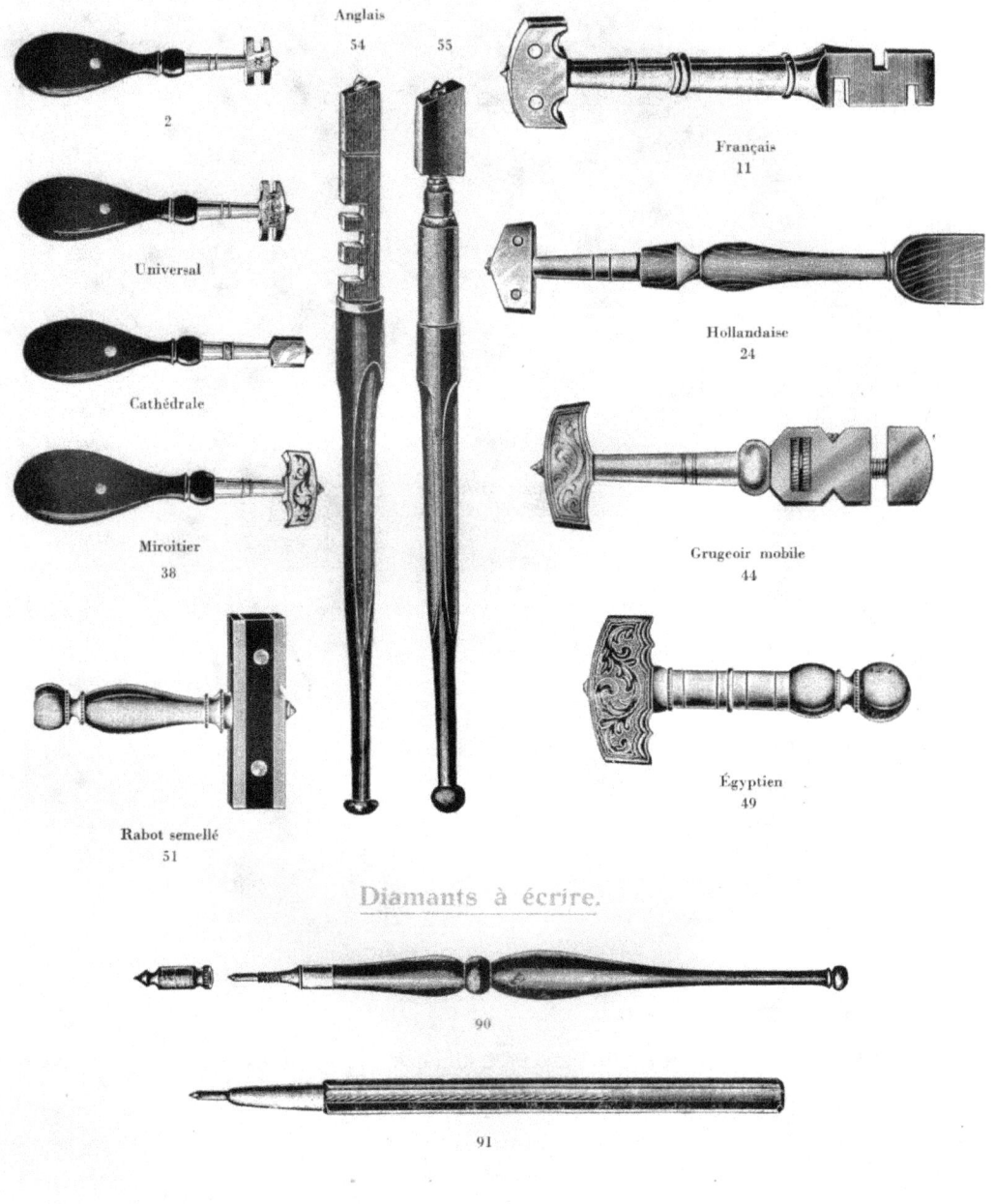

Coupe-verres en différents modèles.

Tous autres modèles peuvent être obtenus sur demande.

Anglais
54   55

2

Français
11

Universal

Cathédrale

Hollandaise
24

Miroitier
38

Grugeoir mobile
44

Égyptien
49

Rabot semellé
51

Diamants à écrire.

90

91

ÉTABLISSEMENT TECHNIQUE DIAMANTAIRE

Figure 32. Copy of page 12 from: *L'Établissement Technique Diamantaire à Anvers, Belgique*

1910 - 1935 25th ANNÉES D'EXPÉRIENCE

Chapter Six

Glass Cutter Categories
By Type, Pictures, Descriptions and Patents

To facilitate the identification and comparison of such a large number of different glass cutters that are included in this book, it has been sub-divided into twenty-three separate categories and are listed in Table 10. An additional four categories are included for associated items. Within a given category a number of glass cutters may be different in only the minutest detail. Some are different in name only, others, the color of paint, stain, shape, size (thickness or length), or kind of wood, metal, plastic, and of course wheel diameter or method of securing the wheel.

A picture of each individual glass cutter is not included. A picture of a glass cutter that represents a very close likeness to others is included. Following the picture is a detailed description of all glass cutters of a similar nature. A price range is a great variable because of the small sample size, the spread of time, and the desire of so many collectors other than strictly glass cutter collectors. Specifically, corkscrew collectors are many and avid. Then there are those that specialize in materials such as brass, ivory, or pocket combination tools. The U. S. Patent list in Table 7 is broken down into a list for each category where applicable.

The 425 different glass cutters known to have been acquired into other hands in the last thirty years are noted for each category. These have been obtained by observing eBay and antique sales. A number of these are quite unique in design. There are hundreds more shown in old catalogs and brochures from around the world (See Bibliography – Catalog Section).

A few Associated Items are shown in Category XXIV.
A sampling of Gummed Labels are shown in Category XXV.
A sampling of Glass and Label Scrapers are shown in Category XXVI.
A very important reference for glass cutter collectors is given in Category XXVII. Shown are a collection of PHOTOGRAPHIC TRIMMERS that are not glass cutters, but are often offered for sale as glass cutters. Illustrations of same and description of use are reproduced from an 1884 catalog provided by the George Eastman House Museum, Rochester, N. Y.

Table 10. GLASS CUTTER CATEGORIES

CATEGORY I DIAMOND POINT - WITHOUT BREAKERS

The typical diamond point glass cutter in this category has a steel head, brass ferrule, wood handle with a ball and is 7 to 7.7 inches in length. A few older ones have bone or ivory handles while newer ones may have plastic or aluminum handles. There are a number of variations in this category which could have or should have been listed somewhere else but are noted following the typical with individual pictures.

There are 73 additional glass cutters in this category known to be in other collections.

Price range: $10 to $60, with more for ivory handles.

Typical Category I glass cutters with names, numbers, locations, etc. on the brass ferrule and/or a rosewood or walnut handle with flattened sides(unless noted)

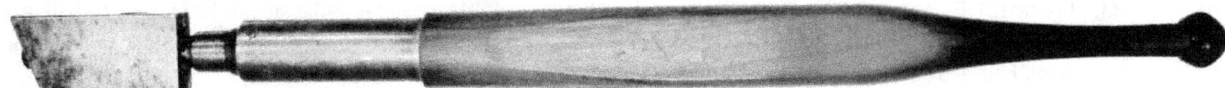

1. ABBOTT MAKER LONDON - S 1 stamped on top of head – bottom of head is rounded – small ball - 7.3"
2. ADAMS, J.H. PATENT NEW YORK - dark finish flattened ball - 7"
3. ADAMS, J.H. NEW YORK - dark finish flattened ball - 6.4"
4. ANTILL, T.E. WORTHING ENGLAND - C 3 stamped on top of plated head - small ball - 7.3"
5. BEANCO MANCHESTER - round tapered handle - flattened ball - 6.95"
6. BENSON. BRADFORD. - A stamped on head - fruitwood finish medium ball - 7.8"
7. BIDDLE & KING PATENT LONDON - a small C stamped on top of head - small ball - 7.1"
8. BIDDLE & KING PATENT LONDON - a small P stamped on top of head - medium ball - 7.3"
9. BIDDLE & KING PATENT LONDON - a small 6 stamped on top of head - small ball - 7.25"
10. BORTON, H. & C° GLASS MERCHANTS LONDON E2 - S A stamped on top of head - bottom of head is rounded - medium ball - came in walnut hinged lid box stamped: A. W. CHIPPERFIELD - 7.4"
11. BORTON, H. PATENT LONDON - a small B stamped on top of head - small ball - 7.3"
12. BROOKS PHILLIPS & C° PADDINGTON GREEN LONDON - A S stamped on top of head - small ball - 7.35"
13. BROOKSTONE WARRANTED JAPAN(small letters) - 2 A stamped in large on top of head that is .5" high vs. .55" for I-14 & 15 - fruitwood color plastic handle with small ball - 7.3"
14. BROOKSTONE WARRANTEED JAPAN(medium letters) - 2 A stamped in large on top of head - walnut finish on wood handle with small ball - 7.15"
15. BROOKSTONE WARRANTED MADE IN JAPAN - 2 A stamped in large letters on top of head - fruitwood color plastic handle - medium ball - 7.1"
16. BUCK & HICKMAN LTD BIRMINGHAM - P D stamped on top on head - bottom of head is rounded - medium ball - 7.7"
17. BUCK & HICKMAN LIMITED MAKERS LONDON - a small A stamped on top of head - medium ball - 7.25"

17-A. BUCK & RYAN – LONDON – A on top of head – walnut handle with ball – 7.4"

18. BUCK, G. PATENT LONDON - a small S stamped on top of head - bottom of head is rounded - small ball - 7.3"
19. BURGON LONDON - small head - small flattened ball - 6.4"
20. BUSH & CHIPPER MAKERS LONDON - a small A stamped on top of head - medium ball - 7.2"
21. BUSH & CHIPPER MAKERS LONDON - small 2 S stamped on top of head - bottom of head is rounded - medium ball - 7.4"
22. BUSH & CHIPPER MAKERS 9 PERCIVAL ST LONDON - a small B stamped on top of head - small ball - 7.1"
23. CORBETT PATENT BIRM M - small head - small ball - 6.65"
24. CORBETT PATENT LONDON L P stamped on top of large head - bottom of head is rounded - small ball - 7.5"
25. CRAWFORD & C° TOTTENHAM LONDON - D stamped on top of head - I believe the ball was cut off - 6.8"
26. CROWDEN & GARROD LONDON - 1 stamped on top of head - small ball - 7.3"

27. CROWNSHEET WARRANTED - a set screw is recessed above the diamond unit to hold it in place - a large rounded bottom head - medium ball - 7.2"
28. CUCUMBER - bottom of head is rounded fruitwood stain - medium ball - 7.05"
    28-A. CURRIE, A. P. GLASGOW – bottom of head rounded – walnut handle – small ball – 7.4"
29. DEPULLY MAKER 18 SPENCER PLACE GOSWELL ROAD LONDON - small head - thin dark handle small ball - 6.95"
30. DIAMOND TOOLS LTD BIRMINGHAM A 100 stamped on top of head - .4' brass neck and no ferrule - thin handle and large ball - 6.4"
31. ELLIS PATENT LONDON - small head and small ball - 7.05"
32. ENDIA BRITISH MADE - natural light wood finish medium ball - 7.05"
33. FARMILOE, T & W. LIMITED WESTMINSTER 4 - AWH carved into flat side of handle small ball - 7.1"
34. HALL & SONS INVENTORS BRISTOL - small head - plated brass ferrule - slender ivory handle - small ball - 6.75"
35. HOLTHAUS & SON BALTIMORE - medium flattened ball - 7.05"
36. HUNT, JEFF'N L. BOSTON - fruitwood - small ball - 7"
37. INDUSTRIAL TOOLS THE "STAR" BIRMINGHAM ENGLAND(facing the head) - medium ball - 6.9"
38. J. K. O. CO. - very thin finger rest section with slender handle with no ball - 7.25"
39. JAMES, A. PATENT LONDON WARRANTED - S stamped on top of rounded bottom head - small ball - 7.35"
40. JOHNSON, R. W. LEE LONDON - 3 stamped on top of head - small ball - 7.2"
41. KARELSEN NEW YORK - small head - ivory handle - small ball - 6.95"
42. KING, E & F. & C° BOSTON - small head - small flattened ball - 6.9"
43. LOCKETT, CHUCK & C° PATENT LONDON - slightly rounded head on bottom - small ball - 7.25"
44. LORING, C. G. & C° PATENT BOSTON - small head - small flattened ball - 6.65"
45. MARPLES, WM & SONS LONDON - 6013 D stamped on top of head - large ball - 7"
46. MARPLES, WM & SONS LONDON - 6816 Y stamped on top of thick head with rounded bottom - medium ball - 7.5"
47. MARPLES, WM & SONS LONDON - 6616 Y stamped on top of rounded bottom head slightly smaller than I-46 - light natural wood finish(may have been stripped) - medium ball - 7.3"
48. MATHIESON & SONS LTD GLASGOW - 2 stamped on top of head - small ball - 7.25"
49. MORTETON, J. & C° PATENT LONDON WARRANTED 2 - a small s stamped on top of head with rounded bottom - medium flattened ball - 7.25"
50. NETTLEFOLD & MOSER - A on upper right of obverse side of head - large ball - 7.45"
51. NICHOLSON, J A. & C° PATENT LONDON - thick rounded bottom head with P stamped on top - small ball - 7.5"
52. NIPPON DIAMOND Co., TOKYO WARRANTED - large 2 stamped on top of rounded bottom head - small ball - 7.55"
53. NURSE & C° LONDON - B S stamped on top of rounded bottom head - medium ball - 7.35"
54. PATENT LONDON - rounded bottom on head - medium ball - 6.4"
55. PIDLER & AYRES MAKERS LONDON - a small D stamped on top of rounded bottom head - small ball - 7.5"
56. PILKINGTON BROS LTD St HELENS(reads toward head) - STAR in a big star on reverse side of head with a 6 and an A below the lower two points - rounded bottom on head - small ball - 7.55"
57. PITTS 1893 - medium head - small ball - 7.2"
58. RADCLIFFE ENFIELD ENG. King of diamonds "playing card" logo on obverse side of head - 00 stamped on finger rest - small ball - 7.3"
59. RADCLIFFE, A . PATENT LONDON - a small 2 stamped on top of medium head - small flattened ball - 7"
60. RADCLIFFE, A. JUNR PATENT LONDON - slight rounded bottom on head - small flattened ball - 7.3"
61. RADCLIFFE, A. PATENT LONDON WARRANTED - small head - small ball - 6.75"
62. RADCLIFFE, A. LONDON WARRANTED - large 2 stamped on top of small head - small ball - 7.2"
63. RADCLIFFE'S "KING OF DIAMONDS" REGD - THINSHEET stamped on obverse side of head under the king of diamonds "playing card" logo - small ball - 7.2"
64. RADCLIFFE'S "KING OF DIAMONDS" Regd - REGD stamped on obverse side of head under the king of diamonds "playing card" logo - S 1 stamped on top of rounded bottom head - small ball - 7.4"

65. RADCLIFFE'S "KING OF DIAMONDS" - REG<u>D</u> stamped on obverse side of head with "king of diamonds" logo in upper left corner - medium ball - 7.45"

66. RADCLIFFE'S "KING OF DIAMONDS" - REG<u>D</u> stamped on obverse side of rounded bottom head under the king of diamonds "playing card" logo - P 2 stamped on finger rest - large ball - 7.65"

67. RADCLIFFE'S " KING OF DIAMONDS" - REG<u>D</u> stamped on obverse side of head under the king of diamonds "playing card" logo - C 2 stamped on finger rest - medium ball - 7.75"

68. RADCLIFFE'S "KING OF DIAMONDS" SOLD BY JOHN LINE & SONS LTD. LONDON & BRANCHES - REG<u>D</u> stamped on obverse side of rounded bottom head under the king of diamonds "playing card" logo - A N H carved into finger rest - medium ball - 7.4"

69. RAMSEY, A. & SONS Cº - 5 stamped on top of rounded bottom head - medium flattened ball - 7.55"

70. RELIANCE LONDON (reads facing the head) - C stamped on top of head - fruitwood finish - medium ball - 7.35"

71. RUDD, A S<u>T</u> HELENS - large 3 stamped on top of head - round handle - medium ball - 7.45"

72. RUSSELL, J. LATE BAXTER PATENT EDINBURGH 687 - small head - medium oval ball - 6.85"

73. SHARRETT & NEWTH LONDON - 3 A stamped on top of rounded bottom head - medium ball - 7.3"

74. SHARRETT & NEWTH LONDON - 4 A stamped on top of rounded bottom head - medium ball - 7.35"

75. SHARRETT & NEWTH LONDON - 5 A stamped on top of rounded bottom head - small ball - 7.25"

76. SHARRETT & NEWTH LONDON 1916 - → on reverse side of rounded bottom head pointing to ferrule - medium ball - 7.35"

77. SHARRETT & NEWTH LONDON ENGLAND AGENTS BROOKS THOMAS & Cº LTD DUBLIN - 4 A stamped on rounded bottom head - end of thick handle has been cut off thus only 6" long

78. SHARRETT & NEWTH LONDON SOLD BY NICHOLS & CLARKE LTD - B stamped on top of head - small ball - 7.15"

79. SHARRETT & NEWTH LONDON SOLD BY WILLIAMS & WATSON LTD LIVERPOOL - 0 stamped on top of head - small ball - 7.1"

80. SHARRETT & NEWTH LONDON SOLD BY WILLIAMS & WATSON LTD LIVERPOOL - 4 A stamped on top of rounded bottom head - small ball - 7.15"

81. SHARRETT & NEWTH LONDON SOLE AGENTS HENRY BROOKS & Cº - I A stamped on top of head - small ball - 7.15"

82. SHARRETT & NEWTH LONDON ENGLAND - rounded bottom head - small dome shape ball - 7.3"

83. SHARRETT & NEWTH LONDON ENGLAND - 2 A stamped on top of .86" long head - medium ball - 7.15"

84. SHARRETT & NEWTH LONDON ENGLAND - 2 A stamped on top of .97" long head - medium ball - 7.08"

85. SHARRETT & NEWTH LONDON ENGLAND - 3 A stamped on top of rounded bottom head - small ball - 7.3"

86. SHARRETT & NEWTH LONDON ENGLAND - 3 A stamped on top of rounded bottom head - small dome shape ball - 7"

87. SHARRETT & NEWTH LONDON ENGLAND SOLD BY BAXENDALE & Cº LTD MANCHESTER - 3 A stamped on top of rounded bottom head - small dome shape ball - 7.1"

88. SHARRETT & NEWTH LONDON ENGLAND SOLD BY BAXENDALE & Cº LTD MANCHESTER - 4 A stamped on top of rounded bottom head - medium ball - 6.4"

89. SHARRETT & NEWTH LONDON ENGLAND SOLD BY BAXENDALE & Cº LTD MANCHESTER - 5 A stamped on top of slightly rounded bottom head medium ball - 7.15"

90. SHARRETT & NEWTH LONDON ENGLAND - 4 A stamped on top of rounded bottom head - medium ball - 7.15"

91. SHARRETT & NEWTH LONDON ENGLAND SOLD BY J. YOUNG & Cº KENNINGTON - 3 A stamped on top of rounded bottom head - medium ball - 6.95"

92. SHARRETT & NEWTH PATENT LONDON - small head .74" long - slender handle - small flattened ball - 6.8"

93. SHARRETT & NEWTH PATENT LONDON - small head .81" long - small ball - 6.9"

94. SHARRETT & NEWTH PATENT LONDON - rounded bottom on head - J. AINSWORTH stamped on side of handle reading towards ferrule - small ball - 7.3"

95. SHARRETT & NEWTH PATENT LONDON - W. FLEMING stamped on reverse side of rounded bottom head - smaller head than I-94 above - ball removed and end refinished - 6.8"

96. SHARRETT & NEWTH PATENT LONDON - ONE POINT stamped on bottom of head small ball - 7.15"

97. SHAW ENGLAND - C stamped on head - ivory colored plastic handle(mold lines very visible) - C stamped on top of head - medium ball - 7.2"

98. SHAW ENGLAND - P C stamped on top of thick rounded bottom head - no ball on end(cut ?) - 7.3"

99. SHAW ENGLAND - S C stamped on top of rounded bottom head - medium ball - 7.35"

100. SHAW ENGLAND - SHAW & SON LONDON stamped on obverse side of head - REPAIRED BY A. SHAW & SON LONDON stamped on reverse side of head - A stamped on top of head - medium ball - 7.85"

101. SHAW PATENT - a pair of recessed dots on top of head - ivory handle - flattened small ball - 6.8"

102. SHAW PATENT - small head - flattened medium ball - 6.95"

103. SHAW, A. & SON 1918 →(toward ferrule) - → stamped on reverse side of head facing ferrule - medium ball - 7.05"

104. SHAW, A. & SON LONDON stamped on obverse side of head 7 / 571 over ↑ and 1944 under the arrow stamped on reverse side of head - .45" long brass step ferrule - medium ball - 6.45"

105. SHAW, A. & SON LONDON stamped on obverse side of rounded bottom head S D stamped on top of rounded bottom head - .5" long brass step ferrule - medium ball - 6.55"

106. SHAW, A. & SON LONDON WARRANTED P F stamped on top of rounded bottom head - D S C stamped in finger rest - small ball - 7.6"

107. SHAW, A. & SON LONDON - B stamped on top of head - medium ball - 7.3:

108. SHAW, A. & SON LONDON - C stamped on top of head - small ball - 7.22"

109. SHAW, A. & SON LONDON WARRANTED - C stamped on top of head - small ball - 7.35"

110. SHAW, A. & SON LONDON WARRANTED MADE IN ENGLAND - P E stamped on top of thick, rounded bottom head - small ball 7.5"

111. SHAW, A. & SON LONDON WARRANTED - S A stamped on top of rounded bottom head - medium ball - 7.5"

112. SHAW, A. & SON LONDON WARRANTED - S C stamped on top of rounded bottom head - medium ball - 7.5"

113. SHAW, A. & SON LONDON WARRANTED - 1941 under ↑ stamped on obverse side of thick, rounded bottom head - small ball - 7.7"

114. SHAW, JOHN & SONS LTD WOLVERHAMTON - S C stamped on top of rounded bottom head - medium ball - 7.5"

115. STAR SHEET WARRANTED - set screw on top of head for fastening cutter unit insert - fruitwood finish - medium ball - 6.9"

116. STAR WARRANTED - large 2 on top of rounded bottom head - fruitwood finish - medium ball - 7.5"

117. STOCK SONS & TAYLORS BIRMINGHAM - small C S stamped on top of rounded bottom head - small ball - 7.35"

118. STOCK, W. & C° GLASS WORKS LEIGH NEAR MANCHESTER - small S stamped on top of rounded bottom head - medium ball - 7.3"

119. TYZACK, S. & SON 343 & 345 OLD ST LONDON - medium ball - 7.25"

120. WATSON & C° PATENT LONDON - very small head - ball end is chewed off - 6.1"

121. WILSON stamped in small letters on top right of reverse side of rounded bottom head - a small B stamped on top right of obverse side of head - large ball - 7.3"
    121-A. WILSON stamped on reverse of head - H571 stamped on obverse of head - slender walnut handle - small ball -- 7.3"

122. YOUNG & MARTEN STRATFORD - 3 stamped on top of rounded bottom head - small ball - 7.35"

123. No ID 4 G A4 stamped on top of head - no finish walnut handle with large ball - 7.35"

124. No ID 1 stamped on top of rounded bottom head - B stamped on top right of obverse side of head - came in a walnut box with A. W. CHIPPERFIELD stamped in a recessed rectangle on the hinged cover - small ball - 7.35"

125. No ID - small thick head - flattened medium ball - 7.2"

126. No ID - small brass head - black varnish stain finish - flattened small ball - 6.8"

VARIATIONS

There was a possibility that some of the following variations could have or should have been in another Category such as XXIII MISCELLANEOUS or even in the front listing of this Category, however, here they are:

127. BIDDLE & KING PATENT LONDON - .5" diameter X 3.9" long, solid brass handle, most likely a make-do one of a kind. - 6"

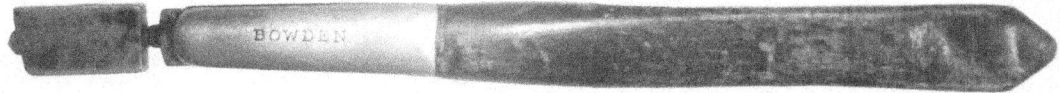

128. BOWDEN PATENT LONDON - small steel head folds back into the handle - 5.65" (open)

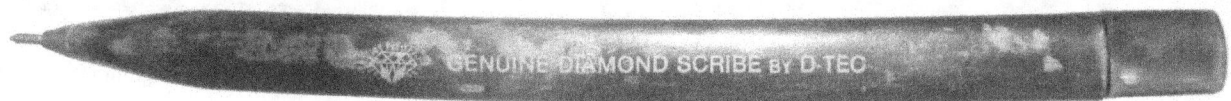

129. D – TEC GENUINE DIAMOND SCRIBE – Diamond "logo" - triangular shape blue plastic handle with carbide tip as cutter or scribe - 7"

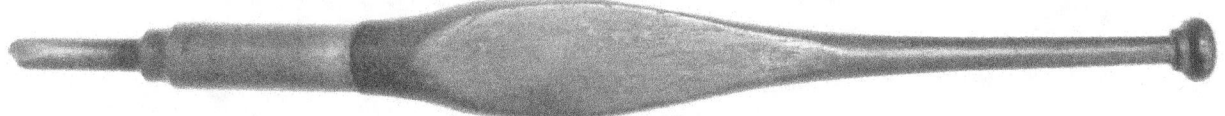

130. DICKINSON, THOS. L. MAKER N. Y. in very small letters at beginning of ferrule - small ball - 6.55"

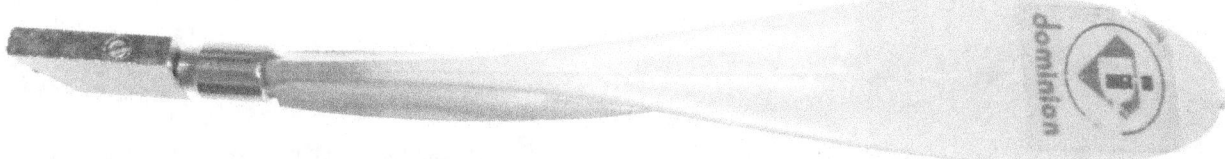

131. **dominion** on clear label near end of tan plastic ergonomic fitting handle - i on a diamond logo - 7"

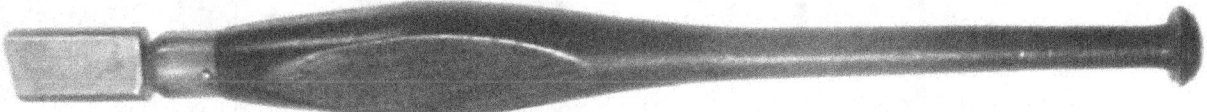

132. ENDIA B on plated steel ferrule - steel head rounded on both top & bottom - medium ball - 6.55"

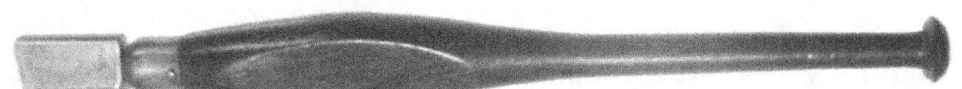

133. EXCELSIOR GLASS CUTTER PAT. SEP. 13th 1864 and JUNE 8th 1869 in very small letters on small brass head - .35" brass ferrule - small flattened ball - 5.125"

134. HALL INVENTOR BRISTOL - small steel head - flat sided handle with tapering to cone end - 5.375"

135. KARELSEN SUPERIOR NEW -YORK - 1.25" nickel plated brass ferrule - flat thin fruitwood handle - small ball - 6.375"

135-A. KARELSEN NEW-YORK – 1.5" brass ferrule – hammer knob on head as on 136 below - ebony handle – flat ball – 6.8"

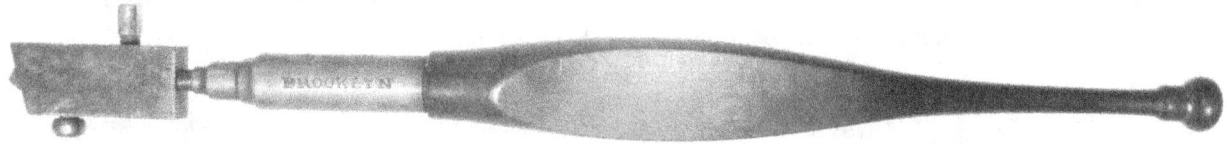

136. LLOYD BROOKLYN N. Y. - 12A stamped on top of head - hammer knob on head - medium ball - 7.25"

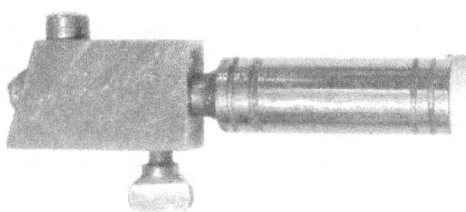

137. MONTGOMERY & Co N. Y. CITY - heavy plated steel head - small letters on 1.5" plated steel ferrule - cream color bakelite handle - medium ball - 7.1"

138. SHARRETT & NEWTH PATENT LONDON - small steel head folds back into brass sided steel center ferrule - small ball - 6.375"

139. SHARRETT & NEWTH PATENT LONDON - small steel head is worn concave on both sides as is the handle - no ball - 5.125"

140. SHARRETT & NEWTH PATENT LONDON - small steel head - ivory handle with small bead like ball that fits over end of handle(only example of this seen) - 5.25"

141. SHARRETT & NEWTH PATENT LONDON SOLD BY WINDER & HARROP - BEEDLES - steel head with rounded bottom - round handle with flattened large ball - 6.125"

142. SHARRET & NEWTH PATENT LONDON - small steel head - short, thin, ivory handle which was roughly carved to make small ball - 4.9"

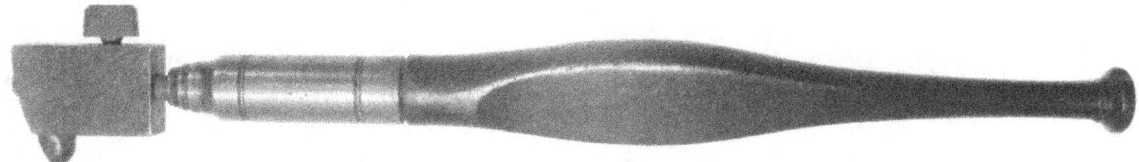

143. SINSZ, P. H. BALTIMORE 3(on front of ferrule) - heavy steel head - nearly black handle - medium flattened ball - 7.25"

144. TECHNICAL DIAMONDS LTD BRITISH MADE - set screw on top of thick, rounded bottom head to secure diamond cutter unit - aluminum ferrule and handle tapered to a cone end "ball" - 7"

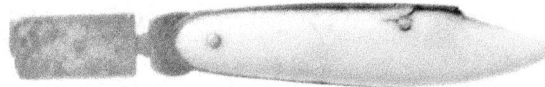

145. No ID - a jackknife type where the small steel head diamond cutter head folds back into the steel and celluloid body - 3.1"

146. No ID - same as I-145 above except for the flattened handle with small ball - 5.9"

147. No ID - 1.8" tapered brass ferrule & .7" brass tip and mini ball on end - with leather case - 4.95"

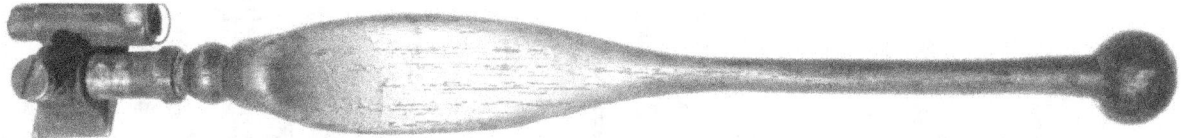

148. No ID - rule guide with a spring loaded oiler tube attached on a 1" cutter unit - a carved ball and "open mouth" leading to a wide finger rest and large ball - 7.05"

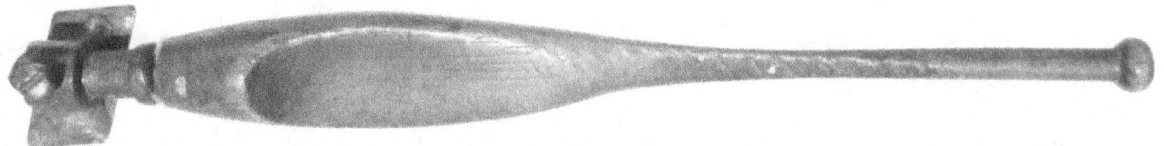

149. No ID - rule guide mounted on .9" cutter unit - no oiler - wide finger rest - slender handle with small ball - 6.25"

150. No ID - same as I-148 above except 1.5" cutter unit and longer handle had been carved to fit glaziers hand - 6.95"

151. No ID - same as I-148 above except 1.25" cutter unit and large ball - 7.25"

152. No ID - a homemade tool - brass rule guide soldered to brass sleeve which is slid onto a 3/8" solid steel rod handle - 6"

153. No ID - 1.2" tapered steel cutter unit - .1" brass ferrule - except for two short finger rests , a round handle with large flattened ball - 6.45"

154. No ID - 1.05" tapered steel cutter unit - .1" brass ferrule - thumb & forefinger rests on dark mahogany handle - no ball - 6"

155. No ID - 1.2" tapered steel cutter unit - .1" brass ferrule - contoured fruitwood handle tapering out to a .42" diameter end - 6.6"

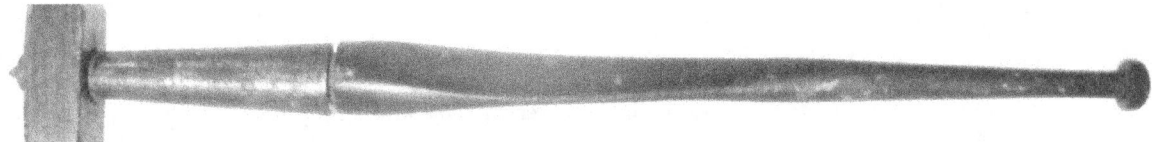

156. No ID - 1.75" tapered steel cutter unit - a homemade wood block next to point servers as a finger rest - slender, dark mahogany handle with mini ball - 6.45"

157. No ID - a carbide tip solid aluminum pencil scribe with pocket clip - no apparent means of tip replacement - finger rest area of .3" diameter pencil is grooved - 5.4"

158. No ID - a carbide tip solid aluminum pencil scribe with pocket clip - .625" "ferrule section unscrews for replacement of .75" long carbide tip unit - 2.3" of .25" diameter handle is knurled - "ball" end has a steel inset for tapper - 4.9"

CATEGORY II: DIAMOND POINT CUTTERS WITH BREAKERS

The typical diamond point steel head glass cutter with four steel breakers on the ferrule and a wood handle is 7 to 7.5 inches in length, unless otherwise noted. A few older ones may have ivory or bone handles. There are several variations within this category which are noted separately by description and/or a picture. They are listed alphabetically under VARIATIONS.

There are thirty four additional different glass cutters in this category known to be in other collections.

Eleven U.S. Patents for this category are listed below:

30,772	56,231	101,111	408,055	464,997	529,957
33,188	64,157	188,058	442,062	482,601	

Price range: $15 to $70, with more for ivory handles and the fold-in or slide-in "jackknife" style.

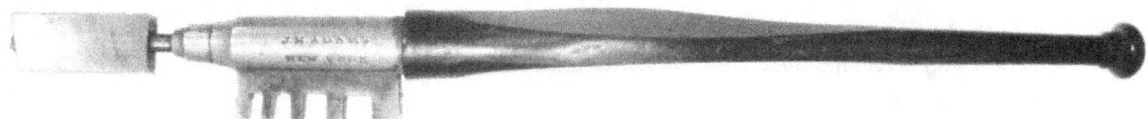

1. ADAMS, J. H. NEW YORK - medium size head - dark handle with medium flattened ball - 7"
2. ADAMS, J. MAKER RESET BY DICKENSON 64 NASSAU ST NEW-YORK - medium size head - dark handle with medium flattened ball - 7.3"
3. ADAMS, J. H. MAKER NEW YORK - medium size head - dark handle with flattened medium ball - 7"
4. ADAMS, J. H. PATENT NEW YORK - medium size head - dark handle with flattened ball - 6.6"
5. BIDDLE & KING PATENT LONDON very small C on top of medium head - cutter end of head has been truncated at both top & bottom - walnut finish on handle with a medium flattened ball - 7.1"
6. BUSH & CHIPPER MAKERS LONDON very small B on top of medium head - walnut finish on handle with a medium ball - 7.1"
7. DEVOE, F. W. & C. T. RAYNOLDS, CO. NEW YORK - plated steel medium head - plated steel ferrule & breakers - walnut finish on handle with a medium ball - 6.85"
8. DIAMOND BRAND SHANGHAI CHINA 5 stamped on top of large head - the brass breakers appear too short and meaningless - 999 A printed on flat side of red varnished handle - 6.95"
   See II-49 for similar glass cutter
9. DICKINSON MAKER NEW YORK CHAS. F. HAAKE SUCC'R TO B stamped on top of regular head - dark handle with medium ball - 7.4"
10. DICKINSON MAKER NEW YORK & PHILA SHAW - dark handle with flattened ball - 7"
11. DICKINSON SOLE MAKER NEW YORK SHAW celluloid handle with a medium ball that screws on - 7"
12. DICKINSON SOLE MAKER NEW YORK & PHILA SHAW PATENT - medium head - dark handle with flattened medium ball - 7.25"
13. DICKINSON SOLE MAKER PHILA SHAW PATENT - five breakers - medium head - walnut handle - medium flattened ball - 6.9"
14. DICKINSON PATENT SOLE MAKER 64 NASSAU ST NEW-YORK SHAW PATENT - short medium head - five breakers - ivory handle - medium flattened ball - 6.4"
    14 – A. DICKINSON, THOS. L. MAKER N.Y. on leading edge of brass ferrule – E on top of steel head – slender walnut handle – thin small ball - 7.15"

15. DUNHAM, G. D. CHICAGO - small head ivory handle - medium ball - 6.9"
16. DUNHAM, G. D. CHICAGO - small head - slightly thicker walnut handle - medium flattened ball - 7.05"
17. EARL, D. & CO CHICAGO on plated brass ferrule - WARRANTED SUPERIOR stamped on obverse of plated steel head - JOHN E. STEPHAN CO. CHICAGO R 5 stamped on reverse of plated, rounded bottom head - fruitwood handle with small ball - 6.35"
18. JAMES, A. PATENT LONDON WARRANTED - medium head - walnut handle with small ball - 7.3"
19. KARELSEN NEW YORK - medium head - dark handle with medium ball - 7"
20. KARELSEN NEW YORK - P stamped on obverse side of medium head - ivory handle - medium ball - 6.9"

21. KARELSEN, N. Y. plated brass ferrule & breakers - plated steel medium head with 112 stamped on obverse side & 2316 stamped on top of head - fruitwood handle with medium ball - 7.35"

22. KARELSEN NEW YORK - small head - wide thin finger rest on dark handle - small ball - 6.6"

23. KARELSEN NEW-YORK - small head - fruitwood triangular handle - medium ball - 6.8"

24. KARELSEN NEW-YORK on plated brass ferrule - EXTRA stamped on obverse side of small plated head - wide finger rests on dark handle - small ball - 6.8"

25. KARELSEN NEW-YORK on plated brass ferrule - EXTRA stamped on obverse side of thick medium head - wide finger rests on rosewood handle - medium ball - 7"

26. KARELSEN NEW-YORK stamped on plated brass ferrule - SUPERIOR stamped on obverse side of thick medium head - rosewood handle with small ball - 7.05"

27. LANDAU, A. & Co. PHILA. stamped on sides of breaker - SUPERIOR stamped on obverse side of medium head - walnut handle with ball end broken off - 6.1"

28. LLOYD BROOKLYN stamped on plated brass ferrule - 5A 11223 stamped on top of plated medium head - thin layer of plated brass or silver solder on diamond face of head - three breakers - dark handle with large ball - 7.15"

29. LLOYD BROOKLYN N.Y. - 626 8 6 stamped on top of medium head with rounded bottom - three breakers - dark & light two tone handle - medium ball - 7.1"

30. MELHUISH, R. Ltd FETTER LANE - 3 A stamped on top of rounded bottom medium head - walnut handle with medium ball - 7.2"

31. RADCLIFFE, A. C. SPOTSWOOD, N. J. stamped on plated brass ferrule - WARRANTED EXTRA SUPERIOR stamped on obverse side of medium head - head of screw holding cutter unit in place is on bottom of head - dark walnut handle with medium ball - 7"

32. RADCLIFFE, A. C. SPOTSWOOD, N. J. stamped on plated brass ferrule - WARRANTED SUPERIOR stamped on obverse side of thick medium head - dark handle with medium ball - 6.9"

33. RADCLIFFE, A. C. SPOTSWOOD, N. J. WARRANTED stamped on plated brass ferrule - small plated head - dark handle with small ball - 7.2"

34. R. P. & D., MANUF'D FOR WARRANTED NEW - YORK medium head - dark handle with end cut off - 5.6"

35. SHARRETT & NEWTH PATENT LONDON rounded bottom, medium head - dark handle with medium ball - 7.35"

36. SHARRETT & NEWTH PATENT LONDON - medium head - dark fruitwood handle with small ball - 7.1"

37. SHARRETT & NEWTH PATENT LONDON - ONE POINT stamped on bottom of medium head - breaker attached with screw in front of 1st breaker - walnut handle - medium ball - 7.15"

38. SHARRETT & NEWTH PATENT LONDON - ONE POINT stamped on bottom of medium head - breaker attached with screw in 1st breaker - walnut handle - small ball - 7.1"

39. SHARRETT & NEWTH PATENT LONDON SOLD BY WHITTER FULLER & C° SAN FRANCISCO - small head - walnut handle - small ball - 6.9"

40. SHAW, A. & SON LONDON - B 3 stamped on top of medium head - dark walnut handle - small ball - 7.2"

41. SHAW, A. & SON LONDON - C 3 stamped on top of medium head - walnut handle - medium ball - 7.25"

42. SHAW, A. & SON LONDON WARRANTED MADE IN ENGLAND - three breakers - S D stamped on top of large head with rounded bottom - dark walnut handle - medium ball - 7.5"

43. SHAW PATENT LONDON SOLD BY KOMMEL NEW YORK - dark walnut handle - small ball - 7.15"

44. SHOEMAKER PHILADELPHIA on plated brass ferrule - EXTRA stamped on obverse of plated medium head - dark handle - medium ball - 7.15"

45. SINSZ, P. H. BALTIMORE on plated brass ferrule – plated rounded bottom breakers - WARRANTED XX stamped on plated medium head - dark walnut handle - medium ball - 6.75"

46. SINSZ, P. H. BALTIMORE - medium head - rounded bottom breakers - dark handle with no ball - 6.5"

47. SINSZ, PHILLIP CO. BALTIMORE on plated brass ferrule - plated rounded bottom breakers - plated medium head - dark handle - large flattened ball - 7"

48. SOLOMAN, L. & SON NEW YORK MADE IN ENGLAND - 1 A on top of medium head - walnut handle - medium ball - 7.1"

49. Supercraft GLASS CUTTER DIAMOND NO.3 TGC1010 807161 Made in China (all data is on the package) - 3 stamped on top of large rounded bottom head - 1" long brass breaker unit is twice the depth as the .85" long breaker unit on II-8 glass cutter - medium ball - 7.1"

50. *Urbanek, Joh. & Cᵉ Wien IX/I Patent* - 5 stamped on medium head - dark walnut handle - flattened medium ball - 8.05"

51. URBANEK, JOH. & Cº WIEN IX / I PATENT - 4 stamped on top of medium head - dark handle - no evidence of ball ever being there - came with rubber loop holding a small steel clip stamped: PAT. MAY 26 96 - nothing in the 432 patents of that date match - 7.15"

VARIATIONS

52. BOKER, HENRY with arrow on label on handle finger rest - Made in Germany stamped on bottom of non-mag. alloy medium head - three breakers - orange stain handle - small ball - 7"

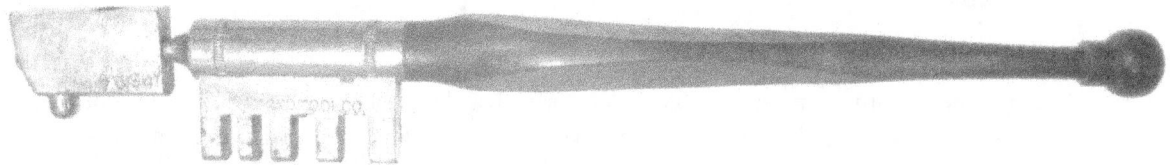

53. DIAMOND TOOL CO. CHICAGO stamped on plated steel breaker unit - 75.941 stamped on lower right of obverse plated steel large head with a tapping knob on bottom - dark handle - large ball - 7.1"

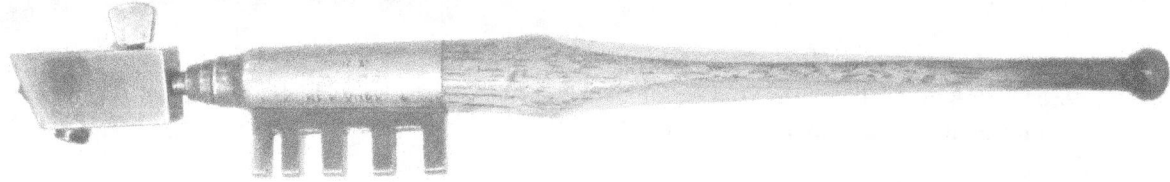

54. DICKINSON SOLE MAKER NEW YORK PHILA. SHAW - PLATE stamped on obverse of large head - thumb screw on top holds head on shaft - tapping knob on bottom - fruitwood handle - medium ball - 7.25"

55. DICKINSON, J. PATENTED BY SEP 3$_D$ 1861, SOLE MAKER NEW YORK stamped on "white brass" side of open slot handle - both small head and breaker unit fold back into the slotted handle - 2151 stamped on side of head - 5.6"

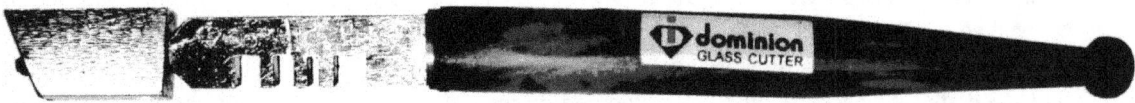

56. **dominion SUPER** stamped on plated steel breaker unit - large plated steel head - .2" brass ferrule - **dominion GLASS CUTTER** printed label on finger rest of walnut finish handle with medium ball - 7"

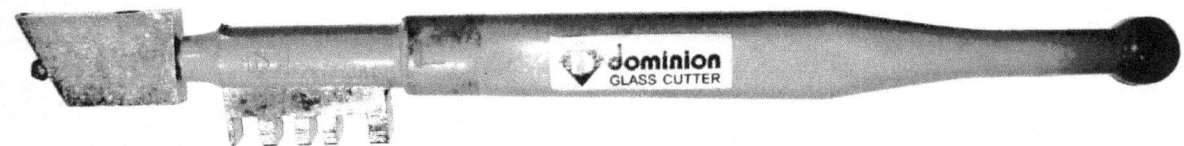

57. **dominion** raised cast letters on yellow painted steel ferrule - **dominion GLASS CUTTER** printed on label on flat side of yellow painted plastic handle with medium ball - 6.8"

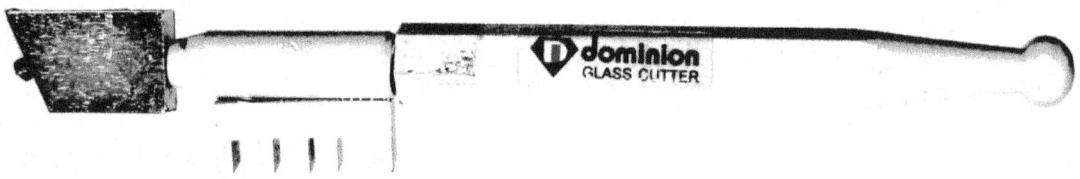

58. **dominion** INDIA stamped on white painted steel ferrule - large plated steel head - dominion GLASS CUTTER printed on label on white painted hexagonal aluminum handle with medium ball - 6"

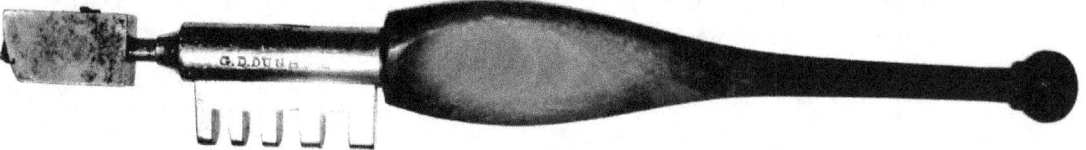

59. DUNHAM, G. D. CHICAGO on plated brass ferrule - small, thick plated head - wide finger rest on walnut handle with medium ball 6.5"

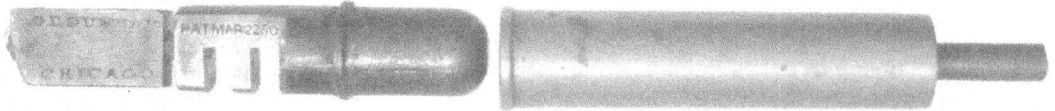

60. DUNHAM, G. D. CHICAGO stamped on obverse of small head - PAT.MAR 22,70 stamped on 2 breaker unit on steel ferrule that slides into metal tube with copper rod extending may have had a typical wood handle attached - the cutter unit can be reversed and inserted into the tube to protect the diamond - 3.875" as is

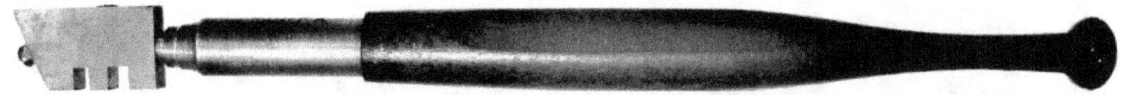

61. FAREAST KOREA stamped on brass ferrule -   3 stamped on top of brass head with 2 breakers - dark handle with medium ball - on box: DIAMONDS ARE FOREVER ND # 4435 - 6.9"

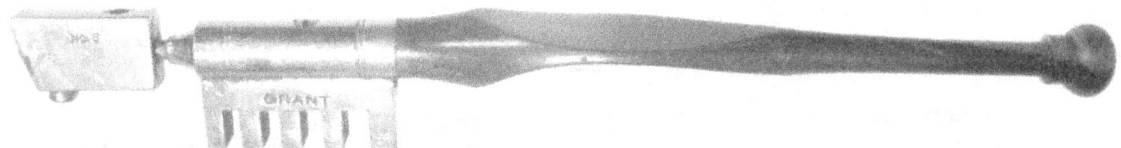

62. GRANT CLEVELAND, O. stamped on plated steel breaker unit - NO. 8 stamped on obverse side of plated steel head with tapper knob - walnut handle with medium –large ball - 7.3"

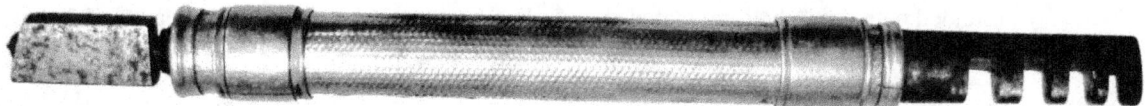

63. KARELSEN, J. E. N-Y PAT JULY 10, 1866 stamped in small letters on handle reading toward the breaker unit rounded on both top & bottom - small head also rounded on top & bottom - both head & breaker slide back into the handle - 5.8" extended

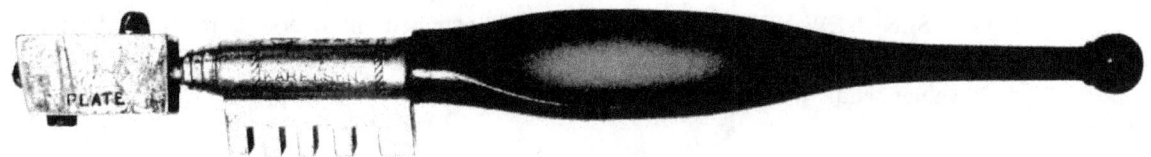

64. KARELSEN NEW-YORK stamped on plated brass ferrule - 5778 stamped on top of large p;lated head - PLATE stamped on obverse of head - slotted screw holds diamond cutter in place - tapping knob on top holds head to shaft - dark handle with medium ball - 7.4"

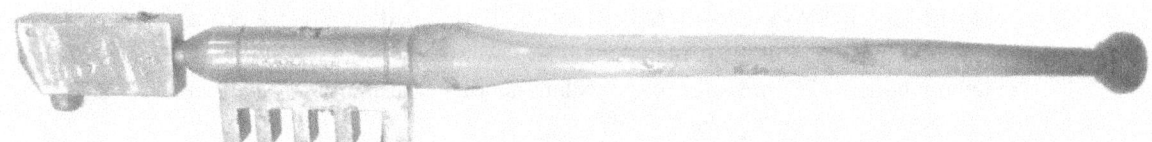

65. KARELSEN NEW YORK stamped on plated brass ferrule -   18888 stamped on top of plated large steel head - 117 stamped on obverse side of head - tapping knob on cutter unit - thin flattened finger rests on blonde fruitwood handle with medium ball - 7.45"

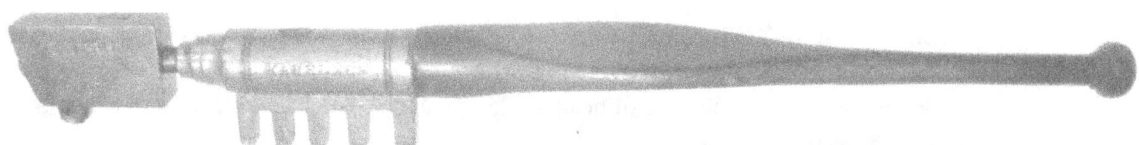

66. KARELSEN NEW-YORK stamped on plated brass ferrule - EXTRA PLATE stamped on obverse of thick, large steel head - tapping knob on cutter unit - dark handle with small ball   - 7"

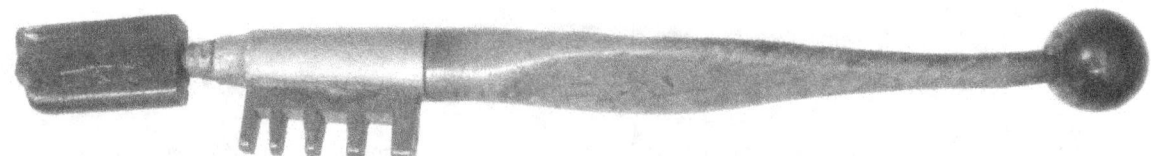

67. KARELSEN NEW-YORK stamped on brass ferrule - 8185 stamped in very small numbers on top of rounded bottom , thick steel head - fruitwood handle with .6" diameter brass ball that screws on end of handle - 6.8"

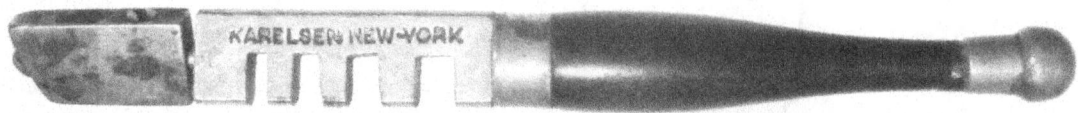

68. KARELSEN NEW-YORK PAT. MAR. 6, 77 stamped on obverse & reverse sides respectively of a rounded both top & bottom, plated steel in-line breaker unit - small steel head - .25" brass ferrule - round handle - small brass ball screws on end of handle - 4.5"

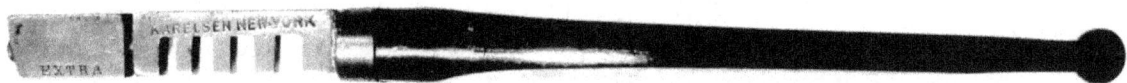

69. KARELSEN NEW-YORK PAT. MAR. 6, 77 stamped on obverse & reverse sides respectively of plated steel in-line breaker unit - EXTRA stamped on obverse of medium head - .25" brass ferrule - dark walnut handle with small ball - 6.9"

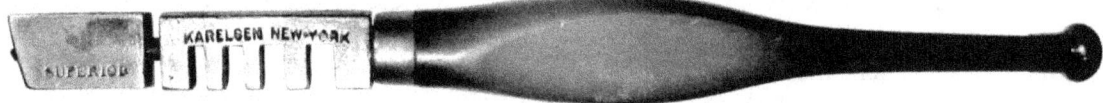

70. KARELSEN NEW-YORK PAT. MAR. 6, 77 stamped on obverse & reverse sides respectively of a rounded both top & bottom plated steel in-line breaker unit - SUPERIOR stamped on obverse of medium head - .25" brass ferrule - walnut handle with small brass ball on end - 6.75"

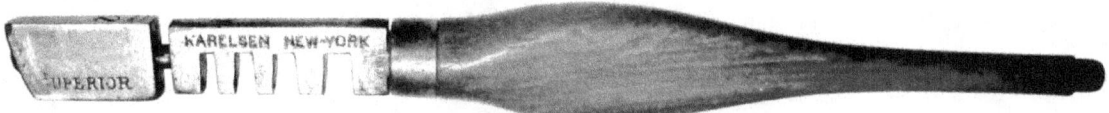

71. KARELSEN NEW-YORK PAT. MAR. 6, 77 stamped on obverse & reverse sides respectively of a rounded both top & bottom plated steel breaker unit - 11118 1024· stamped on top of head - SUPERIOR stamped on obverse of head - .25" plated brass ferrule - fruitwood handle with threaded end for a "brass ball" - 6.3"

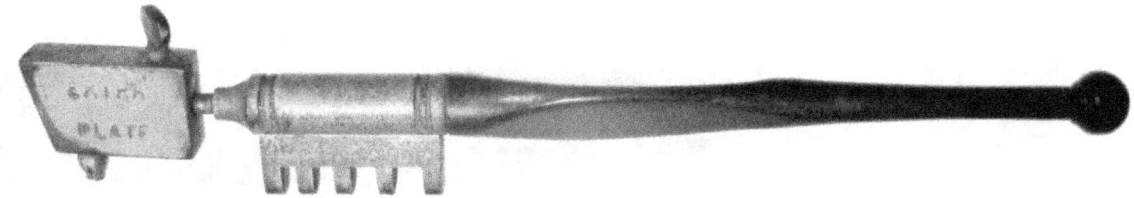

72. LANDAU, A. & Co. stamped on plated steel rounded bottom breaker unit - EXTRA PLATE stamped on obverse of large thick plated steel head - thumb screw holds head to shaft & knob holds cutter unit - dark handle with medium ball - 7.3"

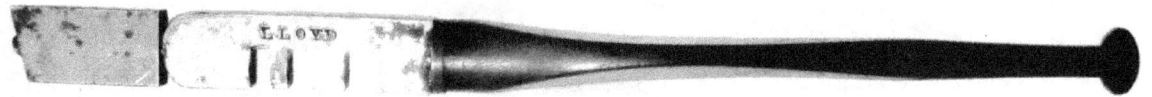

73. LLOYD   BROOKLYN stamped on obverse & reverse sides respectively of plated steel in-line   3 breaker unit - medium head - .05" brass ferrule - dark handle - medium flattened ball - 6.4"

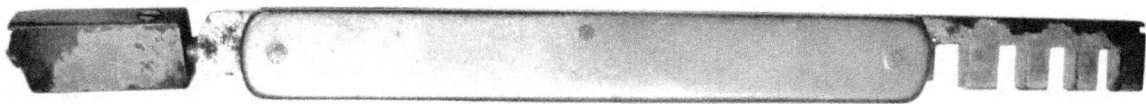

74. RADCLIFFE, A. C. NEW YORK stamped on brass side of open slot handle - both elongated, plated, small cutter head & plated breaker fold back into the slotted handle - 5.9"   see II-55 for similar one

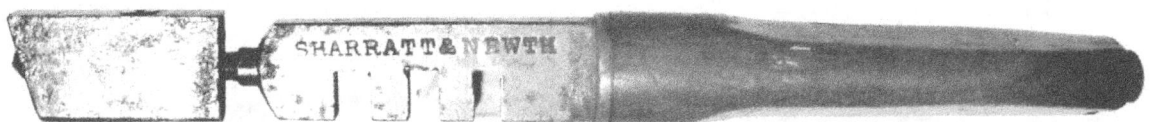

75. SHARRETT & NEWTH   LONDON   stamped on obverse & reverse sides respectively of steel in-line   3 breaker unit that has curved front facing the cutter head - medium head with rounded bottom - .05" brass ferrule - walnut handle cut short - 5.15"

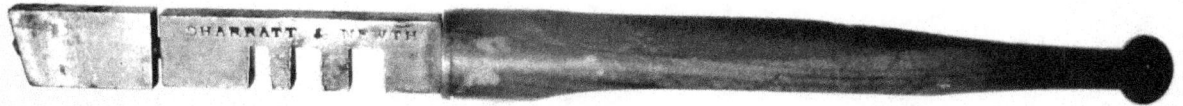

76. SHARRATT & NEWTH LONDON stamped on obverse & reverse sides respectively of steel in-line 3 breaker unit that has square front facing the cutter unit - small head - .05" brass ferrule - walnut handle with medium ball - 6.4"

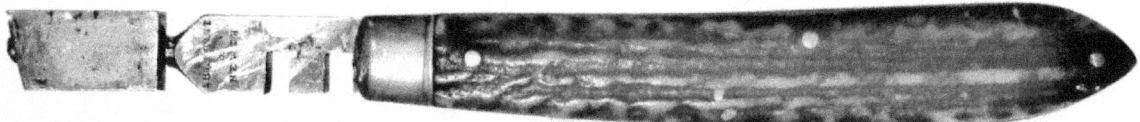

77. SHARRATT & NEWTH stamped in small letters next to cutter head on obverse side of 2 breaker in-line unit that has a rounded surface of the truncated end facing the .35" high head - The cutter head & breaker fold back into the slotted bone sided handle as one piece - 5.5"

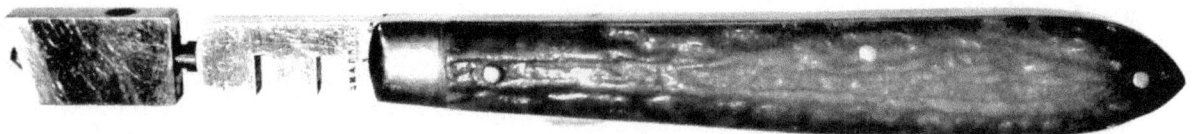

78. SHARRETT & NEWTH stamped in small letters next to handle on obverse side of 2 breaker in-line unit that has a curved end facing the .425" high head - the cutter head & breaker fold back into the slotted bone sided handle as one piece - 5.4"

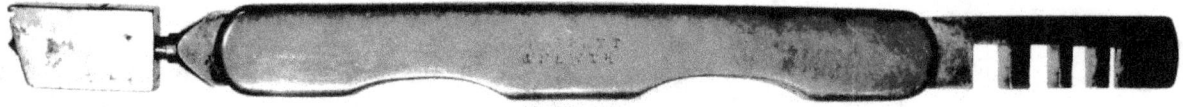

79. SHARRATT & NEWTH stamped on side of brass open slot handle - both working end fold back into the slotted handle - the breaker unit has a finger nail groove to assist opening - 5.75'

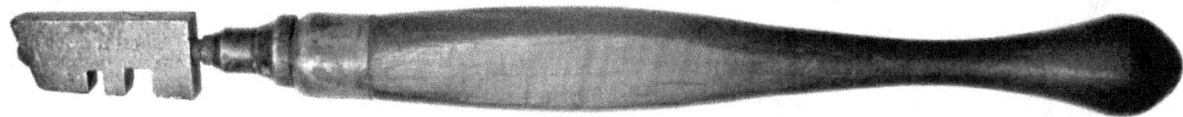

80. TOTTENHAM MAKER stamped on reverse & F. PULLER stamped on obverse of 2 breaker small head - interesting two piece brass ferrule - walnut handle tapering in then out to form a large ball - 6.1"

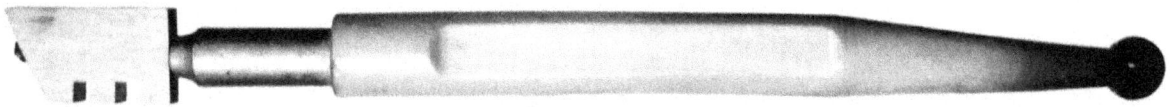

81. No ID on cutter (plastic sleeve: The best glass Tool warranted) - 2 breaker on brass head - natural finish on blonde wood handle with medium ball - 6.8"

CATEGORY III   DIAMOND POINT - BEAVER TAIL

These crescent shaped glass cutter heads have a category of their own because of their "Beaver Tail" handles. Nearly all have a breaker on either side of the cutter head as well as an inlay on the handle.   The Russian cutters have but one breaker on the head and no inlays on the handle. Further details for the cutters are noted in the picture or description beneath the picture.

Thirty six different beaver tails are known in other collections.

No U. S. Patents were found for this category.

Price range: $15 to $100

Instructions for use of this type of Russian and German glass cutter are shown below.

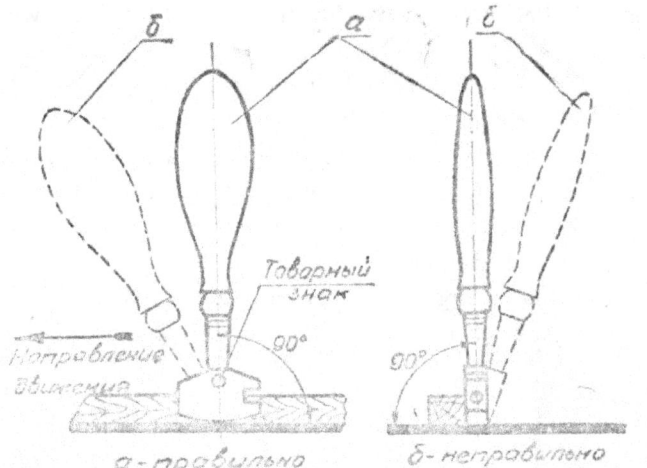

Рославльская тип. Смолоблупр. по печати. Заказ № 4300. 1966 г. Т. 30 000.

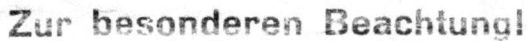

Zur besonderen Beachtung!

Anleitung für die richtige Handhabung des Diamanten

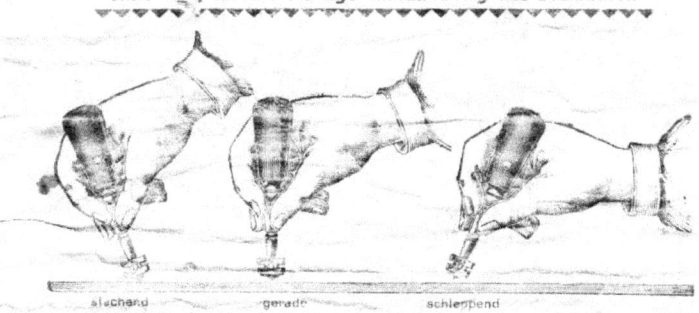

Die Lebensdauer eines jeden Glaser-Diamanten hängt in erster Linie davon ab, wie derselbe behandelt wird. **Der Diamant muß leicht und mit wenig Druck geführt werden** und zwar so, daß der auf dem Heft markierte Stern oder Punkt beim Schneiden (mit der rechten Hand) nach links zeigt.

Wird der Diamant verkehrt geführt, so verliert derselbe sofort den feinen Schnitt oder wird aus der Fassung gerissen und geht unter Umständen sogar verloren.

Beim Schneiden darf der Diamant nicht kratzen, (das Glas darf keinen weißen oder staubenden Schnitt zeigen) sondern nur einen singenden Ton geben.

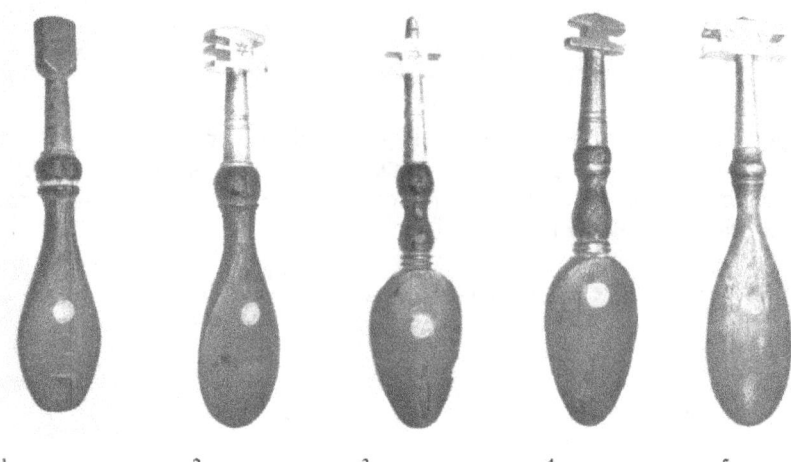

1. One piece 1.75" steel head & ferrule - no breakers - brass inlay with a pair of crossed Beaver Tail glass cutters - 5"
2. Plated steel head with six point star and three breakers - 1.1" brass ferrule - brass inlay with three crossed Beaver Tail glass cutters - 4.75"
3. Plated steel head with six point star - brass inlay with a pair of crossed Beaver tail glass cutters, one showing breakers on the ferrule - 1.1" plated brass ferrule - 5.05"
4. Small steel head with six point star - 1.1" steel ferrule - brass inlay with a pair of crossed Beaver tail glass cutters, one with breakers on the ferrule - 4.6"
5. A pair of six point stars on large plated non-mag. head - 1.05'non-mag. ferrule - brass inlay with single Beaver Tail glass cutter and U. & C. - fruitwood handle - 5.15"

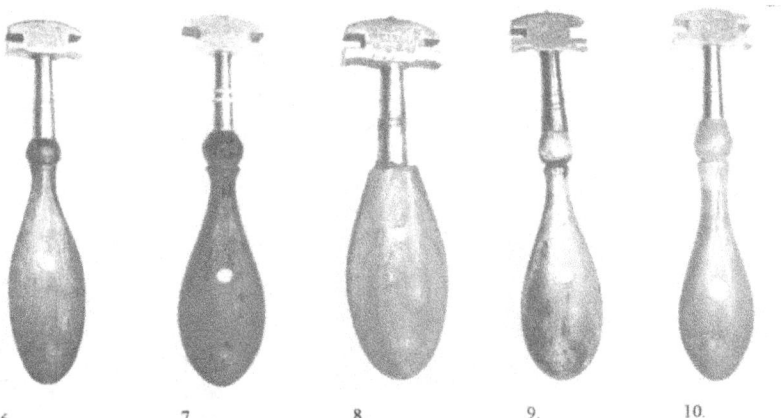

6. Universal in filigree on large plated steel head - 1.2" plated steel ferrule - white inlay - WS 2 stamped on fruitwood handle - 5.2"
7. Universal (reads toward diamond) on large plated steel head - 1.1" plated steel ferrule - EXTRA & logo of man with glass cutter stamped on handle above & below white inlay - 4.9"
8. Universal (reads toward diamond)on large plated steel head - 1.1" plated steel ferrule - mother of pearl inlay on fruitwood handle - 4.1"
9. Universal(reads toward diamond) on large plated steel head - 1.1" plated steel ferrule - white inlay on fruitwood handle that has most of black paint worn away - 4.8"
10. UNIVERSAL (reads toward diamond) on large plated steel head - 1" plated steel ferrule - MADE IN AUSTRIA stamped below mother of pearl inlay on tan plastic handle - 5.15"

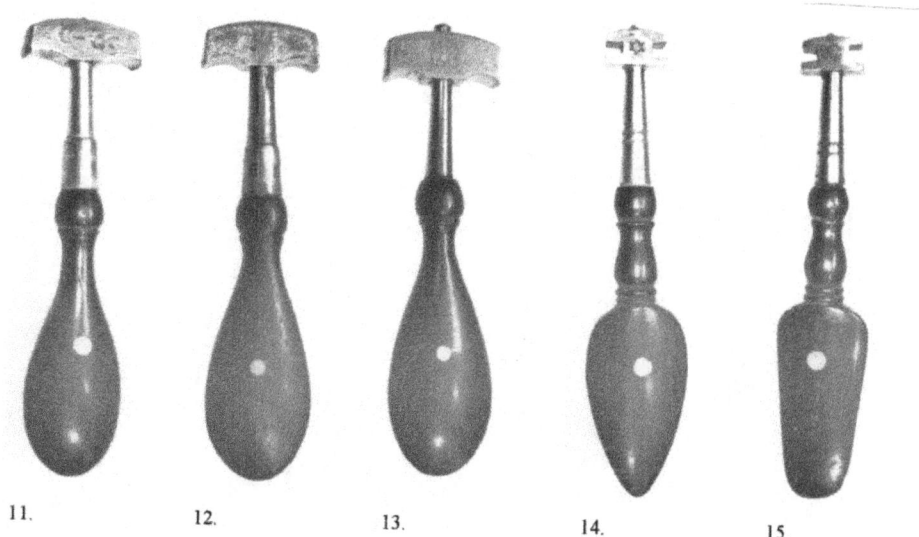

11.   11.   12.   13.   14.   15.

11. Decorative scrolls on obverse of large plated steel head - 1.6" German silver ferrule - M-O-P inlay - 5.75"

12. Decorative scrolls on obverse of large plated steel head - 1.6" plated steel ferrule - white inlay - 5.75"

13. Decorative scrolls on obverse of large plated brass head - 1.2" plated steel ferrule - M-O-P inlay - 5.45"

14. Six point bold star on obverse of small plated steel head - 1.3" plated steel ferrule - M-O-P inlay - 5.2"

15. Six point thin line star on obverse of small plated steel head - 1.2" plated steel ferrule - 4 → stamped on handle next to mother of pearl inlay - 5"

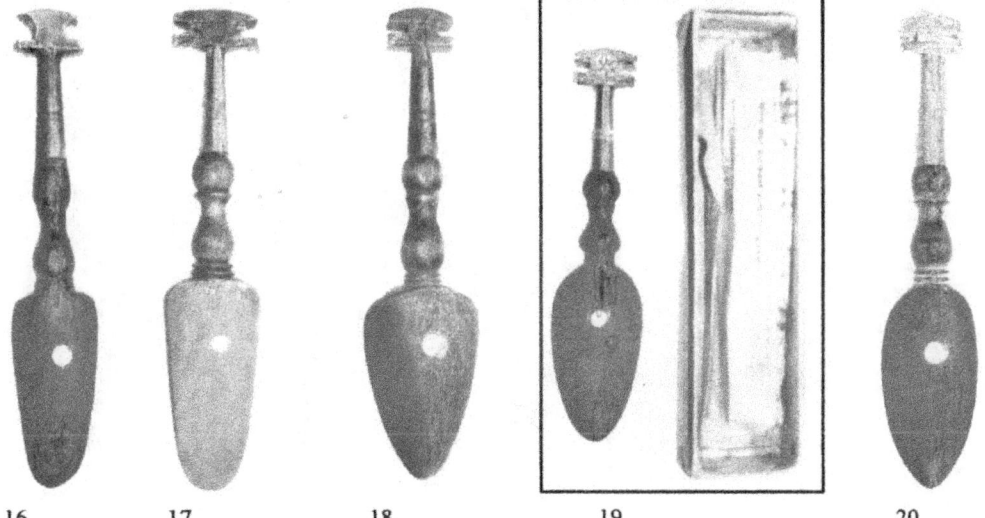

16.   17.   18.   19.   20.

16. Six point star in recessed circle on reverse of small plated steel head - 1.15" steel ferrule - M-O-P inlay on obverse of handle - 5.05"

17. Two 17. six point stars on obverse of medium plated steel head - 1.25" plated steel ferrule - M-O-P inlay - now a natural wood handle but believe it has been striped of ebony finish - 5.55"

18. Six point star on small steel head - 1.05" steel ferrule - LIN stamped next to white inlay - 4.9"

19. Six point star on plated medium steel head - 1.1" plated steel ferrule - T stamped next to white inlay - E.L.D.I.N. stamped inside an oval on handle reverse - came with box with instructions in German - 5"

20. Six point star on small plated head - 1.15"German silver ferrule - A stamped next to M-O-P inlay -5.1"

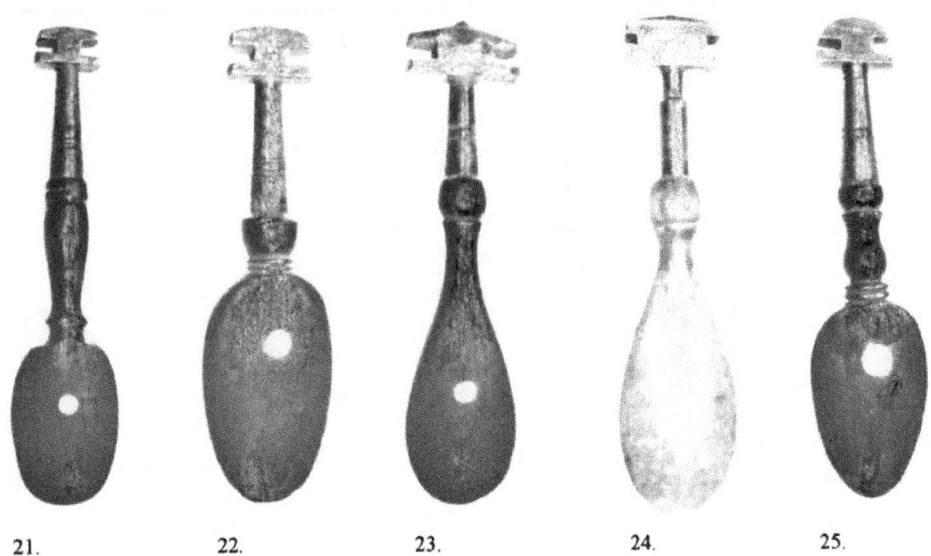

21. Six point star on steel mini head - 10905 on 1.15" plated steel ferrule - M-O-P inlay - 4.65"
22. Six point star on small steel head - 1.1" plated steel ferrule - M-O-P inlay 3.9"
23. A pair of six point stars on large plated steel head - .95" plated steel ferrule - M-O-P inlay - 4.9"
24. SMIT, J. K. & SONS MADE IN ENGLAND stamped on 1.25" plated brass ferrule - 3 stamped next to recess for missing inlay - medium plated steel head - 5.6"
25. Small semi-circle plated steel head - 1.05" plated steel ferrule - S stamped next to large white inlay - 4.6"

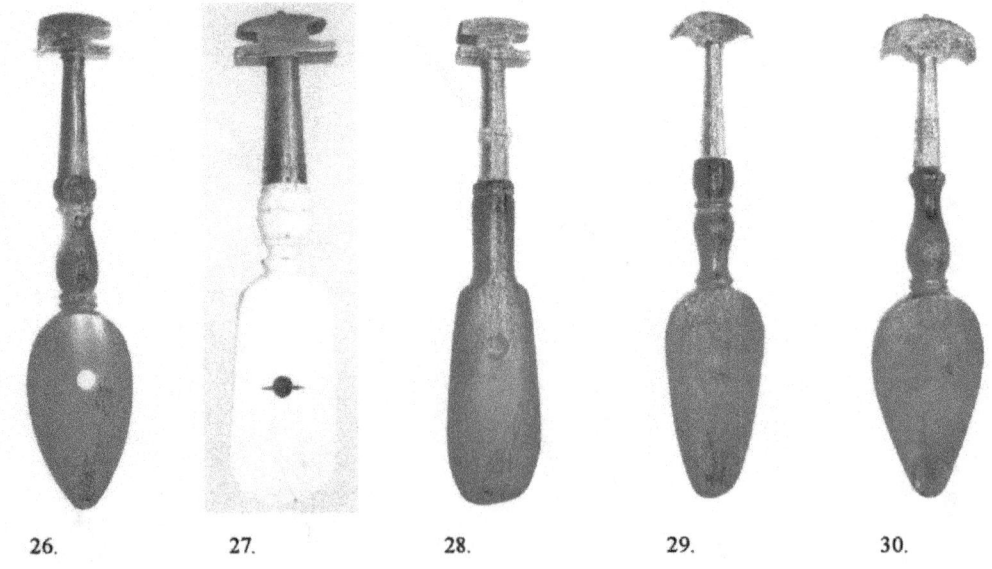

26. Two mini stars on mini plated steel head - 1.2" plated steel ferrule - M-O-P inlay - 4.85"
27. Mini brass head - .9' brass ferrule - black inlay with "wings" - 3.5"
28. Small plated steel head - 1.2" plated steel ferrule - recess with inlay missing - 4.7"
29. S H stamped on mini plated steel head - 1.1" German silver ferrule - H 15 stamped next to the mini German silver inlay - 4.7"
30. A pair of white inlay turned amber color on small plated steel head - 1" German silver ferrule - 4.45"

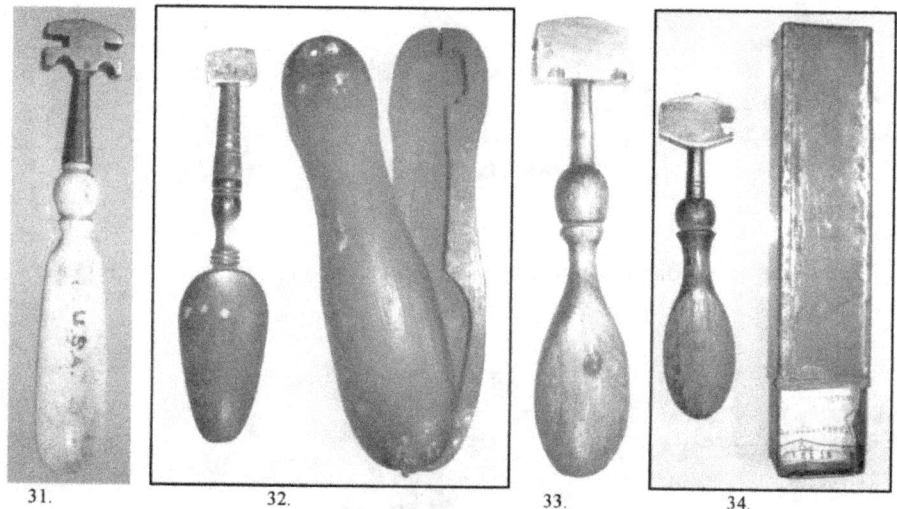

31.   32.   33.   34.

31.   MacHOB, C. F. below four circles with inscription within on obverse of German silver medium head -
1.1" brass ferrule - U.S.A. cut into ivory handle - 5.55"
32. C H on mini brass head - 1.2" plated steel ferrule - small brass inlay - hand carved walnut box - 5.05"
33. left side of partial "sun flower" stars on obverse & a 5 in lower left of reverse with a circle with crossed
glass cutters in center of large brass head - a small E stamped on side opposite the indentation - .9" brass
ferrule - black inlay - 5"
34. 3 – **AT**MUM stamped within a recessed line on large brass head – Russian style but may be Bulgarian -
.75" brass ferrule - black inlay - sliding tin tube box - 5"

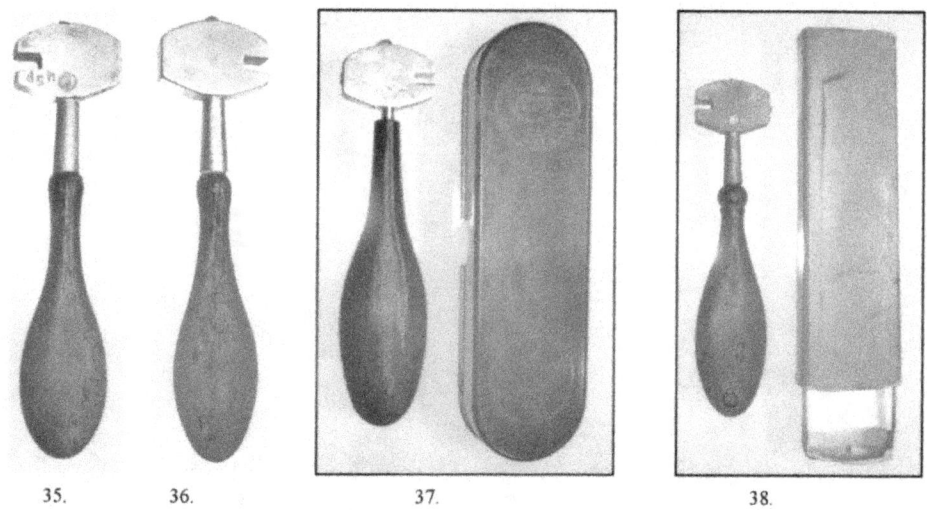

35.   36.   37.   38.

35 45P stamped under breaker on large brass head with set screw, on end opposite breaker, to hold cutter unit
at about a 60⁰ angle - .8" brass ferrule - black plastic handle - Russian circa 1955 - 4.7"
36 U3P   003   X °   stamped on face of large brass head - .8" brass ferrule extends straight through the head
- black plastic handle - Russian - 4.7"
37. u,4p.50k. cast in raised letters on center of black plastic handle - circle logo with wings on head and on top
of black plastic box, also ηOηTABA - Russian - 4.85"
38. Logo only on large brass head – set screw on side opposite breaker holds head to extended.8" brass ferrule
- black plastic handle Russian circa 1966 per instructions in blue slide box - 5.25"

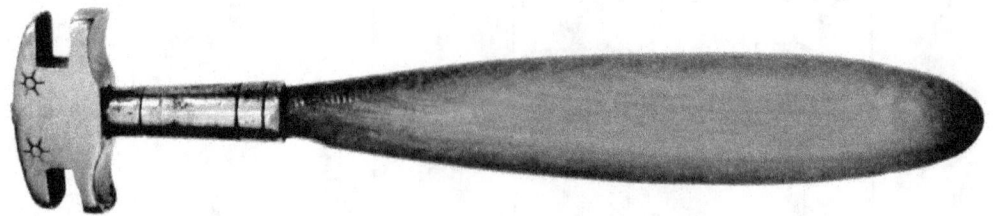

39. No ID - Pair of six point line stars radiating from circle circumference on steel head – 5.25"

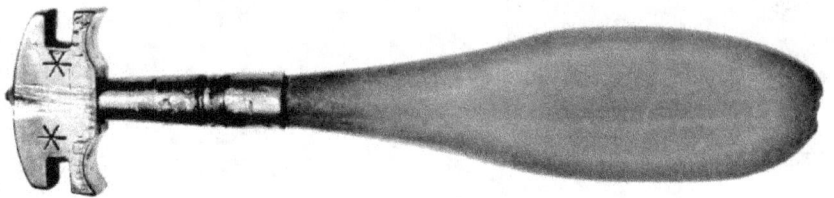

40. No ID - Pair of six point line stars on steel head - 4.6"

CATEGORY IV   DIAMOND POINT   -   CRESCENT HEAD

Crescent head glass cutters are found with a variety of designs of both the head and the handle. Many heads have a pair of either white or black round inlays. The handles range from turned ivory or bone, wood, plastic to heavy round German silver metal with flattened ends usually with four breakers.

Special items in this category are the three miniatures.

No U.S. Patents were found for this category.

Twenty four additional glass cutters are known to be in other collections.

Price range: $25 to $100   Miniatures $400 to $600

This Category is divided into 8 subsets:

    A. IVORY OR BONE HANDLE   usually with a pair of inlay on the head
    B. GERMAN SILVER HANDLE WITH 4 BREAKERS ON FLAT END
    C. WRENCH STYLE
    D. OTHER
    E. MINIATURE
    F. DUTCH
    G. RUSSIAN
    H. NEW

    A. IVORY OR BONE HANDLE

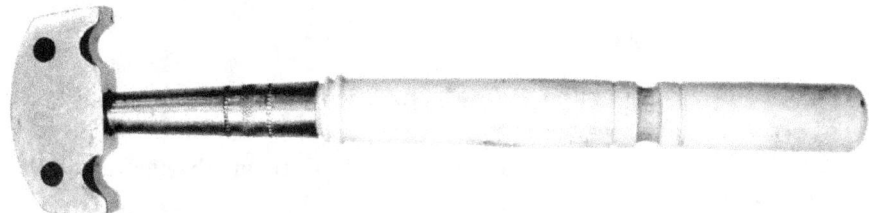

Note: Nos. 1 thru 7 have a flat sided head with arches on bottom of head

1. No ID – German silver head with pair of black inlay – 1.15" plated ferrule – 4.8"
2. No ID – steel head with pair of white inlay – 1.2" plated ferrule – squared end - 4.5"
3. No ID – steel head with pair of white inlay - 1.2" plated ferrule – turnings on handle are different than IV-2 – rounded end – 4.5"
4. No ID – brass head with pair of black inlay – 1.1" brass ferrule – squared end – 4.3"
5. No ID – large steel head with pair of white inlay – 1.2" plated ferrule – squared end – 4.6"
6. No ID – small steel head with pair of white inlay – 1.1" slender plated ferrule – squared end - - 4.3"
7. No ID – small steel head with pair of white inlay – 1.1" slender plated ferrule with 3F at base and different pattern – squared end – same handle as IV-6 - 4.35"

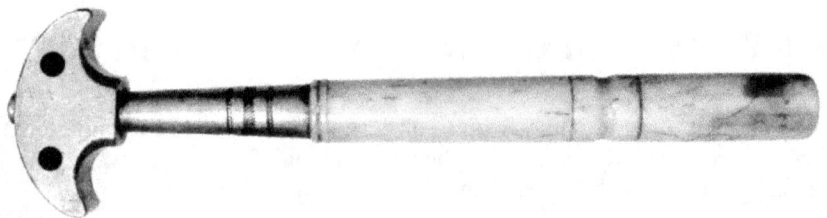

Note: Nos. 8 & 9 have full curved head with arches on bottom of head – ivory or bone handle

8. No ID – German silver head with pair of black inlay – 1.05" plated ferrule – squared end – 4.5"
9. No ID – steel head with pair of white inlay - 1.1" plated ferrule squared end – 4.4"

10. No ID – small steel head with a pair of 8-point line stars and no arches – 1.1" plated ferrule with an F near base – rounded end – 4.15"

B. GERMAN SILVER OR STEEL HANDLE WITH 4 BREAKERS ON FLAT END

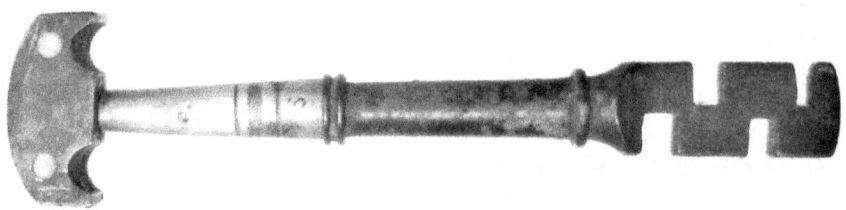

Note: Nos. 11 thru 29 have flat sides on head

11. No ID – steel head with pair of white inlay – 1.2" German silver ferrule with an S & 10 near base – this one has an iron handle – 4.5"
12. No ID – steel head with a pair of white inlay – 1.1" German silver ferrule – plated iron handle with but 2 breakers – 4"
13. AA in diamond on plated German silver(?) head with pair of white inlay – 1.1" plated ferrule – plated steel handle – 4.6"
14. AA in diamond on plated steel head with pair of white inlay – sides of head are slightly rounded – 1.1" plated ferrule – plated steel handle with 100 & small rosette near end of flat end – 4.3"
15. AA in diamond on reverse & 50 on obverse with a pair of white inlay on large plated steel head – 1.1" plated ferrule – plated steel handle – 4.7"
16. AA in diamond on reverse & pair of white inlay on obverse of German silver head – 1" German silver ferrule – German silver handle – 4.5"
17. No ID – steel head with pair of white inlay – 1.2" German silver ferrule – iron handle – 4.55"
18. GRENADE S̲t̲ ETEINNE MF in circle with crown on base of plated brass breaker area – plated steel head with pair of black inlay – plated ferrule and mid handle over steel – 4.4"
19. No ID - plated steel head with pair of white inlay – 1.15" German silver ferrule – plated steel handle – 4.5"

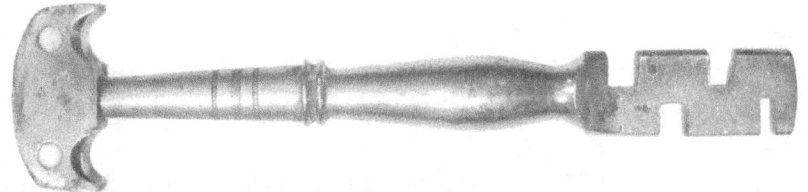

20. No ID – plated steel head with pair of white inlay – 1.1" German silver ferrule with a B near base – round bulbous mid-section of plated steel handle – 4.5"

21. SAINT ETEINNE   MF in circle with crown on obverse of plated steel head with a pair of white inlay – ferrule is part of plated steel handle – 5.5"

22. B & C LONDON A on reverse of German silver head with pair of black inlay – 1" German silver ferrule – German silver handle – 4.25"

23. No ID – small German silver head with a pair of black inlay – 1.05" German silver Ferrule – German silver handle – 4.25"

24. SAINT ETNINNE MF in circle with crown on mid-part of flat breaker area - glass cutter wheel mounted at end of breaker area – head has a pair of larger white inlay – this glass cutter is a cast non- magnetic plated metal – 4.4"

25. No ID - all German silver – pair of black inlay on head – 1.05" ferrule - 10 stamped next to last breaker – 4.3"

26. No ID – all German silver – pair of black inlay on head – 1.2" ferrule – 4.5"

27. No ID – all German silver – pair of black inlay on head – F on base of 1.2" ferrule – 12 stamped next to last breaker – 4.6"

28. No ID – all German silver – pair of black inlay on large head – 4.5"

29. HORLAVILLE   ROUEN on reverse of steel head with a pair of white inlay on obverse – a small L near neck of .33" ferrule – slender handle is German silver – 3.6"

NOTE: 30 – 31 -32 have full curved head with arches on bottom of head

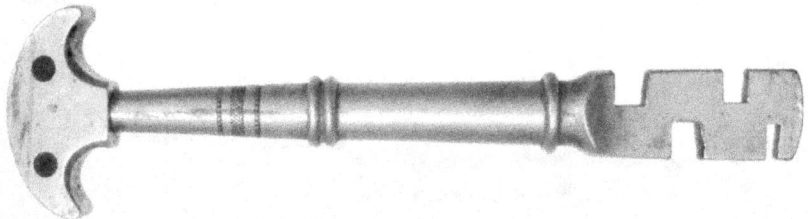

30. No ID – all German silver – pair of black inlay on head – 4.5"

31. No ID – small steel head with pair of white inlay – .9" German silver ferrule – steel handle -4.55"

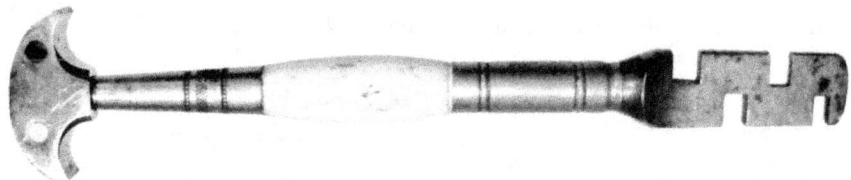

32. No ID – small plated steel head with pair of white inlay – bulbous ivory mid-section bounded by a pair of .9" German silver ferrules – steel breaker section – 4.55"

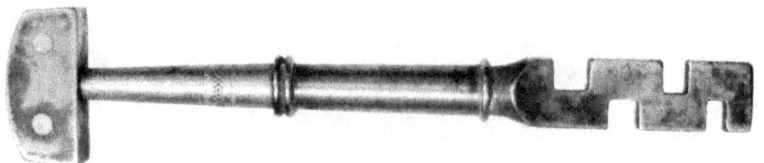

33. No ID – all steel except 1.05" German silver ferrule – pair of white inlays on head – 4.15"

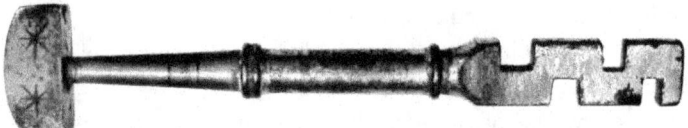

34. No ID – all plated steel except 1.05" brass ferrule – pair of 8 point line stars on head – 4.1"

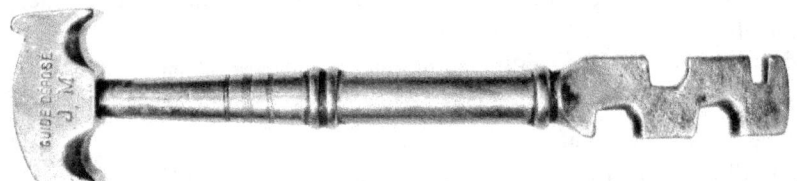

35. GUIDE DÉPOSÉ   J M on head reverse – one black & one white inlay on head obverse - all German silver - note hammer type head – 4.5"

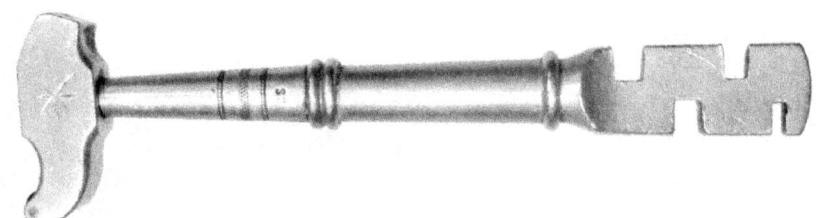

36. DÉPOSÉ on reverse of head – single 8 point line star on head obverse – note the glass cutter wheel on the up-turned end of head - BS stamped into base of 1.2" German silver ferrule – all German silver – 4.6"

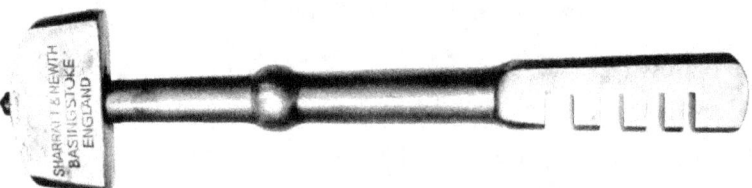

37. SHARRETT & NEWTH BASINGSTOKE ENGLAND on reverse of head – pair of 6 point line stars on head obverse – note alignment of breakers on narrow flat end – all German silver? Split mold lines are visible the length of both sides – 4.2"

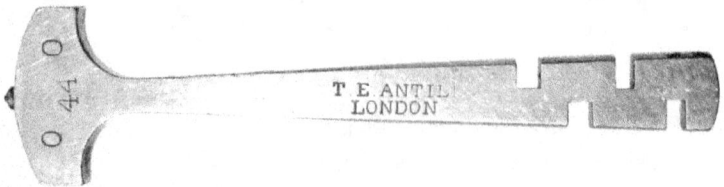

38. T. E. ANTILL   LONDON on obverse of flat handle and a pair of 0's in place of inlays on head with 44 between them - VETRERIE PIZZIRANI BOLOGNA BARI on reverse of flat handle - all German silver – 4.15"

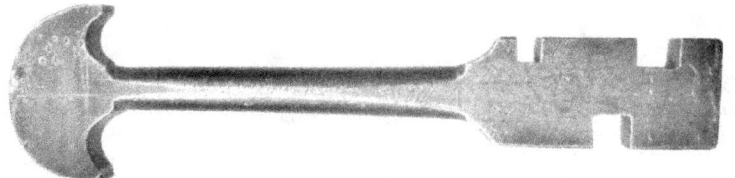

39. No ID – all heavy brass – note only three breakers – 4"

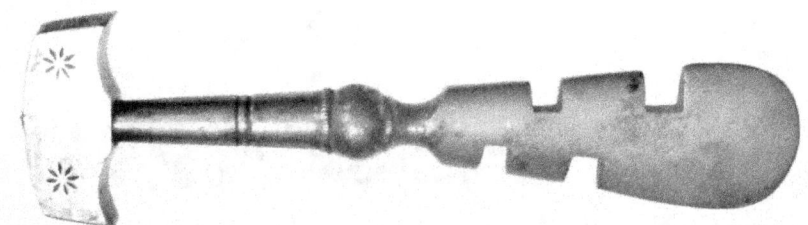

40. No ID – all plated steel – pair of 8 petal stars on head – breaker section tapers to thinner sides - 4.3"
41. No ID – all steel except 1" German silver ferrule – pair of white inlay on broad head – the five breaker tail also tapers to thinner sides and is narrower than IV-40 above – 4.2"

C. WRENCH STYLE BREAKER

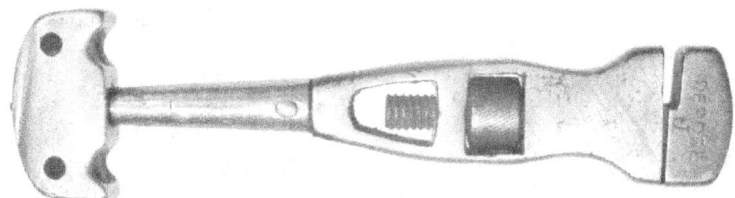

42. DÉPOSÉ   J   at end of steel handle – pair of black inlay on German silver head – 1.1" German silver ferrule – knurled thumbscrew at mid handle to control the breaker width - 4.1"
43. ETIENNE MF in circle with a crown above on base of black steel handle – pair of copper inlay on black steel head – ½" knurled brass screw at end controls the breaker width – 4.6"

D. OTHER

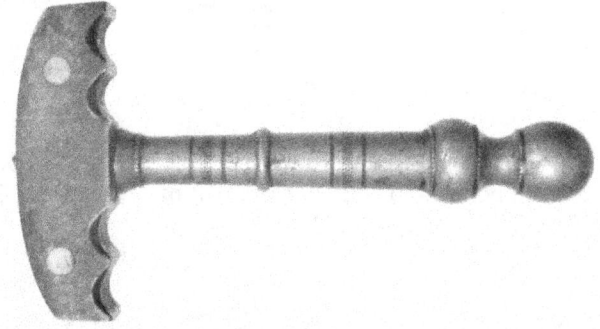

44. No ID - 1.7" wide steel head with pair of white inlay and double arches on bottom of head -2.6" round brass handle – 3.2"

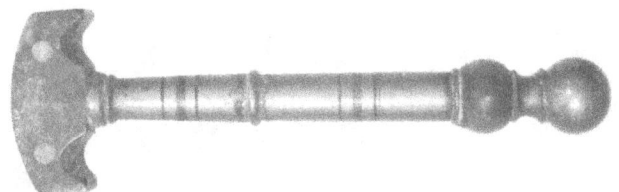

45. No ID – 1.1" wide steel head with pair of white inlay and single arches on bottom of head -   3" brass handle – 3.4"

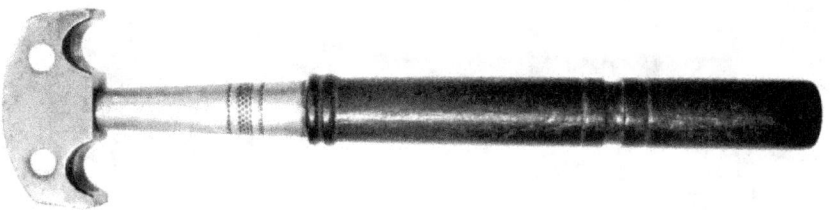

46. No ID – steel head with pair of white inlay – 1.05" German silver ferrule – dark round walnut handle - 4.5"

47. No ID – small plated steel head with pair of white inlay – no arches – 1.1" brass ferrule – dark round walnut handle – 4.1"

48. No ID – small steel head with white inlay with black centers – no arches – 1.15" brass ferrule – dark round walnut handle – 4.6"

49. No ID – small steel head with pair of 8 point line stars – 1.1" brass ferrule – slender dark round walnut handle – 4.45"

E. **MINIATURE**

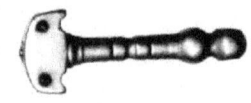

50. Ivory handle - 1.7"   51. 1.1"   52. 1.15"

No ID on any of the three - all German Silver except the ivory handle on 50. All have hole at end of handle for ring attachment per IV-50 - each has a pair of black inlay. These would make very nice ear rings for my wife.

F. DUTCH

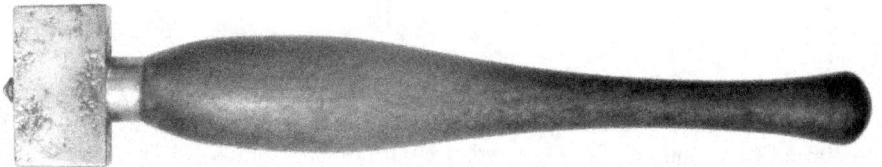

53. No ID – Arrow pointing to the left on rectangular steel head - .2" brass ferrule – walnut handle – 4.7"

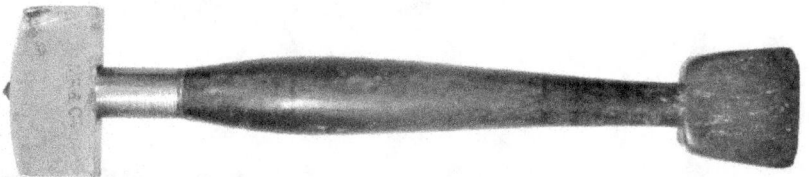

54. PAR & Cº on obverse of steel head – arrow pointing to the left on reverse - .5" brass ferrule – 4.5"

55. No ID – arrow on brass head pointing to left where an E is on end of the head - a K is on the neck end of the .9" brass ferrule – bulbous wood handle with a circular spatula end – 4.6"

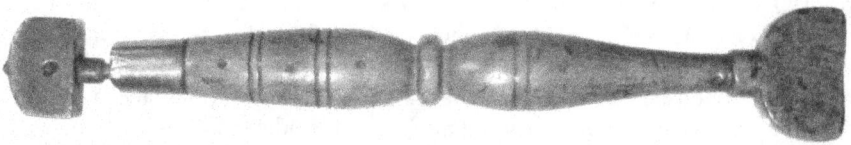

56. No ID – small steel head with a pair of 4 petal stars - .4" brass ferrule – round turned wood handle with spatula end – 4.8"

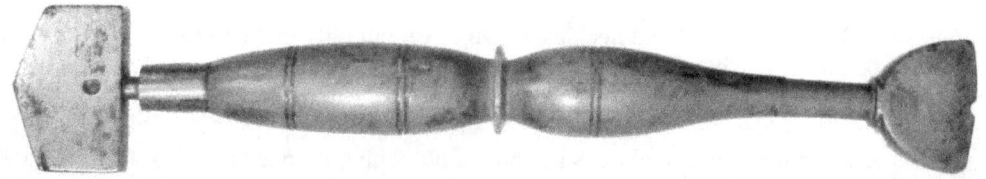

57. No ID – note low "A" frame roof end of steel head with a pair of 4 petal stars - .4" brass ferrule – note: the three circles in line on the upper bulbous part of wood handle and the pair of circles on the semicircular spatula end of handle – 5.2"

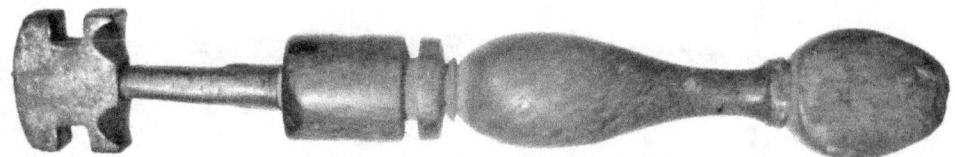

58. No ID – steel head with single breaker on either side - .85" brass ferrule - turned fruitwood finish wood handle with ovoid spatula end – 5.2"

G. RUSSIAN

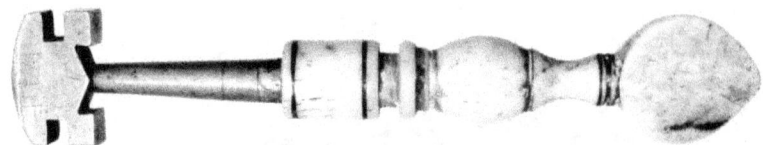

59. ROYCOT3 A. EARYWKNHT surrounding crest and a pair of circles and a 3 on a German silver head with single breaker on either side: note the modified arches – 1.25" German silver ferrule – turned ivory handle with a tapered circular pointed spatula – 4.9"

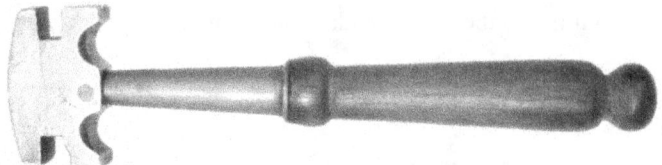

60. CEMEHBb beneath four circles with inscriptions and a 6 on a German silver head with single breakers on either side – 1.25" brass ferrule – slender turned walnut handle – 4.1"

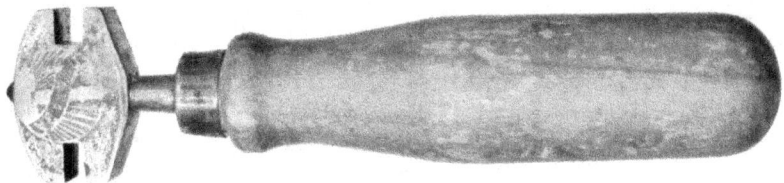

61. ηΟΛΤΑΒΑ on a ribbon banner across a glass cutter in a circle logo on a brass head with single breakers on either side - .35" brass neck - .3" steel ferrule – thick wood handle – 5.3"

62. same ribbon banner and logo, brass head , brass neck and steel ferrule as IV-61 above, however this one has a shorter orange painted thick wood handle – 4.4"

63. same shape brass head as IV -61 & 62 above, however, the banner and logo are smaller – same tapered brass neck which flows smoothly into a sky blue plastic handle ribbed and tapered to a flat square spatula end - 5"

64. same shape brass head and neck as above three, but only one breaker – 009   O(with a p in it)u5p 3 stamped on side with breaker at the left - .8" diam. X .4" long steel ferrule painted black – thick unfinished wood handle – 5"

65. same shape brass head and neck as above , but with only one breaker - 007   O(with a p in it)u5p 3   stamped on side with breaker at the left - brass neck is .75" which unscrews from threaded solid brass handle tightened by two brass nuts - most likely a make-do - 4.9"

I. NEW

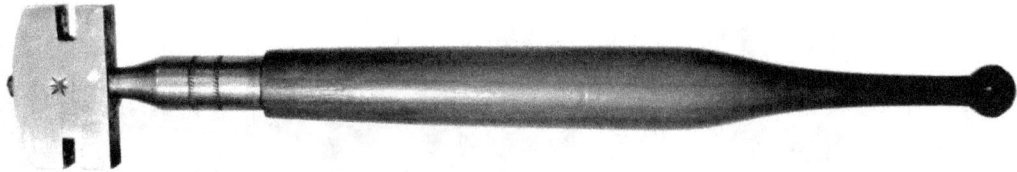

66. SHARRATT & NEWTH LONDON on obverse & a 6 point line star on reverse of steel head with single breakers on either side of head - 1" brass ferrule - walnut handle with small ball – 6.4"

67. DIACARBIDE PRODUCTS INC stamped into one of two elongated finger rests on a solid aluminum handle - solid brass head with single breaker on either side - 6.05"

CATEGORY V: DIAMOND POINT - BLOCK CUTTER

These glass cutters are identified as BLOCK CUTTERS because of their block shape. Six atypical block cutters are shown at the end of the category.

There are 32 different known in other collections.

Four U.S. Patents were found for this category: 85,396   167,575   520,247   1,005,637

Price range: $20 to $75

This category has been subdivided into five subsets by block style: All are plated steel head unless otherwise noted and very similar to subset picture.

A. PAGODA ROOF
B. SLOPE ROOF
C. SKI JUMP SLOPE - SHARP LIP

D. SKI JUMP SLOPE   ROUND LIP
E. OTHER

A. PAGODA ROOF

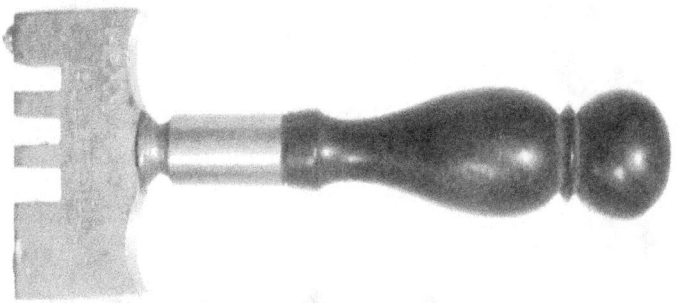

1. DIAMOND TOOL CO. CHICAGO on obverse - I-P XX RULER SIDE on reverse - .85" plated steel ferrule – walnut handle – 3.8"
2. DIAMOND TOOL CO. CHICAGO on obverse - 75,922 RULER SIDE on reverse - .85" plated steel ferrule – walnut handle – 3.8"
3. G. D. DUNHAM CHICAGO on obverse - THIS SIDE TO RULER on reverse - .75" plated steel ferrule - walnut handle .3.65"
4. EARL & CO. CHICAGO 11 on obverse - RULER SIDE WARRANTED on reverse - .75" plated steel ferrule with two deep v grooves is an integral part of the head - walnut handle - 3.5"
5. GRANT TOOL MFRS. CLEVELAND, O. on obverse - A on reverse - .8" plated steel ferrule – walnut handle – 3.85"
6. HANLINE BROS. BALTIMORE on obverse - RULER SIDE on reverse - .7" plated steel ferrule with two just visible grooves is an integral part of the head - walnut handle – 3.75"
7. LLOYD BROOKLYN N.Y. on obverse - THIS SIDE TO RULER on reverse - .7" plated steel ferrule with two medium grooves is an integral part of the head - walnut handle - 3.45"
8. PITTSBURGH PLATE GLASS CO. on obverse - THIS SIDE TO RULER on reverse - .7" plated steel ferrule with two medium grooves and a deep wide one next to head - walnut handle - 3.5"
9. PH. SINSZ CO. BALTIMORE on obverse - RULER SIDE on reverse - .7" steel ferrule with two just visible grooves is an integral part of the head - walnut handle - 3.5"
10. PH. SINSZ CO. BALTIMORE on obverse - THIS SIDE TO RULER on reverse - .75" plated steel ferrule with two medium grooves is an integral part of the head - light walnut handle – 3.65"

11. PH SINSZ BALTIMORE PATD. SEPT. 7, 75. on obverse - THIS SIDE TO RULER on reverse - .7" plated steel ferrule with two just visible grooves is an integral part of the head - walnut handle – 3.4"

12. PH SINSZ BALTIMORE PATD SEPT. 7, 75 XX on obverse - THIS SIDE TO RULER on reverse - .7" plated steel ferrule with two just visible grooves and a wide and deep groove next to head is an integral part of head - slender walnut handle - 3.4"

13. PH. SINSZ BALTIMORE PATD. MAY 22, 94 on obverse - .7" plated steel ferrule with two just visible grooves is an integral part of head - walnut handle - 3.5"

14. PH. SINSZ CO_ BALTIMORE PATENT, MAY, 22, 94 - on obverse .7" plated steel ferrule with two medium v grooves is an integral part of the head - walnut handle - 3.65"

B. SLOPE ROOF

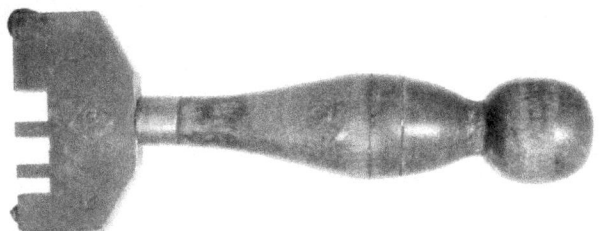

15. DE in a diamond B on obverse - ARROW pointing toward the wheel end on reverse - solid brass head - .25" plated steel ferrule - fruitwood finish handle - 3.5"

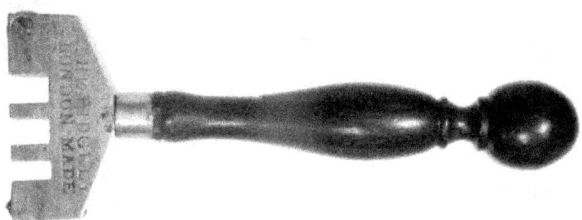

16. THE RIDGELY LONDON MADE on obverse - C. Cresswell 1919 scratched deep into reverse - .25" plated ferrule - walnut handle - 3.3"

17. A. RUDD ST. HELENS ENGLAND on obverse - RULE SIDE 1 on reverse - .2" plated ferrule - walnut handle - 3.55"

18. SHARRATT & NEWTH LONDON, ENGLAND A 2 RULE SIDE on obverse - .2" brass ferrule - light walnut handle - 3.5"

19. SHARRATT & NEWTH LONDON. ENGLAND A 3 RULE SIDE on obverse - RESET BY ??MONOS LTD in a rectangular box on reverse - .2" brass ferrule - dark fruitwood handle - 3.6"

20. SHARRATT & NEWTH LONDON. ENGLAND A 4 RULE SIDE on obverse - walnut handle - 3.6"

21. SHARRATT & NEWTH LONDON. ENGLAND B 1 on obverse - .3" brass ferrule - fruitwood handle - 3.6"

22. SHARRATT & NEWTH LONDON. ENGLAND B 1 RULE SIDE on obverse - MADE IN ENGLAND on reverse - .2" plated ferrule - walnut handle - 3.7"

23. SHARRATT & NEWTH LONDON ENGLAND B 1 RULE SIDE on obverse - .2" brass ferrule - light walnut handle - 3.45"

24. SHARRATT & NEWTH LONDON. ENGLAND B 1 RULE SIDE on obverse - MARSWELLS MADE IN ENGLAND on reverse - walnut handle - 3.45"

C. SKI JUMP SLOPE - SHARP LIP

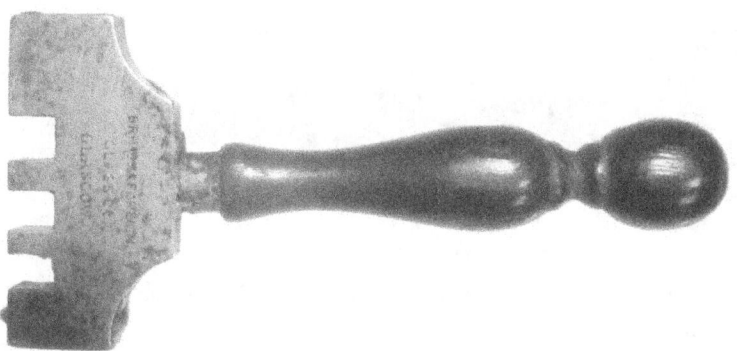

25. BRITISH&FOREIGN GLASS C° GLASGOW on reverse - A   and an ARROW pointing towards the wheel on obverse - .25" brass ferrule 2" wide head - walnut handle - 4.3"
26. INNES-WELD GLASS C° CHICAGO   on reverse - BELGUIM   RULE SIDE on obverse - steel head is ¼ " narrower than V-25 above - .25" brass ferrule - maple handle with walnut finish – 4.7"

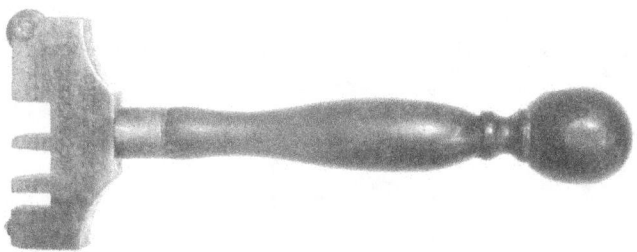

27. CITY GLASS C° GLASGOW   on reverse - B   RULE SIDE   on obverse - .25" brass ferrule - slender walnut handle - 3.55"
28. INNES-WELD GLASS C° CHICAGO on reverse - BELGUIM   RULE SIDE on obverse - .2" brass ferrule - slender fruitwood handle - 3.7"
29. P & T. MACLEOD   PERTH on reverse   -   C and an ARROW pointing to the wheel end - .2" brass ferrule - fruitwood handle - 3.4"
30. SHAW ENGLAND in a rectangle on reverse -   A and an ARROW pointing to the wheel end on obverse - .2" brass ferrule - walnut handle - 3.45"
31. Same as V-30 above except a B on obverse
32. Same as V-30 & 31 above except a C on obverse and a fruitwood handle
33. Same as V-32 except a D on obverse and 3.55"
34. SHAW ENGLAND no rectangle enclosure on reverse -   C   and an ARROW pointing to the wheel end - .2" brass ferrule - walnut handle - 3.3"
35. A. SHAW & SON LONDON in a large diamond on reverse -   B   MADE IN ENGLAND and an ARROW pointing to the wheel end on obverse - .2" brass ferrule - walnut handle - 3.45"
36. A. SHAW & SON LONDON MADE IN ENGLAND on reverse -   D   RULE SIDE on obverse - .2" brass ferrule - fruitwood handle - 3.45"
37. SHAW ENGLAND   A (facing handle)   and an ARROW   pointing to the wheel end on obverse of solid brass head - .2" plated ferrule - dark walnut handle - 3.3"

D. SKI JUMP SLOPE - ROUND LIP

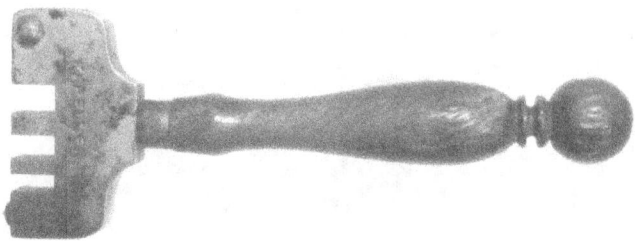

38. KARELSEN, N.Y. EXTRA on reverse - RULE SIDE on obverse - .2" plated brass ferrule - slender walnut handle - 3.5"

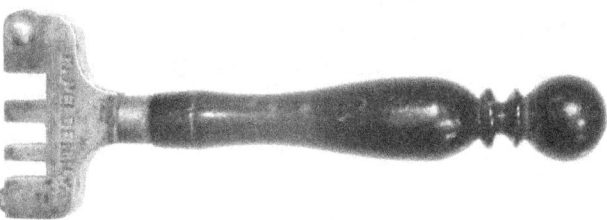

39. KARELSEN, N.Y. on reverse - RULE SIDE on obverse - .2" plated brass ferrule - walnut handle nearly black - 3.5"

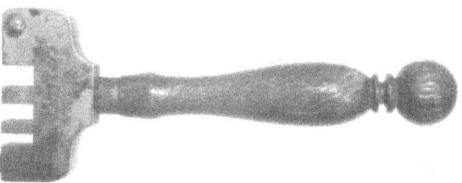

40. SHARRATT & NEWTH B 2 on reverse - RULE SIDE on obverse of solid brass head   - no ferrule - very slender walnut handle - 2.6"

E. OTHER

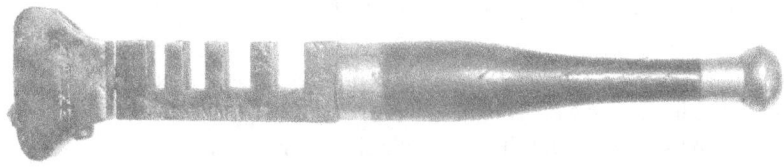

41. KARELSEN NEW-YORK on steel breaker bar - RULE SIDE on steel head   on obverse -PAT. MAR. 6, 77 on breaker bar - EXTRA on head reverse - .25" plated brass ferrule - plated brass ball end - dark walnut handle - 4.3"

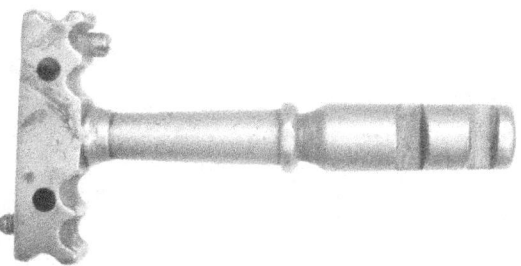

42. L'IDEAL 2 DÉPOSÉ on obverse of German silver head with a pair of black inlay on reverse - German silver handle with 4 breakers - 3"

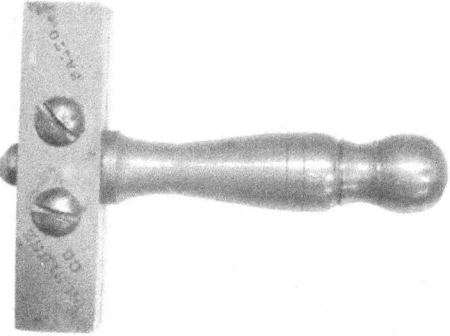

43. PH. SINSZ CO BALTO. on reverse of split steel head held by two steel screws - a pair of white inlay on obverse - ¼" smooth bore hole in end of steel handle - 2.6" (see VIII-43)

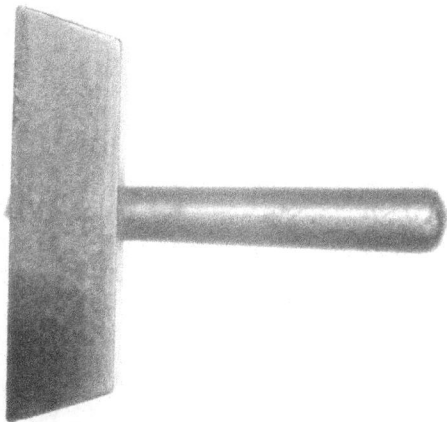

44. No ID – three punch depressions ¼" apart on face of trapezoidal steel head .6" thick X .6" high X 2.45" long base - slightly increasing taper to end of steel handle - 2.6"

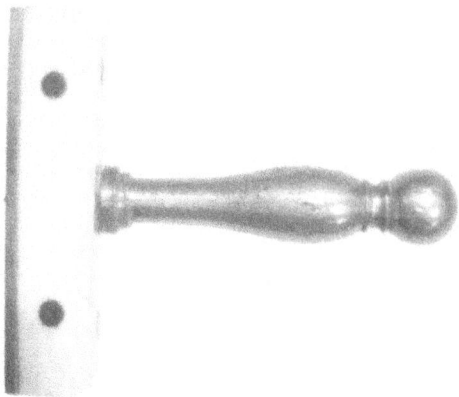

45. No ID - brass handle and diamond plate body of head is ivory with a pair of black inlay on top as well as one face - 2.65"

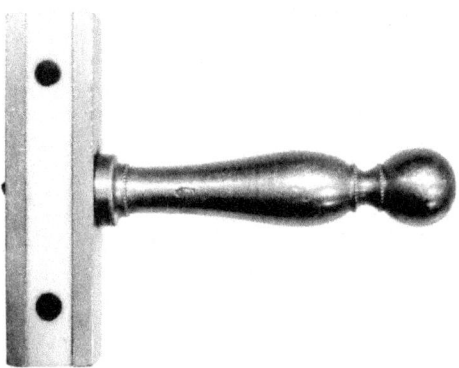

46. No ID – German silver handle - diamond plate & top plate - ivory body with a pair of black inlay on one face - 2.65"

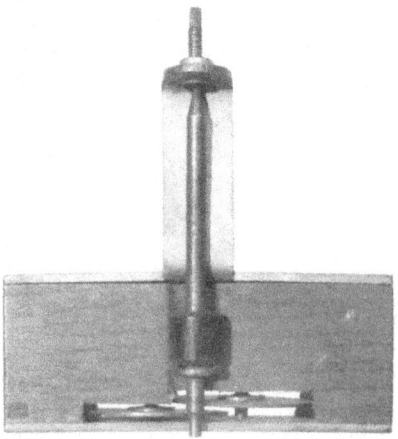

47. MAGIC DIAMOND PAT'D. DEC. 29, 1886(PAT. #85,396) AND MAY 18, 1869* on brass bottom plate - walnut body - brass top plate with attached upright arm holding spindle - 2.25" wide X .9" high X .5" deep at top & .75" deep at bottom - 2.4" height. * No pertinent data was found for this patent date.

CATEGORY VI: EARLY CAST IRON WITH WHEELS

This category began with the businesses of Monce, Barrett, Woodward, and others after the invention of the revolving steel glass cutter wheel. Shortly thereafter, nearly every small tool had a glass cutter wheel attached in some manner.

Thirteen different early iron glass cutters are known in other collections.

Price range: $20 - $50 however, on 4-17-2011 a similar one with a hinged corkscrew that stored between the short legs at the spatula end sold for $382. (Most likely a corkscrew collector)

Six Patents: 102,727   132,219   140,426   150,225   229,228   246,419

This category is divided into six sections:

    A.   **TAPERED NOSE**
    B.   **HOOKED NOSE**
    C.   **MODIFIED HOOKED NOSE**
    D.   **SQUARED SPATULA END**
    E.   **MISCELLANEOUS STYLES**
    F.   **WOOD HANDLE - "LADY LEGS"**

A.   **TAPERED NOSE**

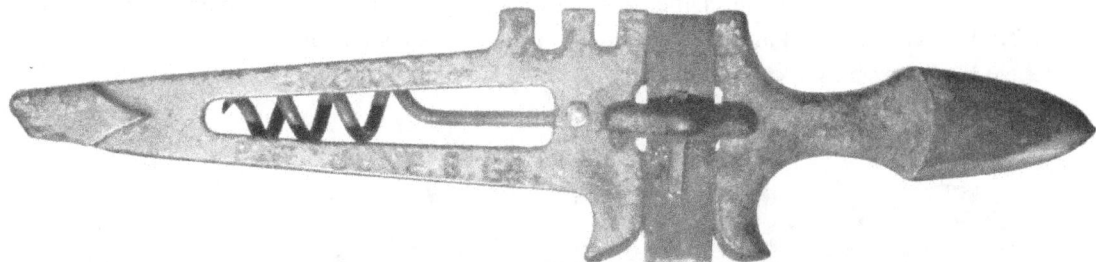

1. MONCE - PAT. JUNE 8, 69 – corkscrew – knife sharpener – pointed spatula end - 5.875"
2. No ID - corkscrew – knife sharpener - pointed spatula end – 5.5"
3. No ID – no corkscrew hole – knife sharpener – cutting wheel is offset like Woodward's – 6 1/8"
4. PAT. APR. 28, 1874(Brook's date) – corkscrew swivel mounted – knife sharpener – 6 1/8"
5. PAT. AUG 17 - 75 (on cutter end) – no corkscrew hole – knife sharpener – 6"
6. PAT. AUG 17 – 75 (on cutter end that is 1/8" longer than VI-5 above) otherwise the same
7. PAT. AUG. 24 – 75 – corkscrew – knife sharpener – 5.75"
8. PAT –AUG 17 – 75 – no corkscrew – knife sharpener – 6 1/8"
9. PAT – AUG 17 – 75 – corkscrew – knife sharpener – 6 1/8"
10. PAT AUG 24 1875 – corkscrew – knife sharpener – 5.625"
11. PAT. AUG. 24 – 1875 – only an indent for corkscrew to be mounted – knife sharpener – 5.75"
11 – A. THE ANDRESS TOOL PAT JUN 8 75 – only an indent for corkscrew – knife sharpener – 5.7"
12. PAT'D JUNE 29. 80 (Adams date) – corkscrew – knife sharpener – 6"

B. HOOKED NOSE

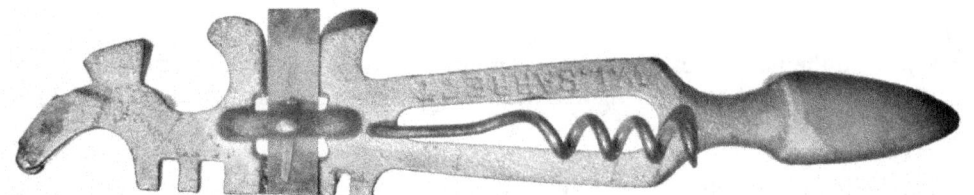

13. W. L. BARRETT – corkscrew - knife sharpener – gold paint – 3 breakers - 5.55"
14. MONCE – PAT JUN. 8 – 69 - indent for corkscrew – knife sharpener – gold paint – 5.75"
15. MONCE – PAT JUN 8 - 69 - corkscrew - knife sharpener – (putty blade broken)
16. THE ARTISANS TOOL – /AT. JULY 22 1874 – indent for corkscrew – knife sharpener – some gold paint – 5.75"
17. THE ANDRESS TOOL – PAT. AUG. 24, 75 – corkscrew – knife sharpener – hammer head has tack puller indent - gold paint – 5.5"
18. NASHUA LOCK CO – PAT AUG 24 75. Corkscrew – knife sharpener –evidence of gold paint – 5.8"
19. PAT. AUG. 24, 75 – corkscrew – knife sharpener – gold paint – 5.625"

19-A   THE TREMONT I. X. L. TOOL – corkscrew – knife sharpener – 2 breakers - 5.8"
20. THE WOODWARD TOOL – PAT. AUG. 24 75 – corkscrew – knife sharpener – gold paint – 5.625"
21. THE WOODWARD TOOL – PAT. AUG. 24 75 – indent for corkscrew – knife sharpener – gold paint – 5.75"
22. PAT. AUG. 24 75(on hook nose) – corkscrew(on under side) – knife sharpener – 2 breakers - 6.125"
23. No ID – corkscrew – knife sharpener – short thick legs by spatula - gold paint – 5.625"
24. No ID – corkscrew – knife sharpener – narrow spatula - gold paint – 5.5"
25. No ID – corkscrew – knife sharpener – gold paint – 5.625"

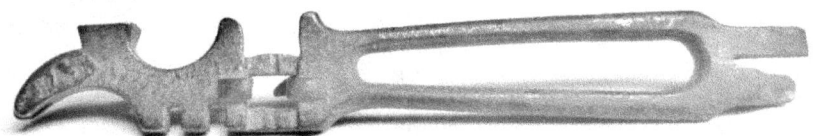

25 – A. PAT. AUG. 24 – 75(on hook nose) – no hole nor indent for corkscrew – the bridge for holding the steel knife sharpener was not cut but cast open as shown as separated hooks - the small pointed tail seen through the small rectangular opening is the sharp blade of a can opener – the long mid ribs are round in cross-section, not flat on one side as others of this style - the upper tail extension is a screwdriver and the lower extension is a tack lifter – these were cast in place, not machined out - 5.5"

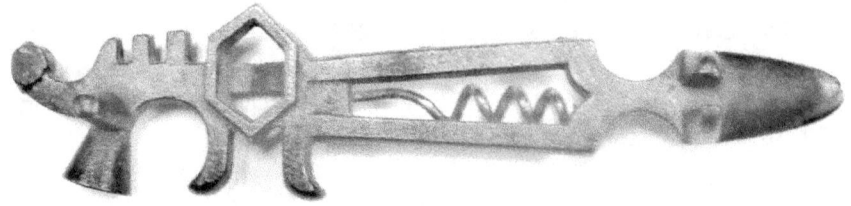

25 - B. PAT JUN 8 69 on flat ribs - ⊙ X Δ – on reverse above breakers – note the hexagonal bridge to hold the missing knife sharpener – corkscrew – hammer – larger wheel holding area – 5.8"

C. MODIFIED HOOKED NOSE

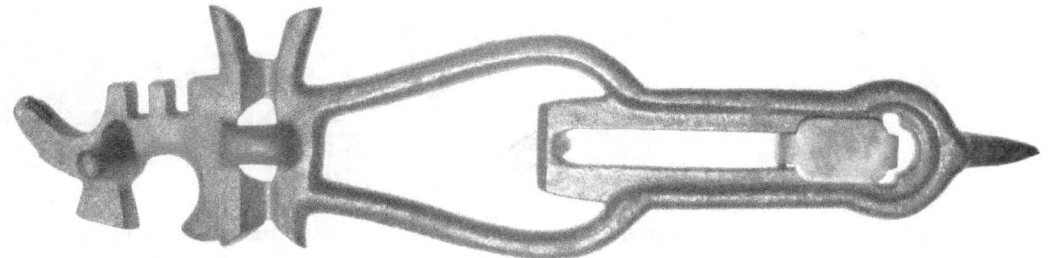

26. No. ID – knife sharpener (triangular hardened steel piece missing) - handle modified with adjustable can opener and pick at end – red paint – 6.3"

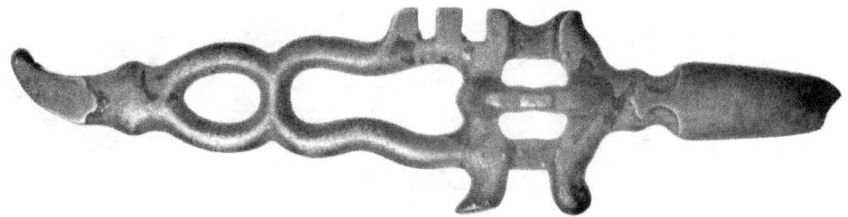

27. No ID – knife sharpener (hardened blade missing) – black paint – 5.25"

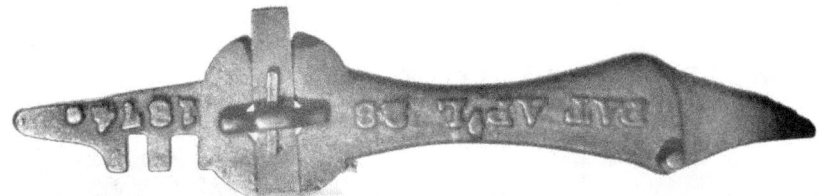

28. PAT AP'L 28 1874. (BROOKS date) - straight nose – knife sharpener – gold paint – 5.15"

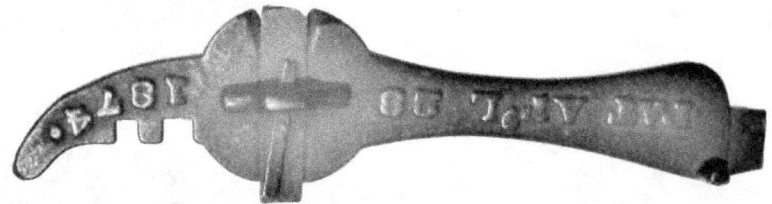

29. PAT AP'L 28 1874. (BROOKS date) – knife sharpener – spatula broken – 4.3" as is

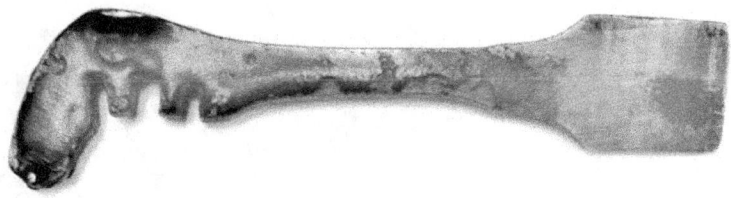

29 –A. No ID - heavy black paint - flat circular finger rest above the three breakers - 4"

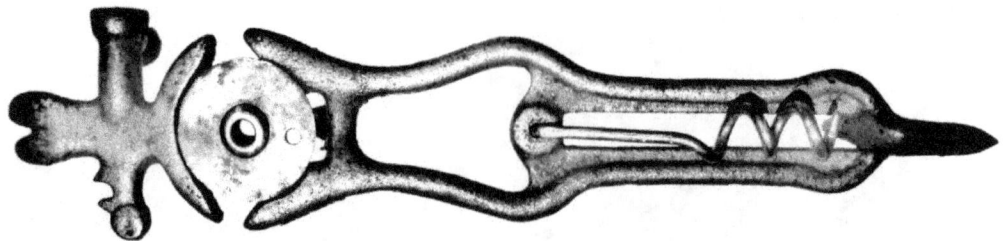

30. No ID – plated steel combination tool – corkscrew – knife sharpener – tack puller – pick – bottle cap opener – hammer – 7.7"

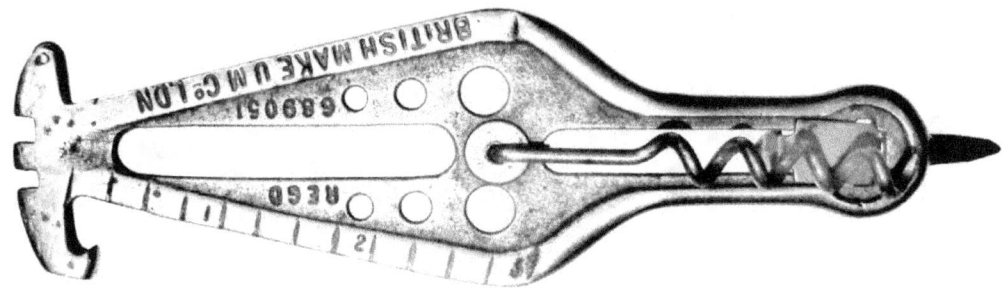

31. BRITISH MAKE U M C° LDN – REGD 689051 – plated steel combination tool - corkscrew adjustable can opener – pick – bottle opener – ruler – 6.4"

D.   SQUARE SPATULA END - VARIOUS STYLES

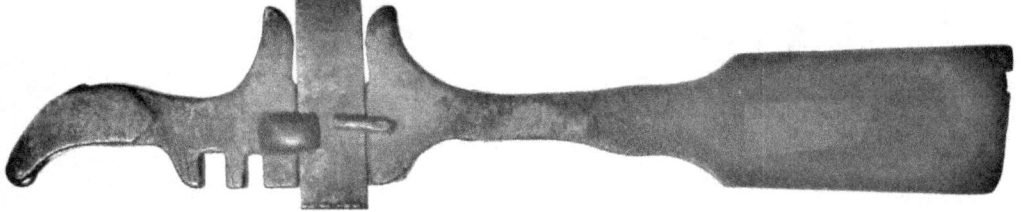

32. No ID – rectangular knife sharpener – gold paint – 5.4"

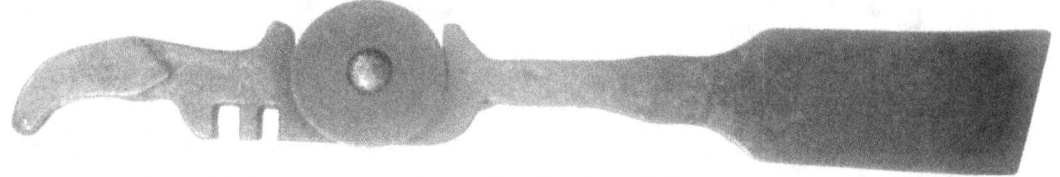

33. No ID – circular knife sharpener – evidence of gold paint – 5.6"

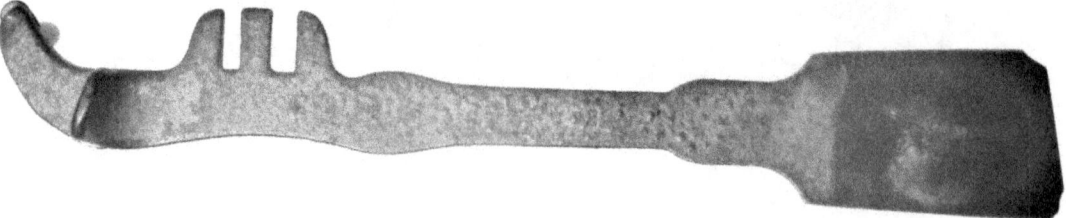

34. MONCE – PAT JUN 8 69 – gold paint – 5.4"
35. PAT. AUG. 24. 75.(WOODWARD date) – rough casting by head – 5.65"
36. PAT. AUG. 24. 75 (WOODWARD date) – some gold paint – 5.5"
37. No ID except a cast raised five point star just above spatula – 5.75"
38. No ID – black paint – 5.4"

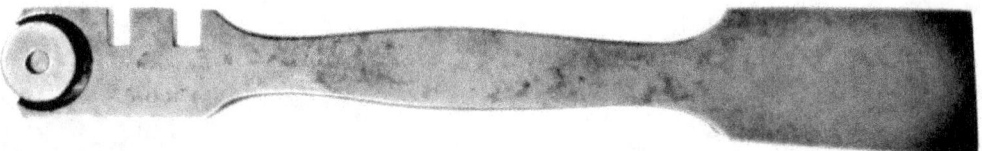

39. Goodell Tool Co. Shelburne, Falls Mass.(on center of handle) – PAT. APL'D FOR NO. 2 (on side of head) – no numbers on 6-wheel turret – 5.2"

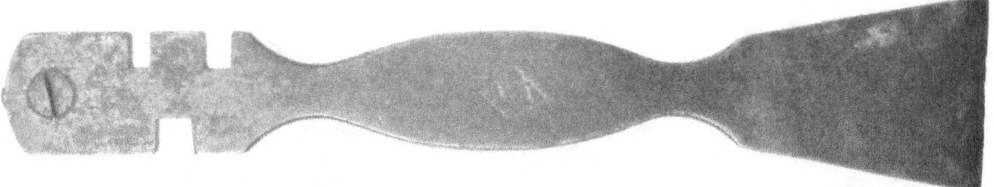

40. A.A in a diamond at mid handle – 6-wheel turret with recessed large numbers – splayed spatula – 5.2"

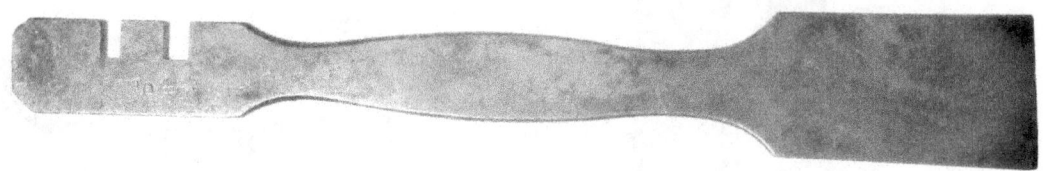

41. Goodell Tool Co. Shelburne Falls, Mass.(on side of head) – No 4 on other side of head -   two wheels mounted at the corners of head – 5.6"

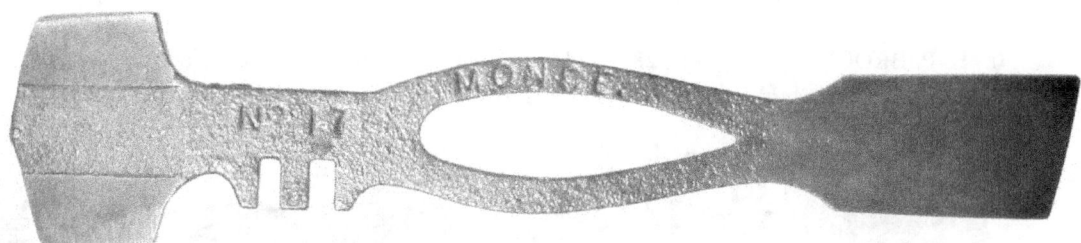

42. MONCE (on center rib) – N° 17 by breakers – plated steel – 5.7"
43. W. L. BARRETT (on center rib) – plated steel – 5.45"

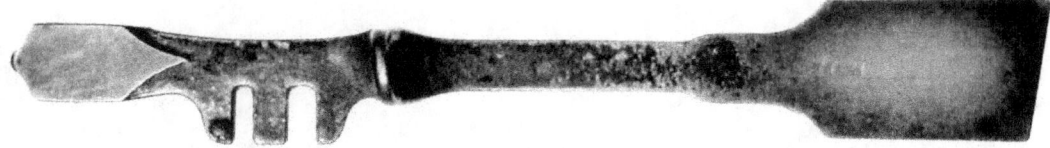

44. PAT. PEND.(on spatula) – thin finger rest – black paint – 5.6"
45. No ID same as VI-44 otherwise – black paint – 5.7"

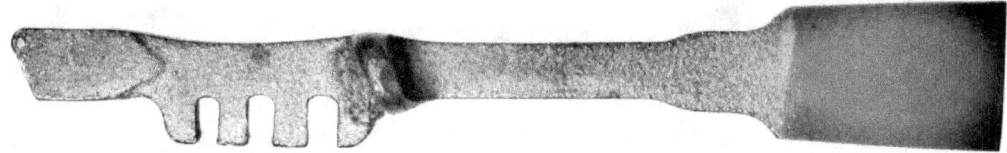

46. No ID – gold paint – normal wheel cut – 5.25"
47. No ID – gold paint – deep wheel cut – 5.45

48. No ID – full thick head – black paint – 5.5"
49. No ID – full thin head – gold paint – 5.45"

E.   MISCELLANEOUS STYLES

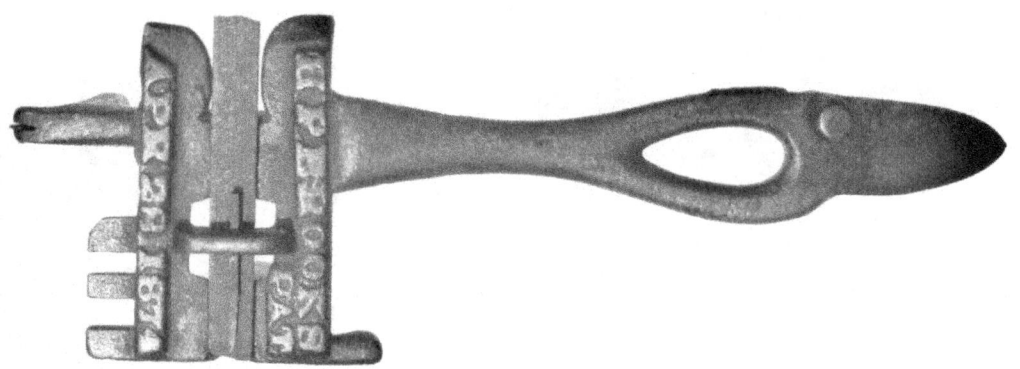

50. H. P. BROOKS PAT. APR. 28, 1874 – cast handle as shown above –triangular knife sharpener – 5.3"
51. H. P. BROOKS PAT. APR. 28, 1874 – cast without handle – triangular knife sharpener – 2.25"

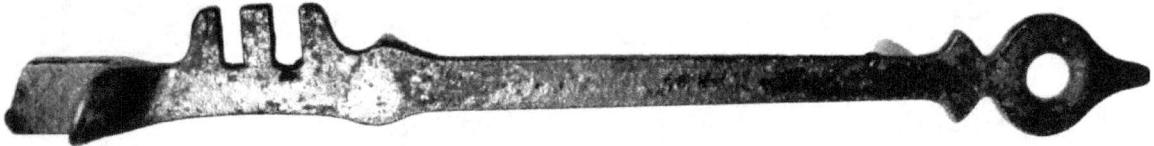

52. No ID – finger and thumb rests – black paint – hole for hanging? – 6"

53. PAT. PENDING(on ruler near finger rest) – gold paint – 5.85"

54. MONCE - circle with a dot in a diamond on side of head – heavy ball end – 5.25"
55. BARRETT – dark maroon paint – heavy ball end – 5.1"
56. No ID – gold paint - heavy ball end – 5.25"
57. No ID – cutter head is of uniform thickness – plated steel – heavy ball end – 5"

F.   WOOD HANDLE - "LADY LEGS"   See ad on page 112.

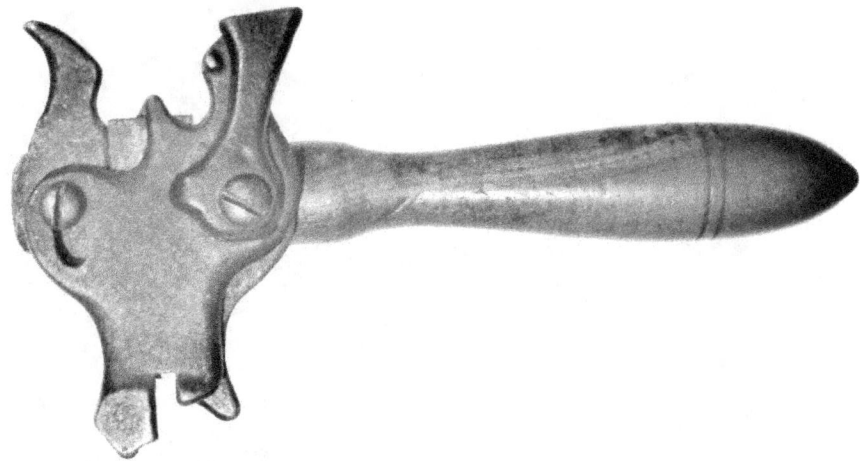

58. PAT. APLD' FOR. – PAT'D MAY 3, 1870(S. C. Stokes date) – stamped in wood next to steel mount – knife sharpener – steel units are identical back to back except for wheel holder end - 5.1"

59. PAT. APLD. FOR. - PAT'D MAY 3, 1870(S. C. Stokes date) – stamped in wood next to steel mount – knife sharpener – steel units are identical back to back - 5.1"

60. PAT'D MAY 3, 1870 - PATD OCT. 15, 1872(S.C. Stokes date) – stamped in wood next to steel mount – knife sharpener – 5.1"

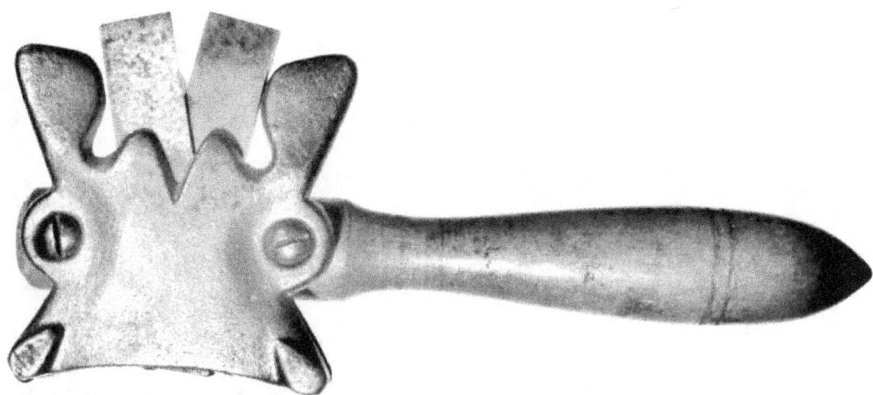

61. No ID – knife sharpener – solid steel back plate is half height – 5.1"

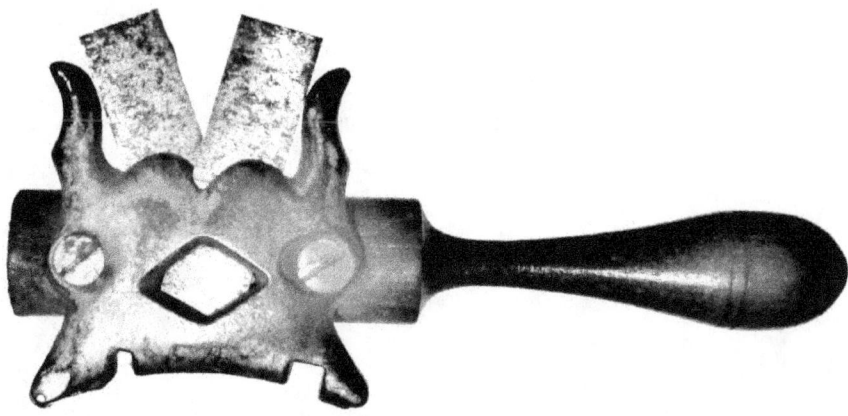

62. No ID – no back plate – knife sharpener – note fancy turned handle – 4.6"

Ad that corresponds with No. 60 on previous page (two patent dates).

CATEGORY VII   PLIERS

Pliers with glass cutters are scarce and the ones with a corkscrew on the handle might be considered dangerous to use. These cutters are collected as combination tools what with the corkscrew, can opener, nut cracker, and screw driver attachments. Only one other is known in another collection.

Price Range: $20 - 50

Fourteen U.S. Patents were found for pliers with glass cutters as follows:

316,430	858,003	1,024,120	1,482,206	2,212,599	2,430,349	4,878,260
751,594	862,049	1,344,264	2,205,717	2,268,257	4,361,498	5,361,498

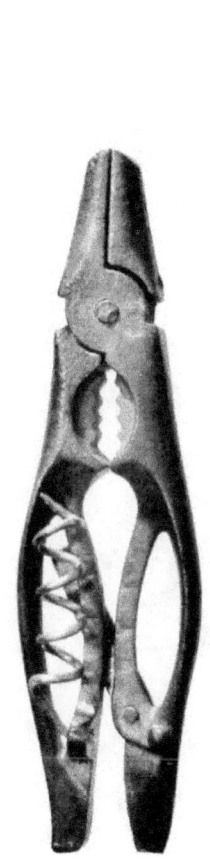 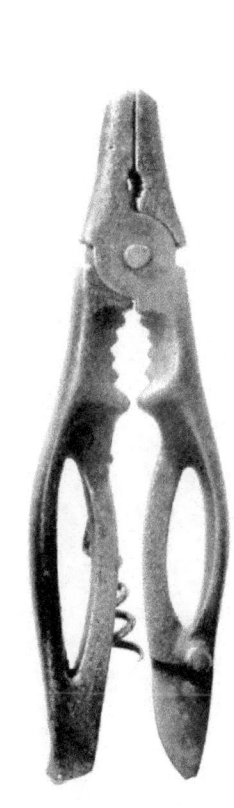 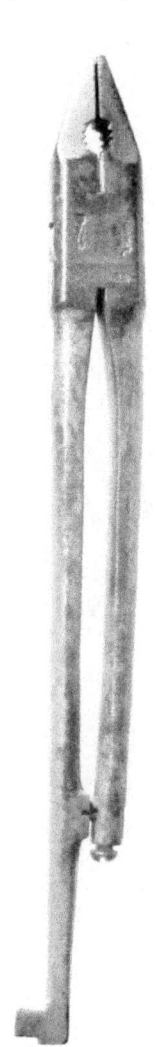

1.   PAT AUG 24 1875 - 5.6"
Corkscrew attached at end
of handle near cutter wheel
and flat blade on other handle

2. No ID - 5.4"
corkscrew attached
near mid handle

3. D. F. & T. CO. UTICA, N.Y.
UTICA PAT. DEC. 9 -03 - 8"
wheel near end of short handle

CATEGORY VIII HEFTY METAL - WHEEL CUTTERS

This category is mostly of French origin, but if not, other European countries. Only one U.S. Patent # 706,196 has been attributed to this category.

Eighteen other cutters are known to be in other collections.

This Category has been divided into four sub-sets.

    A. IRON FLIP TOPS
    B. TURRET CRESCENT HEAD WITH FLATTENED HANDLE WITH BREAKERS
    C. TURRET CRESCENT HEAD WITH ROUND HANDLE WITH BREAKERS
    D. WRENCH STYLE
    E. OTHER

A. IRON FLIP TOPS

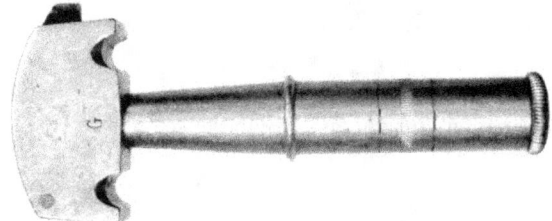

    1. G on crescent head - all German silver - knurled threaded cap at end opens for extra wheel storage - 3.25"

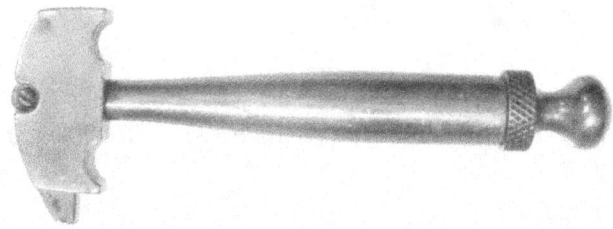

    2. No ID - all brass except flip top - knurled threaded cap with ball at end opens for wheel storage - 3.4"

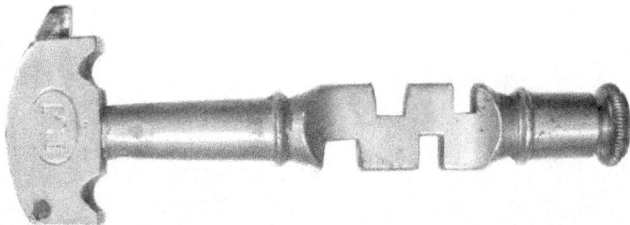

    3. P J in an oval on head - all German silver - 4 breakers on flat mid-section - knurled threaded cap at end opens for extra wheel storage - 3.5"

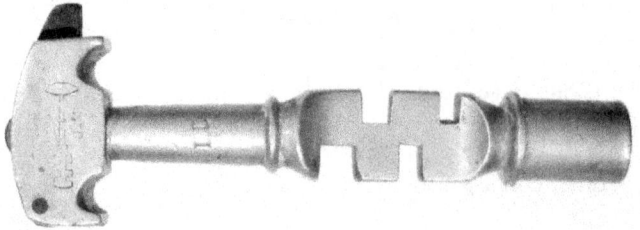

4. DÉPOSÉ on head above GLASS CUTTER logo JM below logo - LL on ferrule - all German silver
   - 4 breakers on flat mid-section - end cap like VIII-3 above missing - 3.6"

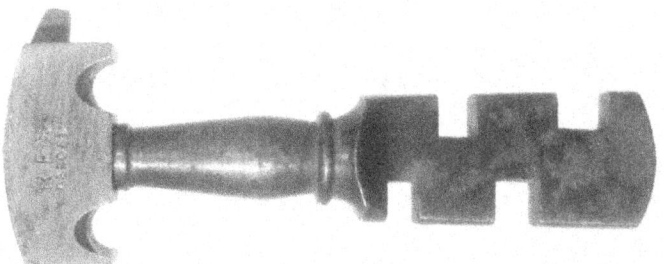

5. REX DÉPOSÉ on head - all steel - 4 breakers on flat end of handle - 3.5"

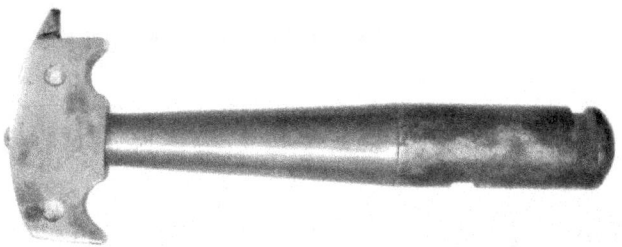

6. No ID - two white inlay on brass head - 1.55" solid brass ferrule - 1.2" steel end of handle with two
   breakers that unscrews for extra wheel storage area - 3.3"

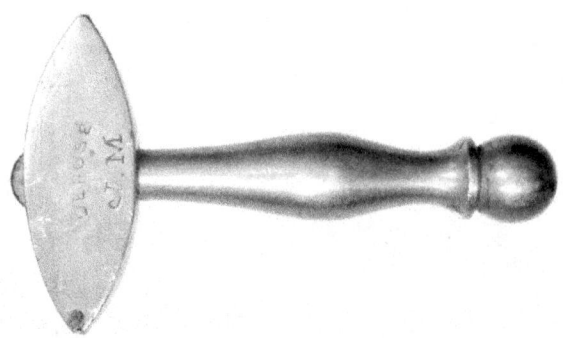

7. DÉPOSÉ J. M. on head – all German silver – 3.2"

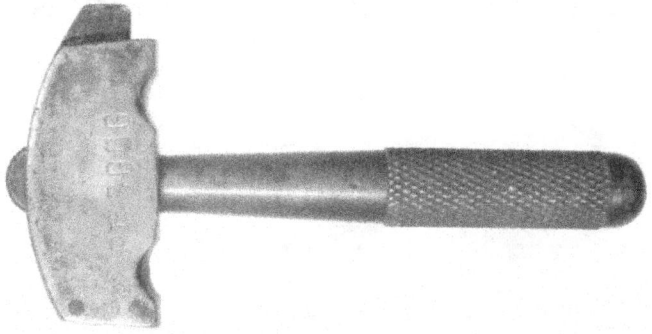

8. BTÉ SGDG on obverse of head - K on reverse of head - all brass - 1.25" end of handle is knurled
   - rounded end has a 1/8" diam. Black plug or inlay - 3.45"

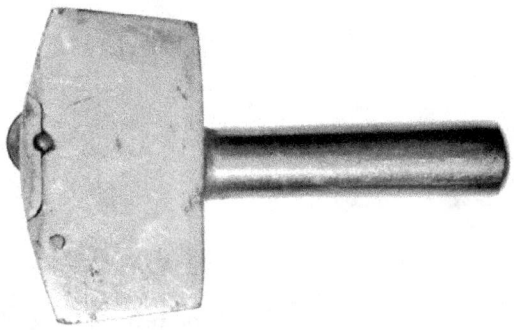

9. No ID - all plated steel - the 3/8" diam. wheel does score glass - 2.7"

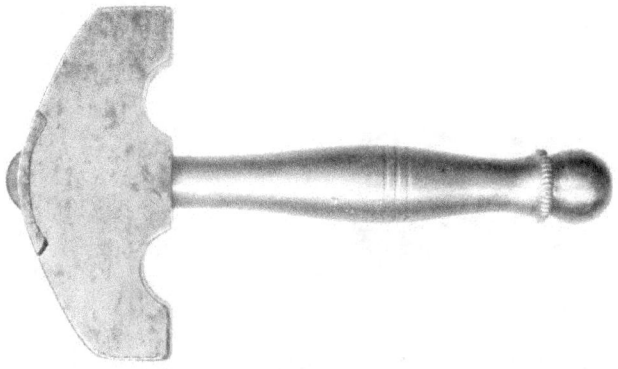

10. No ID - 1.9" wide steel head with pair of arches on bottom - German silver handle with smooth
    bore hole at end - 3.3"

11. No ID - mushroom style handle - all steel
    - screw on top of .6" thick head releases
    plate on bottom that holds a .45" diam.
    wheel in place - 2.9"

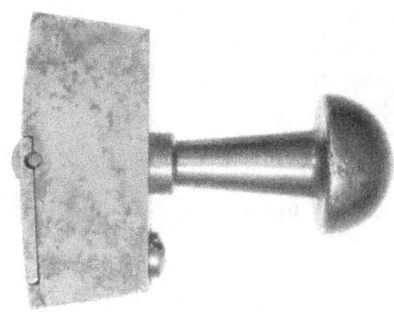

B. TURRET CRESCENT HEAD – FLATTENED HANDLE WITH BREAKERS

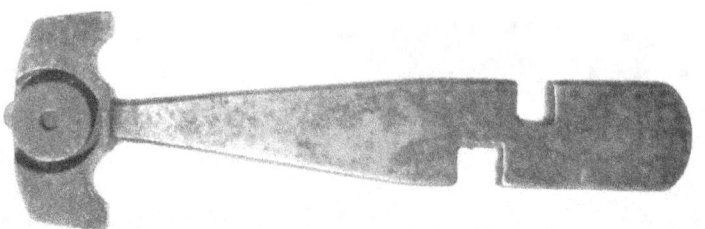

12. No ID - 5 wheel turret - all steel 2 breaker flat handle with single small white inlay 3.75"

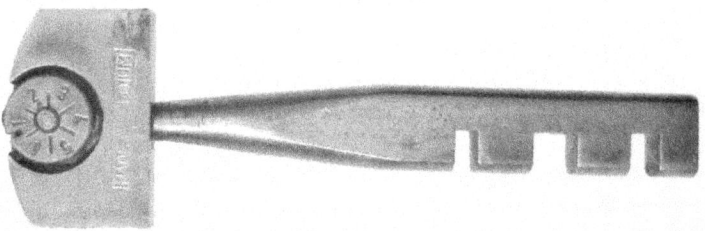

13. *Diaglass* special on obverse - MADE IN BELGUIM in a rectangle on reverse of head with 6 wheel turret with radial lines separating the recessed numbers - all steel - 3.8"

14. *Diaglass* special on obverse - FALLUER & ORBAN GILLY in a rectangle on reverse of head with 6 wheel turret with large numbers - all steel - 3.8"

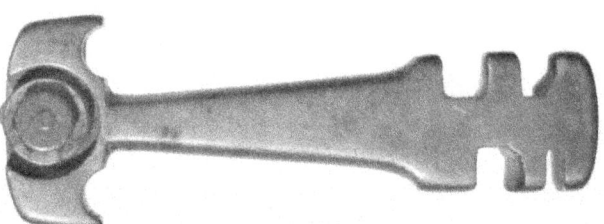

15. No ID - 6 wheel turret - all one piece brass - 4 breaker flat handle - 3.3"

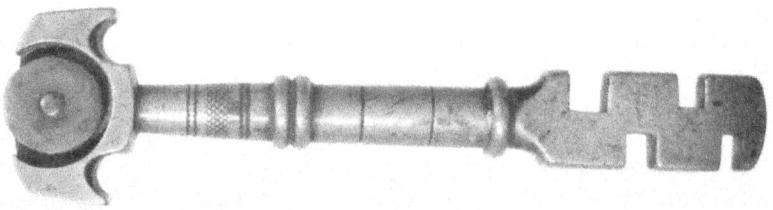

16. No ID - Brassy color German silver - 6 wheel turret with no numbers - 4 breakers on flat end - 4.2"

C. TURRET CRESCENT HEAD WITH ROUND HANDLE WITH BREAKERS

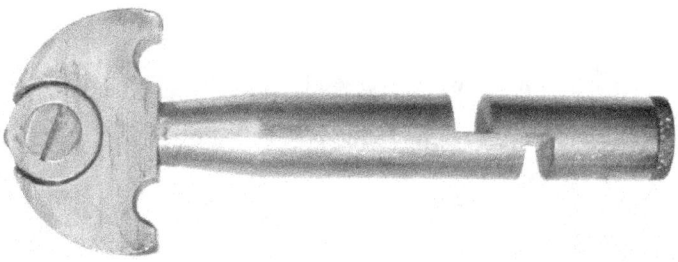

17. AA in diamond on obverse of plated brass head - can you believe a single wheel turret that does not turn? It is - flat male knurled cap at end of plated brass for extra wheel storage - 3.7"

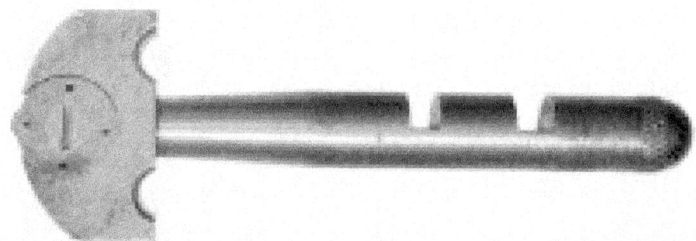

18. AA in a diamond on obverse of steel head -   This single wheel turret has four axle holes with extra axles stored in the rounded knurled cap at end of steel handle - 3.8"

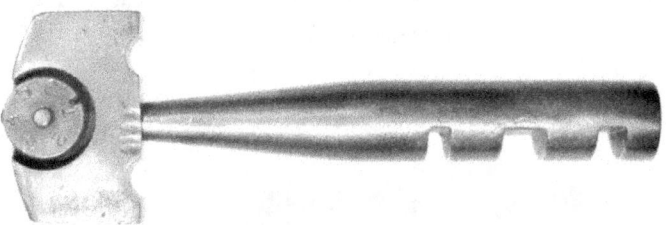

19. ETALI in a circle on right side of obverse - 6 wheel recessed numbers on obverse of steel head - 3 breakers on steel handle - 3.7"

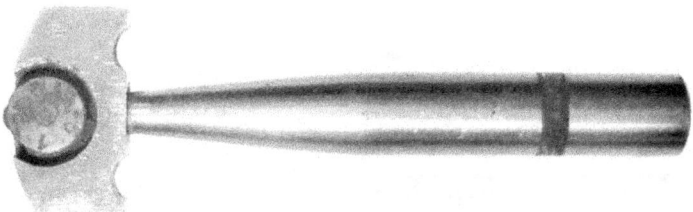

20. "JACCARD" SWISS MADE on obverse - 5 wheel turret recessed large numbers - all steel - 1 breaker on one side & 2 breakers on other side of round handle - 3.8"

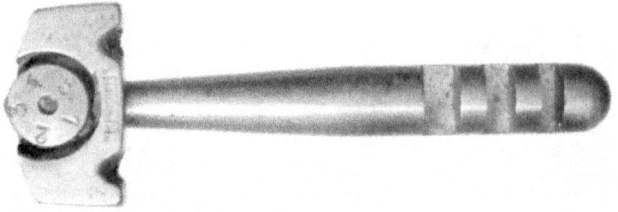

21. "MENIDIAM" on obverse - 5 wheel turret with recessed large numbers - all brass - 3 breakers on turret side of handle - 3.5"

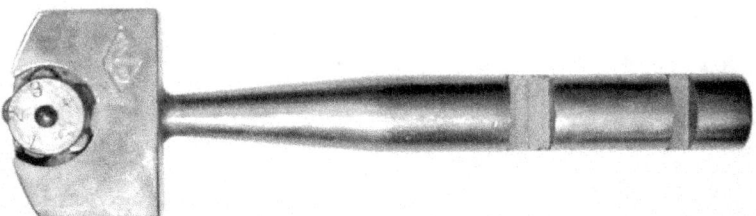

22. TerTrop in diamond on side with 5 wheel turret with large recessed numbers - 2 breakers on turret side of round handle - all plated brass - 4.1"

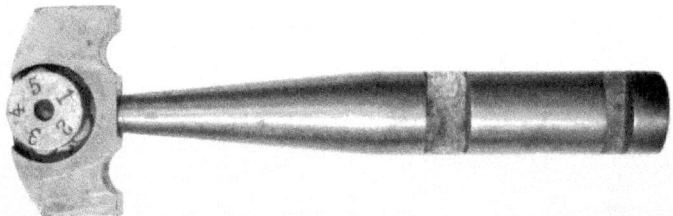

23. No ID - 5 wheel extended turret with large recessed numbers on steel head - 2 breakers on turret side of steel handle & single breaker on the other side - 3.7"

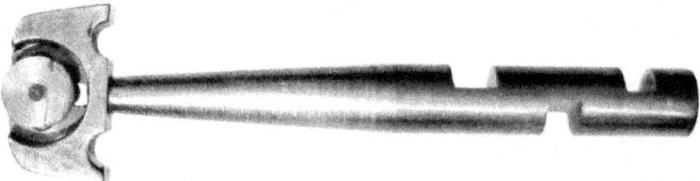

24. No ID - all plated brass - 4 wheel turret with no numbers - threaded hole on head opposite turret for possible use as attachment place for circle cutter extension arm - came in a wood box marked Coupe Verre - 3.8"

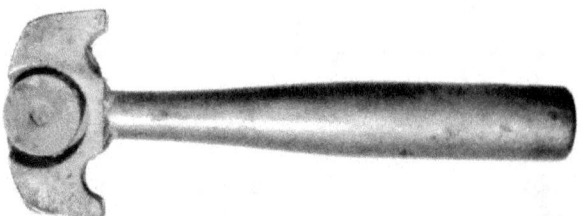

25. No ID - all brass including the 5 wheel turret - two breakers at end of handle opposite side of turret - 3.25"

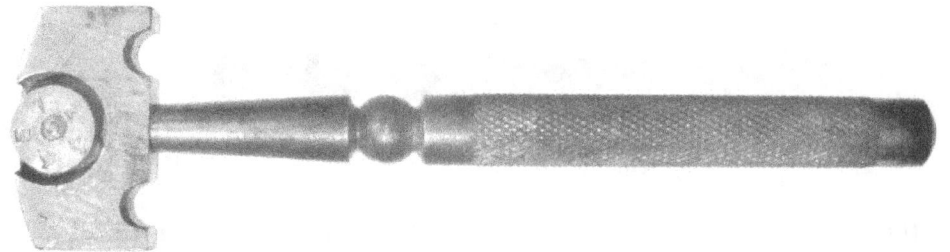

26. AA in a diamond on obverse of steel head with 5 wheel recessed large numbers on reverse - knurled steel handle - 5.2"

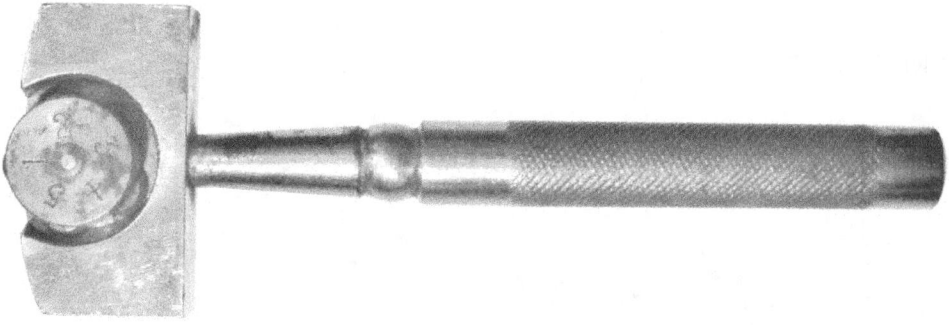

27. RABOT N° 14 on obverse of steel head - "JACCARD" SWISS MADE on end of head - extra large recessed numbers on 5 wheel turret - no breakers - knurled steel handle - 5.2"

27-A. RABOT N⁰ 14 on obverse of steel head (bolder than # 27 above) - no other ID - 5.2"

28. SUISSE on side end of steel head otherwise the same as VIII-27 above - 5.2"

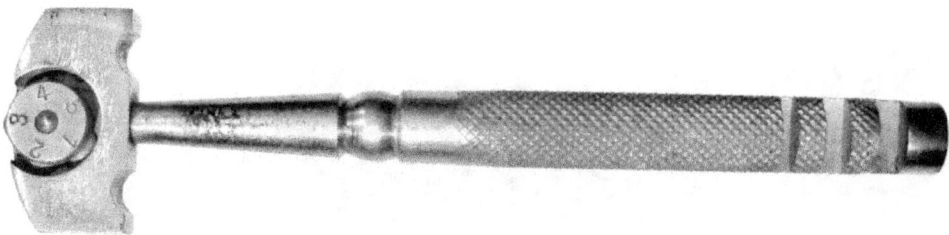

29. No ID - 5 wheel turret with large recessed numbers - knurled handle with 3 breakers near end of handle same side as turret - all steel - 5"

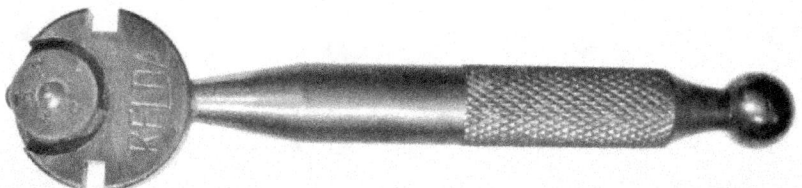

30. <u>RELDA</u> on side of head with 5 wheel large number turret - DÉPOSÉ on other side of steel head with 2 breakers - half knurled handle with ball end - all steel -4.4"

31. <u>RELDA</u> on side of 2 breaker head with 5 wheel small number turret - full handle knurled with ball end - 4.4"

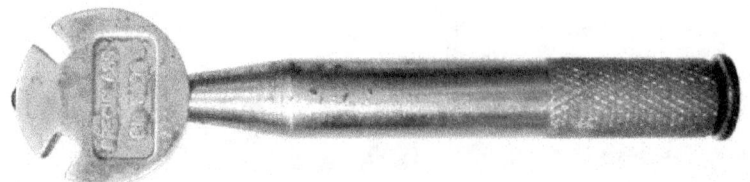

32. PRECIGLASS Bte SGDG in recessed rectangle on obverse - 3 in a recessed circle on reverse - the single cutter wheel is changed by unscrewing the handle from the head - all steel - end 1/3 of handle is knurled - flat knurled cap at end of handles unscrews for extra wheel - 4"

D. WRENCH STYLE

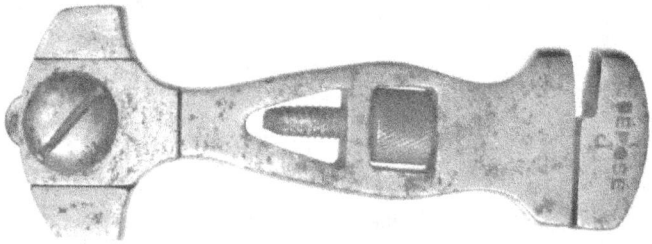

33. DÉPOSÉ J on face of moveable breaker(see IV-42) wrench style - all steel except the brass screw that adjusts the wrench style breaker - large screw holds plate that holds axle in place - 3.6"

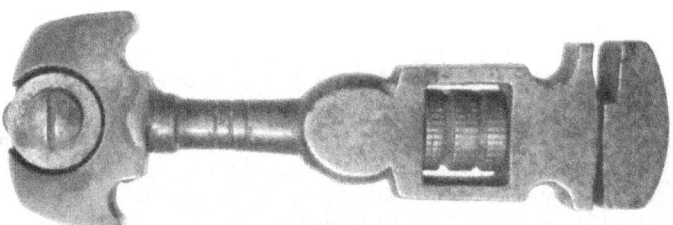

34. DÉPOSÉ A. O on obverse of head - all steel except brass screw that adjusts the wrench style breaker - 3.7"

E. OTHER

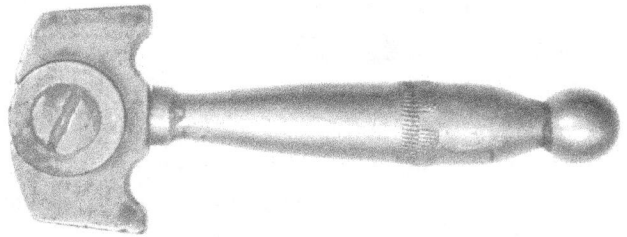

35. AA   in diamond on reverse of steel head   -   single axle & wheel turret   -   German silver handle unscrews near mid handle for extra wheel storage - 3.35"

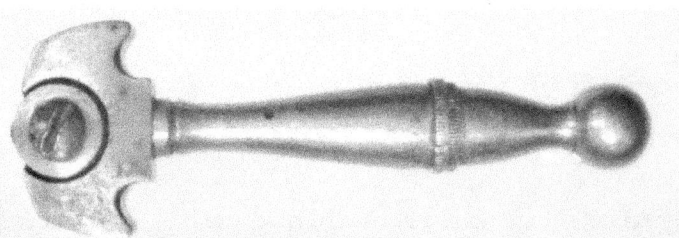

36. DÉPOSÉ   A.O. on obverse of steel head   -   single axle & wheel turret - German silver handle unscrews near mid handle for wheel storage - note smaller head than VIII-33 as well as the rounded ends - 3.6"

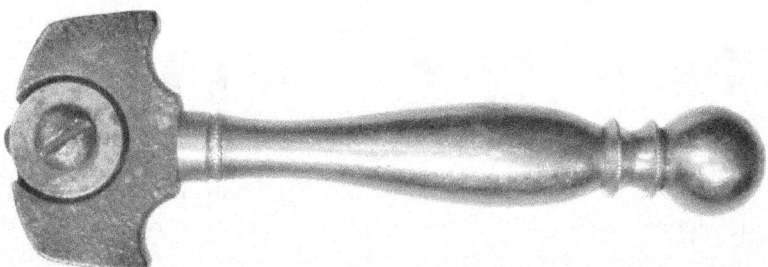

37. DÉPOSÉ   A. O on obverse of steel head   -   single axle & wheel turret - solid German silver handle - 4"

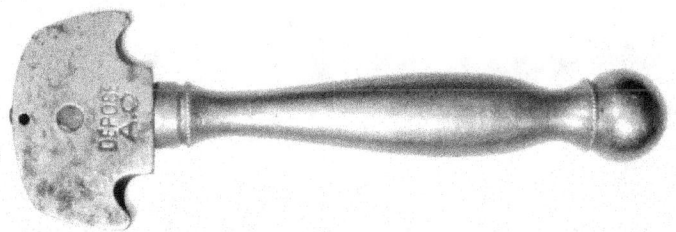

38. DÉPOSÉ   A.O on obverse of steel head   -   top 2/3 rds of reverse head removes to replace wheel - solid German silver handle - 3.7"

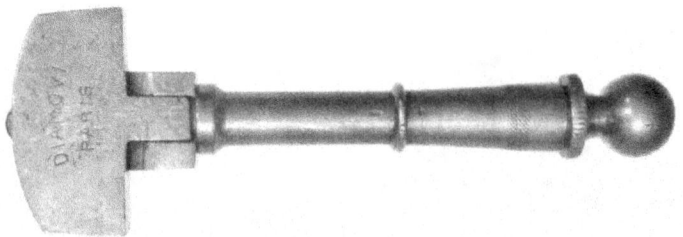

39. DIAMOVI PARIS on female side of head - BREVETE S.G.D.G. on male side of head - hinged split brass head opens when brass handle is unscrewed to replace wheel - knurled cap with ball at end of handle unscrews for extra wheel storage - 3.7"

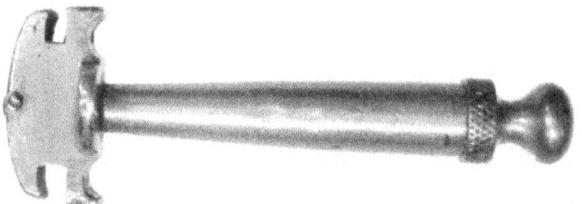

40. No ID - all brass with a protruding fingertip rest at base of head one breaker on either side of head - knurled threaded brass cap with ball on end of brass handle for extra wheel storage – 3.2"

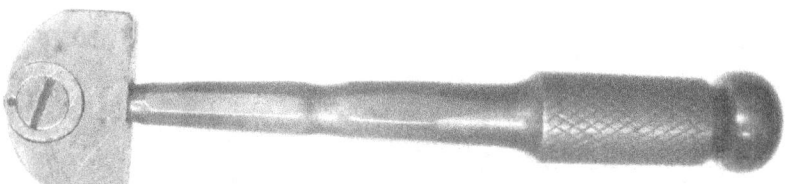

41. No ID - single axle & wheel turret on steel head - first 2/3 of brass handle is 6 sided tapering out to the last 1/3 which is knurled with a smooth brass ball which unscrews for extra wheel storage - 4.7"

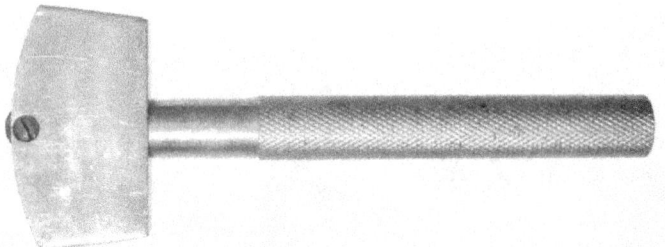

42. No ID - plated brass head & handle - .6" smooth ferrule & 2.2" knurled rest of handle - 3.65"

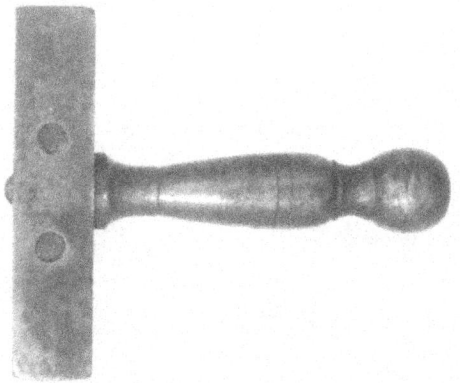

43. PH SINSZ CO.   BALTO. - on obverse of split steel head held by two brass screws otherwise all steel - pair of white inlay on reverse - smooth bore hole at end of handle - 2" wide by 2.4" tall - very similar to V-43 with diamond point block cutter & steel screws

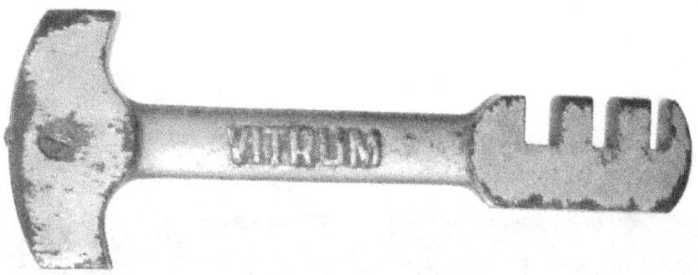

44. VITRUM cast onto obverse side of plated all one piece steel cutter - single axle & wheel turret released by screw on obverse side of head - 3.7"

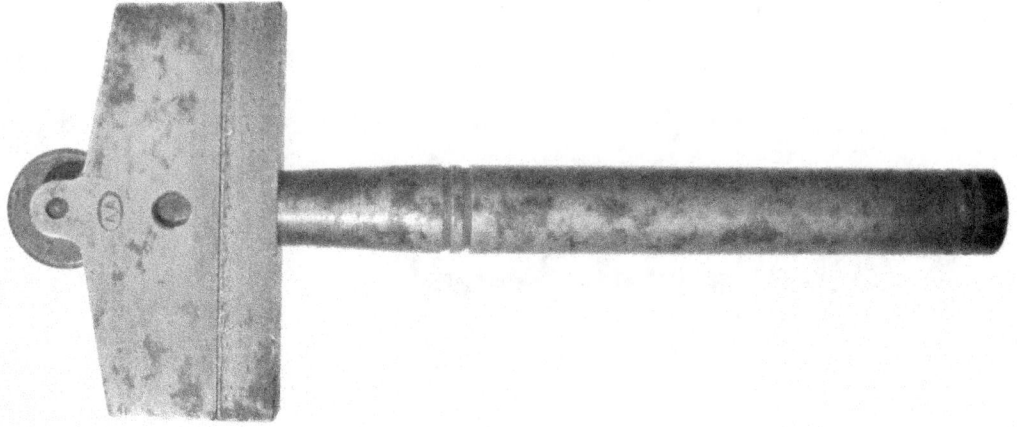

45. AA in a small oval on side of head just below axle - screw head on opposite side of 2.15" wide head holds two plates that hold the axle for the oversize .625" diam. wheel - all steel - two grooves near ferrule & two grooves near end of .45" diam. handle - 5.4"

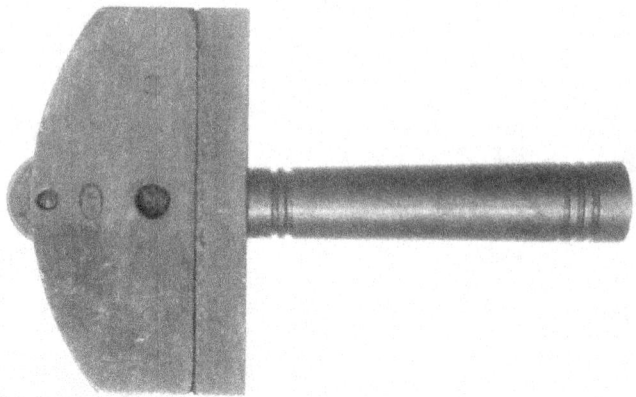

46. AA in a small oval on side of head just below axle - screw head on opposite side of 2.15"wide steel
head holds two plates that holds the axle for the oversize .4" diam. wheel - all steel - three grooves
near end of 2.4" handle & two grooves near head - 3.5" - Came in box: RABOT A MOLETTE
MODELE St GOBAIN Nº 35

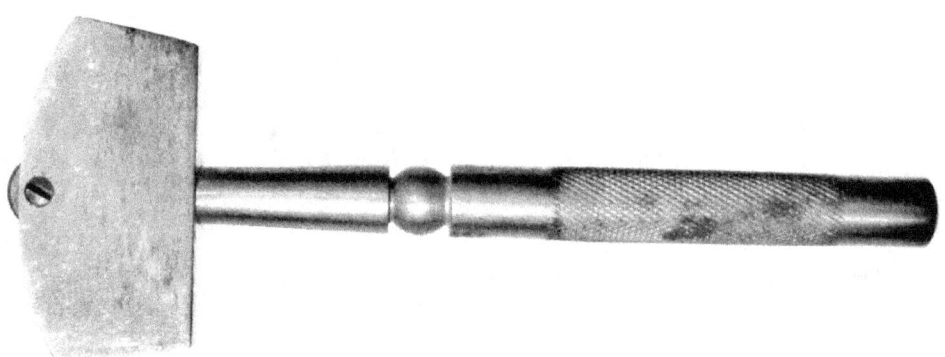

47. No ID - all plated steel - .4" diam. cutter wheel - 5"

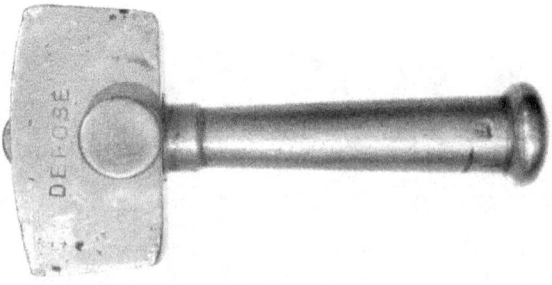

48. DÉPOSÉ   on side of head above flat knurled screw that holds .45" cutter wheel into head - all brass
- 3"

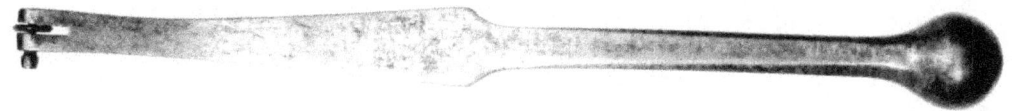

49. No ID - slender arced flat steel handle with ball end - 5.3"

50. No ID - heavy arced flat steel handle with ball end - .5" diam. wheel - 6.7"

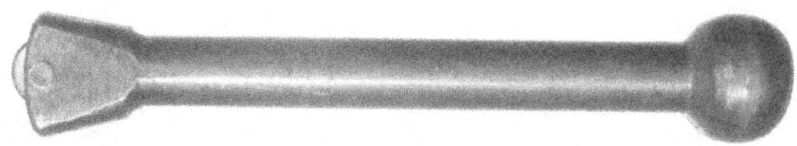

51. No ID - all brass - .375" diam. wheel - 4.2

CATEGORY IX   FRENCH BRASS CRESCENT HEAD - WHEEL

The BRITISH and SWISS also made this same style glass cutter. Variations in the head style and material such as steel, non-magnetic alloys, and some wood handles are shown. Most unscrew in middle of handle to expose a cavity to store extra wheels and an attached screwdriver to effect the wheel change. No U.S. Patents were found for this category.

Only four different are known in other collections.

This category has been sub divided into seven sub-sets. See also Category XV Circle / Oval for this style cutter.
 Price Range $8 - $20

     A.   BASIC FRENCH BRASS CRESCENT HEAD WITH 3 BREAKERS UNLESS NOTED
     B.   ORNATE FRENCH BRASS CRESCENT HEAD
     C.   ORNATE TURRET CRESCENT HANDLE DOES NOT UNSCREW FOR WHEEL STORAGE
     D.   END CAP STORAGE CAVITY
     E.   FLAT HANDLE WITH BREAKERS
     F.   WOOD OR PLASTIC HANDLES
     G.   MISCELLANEOUS

A. BASIC FRENCH BRASS CRESCENT HEAD WITH THREE BREAKERS UNLESS NOTED

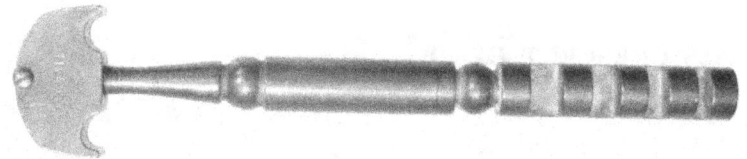

1. FRANCE - OXWALL stamped on screw side of head - 4 breakers - 4"
2. FRANCE stamped on lower left on screw side of head - 4.25"
3. FRANCE stamped on lower left opposite screw side of head - 4.25"
4. FRANCE stamped(half size) on left opposite screw side of head - 4.1"
5. FRANCE stamped on center under screw - the three breakers are closer to end of handle - 4.15"
    5-A. FRANCE stamped on center under screw - .7" long neck to first groove – 4.2"
6. FRANCE WW in a diamond stamped on left on screw side of head - all chrome plated brass - 4.4"
7. MADE IN FRANCE stamped on left on screw side of head - 4.3"
8. BRITISH MADE(large letters) stamped across width of screw side of head - 4.3"
9. BRITISH MADE(large letters) stamped across width of screw side of head - OX in a square in a diamond stamped on reverse - 4.3"
10. Identical handle to IX-9 above, however the left & right sides of the head have been sawn off so that just enough remains to hold the axle screw in place. The OX in a square in a diamond remains as well as SH letters from BRITISH are stamped into ends of a brass pin holding head to handle. This pin is not in evidence in any other cutters in this category except IX-13 & 15 below - 4.3"
11. DURANDAL (large letters) stamped on center under axle hole(screw has been replaced with a make-do bent wire axle) - 4.1"
12. JAPAN stamped on side of handle - entire glass cutter is chrome plated steel - head unscrews as does the 1.1" breaker end of handle - 6"

13. OPTIMA+ is stamped as single letters between the 7 points of a star in a ¼" diam. circle on screw size of head - pin through head to hold handle as in IX-10 above and IX-15 below - 4 5/8"
14. ?H. SEYER stamped in an oval on side opposite of screw on wider steel head - center turning on handle is a trough instead of a bulb - 4.25"
15. T in a small recessed 8-point star(see IX-28) onside of head below a flush mounted wheel - two breakers on side and one on end of handle - pin visible on only one side of head - 4.35"
16. No ID - two breakers on side and one on end of handle - 5 5/8"
17. No ID - 4.6"
18. No ID - head slightly smaller and a short thick neck on handle - 4.15"
19. No ID - slightly smaller head and a slender neck on handle - 4.25"
20. No ID - turning on shoulder only - breakers closer to end of handle - 3 7/8"
21. No ID - small head - four breakers - 4.1"
22. FRANCE on four breaker section of handle - 4.15"
23. No ID - turnings on shoulder only where female handle unscrews from male shoulder with no provision for the small screwdriver - a pair of steel sharpening discs attached at end of handle(see IX-34) - 5.2"
24. ARA raised letters within in a raised diamond outline - one piece cast non-mag. alloy other than brass - 4.1"
25. No ID - white brass head - no evidence plated steel handle unscrews for spare wheel cavity - 4.75"
26. No ID - larger steel head with .5" long flat ends - standard brass handle - 4.3"

B. ORNATE FRENCH BRASS CRESCENT HEAD

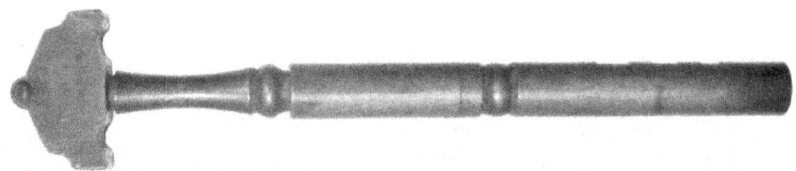

27. FRANCE centered on screw side of head - 4.25"
28. LE DURABLE – PONT ARLIER stamped on screw side of steel head above T in recessed 8-point star (see IX-15) - .35" diam. brass handle - 4.3"
29. C. S. PARIS stamped on screw side of steel head - DÉPOSÉ stamped on reverse - no arches on bottom of head - .35" diam. handle with two breakers on one side and one breaker on the other - 4.25"
30. No ID - minimal arches on bottom of head - thin neck - 4.3"
31. No ID - minimal arches on bottom of head - thick neck - 4.25"
32. VERY BEST – Indian head logo – TRADEMARK all stamped in a square box(.4" on side) on screw side of head - 4.2"
33. MADE IN SWITZERLAND stamped on handle reading towards head - thin neck - 4.05"
34. MADE IN SWITZERLAND stamped on handle reading towards end with pair of steel sharpening discs attached at end of handle(see IX-23) with but two breakers - 4.125"

C. ORNATE TURRET CRESCENT HANDLE DOES NOT UNSCREW FOR WHEELS STORAGE

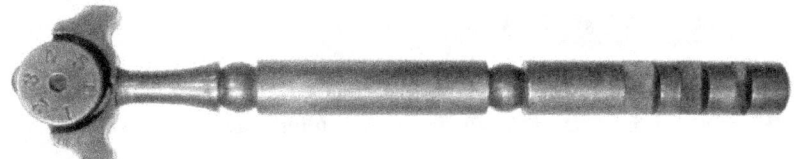

35. FRANCE stamped on breaker part of handle reading towards end - large numbers on extended brass turret - thick neck - 4.3"

36. FRANCE stamped on center part of handle reading towards end - large numbers on flush brass turret - 4.15"

D. END CAP STORAGE CAVITY   **Price Range $20 to $45**

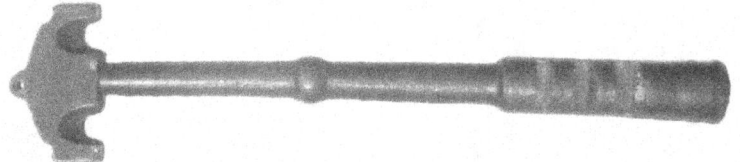

37. NO ID - one piece cast non-mag. alloy - three breakers - brown paint - male end cap - 4"

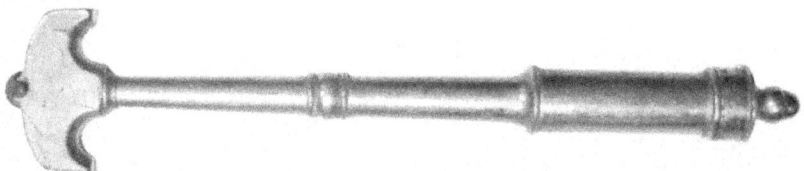

38. No ID - one piece cast plated non-mag. alloy - female cap with ¼" pointed extension - 4.4"

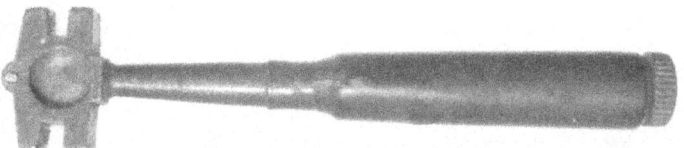

39. GERMANY cast in raised letters on screw side of non-mag. alloy head and .9" ferrule with single breaker on either end of head - reverse has a .35" diam. concave depression - brown paint on steel handle - concave knurled male cap for wheel storage area - 3.8"

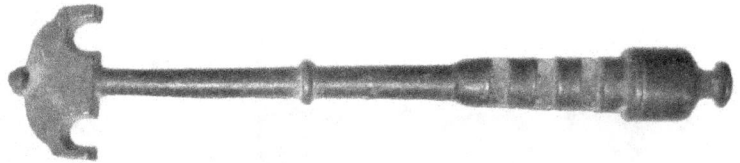

40. MADE IN FRANCE cast in raised letters reading towards head on handle opposite the three breakers - all non-mag. alloy - female cap for wheel storage area - 4.1"

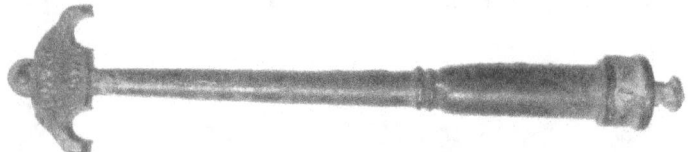

41. MADE   FRANCE cast in raised letters on head facing cutter wheel - one piece non-mag. alloy - female cap - 3.9"

E. FLAT HANDLE WITH BREAKERS   **Price Range $15 to 50**

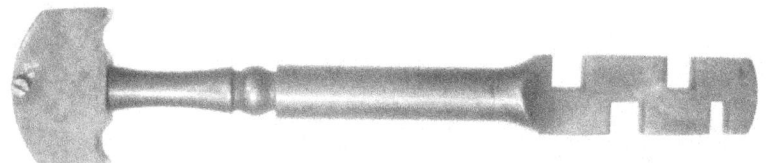

42. No ID - all brass with four breakers - 4.125"

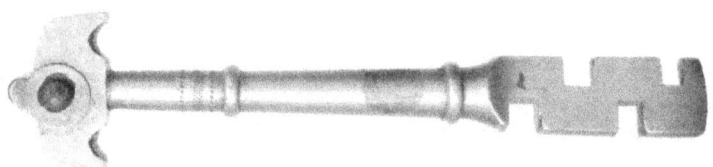

43. DÉPOSÉ A . O stamped on side of head opposite the screw holding a thin disc that holds axle in place - all German silver - 4"

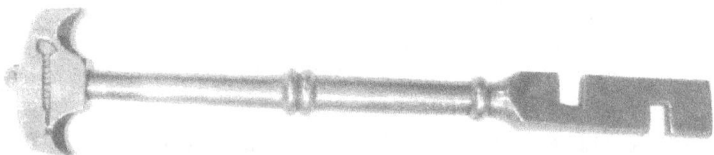

44. B.S.G.D.G. stamped in large letters on obverse side of head - "Clay Pipe" logo with: LE RESCHE in recessed very small letters on reverse of head(see IX-54) - all brass - 4.05"

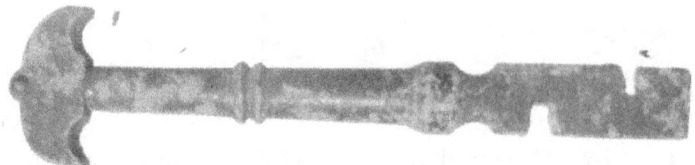

45. No ID - heavy non-mag. alloy one piece casting - evidence of some maroon paint - 4"

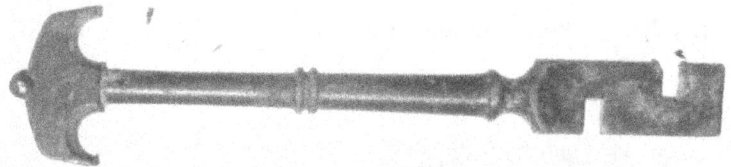

46. No ID - medium weight non-mag. alloy one piece casting - brass pin for axle - 4.2"

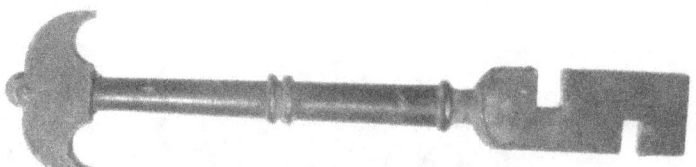

47. No ID - crescent head - non-mag. one piece casting - brass pin for axle - .23" thick head - 3.85"

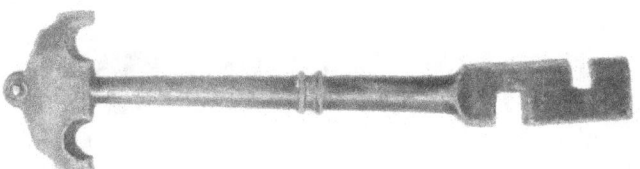

48. No ID - non-mag. alloy one piece casting - brass pin for axle - copper flash finish - .15" thick head - 3.6"

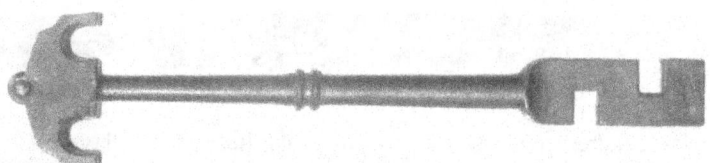

49. No ID - deep arches on head of one piece non-mag. alloy casting - bronze flash finish - brass pin for axle - .2" thick head - 4"

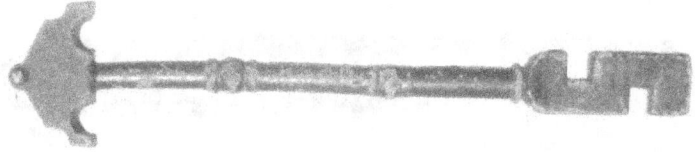

50. Ornate head on one piece non-mag. alloy casting - brass pin for axle - some copper finish - 3.9"

F.   WOOD OR PLASTIC HANDLES Price Range $20 to 30

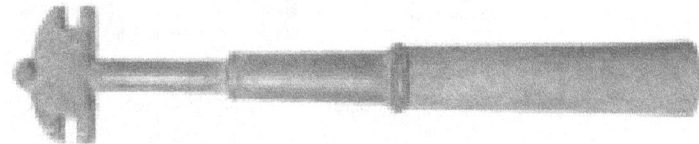

51. No ID - one piece cast non-mag. small head and ferrule - single breaker on ends of head - steel pin for axle - ever so slightly tapered wood handle - 3.8"

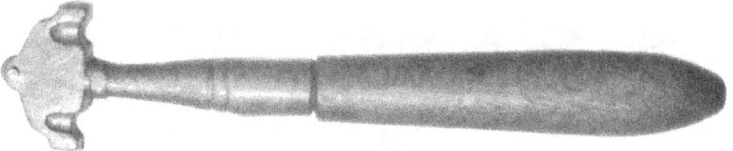

52. No ID - one piece head and 1.25" ferrule non-mag. alloy casting - steel pin for axle - walnut finish on wood handle - 4.1"

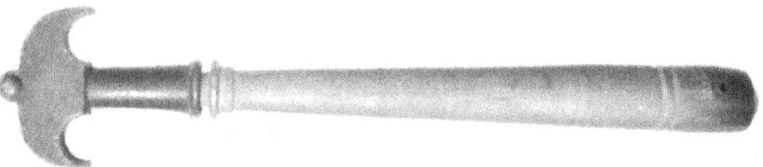

53. No ID - smooth arches on one piece head with a .75" ferrule of non-mag. alloy - brass pin for axle - slightly tapered wood handle that was at one time painted silver or aluminum - 4.4"

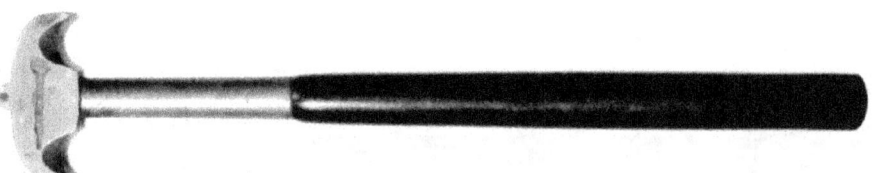

54. B.S.G.D.G. stamped in large letters on obverse side of brass head - "Clay Pipe" logo with LE RESCHE in very small letters stamped on reverse of head - 1.15" brass ferrule - straight round thin rosewood handle - 4.9"

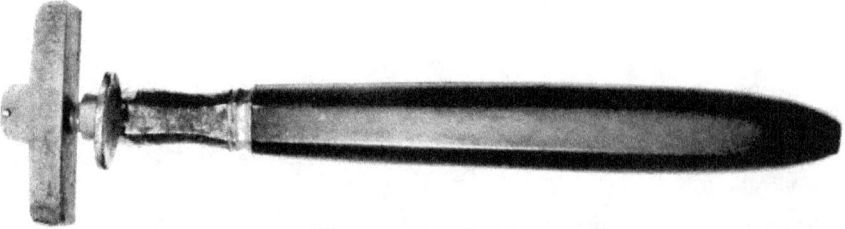

55. COLLIN & C° stamped in small letters on 1.1"plated steel ferrule with plated thumb screw on flattened side of ferrule which may serve as a second finger rest or stop since it does not serve to hold the ferrule in place - the 1.35" X .4" brass head screws on to threaded steel shaft that extends internally nearly to the end of the flat sided rosewood colored plastic handle - 5.1"

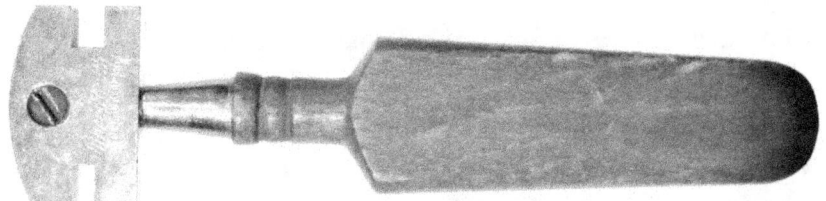

56. *Silberschnitt* MADE IN GERMANY stamped on obverse side of large plated steel head with single breaker on either end - large stamped numbers on nearly flush slotted steel turret - large tapered flat redwood handle - 4.9"

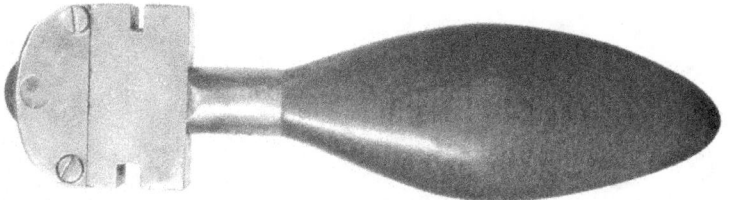

57. No ID - 1.2" wide X .32" thick X 1.2" tall steel head has a .1" thick plate, held by two screws, that retains the axle for the ½" diam. cutting wheel - walnut color plastic "Beaver Tail" handle - 4.8"

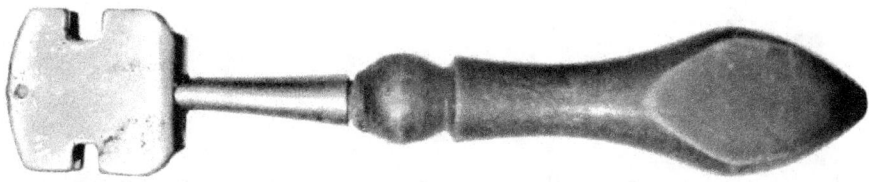

58. No ID - 1" X .9" head is folded over .06" thick plated steel which holds a .3" diam. wheel - 1" tapered steel ferrule - round turned handle has bulb end flattened and tapered toward the end - 5"

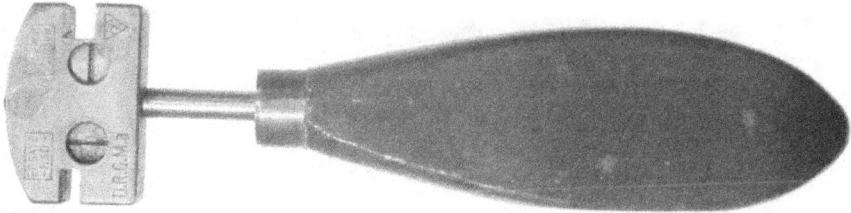

59. ERSATZ -RAD- stamped in a rectangle on upper left corner of brass head - Barthelmes & Salchow stamped in a rectangle on upper right corner of brass head - D.R.G.M.a stamped in lower left corner of brass head - AA in an inverted triangle in lower right corner of brass head - reverse side of head is steel - .15" diam. X .65" long steel neck extends about another 1" into the red painted flat wood handle that is .42" thick - .3" brass ferrule - 4.8"

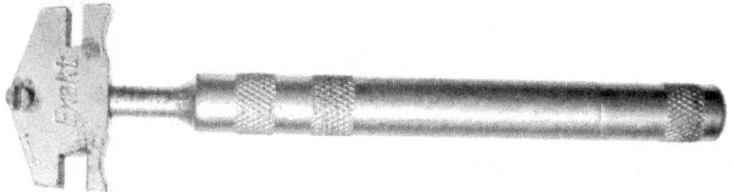

60. Exakt stamped on screw side of plated steel head - plated brass handle with .75" long end piece that unscrews for extra wheel cavity - 4.1"

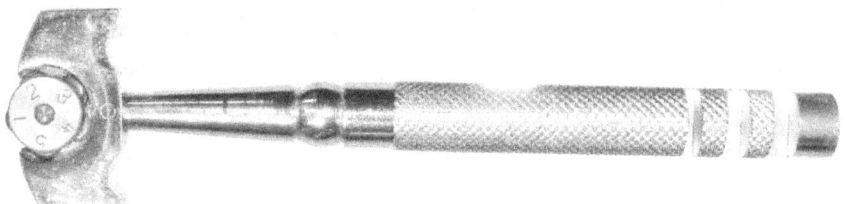

61. SWISS on side of head – 5-wheel turret – all plated steel tool – 3 breakers - 5"

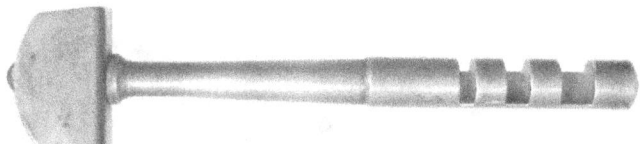

62. No ID - aluminum handle with screw driver unscrews from bottom of bent up steel side holding wheel unit in place - 3.7"

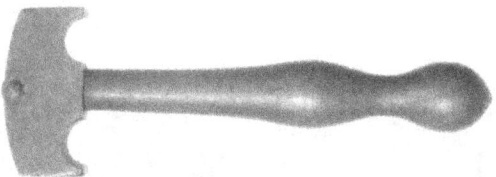

63. No ID - all brass except the axle screw - .35" thick head - one piece turned handle - 3"

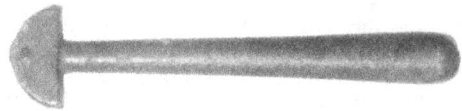

64. No ID - one piece cast non-mag. alloy - head is .6" wide - 2.625"

CATEGORY X   WOOD HANDLE - SINGLE WHEEL
STRAIGHT & BULB & VARIETY

This category contains 72 different glass cutters and are grouped in six different subsets because of their physical differences.

There are also 16 different known in other collections.

Fifteen U.S. Patents are listed below:

91,150	506,466	702,277	766,827	1,129,374	1,169,714	1,884,635
126,302	565,493	742,179	820,092	1,134,307	1,232,366	2,516,668
						2,566,544

Price Range: $6 - $35

The six subsets are:

      A. Diamond Point Style - Breakers on steel ferrule – ball end
      B. Diamond Point Style - No breakers on ferrule – ball end
      C. Short Stained Handle - most common
      D. Extra Wheel Storage Unit
      E. Bulbous Handle
      F. Painted Handle

A. Diamond Point Style - Breakers on ferrule - ball end

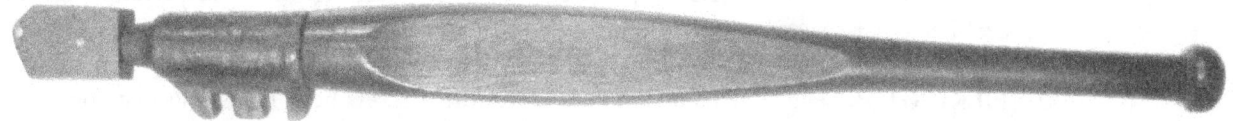

1. MILLERS FALLS CO. - MILLERS FALLS, MASS. – one-piece cast iron ferrule with two breakers painted black – dark mahogany finish - 6 7/8"
2. No ID – otherwise same as X-1 above
3. No ID – otherwise same as X-1 & 2 above except thinner handle
4. No ID – otherwise same as X-1 & 2 & 3 above except smaller iron head & walnut finish – 6 ¾"

B. DIAMOND POINT STYLE - No breakers on ferrule – ball end

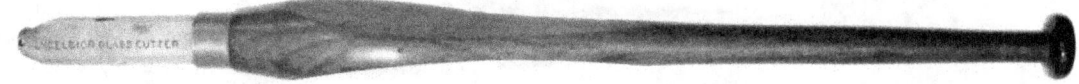

5. EXCELSIOR GLASS CUTTER – PAT. SEPT 13th 1864 and JUNE 8th 1869 on brass head (did not find a pertinent patent dated 9-13-1864) – 5 7/8"

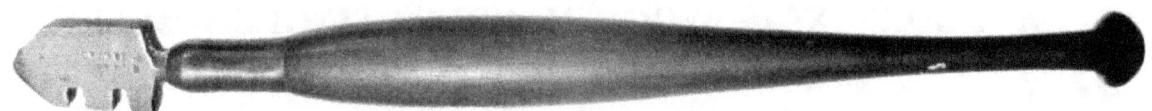

6. CROWDEN & GARROD on brass head with 2 breakers – round tapered dark walnut handle – 6 ¾"

7. (ERIE) on folded over steel head with single breaker – cutter wheel offset - .6" brass ferrule – three flattened finger rests on dark walnut handle - 6.6"

8. J.H. & C° stamped in a square on brass head with 2 breakers & a recess for spare wheels - .6" brass ferrule – round tapered fruitwood handle – 6.1"

9. RICHARDSONS IMPROVED GLASS CUTTER on brass head with no breakers – cutter wheel offset - .65" brass ferrule - a pair of flattened finger rests on dark walnut tapered handle – 6.2"

10. SHEFFIELD on base of brass head with single breaker – cutter wheel offset - .65" brass ferrule – a pair of flattened finger rests on dark walnut tapered handle – 6.6"

11. No ID – with single breaker on opposite sides of steel head .7" brass ferrule – a pair of flattened finger rests on slender tapered dark walnut handle – 6.7"

12. No ID – two breakers on same side of steel head - .75" brass ferrule – a pair of flattened finger rests on slender walnut handle -6.8"

13. No ID – two breakers on same side of steel head - .8" brass ferrule – round tapered dark walnut handle – 6.6"

14. No ID – no breakers on thick steel head – cutter wheel offset – .7" chrome plated ferrule – round tapered fruitwood handle with a tapered ball – 5.8"

15. No ID – no breakers on steel head –cutter wheel offset - .8" brass ferrule – round tapered walnut handle – 6.6"

16. PILKINGTON BROS LTD ST. HELENS on 1.5" brass ferrule – screw head holds thin plate on steel head that secures wheel axle in – a pair of flattened finger rests on light stained medium size walnut handle - 7.35"

17. PILKINGTON BROS LTD on 1.45" brass ferrule – screw head holds thin plate on steel head that secures wheel axle in – a pair of flattened finger rests on a light stained thick size walnut handle – 7.2"

18. PILKINGTON BROS LTD small letters on 1.4" brass ferrule – screw head holds large thin plate on steel head that secures wheel axle in – a pair of flattened finger rests on light stained walnut handle with a half ball end – 7.1"

19. *Richard* ENGLAND on blackened steel head & on 1.55" chrome plated ferrule – a pair of flattened finger rests on light stained walnut handle – 7.35"

20. A. SHAW & SON LONDON WARRANTED on 1.5" brass ferrule – screw head on steel head holds large tapered steel plate that holds wheel axle in – a pair of long flattened finger rests on a medium stained walnut handle – 7.3"

21. SHAW ENGLAND large letters on 1.5" brass ferrule – a pair of flattened finger rests on a medium stain walnut handle with large round ball – 7.2"

22. SHAW ENGLAND same as X-21 except for a large flattened ball- 7.1"

23. No ID – brass screw head on steel head holds thin plate that holds wheel axle in – note hex nut between steel head & 1.5" brass ferrule – a pair of flattened finger rests on a tapered light walnut handle with small ball – 7.4"

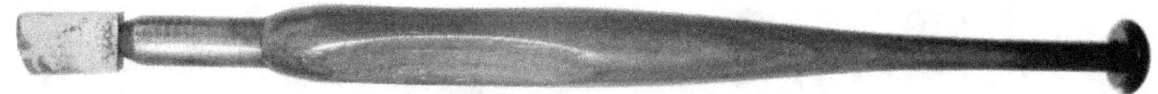

24. No ID – note small steel head - .8" brass ferrule – a pair of short flattened finger rests and narrow ball end of walnut handle – 6.75"

25. SANKYO TRADE MARK ID on box - No ID on glass cutter – plated steel head & ferrule all one piece – brown molded plastic handle – 7"

    25-A. WDK TRADEMARK WARRANTED - 1.4" brass ferrule – nickel plated large steel ball - 7.45"

C. SHORT - STAINED HANDLES - most common with 3 breakers unless noted

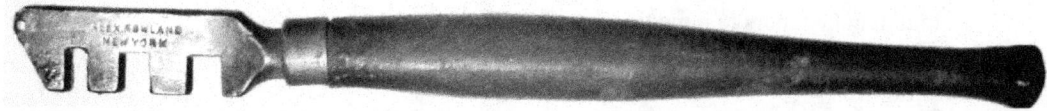

26. ALEX. ROWLAND NEW YORK on side of steel head – dark mahogany varnish finish walnut handle – 5.7"

27. DIAMANTOR - GERMANY on side of head with a pivoting clamp to hold wheel axle in – pair of short recessed finger rests on top and bottom of red varnish finished handle – 5.15"

28. DIAMANTOR – GERMANY on side of head – DIAMANTOR in gold print on side of handle with a pair of short recessed finger rests top and bottom of deep red varnish finished handle - 5.2"

29. GOODELL-PRATT CO GREENFIELD, MASS. U.S.A. on one side of 2 breaker head and Made In U.S.A. on the other – GOODELL-PRATT in gold lettering on side of mahogany varnish handle – 5.5"

30. Goodell Tool CO – Shelburne Falls Mass U. S. A. on side of 2 breaker head –dark mahogany varnish handle – 5.5"

Note: neck between head & ferrule on No's 31 thru 39

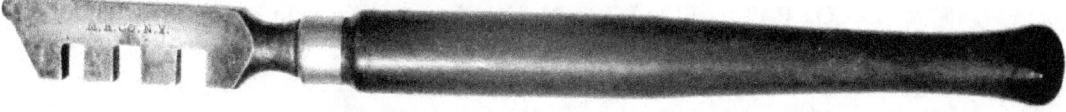

31. M. H. CO. N.Y. on side of head – note neck between head and short plated brass ferrule – dark mahogany varnish handle with thicker tapered end – 5.85"

32. No ID – plated ¼" ferrule - slender handle – dark mahogany varnish with modified ball on handle – 5.8"

33. No ID – brass .2" ferrule – slender handle – dark mahogany varnish with modified ball on handle - 5.95"

34. No ID – brass ¼" ferrule – slender handle – dark mahogany varnish with fuller modified ball on handle – 5.85"

35. No ID – brass ¼" ferrule – medium size handle with dark mahogany varnish with fuller modified ball on handle – 5.7"

36. No ID – thick head – plated .4" ferrule – medium size handle with light mahogany varnish with fuller modified ball on handle – 5.85"

37. No ID – plated .2" ferrule – slender dark mahogany varnish handle tapering to a triple ball end(similar to a honey dipper) – 5.9"

38. No ID – head flares out to form a thick neck – plated .4" ferrule – medium mahogany varnish on thick handle tapering to medium modified ball – 5.8"

39. No ID – head flares out to form a thick neck – plated .4" ferrule – walnut handle tapering to medium modified ball – 6"

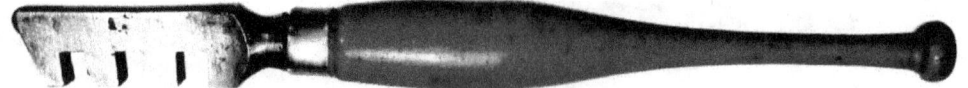

40. No ID – head flares out to form thick neck – plated ¼" ferrule – first 1/3 of handle is full & tapers abruptly to a thin handle an & ball – red paint – 5.3"

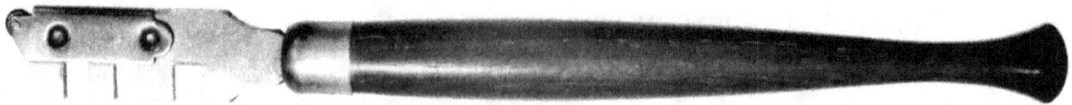

41. No ID – wheel axle support is dual crimped fold over on thin head – plated .4" ferrule – slender dark walnut handle tapers to a medium modified ball – 6.2"

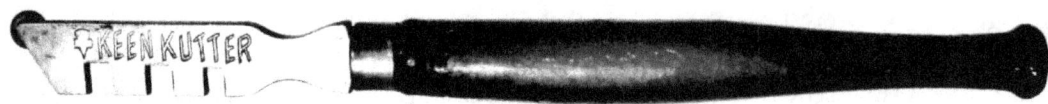

42. **KEEN KUTTER** & logo on side of split head – ¼" plated ferrule – very dark mahogany varnish thick handle – 5.7"

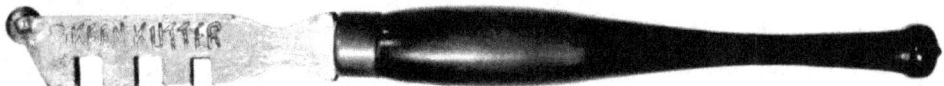

43. **KEEN KUTTER** & logo on side of split head – ¼" plated ferrule – very dark mahogany varnish on handle shaped like X-40 above – 5.35"
44. S. & H. CO. PAT. APLD FOR   No. XXX   on side of split head – ¼" plated ferrule - very dark mahogany varnish – 5.7"

45. No ID – note shape of head rounded both top & bottom with 2 breakers – .3" plated ferrule - natural wood finish – minimal flare out at ball end – 5.5"

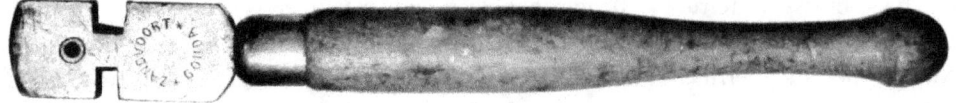

46. ZANDVOORT * GOUDA * circular layout on head obverse - K & M in a triangle on plate that holds wheel axle in and covers 4 extra wheel storage recesses – natural wood finish – 5.5"
47. MADE IN SWITZERLAND on head obverse – same plate on head reverse – natural wood finish – 5.5"

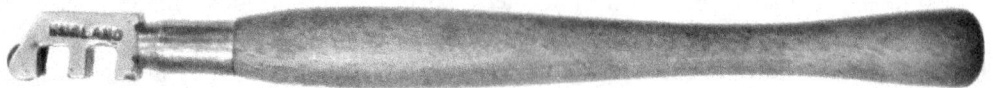

48. ENGLAND on brass head with 2 breakers – 9/16" brass ferrule – fruitwood finish – 5.5"
49. Same as X-48 above except handle finish is darker and the end is rounder – 5.45"

50. No ID – brass head with single breaker - .5" brass breaker – evidence of red mahogany finish -5.6"

D. EXTRA WHEEL STORAGE UNITS - note: Glass cutters No's X-46 & 47 included in previous subset C contain extra wheel storage recesses

51. No ID – recessed bent wire axle for wheel on thick head – mahogany varnish – knurled brass unit at handle end for extra wheel storage – 5.9"

52. No ID – screw head retains bent wire axle for wheel on thin head – ¼" plated ferrule – dark walnut finish – ball end plug at end of handle is actually the ball end of another glass cutter – 5.8"

53. No ID – same as X-52 above except the end of the handle flares outward more – 5.8"

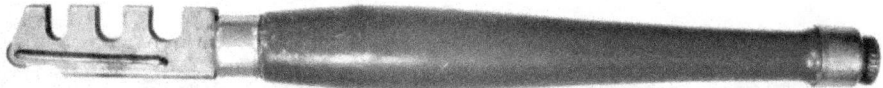

54. No ID – axle wire bent to extend 7/8" along side of rounded top head – note the unique arched breaker slots – ¼" plated ferrule – red mahogany varnish – ¼" ferrule at end of handle has a threaded, knurled steel unit for closing the extra wheel area – 5"

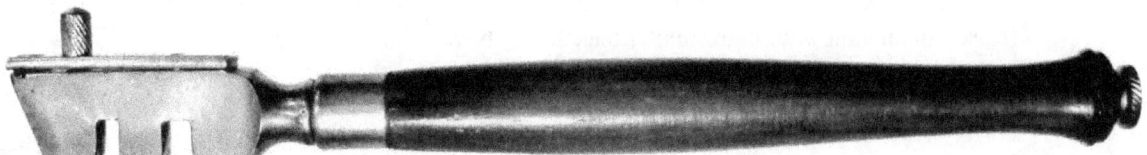

55. PATENTED on 1 1/8" long strip that holds axle in place using rounded top knurled threaded knob, could be used as a tapper – dark walnut finish - plated brass knurled unit for closing the extra wheel area – 5.8"

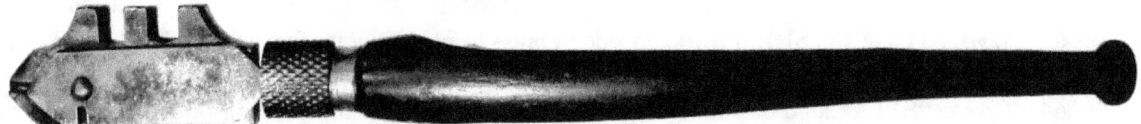

56. No ID – however, this is the same as MILLERS FALLS No. 25 in catalog using a threaded plated knurled brass ferrule to release pivoted cover over large recess in head – dark walnut finish on handle with 2 long flat finger rests – 6.85"

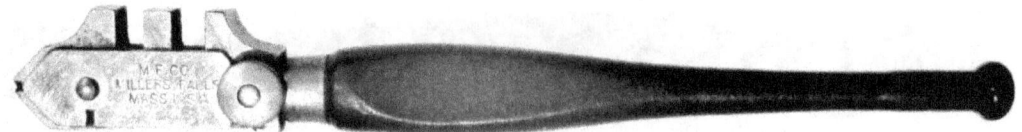

57. M.F. CO. MILLERS FALLS MASS. U.S.A. on pivoted cover over large recess in head and held in place by a knurled steel screw – ¼" plated ferrule – dark walnut finish – 5.5"

58. M.F. Co. MILLERS FALLS MASS. U.S.A. same head & ferrule as X-57 above except is 6.5"

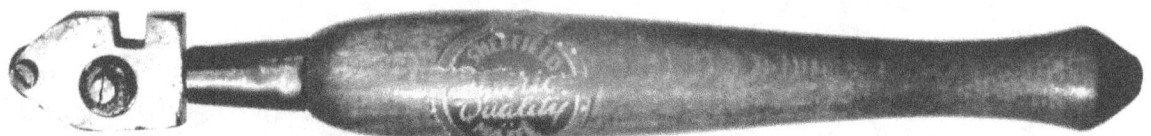

59. SHEFFIELD MADE *Superior Quality* on decal on handle – screw holds extra wheels on side of brass head with single breaker - .6" brass ferrule – walnut finish but not walnut – 5.4"

E. BULBOUS HANDLE

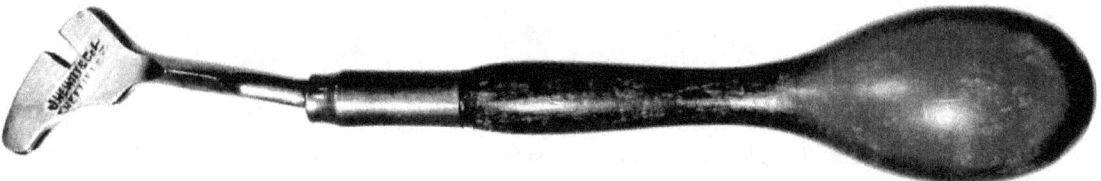

60. J. HEWITT & Co SHEFFIELD PATENT on side of brass head with finger rest - .85"brass ferrule – maple? handle painted black – 6"

61. J. HEWITT & Co SHEFFIELD PATENT on side of steel head with finger rest - .95" brass ferrule – black paint handle with bulb smaller than X-60 above – 5.7"

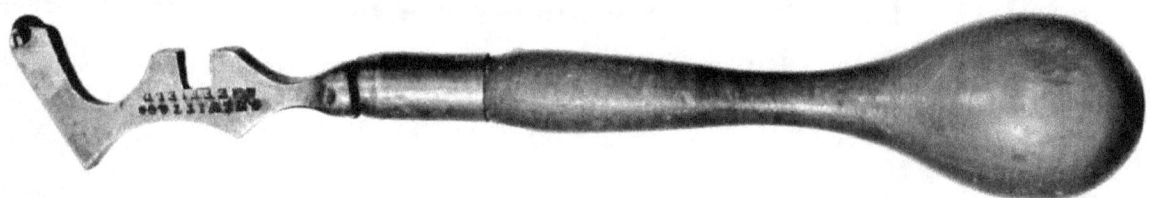

62. J. HEWITT & Co SHEFFIELD on side of brass head - .7" brass ferrule – fruitwood finish – 6.15"

63. J. HEWITT & Co SHEFFIELD on side of brass head - .5" brass ferrule – straight, round, short walnut handle – 4.9"

64. CAMP "BELL" logo on side of cutter tip of steel head - .6" brass ferrule – walnut finish on maple? – 5.5"

65. No ID – black paint on steel head - .5" brass ferrule – fruitwood finish – 5.7"

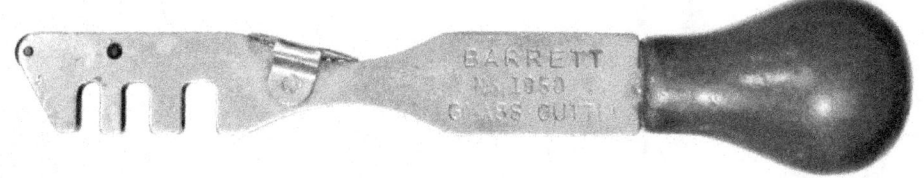

66. BARRETT No. 1950 GLASS CUTTER on side of 3-ply flat steel handle – PAT. APPL'D FOR U.S.A. on opposite side of handle – circular sheet metal finger rest – 5.05"

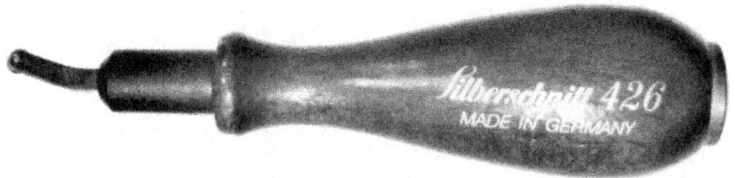

67. *Silberschnitt* 426   MADE IN GERMANY in silver ink on bulbous black painted handle - .7" black aluminum ferrule - .6" 1/8" square steel neck to hold the cutter wheel - .6" diameter brass unit at "ball" end – 4.3"

F. PAINTED HANDLE   all have small recessed finger rest

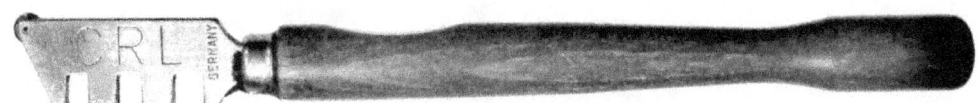

68. CRL GERMANY on head - .2" plated ferrule – sky blue paint – 5.2"

69. DIAMANTOR GERMANY on head - .2" ferrule – green paint – 5.15"

70. DIAMANTOR GERMANY on head - .2" ferrule – DIAMANTOR on side of green handle – 5.15"

71. DIAMANTOR GERMANY on head - .2" plated ferrule – slender green handle – 5.15"

72. *Somaca* on head - .2" plated ferrule – slender orange paint handle – 5.2"

73. No ID – .2" plated ferrule - slender dark green handle -5.2"

CATEGORY XI   TURRET HEAD - WOOD HANDLE

This category contains 112 different glass cutters and are listed alphabetically with physical differences noted either in the description or a picture. Many of the differences of the glass cutters are very minute. Examples are whether the letters USA are like this or like U.S.A. or small or large letters.

There are fifteen different glass cutters known in other collections.

Seven U.S. Patents found for this category are listed below:

557,200   47,633   911,342   1,134,292   1,419,310   2,221,405   4,197,639

This large group is divided into but three sub-sets as follows:

> **A. TYPICAL ROUND HANDLE WITH ROSEWOOD OR MAHOGANY FINISH & TWO BREAKERS**   Price Range: $6 - $20
> **B. FLAT HANDLE** Price Range: $6 - $20
> **C. OTHER**   Price Range: $20 - $40

A. TYPICAL ROUND HANDLE WITH ROSEWOOD OR MAHOGANY FINISH & TWO BREAKERS

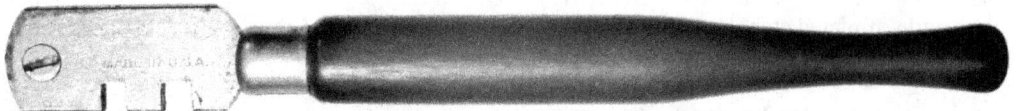

1. BARRETT - MADE IN U.S.A. stamped on plated steel head, the top and bottom of which are slightly rounded - no numbers on plated brass turret - .4" plated brass ferrule - 5.5"
2. BOKER, HENRY - GERMANY stamped on plated steel head, next to extended brass turret with large recessed numbers - .4" plated steel ferrule - 5.3"
3. CHANDOS - ENGLAND raised cast letters in a recessed rectangle on obverse side of non-mag. alloy head - large recessed numbers on slightly extended non-mag. alloy turret - .45" brass ferrule - 5.6"
4. CRAFTSMAN stamped in gold paint on side of blue-green handle - plated steel head with rounded top & bottom - faint large recessed numbers on extended steel turret - .4" plated brass ferrule - 5.5"
5. CRAFTSMAN stamped in gold paint on side of dark blue handle - steel head slightly rounded both top & bottom - recessed large numbers on extended steel turret - .4" plated brass ferrule - 5.5"
6. CRAFTSMAN stamped in gold paint on side of celery green handle - MADE IN USA stamped on obverse of plated steel head that is rounded both on top & bottom - .4"plated brass ferrule - 5.5"
7. CRAFTSMAN stamped on opposite(reverse) side of the dark green handle than the three above - no evidence of paint color on the letters - large recessed numbers on extended steel turret - .4" plated brass ferrule - 5.5"
8. CRAFTSMANBB stamped into reverse side of dark green handle like XI-7 above - recessed medium numbers on extended steel turret - .4" plated brass ferrule - 5.5"
9. CRESCENT stamped on obverse side of steel head - small recessed numbers on extended brass turret - .3" brass ferrule - 5.4"
10. DIAMANTOR stamped near top of reverse side of plated steel head - 200 BEST-BEST 200 stamped near top of obverse side of head - D.R.G.M.249500 *stamped on face of partial extended steel turret with small numbers near outer edge - .25" brass ferrule - slender walnut handle with a three groove ball end(like a honey dipper) 5.8"

11. DRAPER stamped in an extended stamped oval above WEST GERMANY stamped on obverse side of plated steel head - medium recessed numbers on a slotted hex steel turret - .25" plated steel ferrule - red-orange stain on handle - 5.2"

12. DRAPER in an extended oval above WEST GERMANY as raised letters in a recessed rectangle on obverse side of plated non-mag. alloy head - large recessed numbers on a slotted non-mag. alloy hex extended turret - plated steel ferrule - sky blue paint on handle - 5.2"

13. DUNLAP stamped in an oval on obverse of plated steel head with rounded both on top and bottom - extra large recessed numbers on an extended steel turret - .4" plated steel ferrule - 5.1"

14. EVERCUT stamped in rectangle on obverse of plated steel head - MADE IN BELGUIM stamped in rectangle on reverse of head - large recessed numbers on extended steel turret - EVERCUT stamped in gold paint on side of slightly fatter handle - .4" plated steel ferrule - 5.4"

15. "FIX'N'SAVE" stamped on obverse side of plated steel head - WEST GERMANY stamped in small letters next to .4" plated steel ferrule - extra large recessed numbers on brass extended turret - 5.1"

16. & 17. & 18. SEE CATEGORY XXII FLETCHER-TERRY

19. FOREIGN stamped in small letters on top of steel head - large recessed numbers on extended brass turret - .4" plated steel ferrule - 5.6"

20. GOODELL-PRATT CO. GREENFIELD, MASS. U.S.A. PAT. MAR. 31, 96 stamped in obverse of steel head with both top & bottom rounded - No. 01 stamped in on reverse of head - medium recessed numbers on extended steel turret - .4" plated brass ferrule - black finish - 5.4"

21. GOODELL-PRATT CO. GREENFIELD, MASS. U.S.A. PAT. MAR. 31-96 stamped on obverse side of plated steel head - No. 1 stamped on reverse of head - large recessed numbers on extended steel turret - .4" plated brass ferrule - 5.5"

22. GOODELL-PRATT CO. GREENFIELD, MASS. U.S.A. PAT. MAR. 31, 96 - stamped in obverse side of plated steel head - No. 1 stamped in reverse side of head - medium recessed number on extended steel turret - .4" plated brass ferrule - 5.5"

23. Goodell-Pratt Co. Greenfield, Mass. U.S.A. Pat. Mar. 31-96 stamped on obverse side of plated steel handle - NO. 1 stamped on reverse of head - medium recessed numbers on extended steel turret - .4" plated brass ferrule - 5.6"

24. GOODELL-PRATT CO. GREENFIELD, MASS. MADE IN U.S.A. stamped in obverse side of steel head with both top & bottom rounded - No. 01 stamped on reverse side of head - medium numbers on extended steel turret - .4" plated brass ferrule - 5.6"

25. GOODELL-PRATT CO GREENFIELD MASS MADE IN USA stamped on obverse side of steelhead with both top & bottom rounded - No. 01 stamped on reverse of head - medium recessed numbers on extended steel turret - .4"plated steel ferrule - 5.55"

26. GOODELL-PRATT CO. GREENFIELD, MASS. NO. 1 MADE IN U.S.A. stamped on obverse side of plated steel head - medium numbers on extended steel turret - GOODELL-PRATT stamped in gold letters on side of wood handle - .4" plated brass ferrule - 5.4"

27. GOODELL-PRATT CO. GREENFIELD, MASS. MADE IN UNITED STATES OF AMERICA stamped on obverse side of plated steel head - No. 1 stamped on reverse of head - medium recessed numbers on extended steel turret - .4" plated brass ferrule - GOODELL-PRATT stamped in gold paint on side of handle - 5.5"

28. Same as XI-27 above except the numbers on turret are large & bold

29. Same as XI-27 above except raised numbers on nearly recessed non-mag. alloy turret and serif's on the N in No.

30. Same as X-27 above except for smaller No. 1 and smaller numbers on turret - 5.55"

31. GOODELL-PRATT CO GREENFIELD MASS MADE IN USA stamped in obverse of plated steel head - No. 1 stamped on reverse side of head large recessed numbers on extended steel turret - .4"plated steel ferrule - GOODELL-PRATT just barely visible stamped on side of brown stained wood handle - 5.5"

31A. GOODELL-PRATT CO same as -31 above except bold nos. on turret and red stain handle – 5.5"

32. GOODELL –PRATT stamped in a rectangle above NO. 1 MADE IN USA stamped on obverse of plated steel head - large recessed bold numbers on extended steel turret - .4" plated brass ferrule - GOODELL-PRATT stamped in small gold letters on side of wood handle - 5.5"

33. GOODELL-PRATT CO. GREENFIELD, MASS. MADE IN U.S.A. PAT. MAR. 31. 1896. Stamped on obverse of plated steel head - No. 1 stamped on reverse of head - medium recessed numbers on extended steel turret - .4" plated brass ferrule - GOODELL-PRATT stamped in gold letters on side of wood handle - 5.4"

34. GOODELL-PRATT CO. GREENFIELD, MASS. U.S.A. PAT. MAR. 31-96 stamped on obverse side of plated steel head - slot head screw bolt holds circular plate stamped: 6 EXTRA WHEELS, over recess on reverse side of head for extra wheels - medium recessed numbers on extended steel turret - .4" plated brass ferrule - 5.6"

35. Goodell Tool Co Shelburne Falls Mass. stamped on obverse side of steel head - PATENTED MAR. 31'96 No. 1 stamped on reverse of head - small recessed numbers on extended steel turret - .4" plated brass ferrule - 5.6"

36. Goodell Tool Co Shelburne Falls Mass stamped on obverse side of plated steel head - PATENTED MAR. 31, 96 No. 1 stamped on reverse of head - no numbers on extended steel turret - deep cut narrow breakers - .4" plated brass ferrule - 5.5"

37. Goodell Tool Co Shelburne Falls Mass. stamped on obverse of plated steel head - No. 1 PATENT 557,200 stamped on reverse of head - faint medium numbers on extended steel turret - .4" plated brass ferrule - 5.5"

38. Goodell Tool Co. Shelburne Falls Mass. stamped on obverse of plated steel head - PATENTED MAR. 31.'96 No.1 stamped on reverse of head - medium recessed numbers on extended steel turret - .4" plated brass ferrule - 5.5"

39. Goodell Tool Co Shelburne Falls Mass. stamped on obverse of steel head - PATENTED MAR. 31, 96 No. 1 stamped on reverse of head - no numbers on extended steel turret - .4" plated brass ferrule - 5.6"

40. Goodell Tool Co. Shelburne Falls, Mass. U.S.A. Pat. Mar. 31-96 stamped on obverse of plated steel head - No. 1 stamped on reverse of head - large recessed numbers on steel turret - .4"brass ferrule - 5.5"

40A. Goodell Tool Co. Shelburne Falls, Mass. U.S.A. Pat. Mar. 31-96 stamped on obverse of plated steel head in bolder letters than XI-40 above - medium recessed numbers on steel turret - .4" plated brass ferrule – 5.5"

41. Goodell Tool Co. Shelburne Falls, Mass. Pat. Mar. 31-96 stamped on obverse of steel head with both top & bottom rounded - No. 01 stamped on reverse of head - faint large numbers on extended steel turret - .25" brass ferrule - flattened wood ball at end - 5.15"

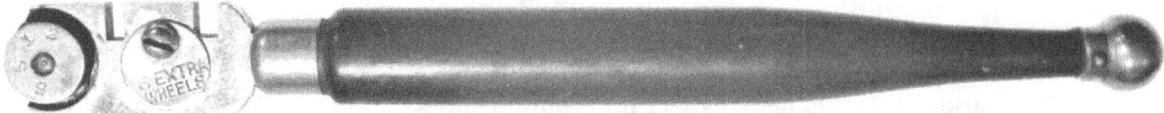

42. Goodell Tool Co. Shelburne Falls, Mass. U.S.A. Pat. Mar. 31-96 stamped on obverse of plated steel head - slot head screw bolt secures circular plate stamped: 6 EXTRAS WHEELS, over reces on reverse for extra wheel storage between breakers - large recessed numbers on extended turret - .4" plated brass ferrule - plated steel small ball at end of handle - 6.2"

43. "GOVERNOR" MADE IN U.S.A. stamped on obverse side of plated steel head with both top bottom rounded - medium numbers recessed on extended steel turret - .4" plated brass ferrule - 5.55"

44. GUYS (HANDTOOLS) LTD. raised letters in a recessed, yellow paint background, rectangle on obverse side of non-mag. alloy head - raised numbers on extended non-mag. alloy turret - .5"plated steel ferrule - 5.5"

44-A. "HAGA" BRILLANT SCHNITT stamped on obverse face of rounded top & bottom steel head – 5.5"

45. H & B SERIES 3 raised letters in a recessed , red paint background, rectangle on obverse side of non-mag. alloy head - raised numbers on extended non-mag. alloy turret - .5" plated brass ferrule - box says: MADE IN ENGLAND - 5.5"

46. H. W. V. & C° L$_{TD}$ ENGLAND raised letters in a recessed, red paint background, rectangle on obverse side of extended non-mag. alloy head - raised large numbers on non-mag. alloy turret - 5.5"

47. IMCO in a small diamond stamped on obverse side of plated steel head with both top & bottom rounded - small recessed numbers on extended steel turret - .25" plated brass ferrule - 5.55"

48. IMCO in a large diamond with No 37 under it stamped on obverse of steel head with both top & bottom rounded - medium recessed numbers on extended brass turret - .25" plated brass ferrule - tapered short handle with a flat ball end - 5.1"

49. IMCO in a large diamond with No 37 under it stamped on obverse of steel head with both top & bottom rounded - large recessed numbers on extended steel turret - .25" plated brass ferrule - tapered short handle with a flat ball end - 5.1"

50. JAPAN stamped in small letters on bottom of plated steel head with three breakers - medium recessed numbers on brass turret - .4" plated brass ferrule - 5.45"

51. JOBO MADE IN GERMANY raised letters in a recessed rectangle on obverse side of plated non-mag. alloy head - slotted hex extended steel turret with large recessed numbers - .25" plated steel ferrule - orange-red finish on thinner handle - 5.25"

52. Jordan Germany stamped in a diamond on obverse side of plated steel head - medium recessed numbers near edge of extended brass turret - .3" plated brass ferrule - 5.5"

53. MADE IN GERMANY stamped on reverse side of plated, square nose, non-mag. alloy head - large raised numbers on extended non-mag. alloy turret - .3" plated steel ferrule - 5.5"

54. M.F.CO. MILLERS FALLS, MASS. PAT. JUNE 13 1922 MADE IN U.S.A. Nº300 stamped on obverse side of plated steel head - large recessed numbers on flush steel turret - .25" plated brass ferrule - flatted ball at end of handle - 5.65"

55. MILLERS FALLS CO. GREENFIELD, MASS. MADE IN USA stamped on obverse side of plated steel head - No.1 stamped on reverse of head - large recessed numbers on extended steel turret - .4" steel ferrule - MILLERS FALLS stamped on side of wood handle - 5.55"

56. MILLERS FALLS CO. GREENFIELD, MASS. MADE IN USA stamped on obverse side of plated steel head - No 1 stamped on reverse of head - large numbers recessed on extended steel turret - .4" plated brass ferrule - MILLERS FALLS stamped in gold paint on side of wood handle - 5.55"

57. MILLERS FALLS (stamped inside company logo) NO1 MADE IN USA (stamped in small letters) on obverse side of plated steel head with both top & bottom rounded - large recessed numbers on extended steel turret - .4" plated brass ferrule - MILLERS FALLS stamped in gold paint on side of wood handle - 5.55"

58. MILLERS FALLS(stamped inside company logo) NO600 MADE IN USA(stamped in small letters) on obverse of plated steel head very slightly rounded top & bottom - large recessed numbers on extended steel turret - .4" plated brass ferrule - MILLERS FALLS stamped in gold letters on side of wood handle - small plated steel ball end - 5.8"

59. OAK LEAF (inscribed within an oak leaf) F.66 stamped on obverse side of plated steel head with both top & bottom rounded - small recessed numbers on extended steel turret - .4" plated brass ferrule - 5.55"

60. READING stamped on obverse side of steel head with both top & bottom rounded - small recessed numbers on extended brass turret - .4"brass ferrule - 5.6"

There are six RED DEVIL wood handle turret head glass cutters listed in: CATEGORY   XXI   RED DEVIL

61. "REV-O-NOC" (anything to it that backwards it spells CONOVER?) stamped on obverse side of plated steel head - medium recessed numbers on extended plated brass turret - .4" plated brass ferrule - 5.35"

62. SHAW ENGLAND raised letters in a recessed, red paint background, rectangle on obverse side of non-mag. alloy - large numbers on extended steel turret - .4" plated steel ferrule - walnut stain finish - 5.5"

63. SHAW ENGLAND raised letters in a recessed ,black paint background, rectangle on obverse side of non-mag. alloy - large recessed numbers on extended steel turret - .1" plated brass ferrule - evidence of black stain finish - 5.4"

64. *Spardia* on obverse of plated steel head - large recessed numbers on slotted, hex, extended steel turret - .45" plated steel ferrule - metallic red painted handle - 5.2"

65. SPIRALUX recessed letters in a recessed rectangle on obverse side of non-mag. alloy head - MADE IN ENGLAND recessed letters in recessed rectangle on reverse - large raised numbers on extended non-mag. alloy turret - .5" plated steel ferrule - red paint handle - 5.55"

66. STANDARD Nº 1 MADE IN U.S.A. stamped on obverse of plated steel head with both top & bottom rounded - medium numbers on extended steel turret - .4" plated brass ferrule - 5.6"

67. *Steelcraft* stamped on reverse of plated steel head - GERMANY(in very small letters) on obverse of head next to the ferrule - large recessed numbers on extended brass plated turret - .4" plated steel ferrule - 5.1"

68. *Steelcraft* stamped on obverse of plated steel head - WEST-GERMANY(in very small letters) on reverse next to ferrule - large recessed numbers on brass plated extended steel turret - .4" plated steel ferrule - 5.2"

69. SUPREME stamped on obverse side of plated steel head - WEST-GERMANY(in very small letters) on reverse next to ferrule - large recessed numbers on extended brass plated turret - .4" plated steel ferrule - 5.2"

70. SWITZERLAND, MADE IN (very small letters) stamped on top of plated steel head with both top & bottom slightly rounded - large recessed numbers on extended steel turret - .4"plated steel ferrule - 5.6"

71. SWISS MADE ORIGINAL stamped on obverse side of plated steel head with both top & bottom slightly rounded - large recessed numbers on extended steel turret - .45" plated steel ferrule - box says: Glasscutter, first quality (N^0 2A) in four languages - 5.5"

72. UNIVERSAL ORIGINAL MADE IN GERMANY stamped on reverse side of plated steel head with both top & bottom rounded - extra large recessed numbers on extended brass plated non-mag. alloy turret - .45" plated steel ferrule - red-orange paint - 5.15"

73. UNI CORP. (small letters) MADE IN GERMANY stamped on obverse of plated steel head - large recessed numbers on extended brass turret - .45' plated steel ferrule - 5.2"

74. UNI CORP. (large letters) MADE IN GERMANY stamped on obverse side of plated steel head - large recessed numbers on extended brass turret - .4" plated steel ferrule - orange-red stain - 5.2"

75. UNIPRISE stamped on obverse side of plated steel head - large recessed numbers on extended brass plated steel turret - .45" plated steel ferrule - 5.15"

76. VERIBOR N° 2 GERMANY(very small letters next to ferrule) stamped on obverse of plated steel head - large recessed numbers on extended steel turret - .45" plated steel ferrule - 5.2"

77. VERIBOR MADE IN GERMANY(small letters) stamped on obverse side of plated steel head - recessed large numbers on extended hex steel turret - .25" plated steel ferrule - red stain handle - 5.2"

78. WEST-GERMANY & acorn logo raised letters in a recessed rectangle on reverse side of plated non-mag. alloy head - medium recessed numbers on slotted, hex, non-mag. alloy turret - .45" plated steel ferrule - 5.15"

79. W-GERMANY & acorn logo under on reverse side of plated steel head with both top & bottom rounded - raised large letters on extended ,hex, brass plated, non-mag. alloy turret - .45" plated steel ferrule - metallic red paint - 5.2"

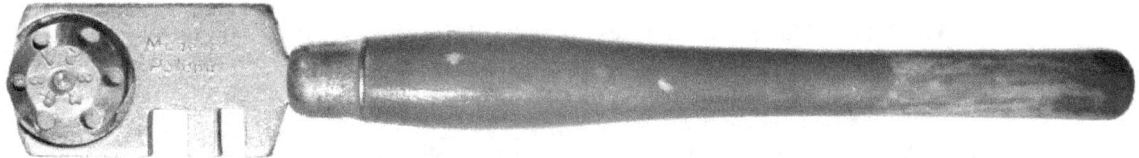

80. Made In Poland on turret side of plated steel .8" high X 1.5" long X .1" thick head - large numbers on top center area of extended, truncated cone of a .6" diam. plated steel turret - .4" plated steel ferrule - round red handle - 6"

81. Made In Poland on turret side of plated steel .8" high X 1.5" long X .1" thick head - large numbers in center of extended, flat .6" diam. plated steel turret - a .75" finger rest on walnut stain handle places the two breakers on the top of head while cutting - contour of handle is like: CATEGORY X-69 & 70 DIAMANTOR - 5.7"

B. FLAT HANDLES

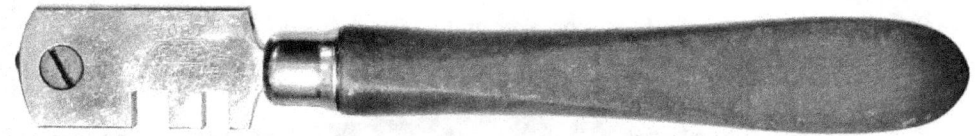

82. C. K. (in a short elongated hexagon) 5087 GERMAN MAKE stamped on obverse side of plated steel head - large recessed numbers on extended steel turret - .4" plated steel ferrule - light walnut stain - 5.2"

83. C. K. (in a short elongated hexagon) 5087 WEST-GERMANY stamped on obverse side of plated steel head - KEEP CLEAN LIGHTLY OILED stamped on reverse - extra large recessed numbers(no 1, a .05" diam. hole instead) on extended steel turret - .25" plated steel ferrule - light walnut stain handle - 5.3"

84. SHAW ENGLAND raised letters in a recessed rectangle on a plated non-mag. alloy head - large recessed numbers on extended steel turret - .4" plated steel ferrule - light walnut stain finish - 4.9"

85. SHAW ENGLAND: same as XI-84 above except larger numbers on turret and redder walnut finish on longer handle - 5.15"

86. SHAW ENGLAND: same as XI-85 above except the flat handle is slightly convex on both top & bottom of the shorter handle - 5.05"

87. *Silberschnitt* MADE IN GERMANY stamped on obverse side of plated steel head - extra large recessed numbers on extended, hex, steel turret - .22" rectangular shape .55" X .3" plated steel ferrule & this cross-section continues down the tapering walnut handle - 5.3"

88. *Silberschnitt* stamped on obverse side of plated steel head - EHREKE DIEBURG TEL. 671 stamped on reverse - large recessed numbers on extended steel turret - .4" plated steel ferrule - reddish walnut handle - 5.3"

89. *Silberschnitt* stamped on obverse of plated steel head - H & S in over lapping rhombuses (tilted squares) stamped on reverse - large recessed numbers on extended steel turret - .42" plated steel ferrule - reddish walnut handle - 5.3"

90. *Silberschnitt* MADE IN GERMANY stamped on obverse side of plated steel head - large recessed numbers on extended, hex, steel turret - .42" plated steel ferrule - fruitwood stain handle - 5.2"

91. *Silberschnitt* MADE IN GERMANY stamped on obverse of plated steel head - slot in place of 1 with large recessed numbers on hex, extended steel turret - .3" plated steel ferrule fruitwood stain handle - 5.35"

92. STANLEY (in a modified rectangle) 14-040 stamped on obverse of plated steel head - large recessed numbers on extended hex, steel turret - slot in place of 1 on turret - .3" plated steel ferrule fruitwood stained handle - 5.3"

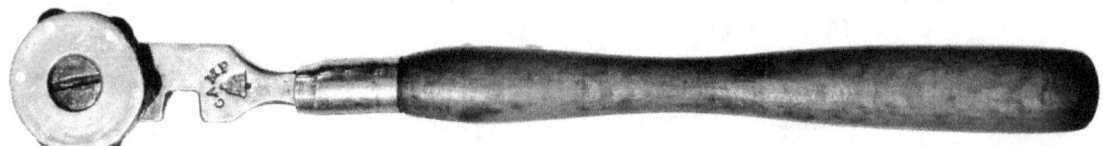

93. CAMP(BELL logo) on neck of brass breaker unit - .75" brass no number turret - .6" brass ferrule - slender shaped walnut handle 5.9"

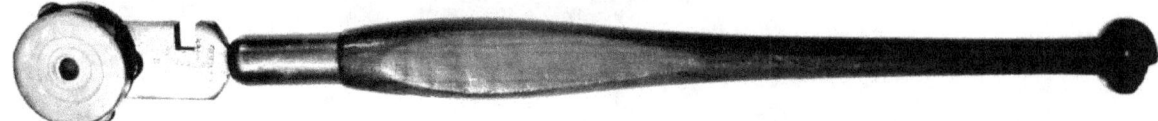

94. GOVERNOR & logo of governor on reverse of steel breaker unit - MADE IN ENGLAND stamped in a rectangle on obverse of steel breaker unit - .75" diam. brass no number turret - .75" brass ferrule - two 1.9" finger rests on walnut handle with ball end - 7.3"

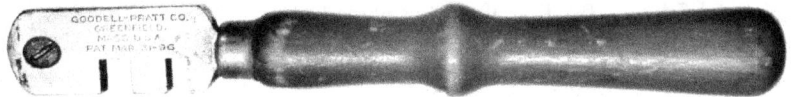

94-A. GOODELL-PRATT Co. GREENFIELD, MASS. U.S.A. PAT. MAR. 31-96 No. 1 - 2" plated brass ferrule – recessed numbers on extended turret - 4.4"

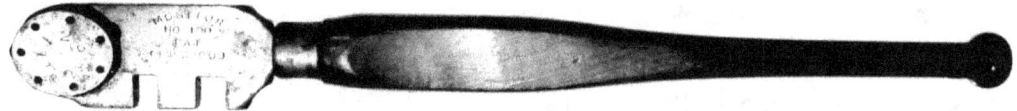

95. M.F. CO. MILLERS FALLS MASS. U.S.A. stamped on reverse side of plated steel head - MONITOR NO. 100 PAT. FEB. 2, 1909 stamped on obverse next to extended steel turret with seven wheels and recessed medium numbers - .25" plated brass ferrule - walnut handle with ball end - 5.4"

96. MILLERS FALLS CO. MILLERS FALLS, MASS. stamped facing away from breakers on plated steel head - MONITOR NO 100 PAT. FEB. 2, 1909 stamped on turret side of plated steel head - seven wheel, extended plated steel turret with recessed medium numbers - .25" plated steel ferrule - walnut handle with ball end - 5.45"

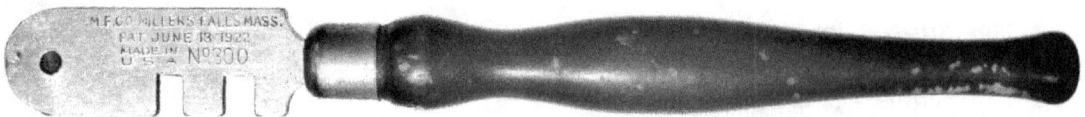

97. M.F. CO. MILLERS FALLS, MASS. PAT. JUNE 13 1922 MADE IN U.S.A. N° 300 stamped on obverse side of 1.6" long plated steel head - medium numbers on .53" diam. 6-wheel extended steel turret - .4" plated brass ferrule - contoured mahogany finish handle - 5.8"

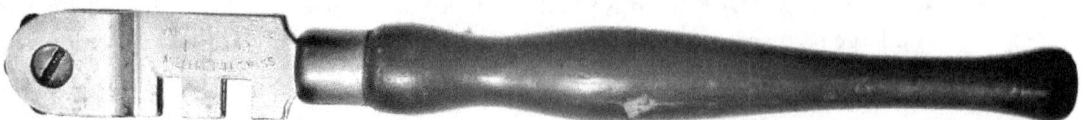

98. MILLERS FALLS CO. N° 300 MILLERS FALLS, MASS. stamped on obverse of plated steel head of split construction where steel turret is held between the spread ends - one turret number at a time shows at end of head - .4" plated brass ferrule - contour walnut handle - 5.8"

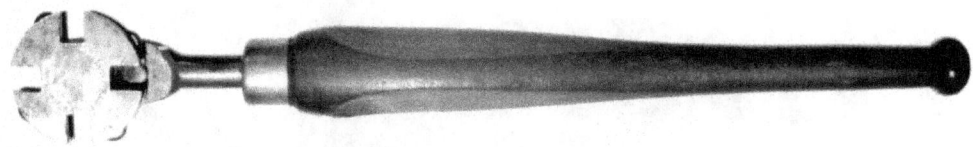

99. MILLERS FALLS CO. MILLERS FALLS MASS stamped in a circle on center of .75" diam. 4-wheel & 4-breaker extended steel turret - knurled turret fastener has a screwdriver slot - steel neck - .25" plated brass ferrule - walnut handle with small flat ball - 5.2"

100. MILLERS FALLS CO. same as XI-99 except no screwdriver slot in knurled turret fastener - 5.1"

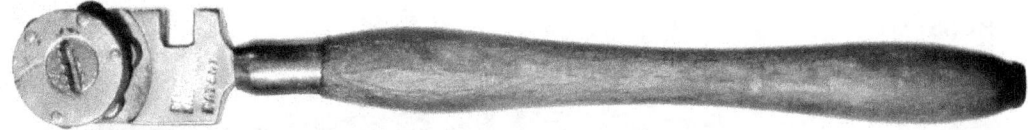

101. NEW SHEFFIELD PATENT on turret side of single breaker brass head near the .5" brass ferrule - no numbers on .6" diam. extended brass 6-wheel turret - contoured natural wood handle - 5.6"

102. G-T-L BRITISH MADE in an oval on obverse of single breaker brass head - no numbers on 6 wheel .55" diam. extended brass turret - .4" brass ferrule - decal on natural wood handle: ALL BEST BRITISH TOOLS G-T-L MADE IN SHEFIELD - 5.4"

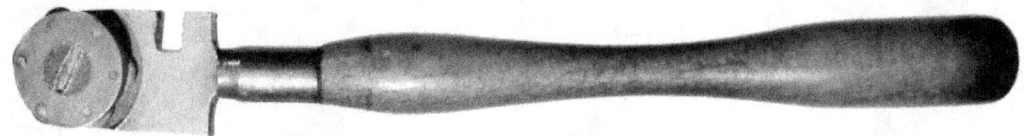

103. No ID - single breaker brass head - no numbers on 6 wheel .625" diam. extended brass turret - .6" brass ferrule - contour natural wood handle - 5.5"

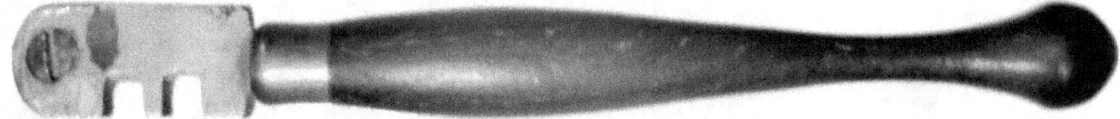

104. No ID - two breakers on thick brass head - no numbers on .44" diam. extended brass turret - .4" brass ferrule - note "ball" end of walnut handle - 5.9"

105. No ID - 3 breakers on plated steel head - medium numbers on brass plated extended steel turret - .4" plated brass ferrule - mahogany handle - .35" plated brass ferrule at 1.2" long screwdriver (but sharpened to a sharp chisel edge) - 6.4"

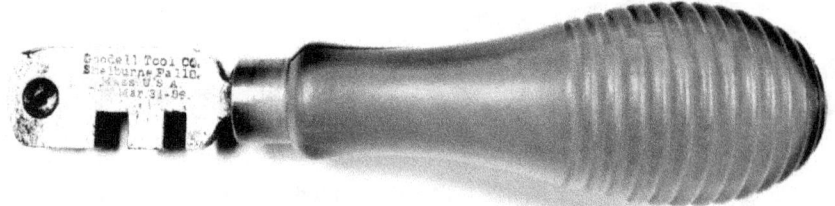

106. Goodell Tool CO. Shelburne Falls, Mass. U.S.A. Pat. Mar. 31-96 stamped on obverse of steel head -
No. 1 stamped on reverse of head - **.3"** brass ferrule –dark stained bulbous handle with 13 grooves
(like a honey dip stick) – 4.7"

D.   RUSSIAN

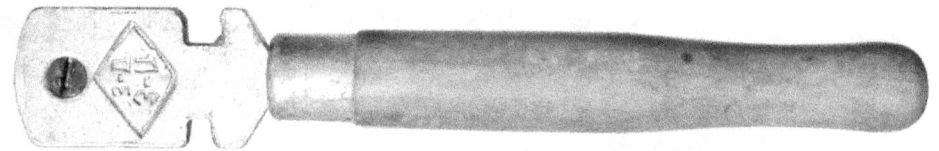

107.   and 108 thru 112 below. These Russian glass cutters have various logos or data on **.8" X 1.35" X .16"**
aluminum heads with 2 breakers - 3-wheel brass extended turrets with no numbers - **.45"** aluminum
ferrules - natural wood handles 5" or 5.1"

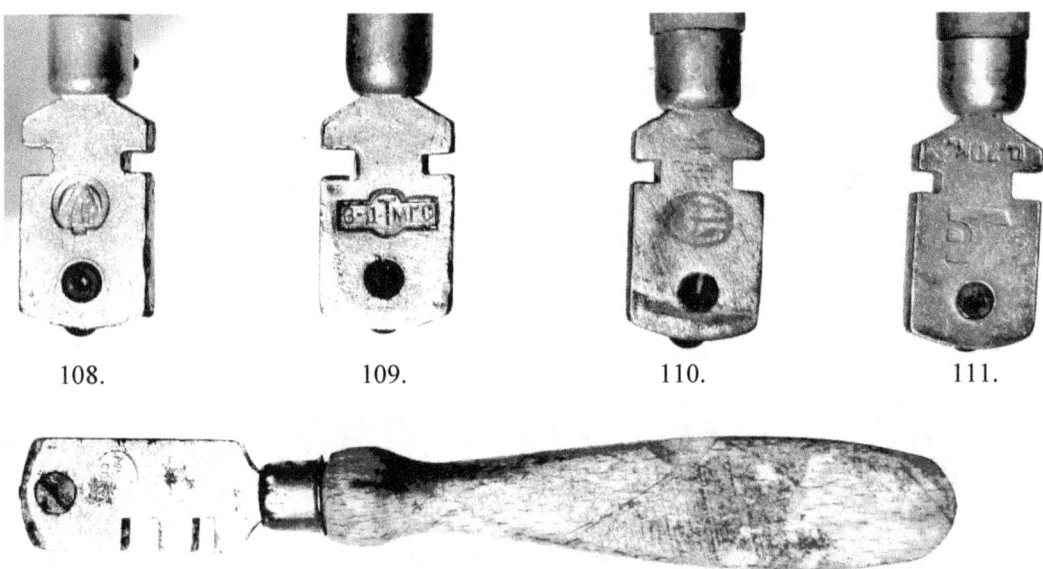

| 108. | 109. | 110. | 111. |

112. ID stamped in an oval on obverse of plated steel head   - large numbers on extended steel turret - **.4"**
plated steel ferrule - natural wood flat(almost a narrow "beaver tail") handle - 5.2"

CATEGORY XII TURRET & MULTI-WHEEL - METAL AND/OR PLASTIC HANDLE

Glass cutters in this category are quite individualistic. Some could probably fall in other categories, but here they are. No U.S. Patents were found for this category. There is but one other cutter known different by others. There are eight of this style in Category XXI RED DEVIL and only one in Category XXII FLETCHER.

Two subsets:

A. **METAL HANDLE**   B. **PLASTIC HANDLE**

Price Range: $30 - $65   Price Range: $ 8 - $15

A.   **METAL HANDLE**

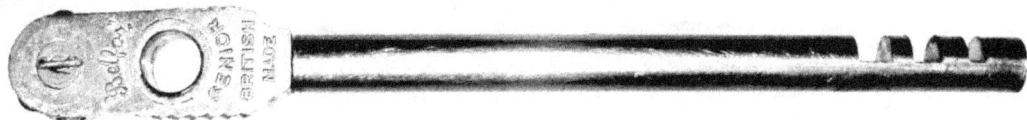

1. "*Belfor*" SENIOR – BRITISH MADE on obverse of plated non-mag. head - large numbers on non-mag. turret - .3" diam. non-mag. round handle unscrews from head and resulting threaded hole extends into the .2" diam. hole in head - 5.5"

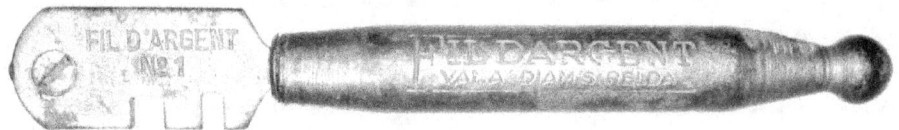

2.   FIL D'ARGENT No 1 on obverse of steel head - large numbers on 5 wheel steel turret - FIL DARGENT VANA'DIAM'S RELDA on solid steel handle - 4.8"

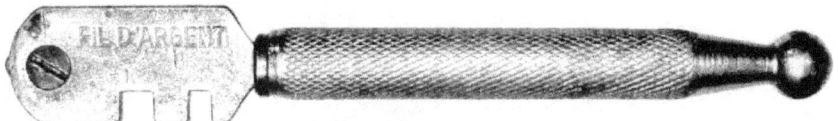

3.   FIL D'ARGENT on obverse of steel head - large numbers on 5 wheel steel turret - .05" steel ferrule - .4" diam. solid steel handle is finely knurled - 4.6"

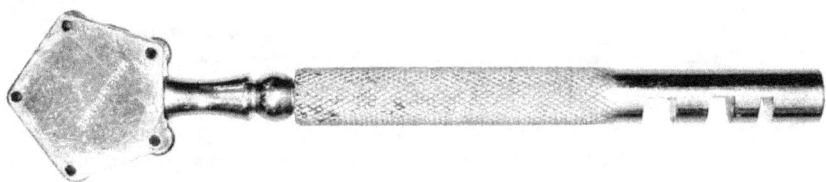

4.   MADE IN FRANCE on obverse of plated non-mag. five sided head - DÉPOSÉ & extra large numbers on 5 wheel turret - finely knurled plated brass handle with three breakers unscrews to be used at the other 4 sides of head - 4.5"

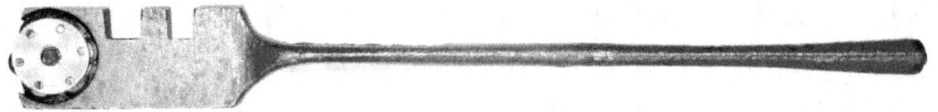

5. SINGER in recessed rectangle on bottom of handle - cross-hatch finger rest in an oval - no numbers on 6 wheel flush steel turret - maroon paint - 5.2"

6. Same as XII-5 above except extended 6 wheel steel turret is numbered - red paint - 5.2" Box says this is a No. 66

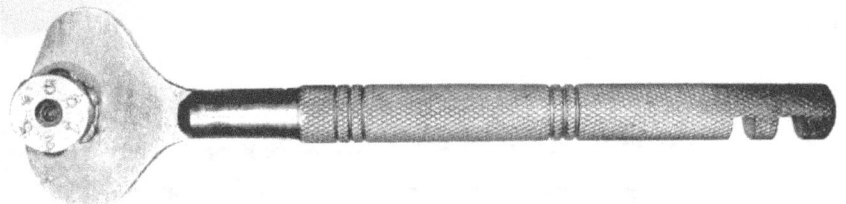

7. UNIVERBEL in a rectangle on plated steel thin head - large numbers on 5 wheel steel turret - smooth part of solid handle(ferrule) is grooved to accept attachment of the thin neck of the head - rest of the .35" diam. handle is finely knurled with two breakers - 4.9"

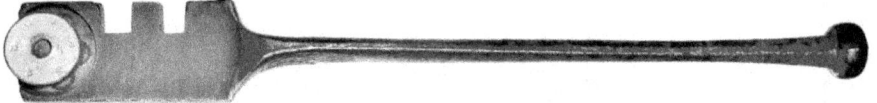

8. UTICA in a recessed rectangle on bottom side of flattened steel handle - cross-hatched finger rest on top side - very small numbers on 6 wheel steel turret - red paint wheel shape ball end - 5"

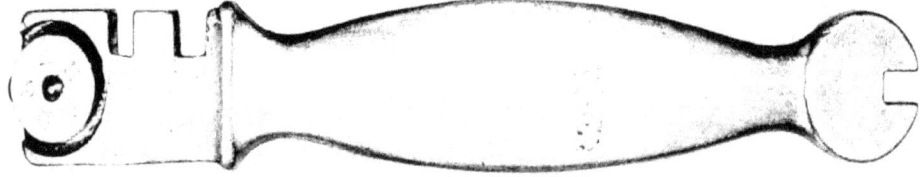

9. No ID - one piece aluminum .25" thick - large numbers on aluminum 5 wheel turret - 5.1"

10. No ID - 3 wheels mounted fixed on end of 2 breaker head - some evidence of maroon paint - 4.7"

10-A. No ID – same as XII-10 above except very good maroon paint and the portion of head holding the 3 wheels is where the extra length is – 4.75"

B. PLASTIC HANDLE

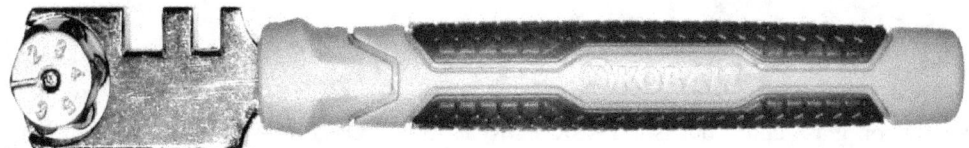

11. KOBALT K in a circle molded onto grey plastic mid-handle of an ovoid cross-sectional handle -
     hexagonal knobs on the deep blue component of handle - no ID on plated non-mag. head - large
     numbers on slotted non-mag. hex 6 wheel turret - slot replaces the 1 - 5.2" item # 239124 on pac

12. *Richard* ENGLAND in a recessed rectangle on obverse of plated non-mag. head -   large
     numbers on 6 wheel steel turret - yellow plastic handle with a1.4" concave finger rest - small ball –
     5.8"

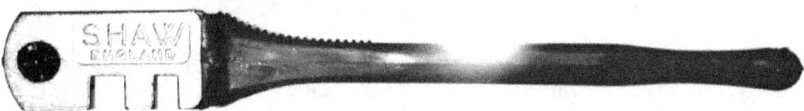

13. SHAW ENGLAND in a recessed rectangle on non-mag. matte finish head - medium numbers on a
     steel 6 wheel turret - blue plastic handle with lined finger rest and SHAW on under side - 4.8"
14. SHAW ENGLAND in a recessed rectangle on shiny plated non-mag. head - large numbers on steel
     turret - otherwise same as XII-13 above - 4.8"

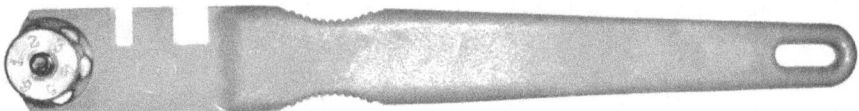

15. SHAW ENGLAND in shallow recessed rectangle on head of a one piece blue plastic glass cutter with
     elongated hole at end of handle for hanging - large numbers on steel 6 wheel turret - lined finger
     rests both top and bottom - 5"

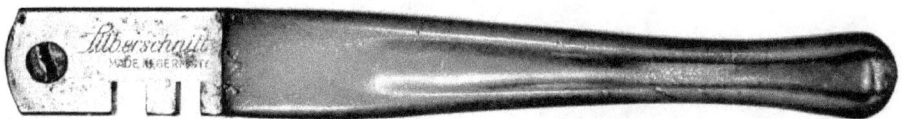

16. *Silberschnitt* MADE IN GERMANY on obverse of plated steel head - large numbers on steel hex
     turret - blue-grey plastic handle 5.15"

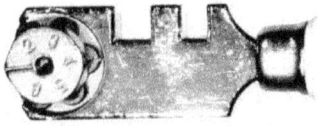

17. No ID on glass cutter(but is a TASK FORCE from LOWES) - non-mag. plated head - slotted 6 wheel hex steel turret   slot is in the 1 spot - .25" plated steel ferrule - natural wood-like plastic handle - 5.15"

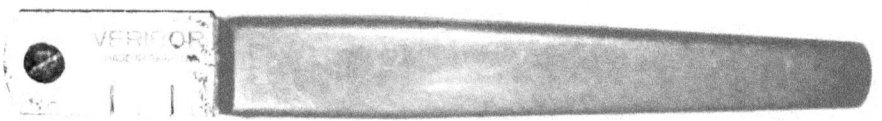

18. VERIBOR MADE IN GERMANY on obverse of plated steel head - large numbers on steel turret - orange-red tapered flat plastic handle - 5.1"

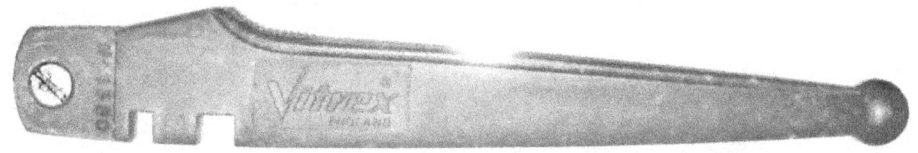

19. VITREX ENGLAND in a recessed rectangle on obverse side of handle below lined finger rest - No. 1380 on obverse of head - large recessed numbers on non-mag. turret - all red plastic construction - 5.2"

20. No ID - thin plated steel head - extra large numbers on a brass turret - flat yellow plastic handle - 4.65"

CATEGORY XIII   TUBING & ROD CUTTERS

Tubing and rod glass cutters come in a number of designs and are well represented in the US Patent literature. Many are quite similar, so they are not pictured but are very adequately described. Sixty two U.S. Patents have been relisted from the master U.S. Patent list.

207,809	476,626	934,487	1,124,784	1,482,206	2,261,214	2,839,871
310,914	483,778	936,674	1,169,579	1,535,903	2,425,093	3,084,431
333,235	505,211	950,273	1,170,588	1,579,980	2,476,680	3,318,500
363,563	513,965	996,285	1,308,260	1,691,530	2,556,434	3,395,493
365,190	673,312	1,024,983	1,359,751	1,922,426	2,577,486	3,403,442
433,537	805,309	1,028,870	1,375,958	1,951,140	2,582,078	3,406,886
454,233	849,149	1,096,782	1,411,524	2,125,864	2,612,001	4,046,299
457,732	862,049	1,101,032	1,435,955	2,199,807	2,631,411	4,351,459
467,500	887,604	1,123,336	1,462,030	2,250,159	2,674,066	

There are fifteen different tubing glass cutters known in other collections. The following in this collection are shown at less than actual size.

There are eight sub-sets in this category:

    A. **SINGLE SHAFT**
    B. **LOOP END**
    C. **OFFSET LOOP END**
    D. **PIN HINGE**
    E. **CIRCLE END SPRING WITH TRIGGER**
    F. **WOOD HANDLE WITH TRIGGER**
    G. **PLIER STYLE SHORT TOOL**
    H. **PLIER STYLE LONG TOOL**
    I. **LAB UNITS**

Price range: $ 10 to $35

A.   SINGLE SHAFT

1. RED DEVIL - S & H CO. N.Y. - 8.4"

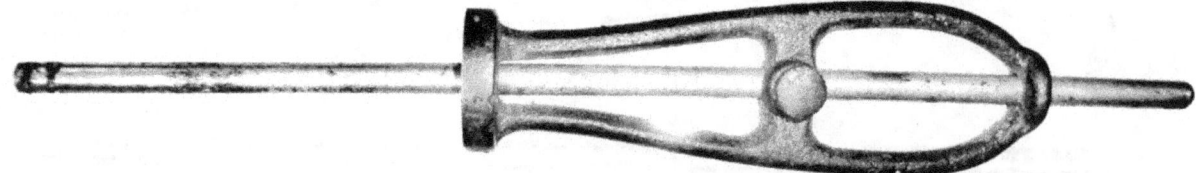

2. No ID - no breakers - cast iron body – steel glass cutter rod is adjustable w/set screw on
      cross-over bar – 7.5"

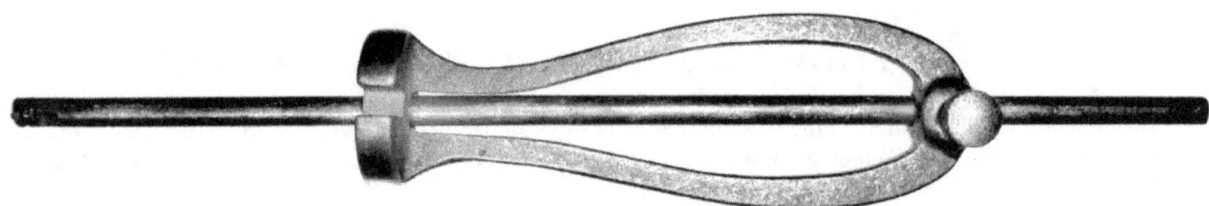

3. No ID - 2 breakers on glass tube stop - cast iron body — glass cutter rod is adjustable with set screw at end of loop - no cross-over bar, - 7.5"

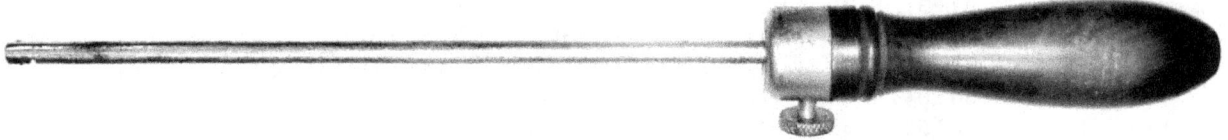

4. No ID(on cutter) – THE McREA & ROBERTS CO.'S GAUGE GLASS CUTTER (on box) - turned rosewood handle - .5" plated steel ferrule - 9.5" long

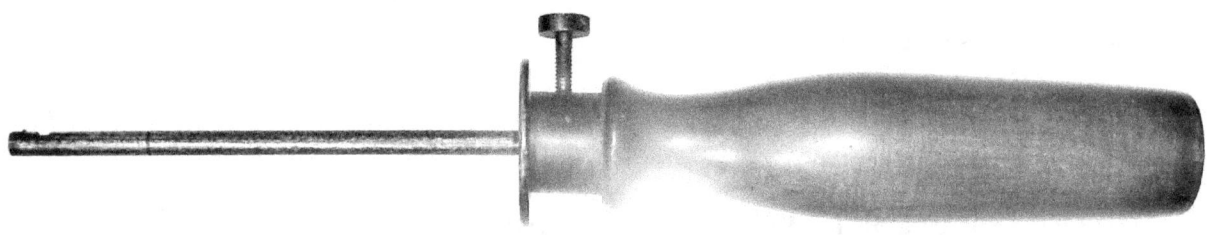

5. No ID - wood handle with a 1.25" diam. brass stop plate with .5" ferrule attached with an adjustable set screw – 9"

B. LOOP END

6. No ID - tube guide is a flattened and grooved end of steel rod at a 45⁰ angle - adjustable tube stop - 10"

6-A. RAINBOW PACKING – PEERLESS PISTON PACKING – PEERLESS RUBBER MFG. CO. NEW YORK - tube guide is the rod end flattened and split into a vee - no adjustable tube stop – 8.125"

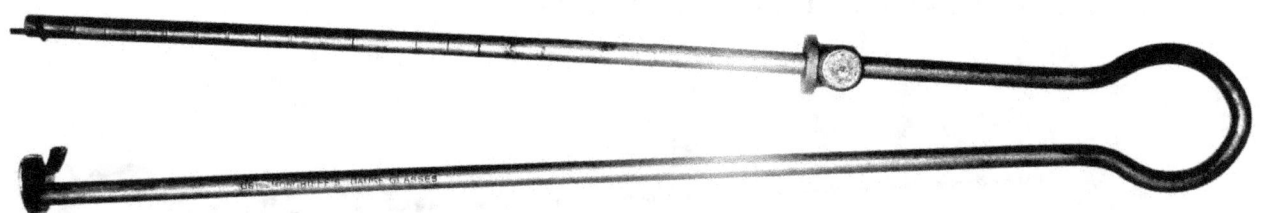

7. USL MONCRIEFF'S GAGE GLASSES – thin sheet steel tube support swaged onto end of 5/32" diameter steel rod with scale - 10"

8. No ID - thin sheet steel tube support swaged onto end of 5/32" diameter steel rod with no scale - adjustable tube stop - 10"

9. No ID - 7/32" diameter plated steel rod with 1/4" scale with no numbers - .4" wide solid steel tube support - adjustable tube stop - 10 3/4"

C. OFFSET LOOP END

10. PAT. JUNE 11, 1912 on center of plated steel rod with ¼" scale without numbers with an offset loop handle - .2" diameter knurled set screw adjustable tube stop - pressed folded over sheet steel trigger - 1" pressed metal tube support swaged on end - 11"

11. Chesterton box - No ID on cutter - .2" diameter plated steel rod with offset loop handle - stamped out trigger unit – ¼" scale - .3" steel tube support swaged on end - 10"

D. PIN HINGE

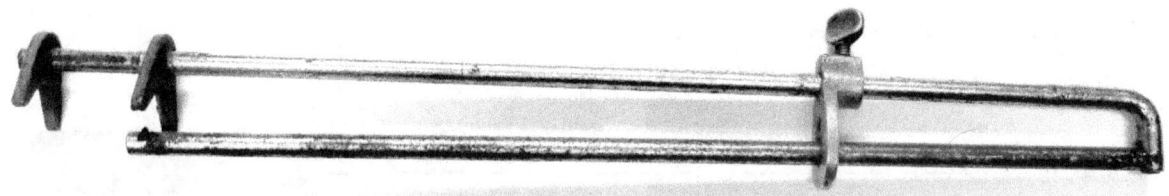

12. No ID (like postcard ad: W. & G. GAGE) - a pair of tube supports are composition material – The plated steel shaft holding the cutting wheel is the male part of the hinge - 12"

13. No ID - identical to XIII-12 above except the shaft holding the wheel is the female part of the hinge – 12"

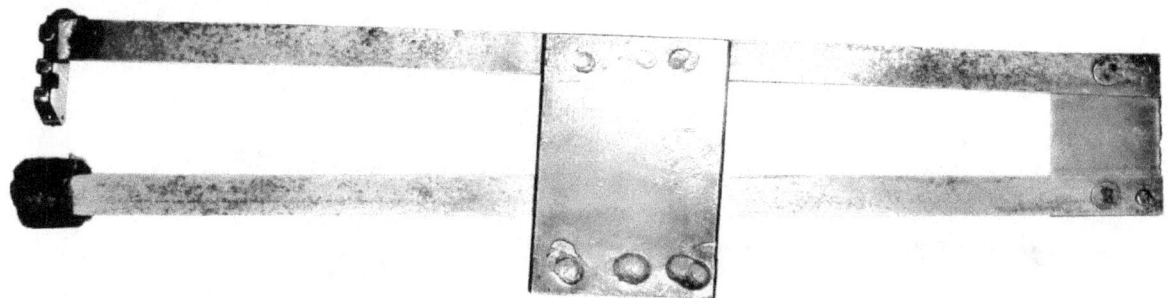

14. No ID - homemade heavy steel unit with arms of 3/8" square stock and 9.25" long – a washer silver soldered to a bolt applies the pressure against the wheel

E.   CIRCLE END SPRING STYLE WITH TRIGGER

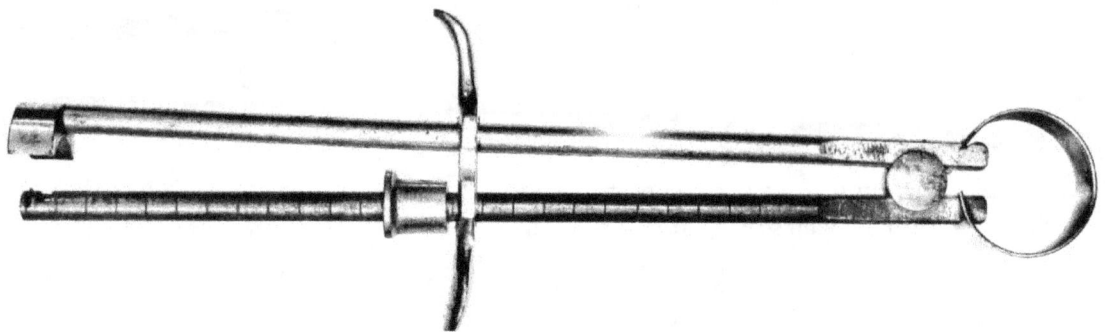

15.   PAT APL'D FOR stamped on heavy cast plated brass trigger - 1/4" plated steel rod with 1/4" scale - .4"
plated steel tube guide - 8.75"

16.   ASHCROFT MANUF. CO.(on box) - PAT. JUNE 7, 1892 – OCT. 4, 1892 stamped on heavy cast
plated brass trigger – ¼" plated steel rod with ¼" scale - .4" plated steel tube guide - 8.75"

17.   PAT. JUNE 7, 1892 – OCT. 4, 1892 stamped on heavy cast plated brass trigger - 1/4"
plated steel rod with 1/4" scale - .4" plated steel tube guide – circle spring is heavier
gauge than XIII-16 above 8.75"

18.   PAT JUNE 7, 1892 - OCT 4, 1892 stamped on pressed steel trigger - 1/4" scale – fluted plated brass
tube guide - 8.75"

19.   Chesterton's box - No ID on cutter – pressed, plated steel trigger - 1/4" scale on plated steel rod - .35"
pressed, swaged plated steel tube guide – 8 5/8"

F.   WOOD HANDLE WITH TRIGGER

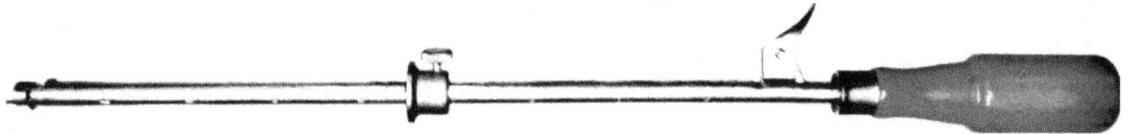

20.   PAT. JUNE 27, '11 - black smooth handle –pressed steel trigger – 1/8" scale on ¼ "
diameter plated hollow steel rod - .35" plated brass ferrule - 13"

21.   FLETCHER-TERRY BOX - No. 35(WILKINS PATENT) - No ID on cutter - orange painted fluted
wood handle - 1/8" scale on hollow steel rod - .45" plated steel ferrule - 13" long

G.   PLIER STYLE - SHORT TOOL

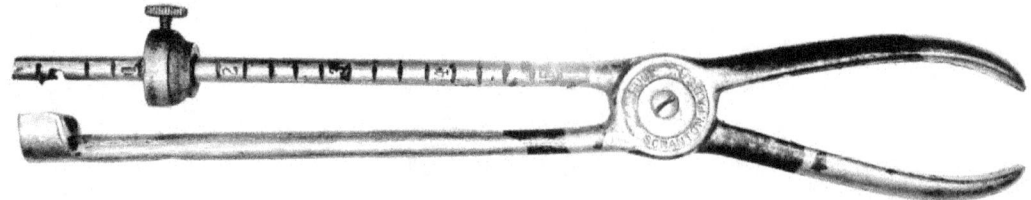

22. A.L. HUNT, SCRANTON, PA. U.S.A. recessed letters on center pivot - nickel
plated steel – ¼ " scale on plated ¼" steel rod - .4' welded on plated steel tube guide - 10"

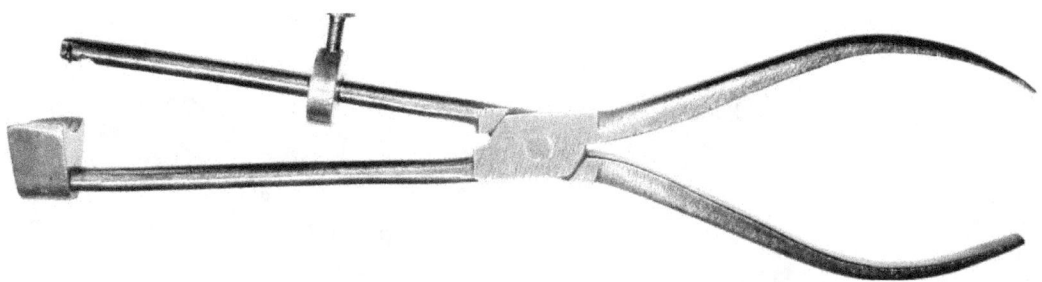

23. No ID - .55"solid brass tube guide & .2" thick X .6" diam. brass tube stop - no scale – 9.5"

H. PLIER STYLE - LONG TOOL

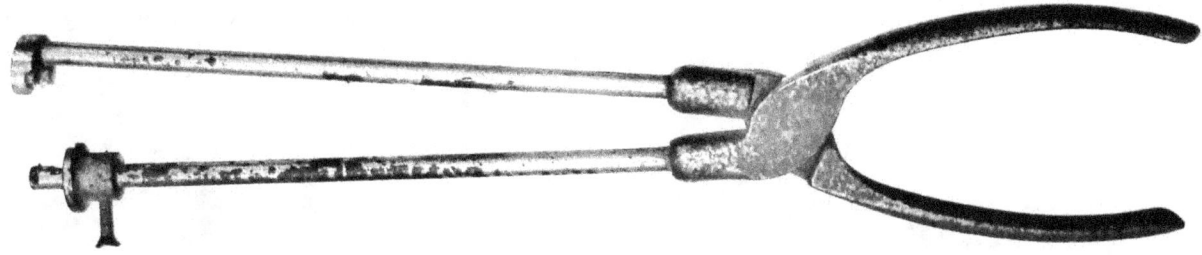

24. Goodell-Tool Co. Shelburne Falls, Mass. stamped on .22" wide plated steel tube guide - 1/16" scale on ¼" diameter plated steel rod - .5" adjustable steel tube stop - 12.5"

25. BARRETT - MADE IN U.S.A . cast on outside of both black painted cast steel handles - 4-ply steel tube guide swaged on end of ¼" diam. plated steel rod - .6" adjustable steel tube stop - 1/16" scale - 12.5"

26. No ID , however may be RED DEVIL No. 1079(see catalog) - sheet steel tube stop - 4-ply steel tube guide swaged on end -¼" diameter plated steel rod with 1/16" scale - 12.5"

27.   RED DEVIL, IRV. N.J. U.S.A. No. 90 stamped on center of ¼" steel rod with .3" wide steel tube guide - .6"adj. tube stop - 1/16" scale - red paint on handle - 12.5"

28. CHICAGO SPECIALTY MFG. CO SKOKIE ILLINOIS, SPEEDY Gauge Glass Cutter No. 3871(on box) No ID on cutter - 1/16" scale - like new plating - 4-ply steel tube guide - sheet steel tube stop - 12.5"

29. CHICAGO SPECIALTY MFG. CO.(on box and cutter) - No. 3871(on box) - red paint on handle - 4-ply steel tube guide - sheet steel adj. tube stop - 1/16" scale - 12.5"

30. ERNST WATER COLUMN & GAGE CO. LIVINGSTON N.J. stamped on ¼" diam. plated steel rod with .3" wide steel tube support - black paint handle with one inch red tips - .6" solid steel tube stop - 1/16" scale - 13 3/8""

31. MILLERS FALLS CO. GREENFIELD, MASS. MADE IN U.S.A. NO. 218(on box) and stamped on ¼" diam. plated steel rod with .3" thick steel tube guide - black paint handle with 3/4" red paint tips - .6" solid steel tube stop - 1/16" scale - 13"

32. GOODELL- PRATT CO. GREENFIELD, MASS MADE IN U.S.A. - 12.5" long(otherwise exactly the same as XIII-31 MILLERS FALLS above)

I.   LAB UNITS

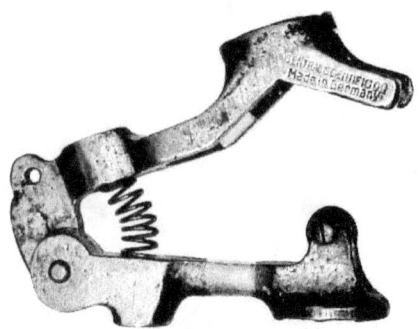

33. CENTRAL SCIENTIFIC C°
Made in Germany stamped on
tube guide arm – all brass except
steel coil spring - 2.7"

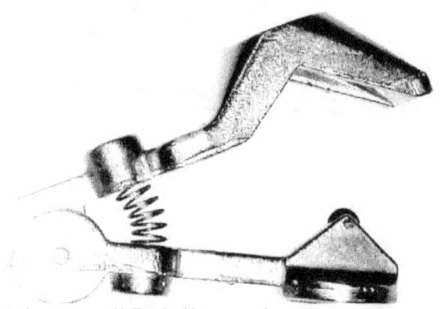

34. H in a modified diamond on cutter arm -
MADE IN U.S.A. in recess under tube
guide – No other ID, but this design is of
Griffin Glass Cutter, Macalaster Bicknell Co. -
all plated zinc alloy - steel coil spring – 2.85"

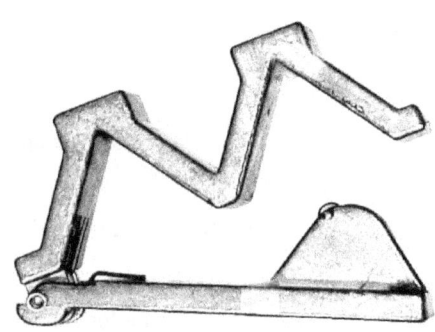

35. No ID on cutter - WAL—Rich Corporation
Corona, NY 11368 # 1801006 - zinc alloy – 2.6"

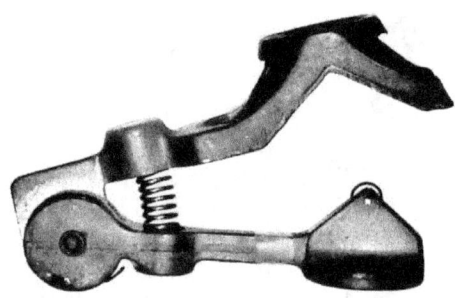

36. H in a modified diamond on cutter arm -
all   brass except spring - 2.75"

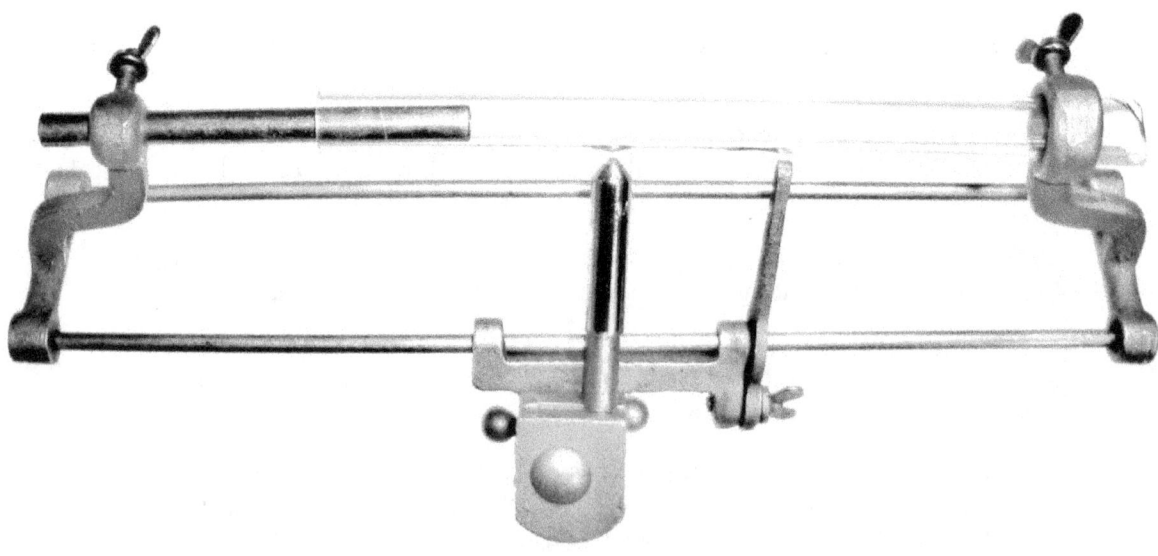

37.   No ID - diamond mounted on end of tool unit stamped 1/4 which is clamped into free
sliding unit with short adjustable actuating handle - will only accept .6" OD & .3" ID
tubing - apparatus is 11.25" long

CATEGORY XIV   BOTTLE & JAR CUTTERS

The late 1940's through the early 1970's was the peak time for changing beer and soda bottles into drinking vessels or flower vases. Today these cutters are popular items on internet auctions. There are six different known in personal use or other collections. Nineteen U.S. Patents from the master list for this Category are relisted below along with a Design Patent.

427,002	1,584,572	2,447,988	3,572,564	3,744,692	3,902,643
596,205	2,209,701	2,503,517	3,699,828	3,839,006	4,028,801
999,668	2,425,093	2,566,434	3,744,359	3,845,555	5,012,393
					6,811,477

Design Patent # 233,308   Price Range: $ 10 - $25

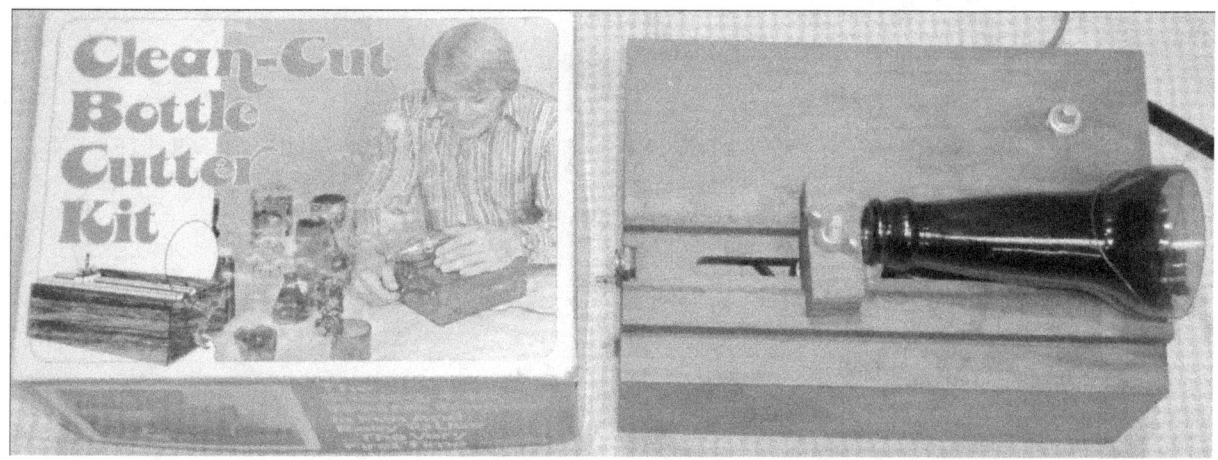

1.   Clean-Cut Bottle Cutter Kit   No. 7091 - No ID on cutter unit - Manufactured by AMERICAN HANDICRAFTS 1920 8TH Avenue FORT WORTH, TEXAS 76110 - Wood box 8.5" X 6" X 3.5" tall is open on the bottom - where 110 ac house electricity with a push on/off switch is fed into a transformer whence to the nichrome wire that wraps around the bottle to be cut.

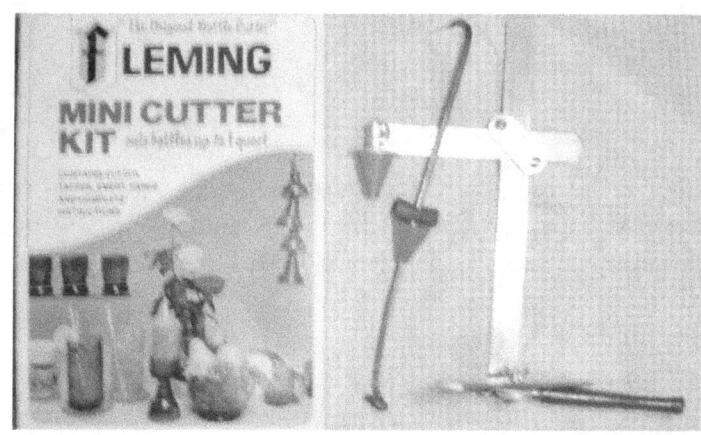

2.   FLEMING MINI CUTTER KIT by FLEMING BOTTLE   AND JUG CUTTER, INC. SEATTLE, WASHINGTON 98188 © 1971 U.S. PATENT NO. 3,572,564   - uses a VERIBOR MADE IN GERMANY turret glass cutter a with red painted handle(see XI-77) - aluminum and blue plastic construction - 10" high

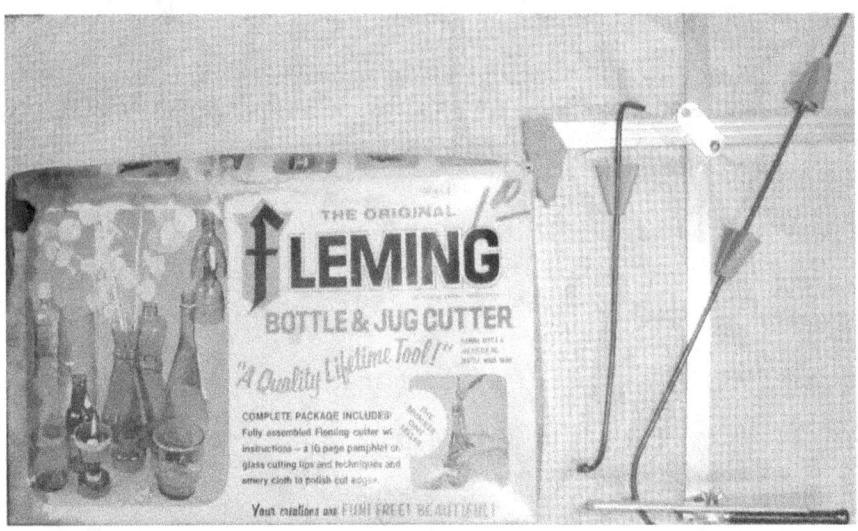

3. FLEMING THE ORIGINAL PATENTED by FLEMING BOTTLE AND JUG CUTTER, INC. SEATTLE, WASHINGTON 98188 copyright 1972 - U. S. PATENT 3,572,564 - uses a VERIBOR MADE IN GERMANY turret glass cutter with a red painted handle(see XI-77) - aluminum and yellow plastic construction - 14" high

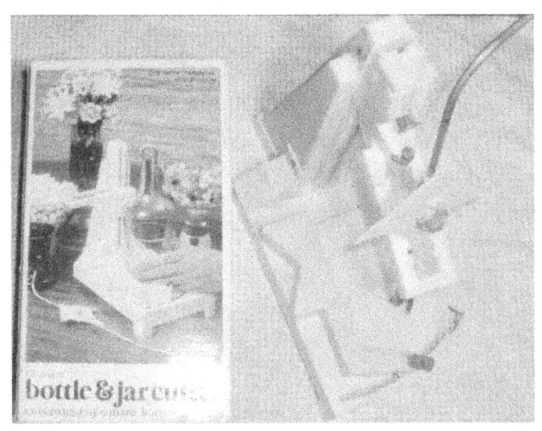 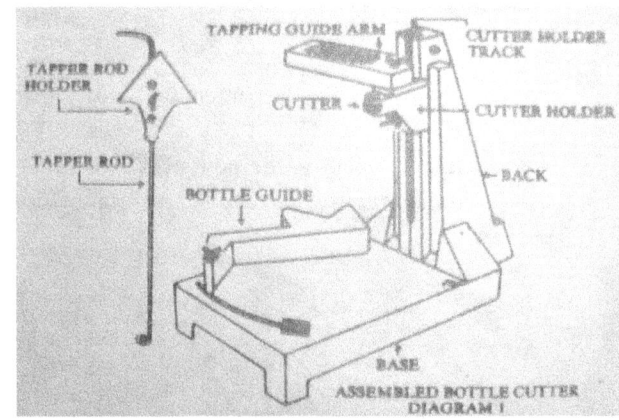

4. Ronco Bottle & Jar Cutter – No ID on cutter unit - by RONCO TELPRODUCTS, INC., 910 N. MICHIGAN AVENUE, CHICAGO, ILLINOIS 60611 - COPYRIGHT 1972 - all yellow plastic construction except the steel rod for tapping - Made in America - uses a 5-wheel turret glass cutter - 11.5" high

CATEGORY XV CIRCLE - OVAL

This category is so diverse it has been divided into nine subsets.

A. **DIAMOND POINT - PIVET BEAM**
B. **DIAMOND POINT - ROTARY BED**
C. **WHEEL - ROTARY BED or CRANK HANDLE**
D. **WOOD KNOBS**
E. **METAL KNOBS**
F. **FLIP HEAD PIVOT UNIT - SUCTION CUP BASE**
G. **6 - WHEEL TURRET**
H. **VITREX STYLE**
I. **OTHER**

There are forty eight different circle-oval cutters known to be in other collections.

Fifty seven U.S. Patents for this category are listed below:

308,466	1.056,353	1,420,867	2,302,174	4,044,464	5,044,245
396,600	1,101,604	1,421,921	2,375,378	4,112,793	5,438,757
520,247	1,109,274	1,424,625	2,507,841	4,275,633	5,507,212
683,023	1,141,192	1,422,926	2,515,445	4,339,877	5,558,565
702,732	1,146,176	1,511,016	2,576,291	4,437,958	6,202,530
717,259	1,153,092	1,883,445	2,612,689	4,541,176	
910,129	1,179,706	1,927,865	2,943,392	4,872,289	
939,843	1,183,144	1,988,565	3,047,953	4,916,820	
958,941	1,219,461	2,048,935	3,224,098	4,939,968	
959,311	1,402,961	2,122,258	3,537,345	5,014,436	
983,173					
992,819					

Price Range: There is an extensive diversity in style and market varies to an extent that the price range is very broad: $20 - $300

A. DIAMOND POINT - PIVOT BEAM

1. BENRATH   51 – C543 at end of the 3/16" X ½" 16" steel beam that folds into the slotted base of brass pivot - cutter slide unit is brass - ¼ scale

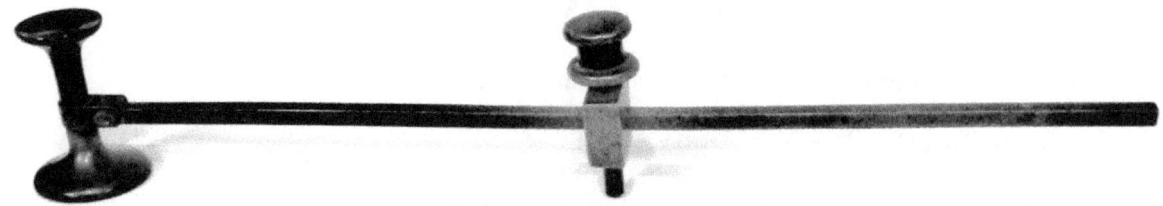

2. DICKINSON - MAKER - NEW YORK on cutter unit dual knurled brass slide - pivot 2.5" high - no scale on the ¼" square 15" brass beam

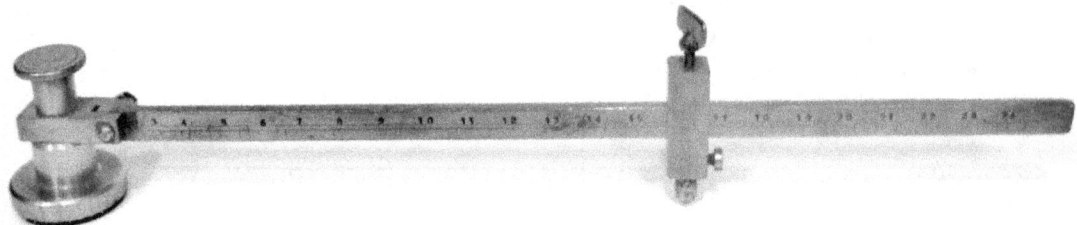

3. SHARRATT & NEWTH - LONDON - NO 44 on reverse end of 1/8 X 1/8 X 13" brass beam with ¼" scale - pivot is 1.7" high - all brass

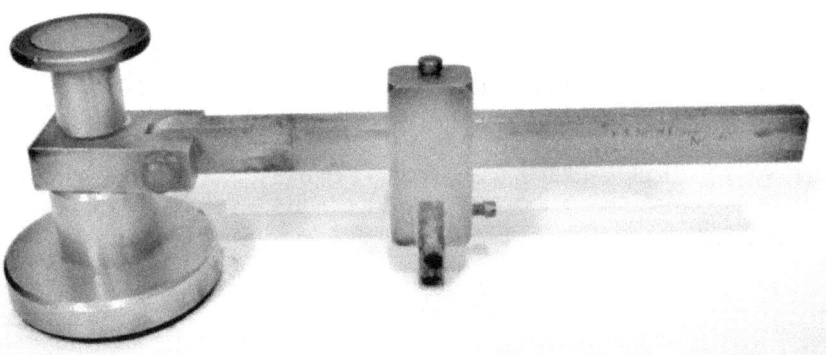

4. SHARRETT & NEWTH - LONDON NO 42 on side of ¼" X ½" X 7" brass beam with ¼" scale on top - pivot is 2.1" high all brass

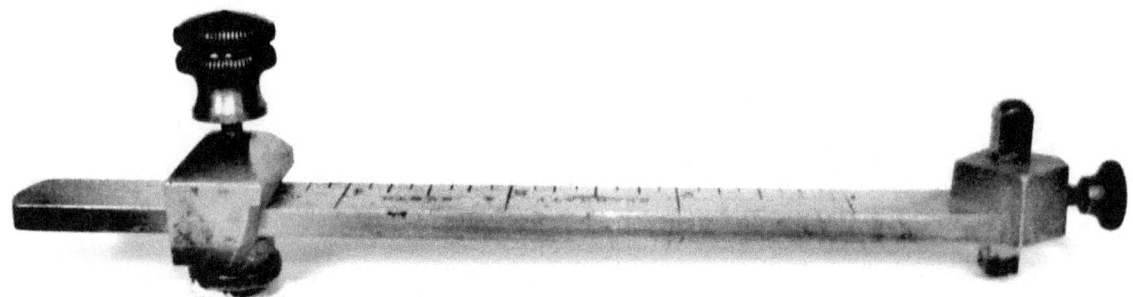

5. SHARRATT & NEWTH - LONDON on top of .2" X .6" x 6" brass beam with steel cutter unit inserted into the .42" high holder at end of beam - dual knurled knob atop slide unit controls location - base is incomplete as it looks as if the rotatable round brass wheel should slide into something to rotate

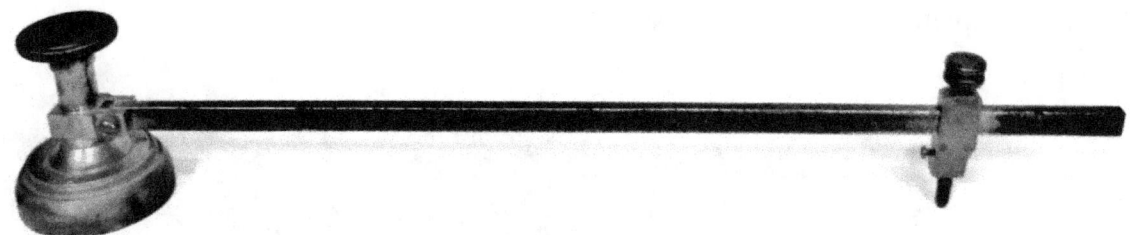

6.	SHAW - ENGLAND on end of ¼" X 3/8" X 16 ¼" steel beam with a ¼" scale - brass dual knurled knob cutter slide - brass and wood base pivot 2.5" high

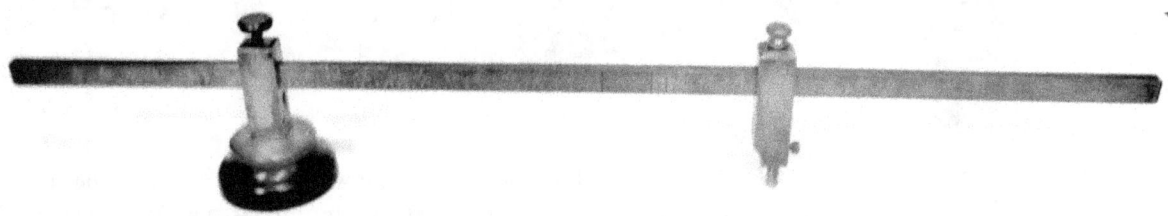

7.	No ID - 3 on top end of .2" X .4" X 19.75" brass beam with dual scale: one end 3" to 18", the other end 18" to 36" - cutter unit brass slide - 3" high pivot with wood base

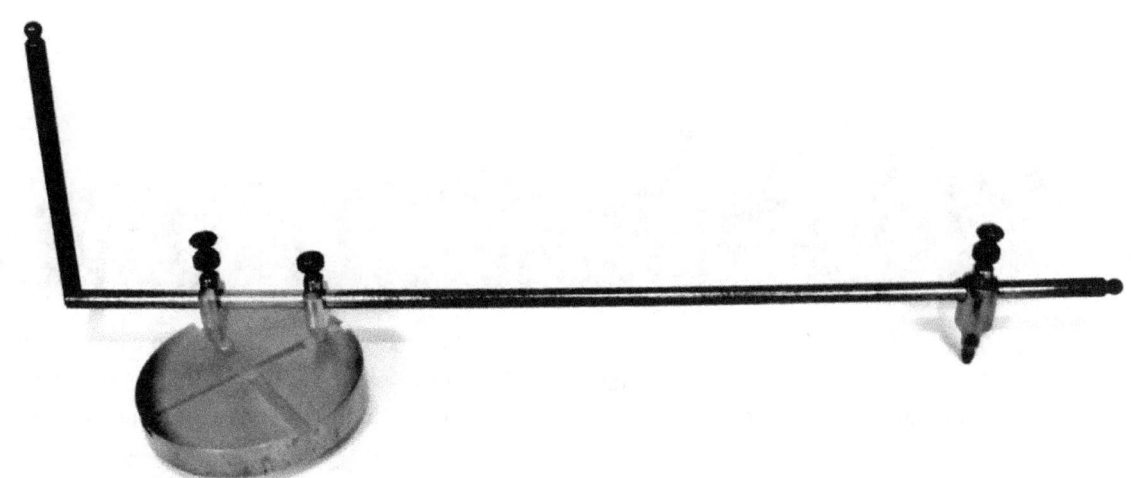

8.	No ID - brass slide cutter unit, dual knurled knobs - ¼" round steel beam 15" long with flattened top surface - no scale - 4" hinged extension - base steel disc 3.1" diam. slotted on top for track to guide two adjustable brass slides to control the oval axis. Four removable points on underside of steel base(when in place tool is unusable as a glass cutter)

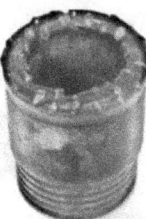

9.	No ID - Threaded diamond studded steel hole saw - 1 ½" dia.

B. DIAMOND POINT – ROTATING BED

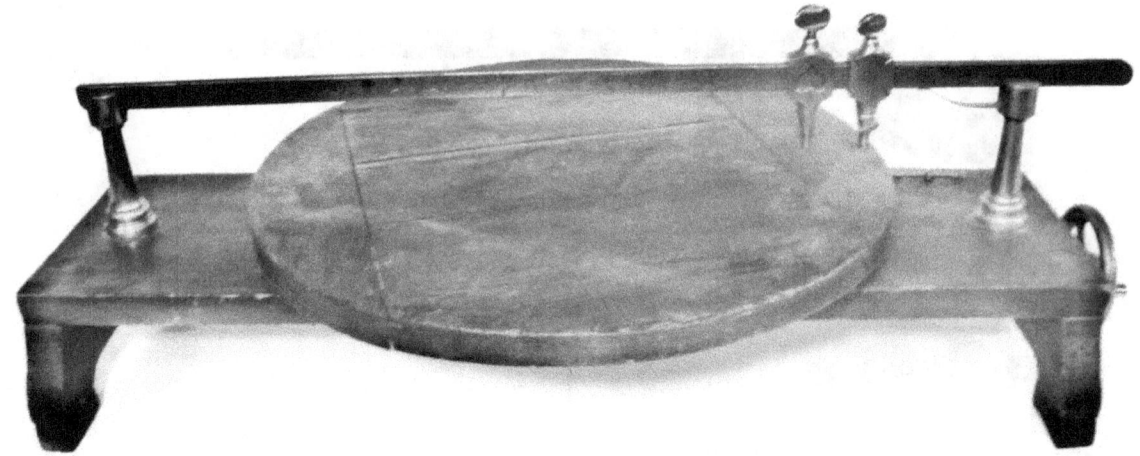

10. ELITE - wood base 7" X 25" X 4" high(originally 3 ¼" ,however, a ¾" extension has been added to each of the four feet) - one very similar to this is shown in: "Industrial Diamonds and Diamond pointed Tools", The Diamond Drill Carbon Co., New York - Hinged steel beam is 3/8" X 5/8" X25 ½" with two brass slides(trammels) with diamond points. One slide marked: F.S 12 23, the other slide marked: PARIS 4 J.C. J.C. and a logo: hammer through a C

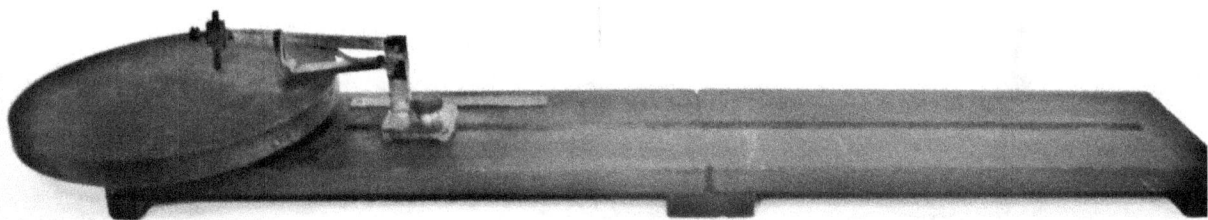

11. SHARRETT & NEWTH - LONDON - 12" diam. solid walnut rotating disk - solid walnut base 39" X 7" X 1 ¾" high - Cutting unit: 12" brass scale - 2 3/8" square brass base to sliding unit holding a spring loaded 7 ¼" beam holding the cutting tool - Why the separate add-on extended bed?

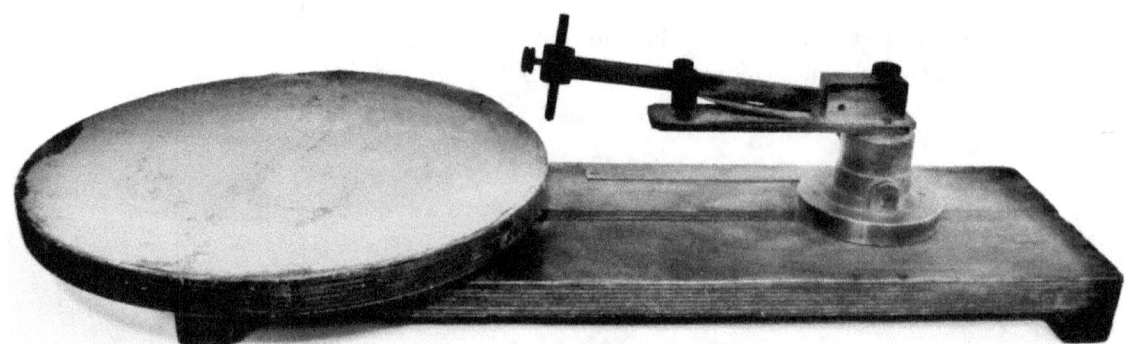

12. SHARRETT & NEWTH - LONDON - 12" diam. wood(16 ply) rotating disk - wood base(16 ply) 21" X 6 5/8" X 1 ½" - 12" brass scale - 3 ½" brass base to sliding unit holding spring loaded 6/3/4" X ¼" X ½" brass beam holding cutting tool

C. WHEEL - ROTATING BED or CRANK HANDLE

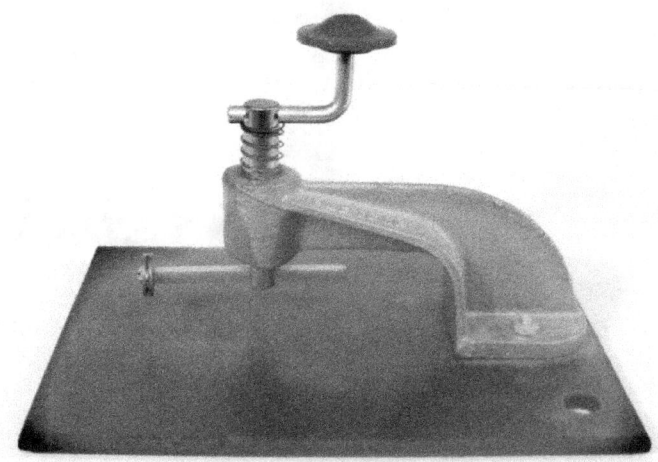

13. FLETCHER - MADE IN USA – NO 32 - on green painted steel arm - red plastic knob - dark green fiber board base: 5 7/8" X 7 7/8" X ¼" - plated brass 3" beam arm with a 3 wheel turret - See: 1963 Fletcher-Terry catalog

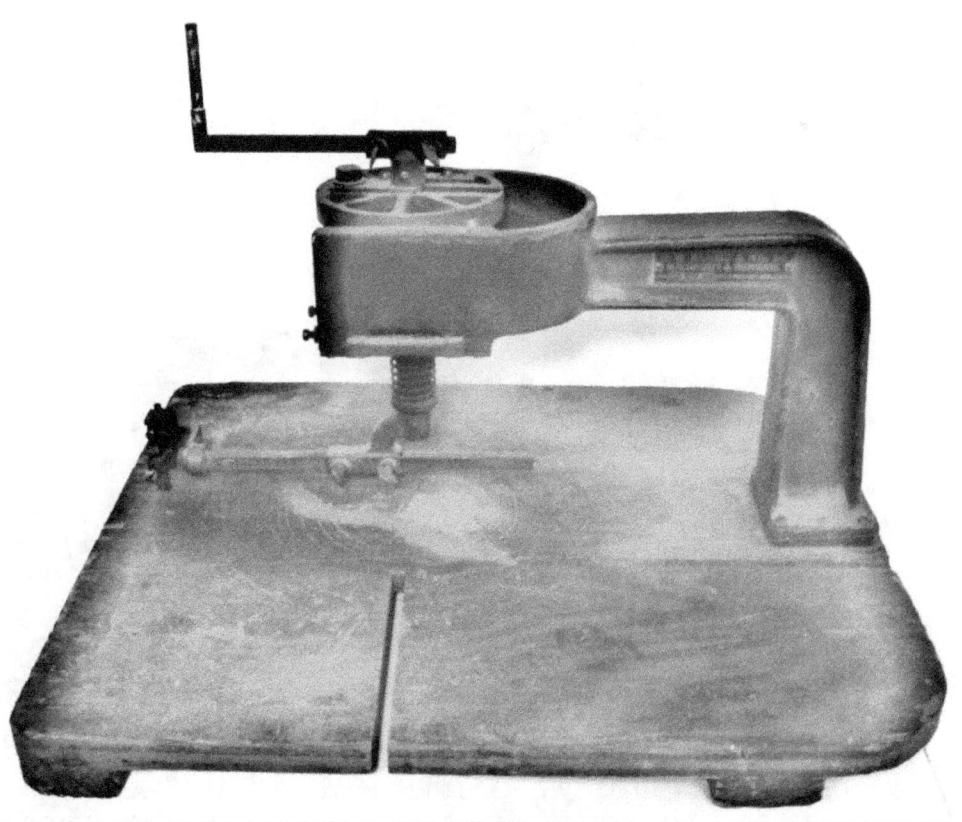

14. KLAGES, G.W. & SONS INC MACHINISTS & ENGINEERS - No. 387 - PITTSBURGH, PA USA - wood base: 17 ½" X 15 ¼" X 1 ½" - 8" steel beam with brass "gimble" cutter attachment - crank handle wood knob missing - maroon paint on heavy steel cantilever arm

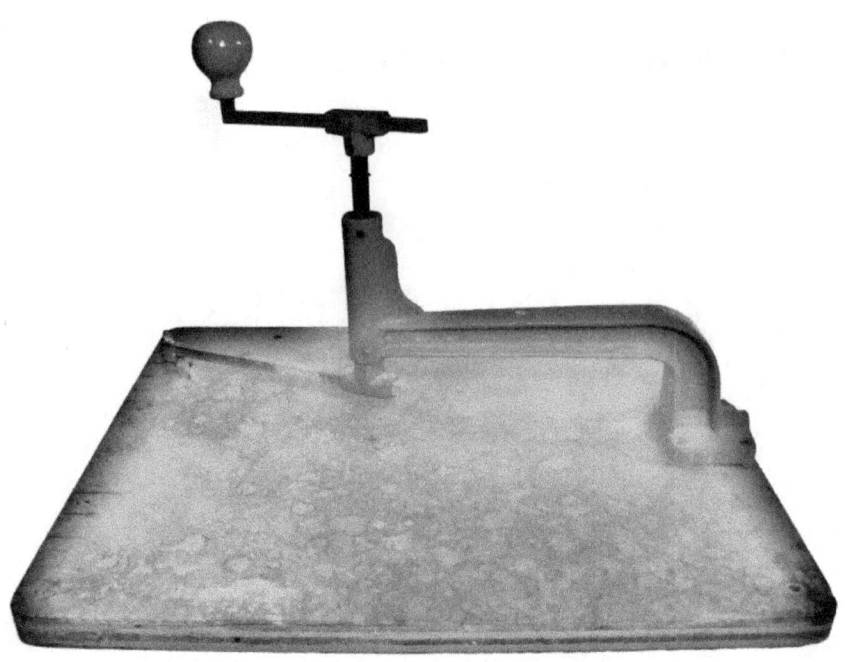

15. RED DEVIL GLASS CUTTER & TOOLS, IRVINGTON N.J. U.S.A. cast into heavy cast iron cantilever arm - plywood base: 18 3/8" X 15 3/8" X ¾" with a 1/8" fiberboard surface - 5/16" square 8" steel beam with scale

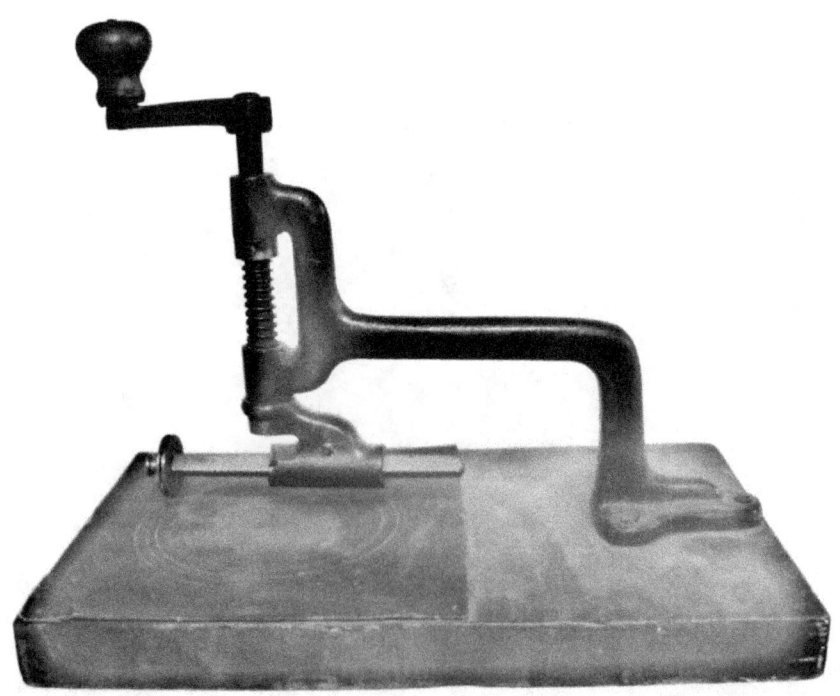

16. RUSSELL, JOHN, CUTLERY CO. TURNER FALLS, MASS. ALEX ROWLAND PATENT on 6-wheel turret on end of 5" brass beam 5/16" square with scale - ALEX ROWLAND PATENT NEW YORK, N.Y. , U.S.A.(stamped into wood base) 7 ¼" X 12 ½" X 1 1/8" - AD label glued to bottom of base

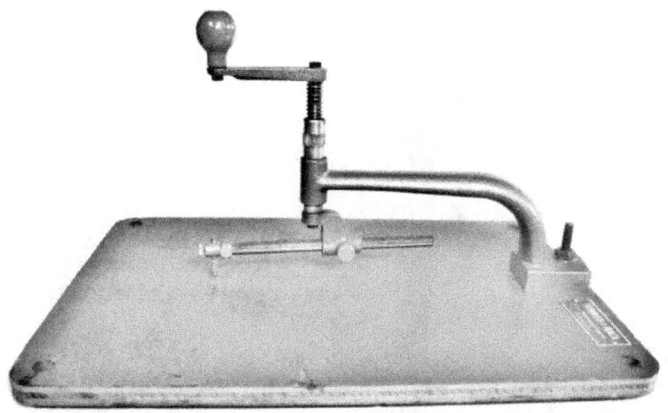

17. SOMMER & MACA - glass manufacturing company - CHICAGO 50, ILL. On an aluminum label - VERIBOR (stamped into wood knob's aluminum arm - *Silberschnitt* stamped into reverse of 6-wheel steel hex. turret at end of brass beam – flat on top with scale - plywood base: 19 ½" X 14 ½" X ¾"

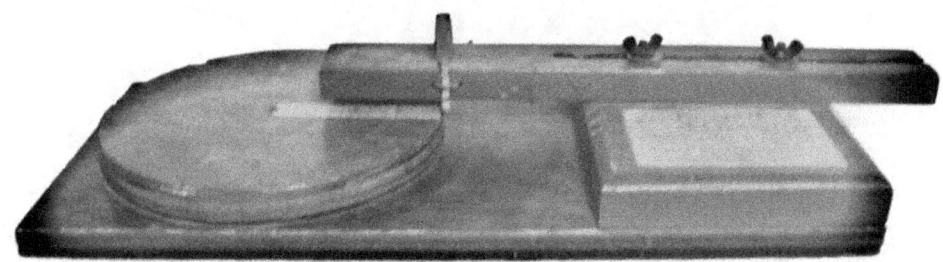

18. TRU-CUT - CIRCULAR CUTTER CUTS 1" to 8" DIAM. H.I. MacDONALD, 1119 MONTELLO ST. BROCTON, MASS. - plywood base 18" X 8" X ¾" - glass cutter is a cut off non-mag. standard basic style -scale is inlaid on rotating 8" diam. table - natural wood finish

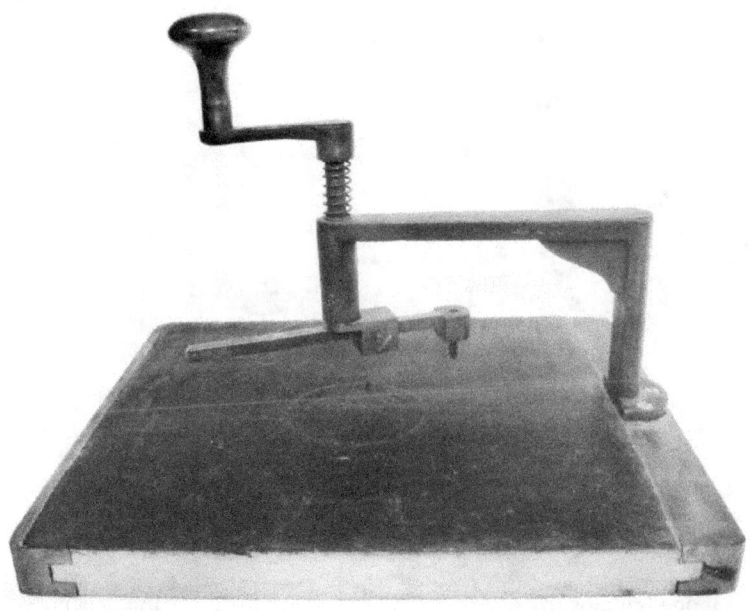

19. No ID - wood base is tongue & grooved 14" X 16" X 1 ¼" with a 3/32" black leatherette covering - Cutter is a cut off standard basic style stamped L-06 at the end of a 7 ½" steel beam ¾" square - no scale

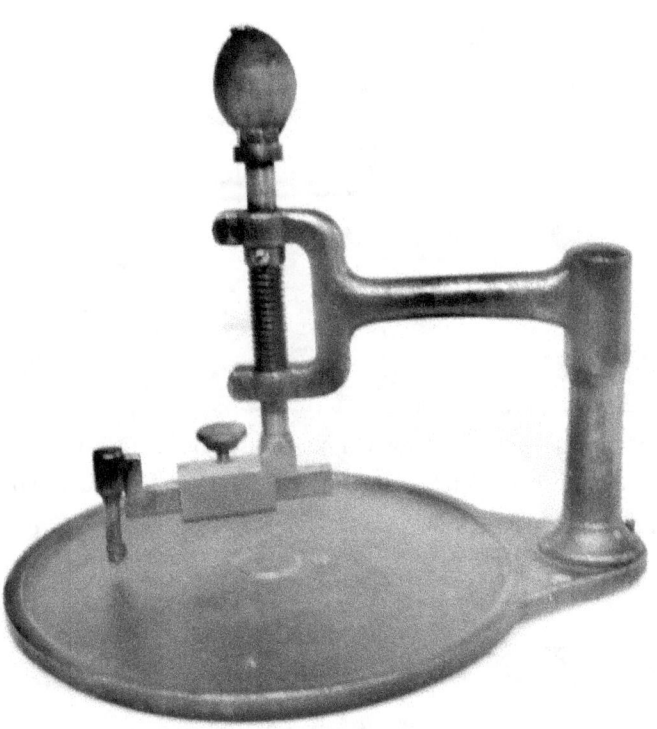

20. No ID - this cast iron unit has a 6 ¼" diam. base with a 5 ¾" diam. recessed area(pad missing) - the post is both screwed and pinned in place - the cutter arm and holder are cast as one piece - cutter wheel is pinned with a wire loop - no scale

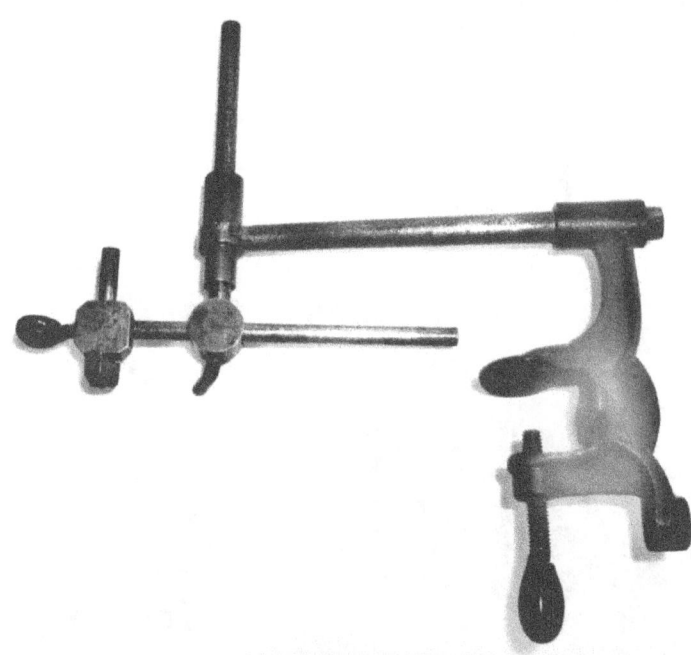

21. No ID - This model clamps to edge of work table using the table top as a base for the glass to be cut - no scale - steel cutter beam is 5 ¾" X ¼" diam. Glass cutter that fits is a brass French crescent style marked – FRANCE

D. WOOD KNOB(S)

22. PAULSON stamped on underside of 11 ½" X 1/8" square steel beam with scale - blonde wood knobs - single wheel bent wire axle

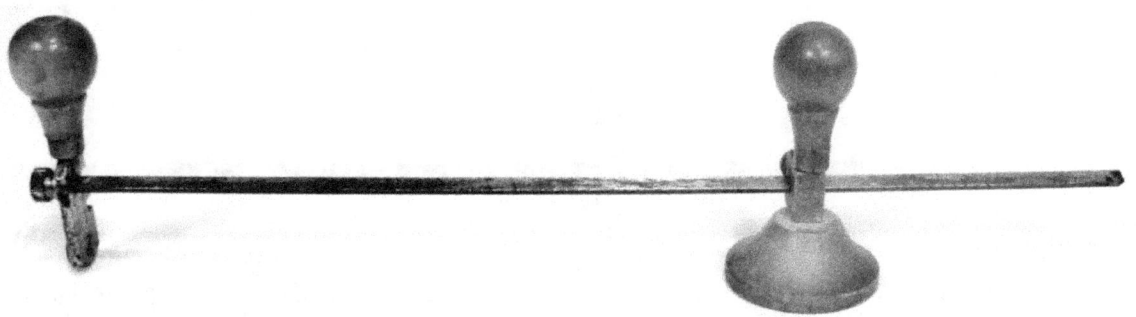

23. SINGER – No. 1 – MADE IN U.S.A. stamped on 6-wheel turret head - 11 ½" X 1/8" square steel beam with scale - blonde wood knobs

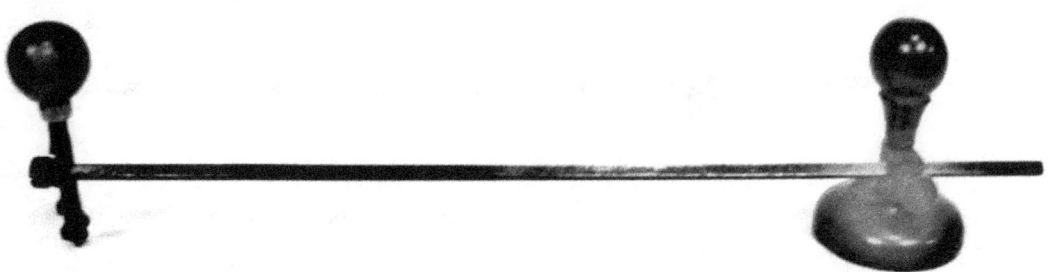

24. No ID - 11 ½" X 1/8" square steel beam with scale - mahogany color knobs smaller than knobs on XV-22 above

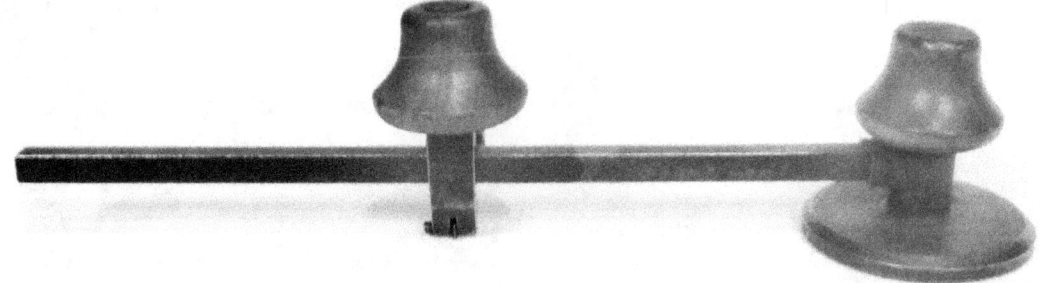

25. KLAGES, G.W., PITTSBURG - 392 stamped on end of 6 ¾" X ¼" steel beam with scale - single wheel - screw as axle - red paint on 1.92" diam. flat steel base - pagoda roof style fruitwood knobs

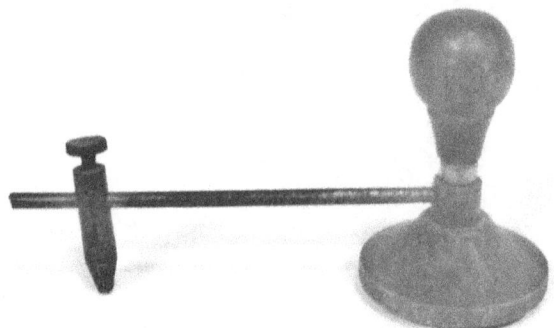

26. IMCO in a diamond on top of same style single wheel cutter unit as XV-27 below - 4 ¾" X 1/8" diam. steel beam - no scale - fruitwood knob and 1.7" diam. wood base with black rubber pad almost like the FLETCHER "LITTLE BEAUTY" in the 1935 Catalog No. 226

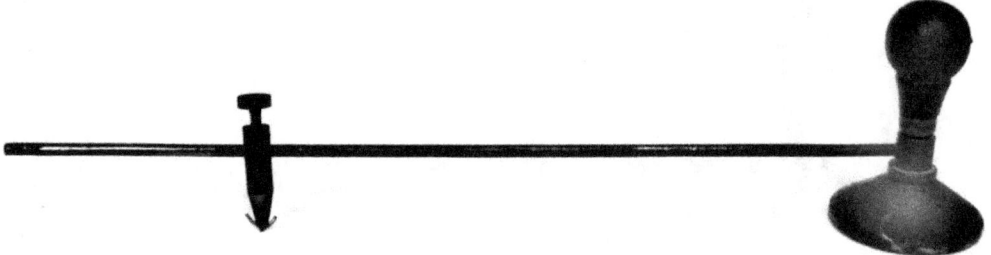

27. RED DEVIL stamped on side of same style single wheel cutter unit as XV-26 above - 10" X 1/8" diam. steel beam - no scale - mahogany finish on knob and 1.75" wood base with black rubber pad

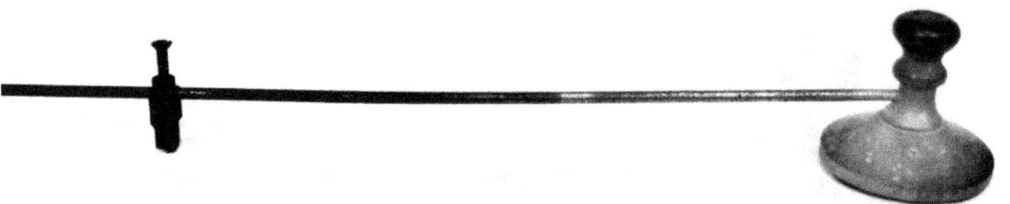

28. No ID - 10" X 1/8" diam. steel rod - no scale - single wheel steel cutter unit is square - 1 7/8" diam. wood base - red felt pad

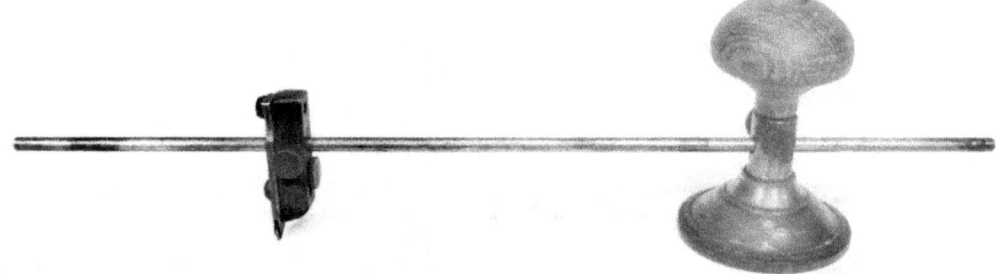

29. No ID - 12 ½" X 3/16" diam. steel rod - no scale - a three breaker, split head glass cutter is attached to a 3/8" X 3/8" X 1 5/8" brass cutter unit by two screws - the walnut finish 2 ¼" diam. wood base is beaded at the edge of base and at top next to the brass collar - the 1 5/8" diam. unfinished wood knob looks out of place - a steel weight is recessed in the base - no pad

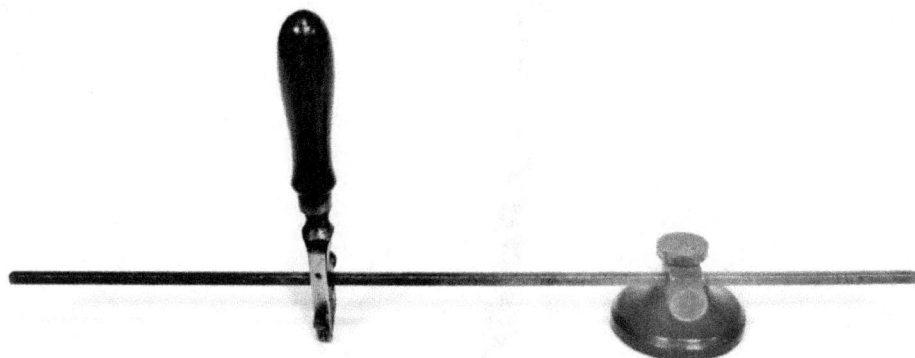

30. PATENT stamped on plate atop a two breaker cutter head that holds axle in place(see XV-33) - ¼" plated brass ferrule and a very nice 2" walnut handle - No other ID - 10 ½" X 3/16" square steel beam with scale - 1 5/8" wood base with mahogany finish and black rubber pad

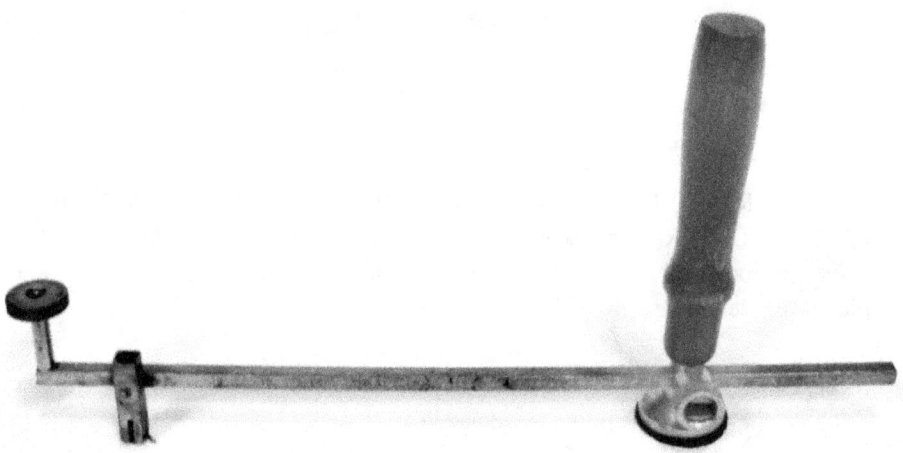

31. No ID - 9" X .18" square steel beam with Scale - single wheel on a 1" X ¼" square steel cutter unit riveted to the beam with no evidence of bolt hole to hold wheel axle as in cutter below - dark blue painted wood handle 3 ¾" tall above the beam - 1" black rubber pad

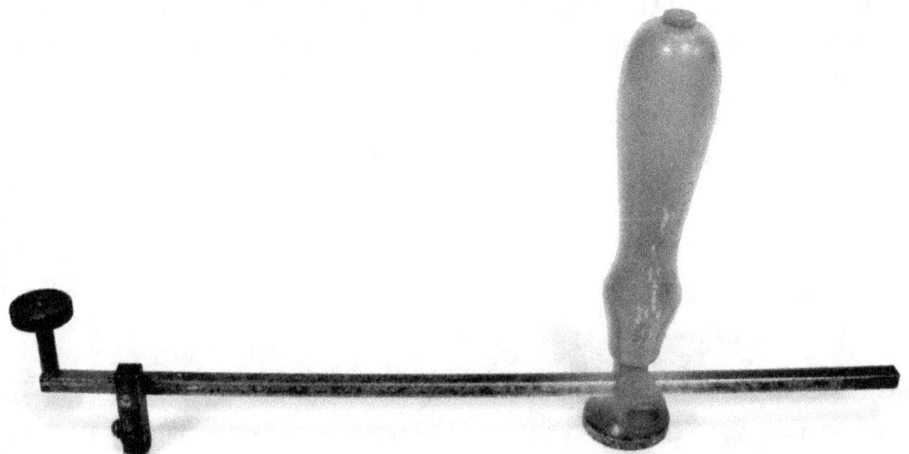

32. No ID - same as XV-31 above except for a slightly different shaped handle, a threaded brass knurled plug on top for extra wheel storage and a round head bolt holds the bent end of wheel axle – pad missing - one like this was listed on eBay in 2006 as a W. M. Barrett, not a W. L. Barrett.

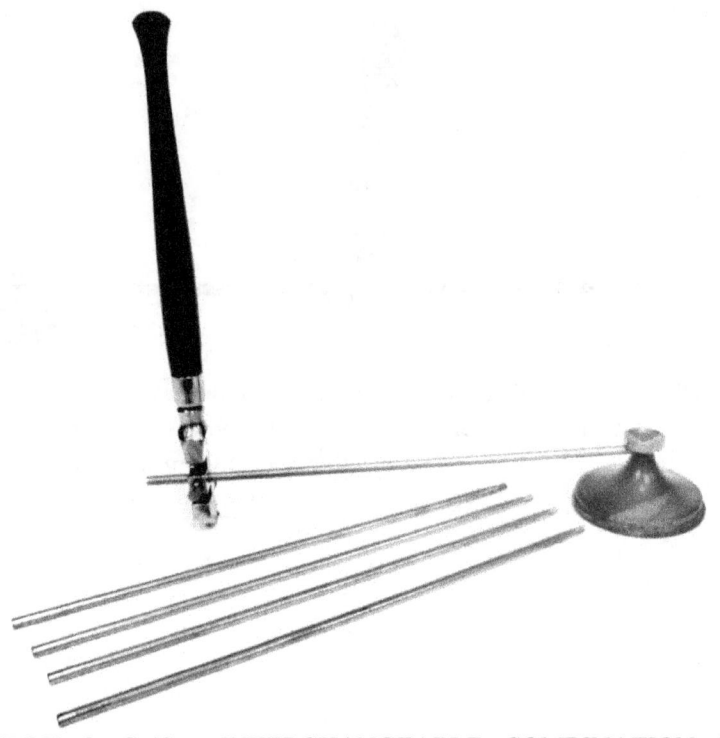

33. FLETCHER, TERRY & Co'S.   INTERCHANGEABLE COMBINATION STRAIGHT AND
    CIRCLE CUTTER(on black box only) - See XV-30 for same cutter head - five extra 6-inch long
    extension rods - 1 ½" diam. walnut base with grey rubber ring pad - plated 2-breaker head - .4"
    plated ferrule - glass cutter 5.9"

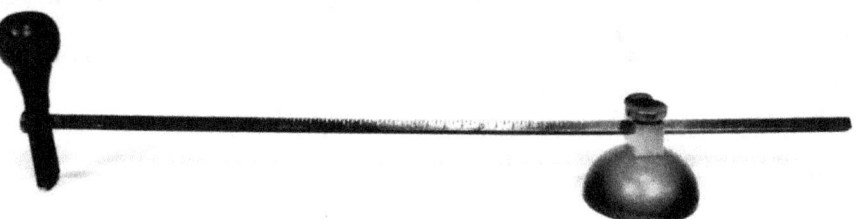

34. RED DEVIL - TRADE MARK – S. & H. Co. N.Y. U.S.A. on top of knurled screw holding 1.7"
    diam. solid steel pivot to the 12 ½ X 3/16" square steel beam with two scales - bent wire holds single
    cutter wheel

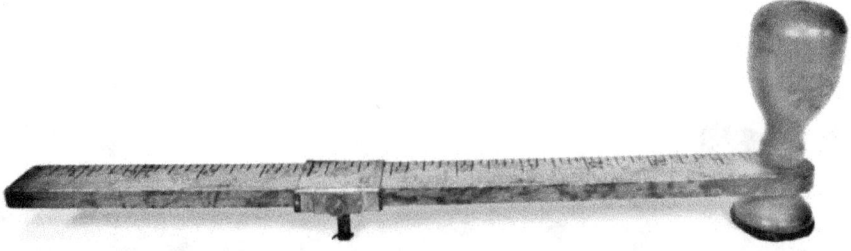

35. No ID - PAT'D FEB. 8, '98 stamped on brass scale slide with 5/8" X .2" diam. cutter unit attached
    on bottom - none of the 289 patents of this date referred to this apparatus, however, this is almost the
    same brass slide as used on a glass cutting board unit with U.S. Pat. No. 1,115,333 dated 10-7-1914 -
    The beam is a 12" X 1" X .3" wood ruler - maple knob & base are 3 ½" tall – black pad

E. METAL KNOBS

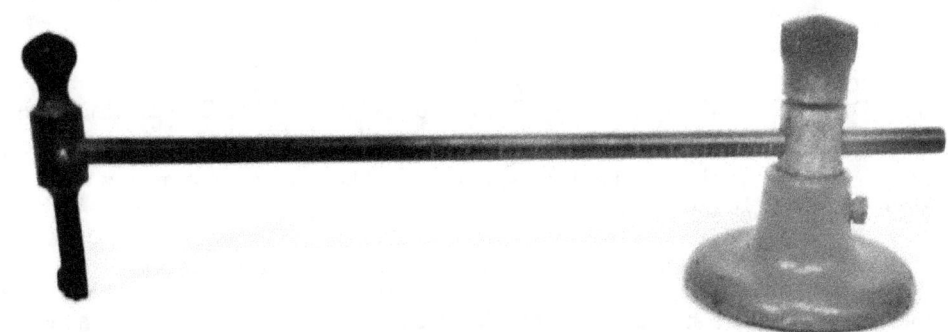

36. M – F – Co MADE IN USA on cutter head - 6 ½" X 3/16" diam. steel beam flat on top with scale on round side - bent wire for wheel axle - cork pad on 1.8" diam. red steel pivot base - 2"tall

37. M. F. Co. GREENFIELD, MASS. U.S.A. on cutter head - 12 ½" X 3/16" diam. steel beam flat on top with scale on round side - bent wire for wheel axle - black rubber pad on 1.8" diam. red steel pivot base - 2 ¼" tall

38. GLAZIER'S I.M. CO. on end of 9" X 3/16" diam. steel beam flat on top with scale on round side - cutter wheel held in place by a pivoting piece of sheet steel - pad missing on 1.8" diam. flattened red steel base - knurled knob below the top pivot secures the pivot to the beam - 2" tall

39. GOODELL-PRATT CO GREENFIELD, MASS. U.S.A. on cutter head - 6 ½" X 3/16" diam. steel beam flat on top with scale on round side - bent wire for wheel axle - black rubber pad on 1 ¾" orange/red steel pivot base - 2.3" tall

40. GOODELL-PRATT Co. SHELBURNE FALLS, MASS on cutter head - 6 ½" X 3/16" diam. steel beam flat on top with scale on side - bent wire for wheel axle - black rubber pad on 1 ¾" diam. red steel pivot base - 2.2" tall

41. G P Co in crest on cutter head - 11 ½" X 3/16" diam. steel beam flat on top with scale on side - bent wire for wheel axle - black rubber pad on 1.8" diam. red steel pivot base - 2.2" tall

42. GOODELL TOOL C SHELBURNE FALLS MASS. U.S.A. on flat side of cutter head - the high knurled knob allows the cutter beam rod to adjust - the low knurled knob keeps it in alignment -- bent wire for wheel axle - pivot arrangement same as XV-38 except this one has a knurled knob on 1.8" diam. red steel base that controls a steel point that extends just past the plane of the base - pad missing - 2.15" tall

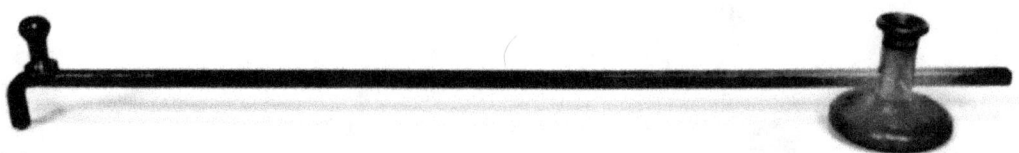

43. RED DEVIL N0 263 cast on red 1 ½" diam. pivot base - MADE IN U.S.A. stamped into top of 12"
X ¼" square steel beam near the cutter unit end with scale on side of beam - cutter wheel is attached
by a bent sheet metal piece that inserts into a round hole in the bent section of the beam - pivot is 1
3/8" tall with black rubber pad

44. RED DEVIL NO 263 cast on red 1 ½" diam. pivot base - FORD script logo is stamped into top of
the 12" X ¼" square steel beam with scale on side of beam - cutter wheel is attached with a bent wire
that also holds a spare wheel -   pivot is 1 3/8" tall with a black rubber pad

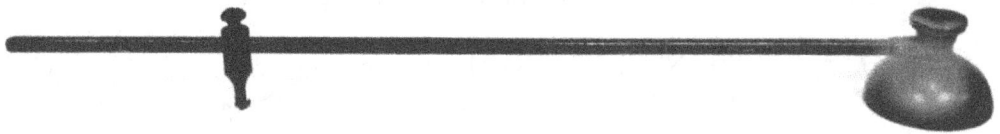

45. No ID - wrap around swivel & hinged 12" X ¼" square steel beam with scale on top - solid black
hemi-sphere pivot base 1.7' diam. - bent wire axle holds wheel -

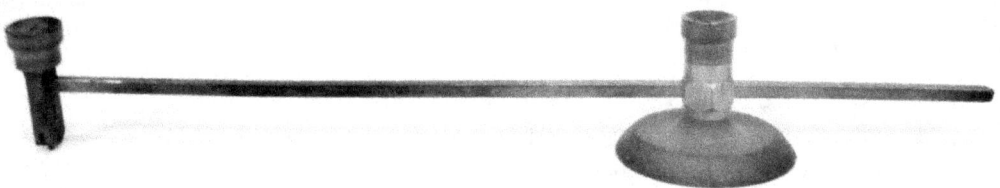

46. MADE IN U.S.A. stamped into bottom of 12 ½" X ¼" square brass beam with scale on top - concave
plated brass knobs atop both the 1 ¾" tall pivot unit & 1 ¾" tall cutter unit - cutter wheel is attached
by a bent wire secured in grooves on either side if the 1.2" X .5" X .2" steel cutter head - 2.35" diam.
steel pivot base has the wrinkly black paint finish - pad missing

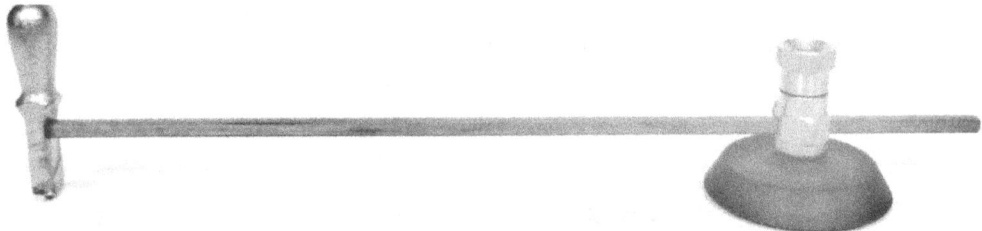

47. No ID - 12" X ¼" square brass beam with scale on top - rough cast plated cutter head unit 2 ½" tall
& .6" diam. at top - cutter wheel is attached by same type sheet metal piece (as in XV-43) pushed into
a hole in the bottom of cutter unit - 2 3/8" diam. .4" thick pivot base with the wrinkly black paint
finish - the top part of the pivot unit is same as XV-46 above except it is made of aluminum - 1.9"
tall with black rubber pad

48. Same as XV-47 above except the beam is plated brass & the rough cast cutter head unit is .5" diam. at
top & wrinkly black base is .3" thick

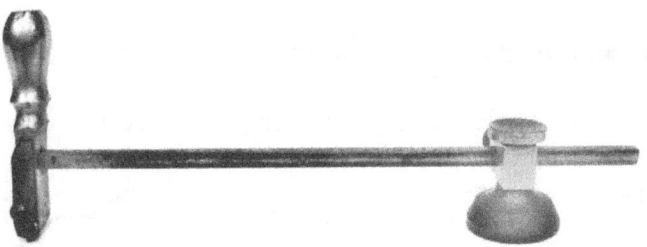

48 –A. No ID – 6.5" X 1/8" square plated brass beam with scale on top – 1" diam. brass pivot base with
black   pad missing – cutter wheel held in place by bolted on steel block – 6.8"

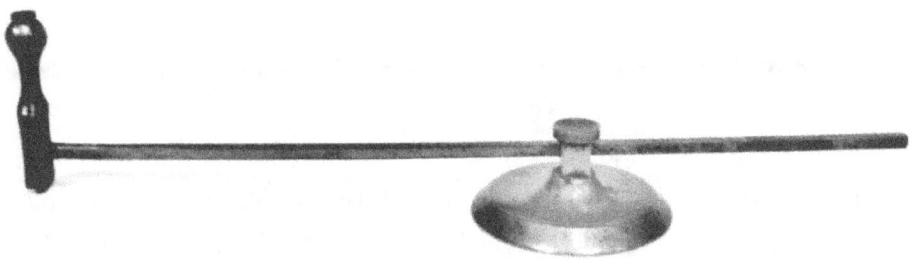

49. No ID - 11 ½" X ¼" square plated brass beam with scale on top - 2.6" diam. plated steel base with
pad missing - pivot unit is 1.2" tall - steel cutter unit has a knurled screw cap at top that opens for
extra wheel storage - cutter wheel is held in place by a bent wire held in place with grooves on either
side of the 2.4" tall unit

50. FRANCE stamped on end of 8" X 3/16" square plated(brass?) beam with top side scale in cms - .4"
diameter knurled knob atop all non-mag. 1 ½" high pivot unit except for internal screw - pivot base
is 1 ½" diam. - knurled steel screw adjusts non-mag. cutter unit - black rubber pad

51. No ID - same as XV-50 above except knob atop pivot is not knurled

52. No ID - 8" X .2" triangular plated (brass?) beam with top side scale in cms. - .65" knurled knob atop
non-mag. 1.4" tall pivot with a 1 ¼" diam. base with red rubber pad

53. No ID - 8' X .2" square steel beam with top side scale in cms. - cutter unit is aluminum(wing nut is
most likely not original) - 1 ½" high pivot unit is aluminum with a flat knurled on top - plated steel
base is 1 3/8" diam. with black rubber pad

54. No ID - 17 ½" X ¼" square steel beam with scale in cms. - brass cutter unit is same but smaller than XV-50, 51, & 52 - 1.3" tall pivot unit is all brass with flat knurled knob atop - pivot base is 1.05" diam. with pad missing

F. FLIP HEAD PIVOT UNIT - SUCTION CUP BASE

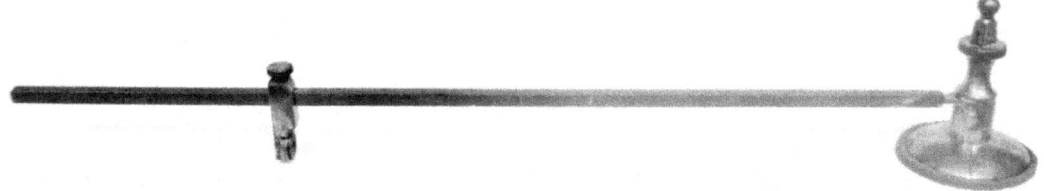

55. *Silberschnitt* (on side of brass cutter unit with large number 6-wheel steel turret) - 15" X ¼" square brass beam with scale in inches - all brass pivot unit 2 7/8" tall & base 2" diam. - red rubber pad

56. *Silberschnitt* (on end of black plastic cutter unit with a large number hex 6-wheel steel turret 8" X ¼" brass beam - pivot unit same as XV-55 above

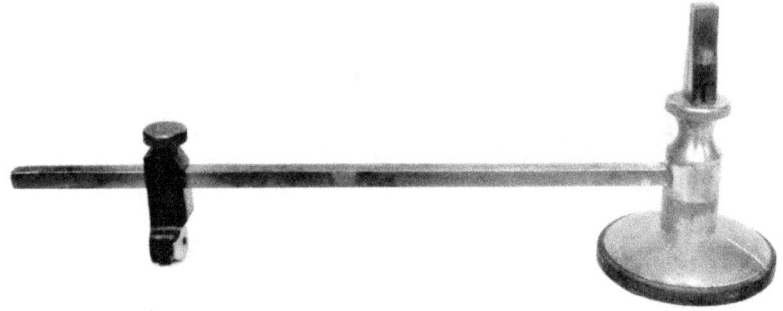

57. *Silberschnitt* (on end of black plastic cutter unit with a large number hex 6-wheel steel turret 8" X ¼" brass beam - all brass pivot unit except the black plastic flip head - black rubber pad

58. *Silberschnitt* (on end of black painted aluminum cutter unit with 1 ¼" diam. plastic ball knob on top and a large number slotted hex 6-wheel steel turret - 8" X ¼" square brass beam with scale in cms. on top & scale in inches on a side - MADE IN GERMANY on side of beam - 3 1/8" tall pivot unit has black plastic flip head & U shape black plastic swivel the rest is brass with 2.1" diam. base - black rubber pad

G. 6 – WHEEL TURRET

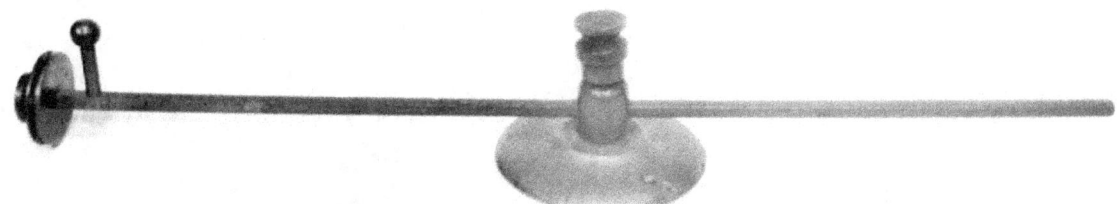

59. ALEX. ROWLAND PATENT - JOHN RUSSELL CUTLERY Co., TURNERS FALLS, MASS. on the center of 2 ½" X 1 7/8" high brass pivot base - ALEX. ROWLAND N.Y. PAT. JAN. 22 '89 on face of the brass 1 ½" diam. 6-wheel turret with large numbers at end of 12 ½" X 3/16" square brass beam with scale in inches on top - knurled wheel on pivot unit adjusts pivot slide - pad missing

60. Same as XV-59 above except data on 6-wheel turret reads: JOHN RUSSELL CUTLERY Co. TURNERS FALLS, MASS. ALEX. ROWLAND PATENT. - knurled wheel on pivot unit is shorter thus unit is only 1 5/8" tall - pad missing

61. ALEX. ROWLAND, NEW YORK, N.Y. U.S.A. - PAT. JAN. 22,'89 on top center of 2 ½" diam. brass pivot base - ALEX. ROWLAND N. Y. PAT. JAN. 22, '89 on face of 6-wheel brass turret at end of 12 1/2 " X 3/16" brass beam with a scale in inches mounted through the 1 1/8" high pivot unit at 45 degrees - an off-set thumb screw adjusts the slide - black rubber pad

62. Same as -61 above except data on center of pivot base reads: ALEX. ROWLAND PAT. JAN. 22, '98

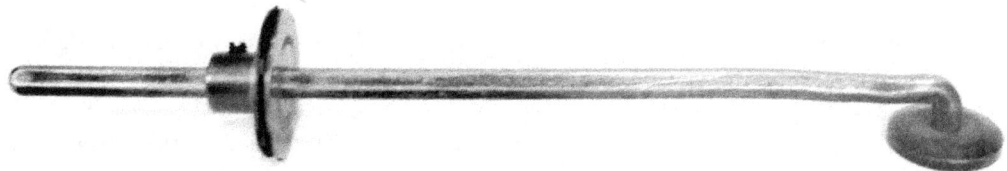

63. JOHN RUSSELL CUTLERY Co. TURNERS FALLS, MASS. ALEX. ROWLAND PATENT on face of 6-wheel brass turret soldered to a brass ring with a set screw for adjusting slide - no numbers on turret - 7" X ¼" hex steel beam with no scale - brass pivot base is .9" diam. - pad missing

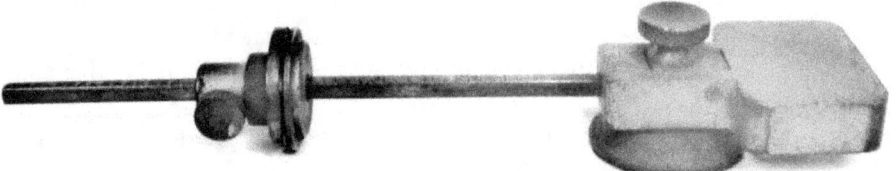

64. PAT. AUG. 1, 1922 - PAT. JULY 4, 1922 atop the brass plated non-mag. 2" X 1 ½" X 9/19" counterweight from which the 6 ½" X 3/16" square brass beam with inch scale on top protrudes & held in place by a set-screw - the 1.6" diam. non-mag. base pivot unit is hinged in the counterweight - no data on the 6-wheel brass turret which locks with a knurled threaded ring toward the knurled set-screw which controls the slide - black rubber pad

65. EUREKA PATENTED JULY 4, 22 - AUG. 1, 22 SOMMER & MACA CHICAGO atop the plated 2" X 1 ½" X 9/16" non-mag. counterweight from which the 12 ½" X 3/ 16" square plated brass beam with scale on the side protrudes & held in place by a set-screw - the 1.6" diam. non-mag. base is hinged in the counterweight - no data on the plated 6-wheel turret which locks with a knurled threaded ring toward the wing nut which controls the slide - black rubber washer like pad

65-A. Same as XV-64 & 65 above except marked: EUREKA PATENTED JULY 4, 22 – AUG. 1, 22 CARL F. DOERR NEW YORK atop the counterweight. This sold on the internet to another collector in Nov. 2010.

H.   VITREX STYLE - See also Category IX "French" Crescent for this style glass cutter

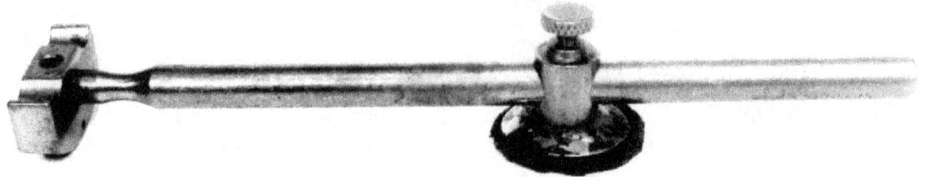

66. VITREX stamped on brass single wheel crescent head - MADE IN SWITZERLAND stamped on 3 breaker end of 5.1" long brass handle - head is threaded for either circle or straight cutter - ¾" diam. steel pivot base with black rubber pad - Box and instructions indicate sold by: VITREX (SALES) LTD 457 CALEDONIAN ROAD LONDON 17 ENGLAND (printed 12/67)

67. VITREX stamped on brass single wheel crescent head - MADE IN SWITZERLAND stamped facing the other direction than XV-66 on 3 breaker end of 5.1" brass handle - head is threaded for either circle or straight cutter - ¾" steel pivot base with white rubber pad

68. VITREX ENGLAND stamped on brass 3 wheel semi-circular head threaded for either circle or straight cutter - the end ½" of 5" long 3 breaker brass handle is knurled - ¾" diam. steel pivot base with white rubber pad

69. Same as XV-68 above except: VITREX ENGLAND is stamped upside down on the 3 wheel brass head

70. FRANCE stamped near single wheel cutter crescent head of first 3 ½" section and front end of 4" center section of 9.2" X ¼" diam. long three section plated brass handle with four breakers and screw driver on third section - pivot unit is unique in that one lifts up on the top knurled knob to engage the slide clamping mechanism - no scale -red rubber pad on 5/8" diam. brass base

71. No ID - 5 ¼" X ¼" diam. handle with scale in cms on top & a .8" 3 breaker end section plated brass - single wheel plated brass crescent head threaded for either circle or straight cutter - pivot unit is 1.2" tall with a .32" diam. ¾" diam. plated brass base with red rubber pad

72. No ID - same as XV-71 above except a 1" 3-breaker section at end of handle

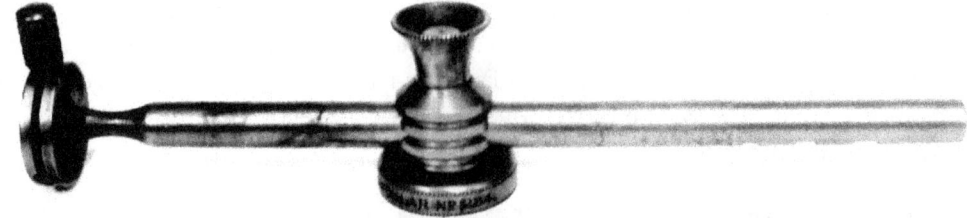

73. VITREX CIRCULAR No 234. stamped on edge of .8" diam. brass pivot base - set-screw in bottom of base controls slide on 5.2" long brass handle - no pad - 3-wheel numbered .75" diam. brass turret with two holes threaded for using as either circle or straight cutter

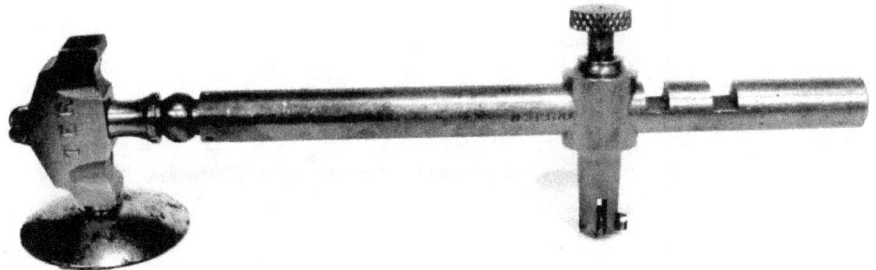

74. TER stamped into ornate style French crescent brass head with single wheel for straight cuts - FOREIGN stamped on mid part of 3 ¼" brass handle section with 3 breakers that unscrews for extra wheel storage - 4 ¼" long extra brass extension section - pivot unit starts with holes on either side of head where one of two different size (.75" & .9" diam.) base plates may be inserted - the single wheel circle cutter unit slides along the brass handle

75. A-B-C (with arrow through) inside an oval on face of ornate style French crescent brass head - ID on box: UTENSILI ABC with arrow in an oval - rest is same as XV-74 above

I. OTHER

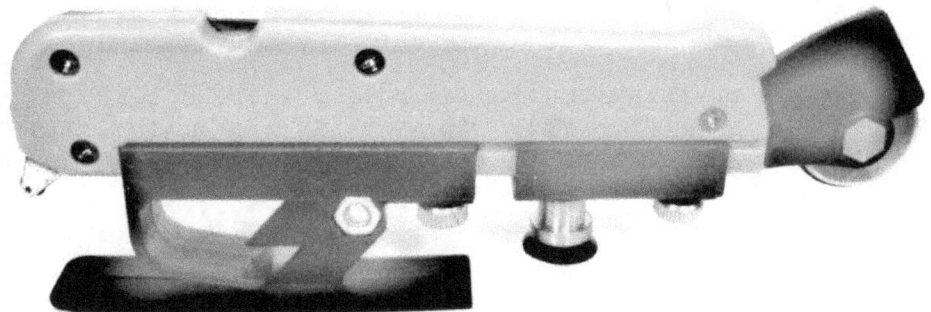

76. No ID on tool - MIRACLE GLASS & TILE CUTTER on box - green plastic body, black plastic attachments - overall length 10 ¼"

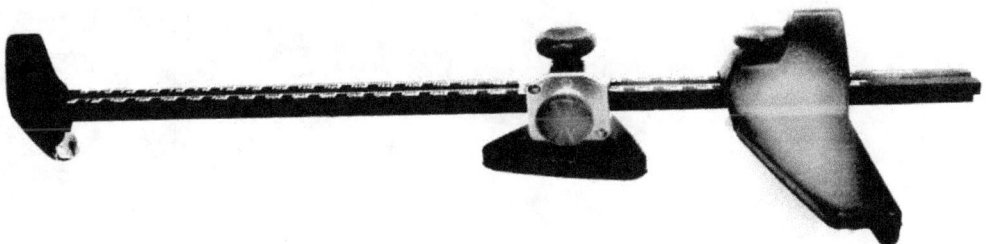

77. GLASTAR cast into non-mag. body of pivot unit and on black plastic straight edge unit - 12 ½" X 5/8" X 3/8" Black plastic beam has both cm and inch scales in white paint - PAT. PENDING

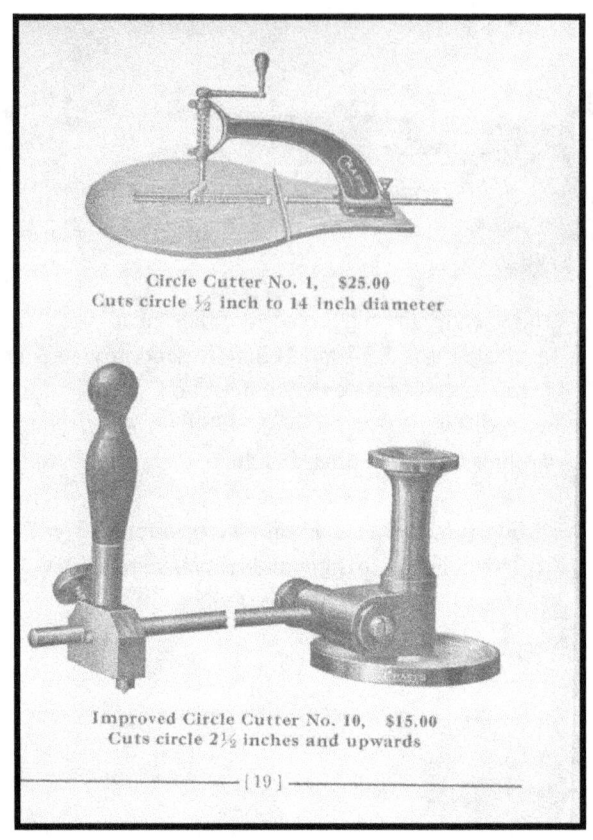

Circle Cutter No. 1, $25.00
Cuts circle ½ inch to 14 inch diameter

Improved Circle Cutter No. 10, $15.00
Cuts circle 2½ inches and upwards

[19]

Excerpt from page 19: <u>DIAMONDS USED IN TOOLS,</u> ARTHUR A. CRAFTS & CO. 125 SUMMER STREET, BOSTON, MASS., U.S.A., EARNSHAW PRESS CORPORATION, BOSTON, 1921
No glass cutters marked " CRAFTS " have been known by the author in the past 30 plus years.

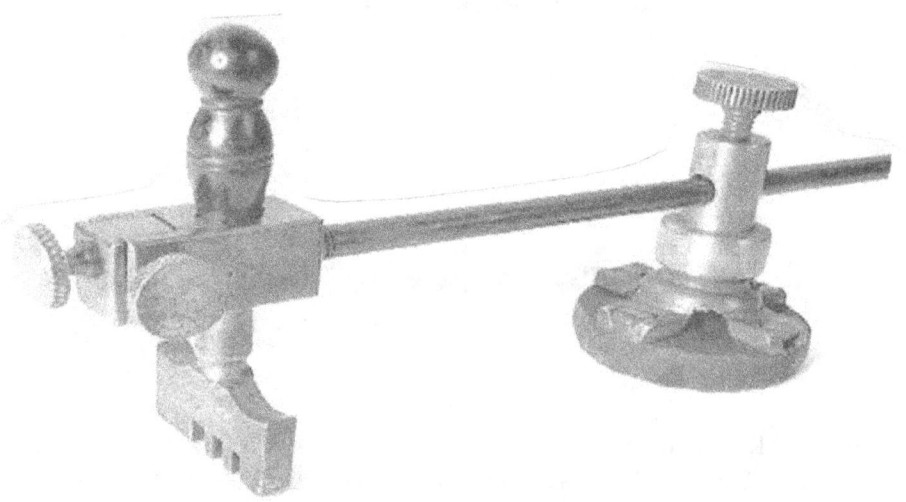

Picture of a circle cutter bought off eBay for another collection in 2002

PH SINSZ - BALTIMORE - PATD SEPT 7, 75 THIS SIDE TO RULER

CATEGORY XVI OPTICAL LENS CUTTER

There is quite a variety of designs for these lens cutters as evidenced by the three shown here, the twelve additional known in other collections and the 27 U.S. Patents listed below.

607,009	813,459	1,122,247	1,456,672	1,581,883	2,246,055	2,774,188
673,988	1,135,507	1,243,145	1,465,366	1,638,063	2,341,201	2,778,115
696,168	1,176,707	1,385,732	1,459,369	1,997,561	2,522,818	2,818,651
772,783	1,186,254	1,427,052	1,574,989	2.044,577	2,732,623	

Price range $40 to $300

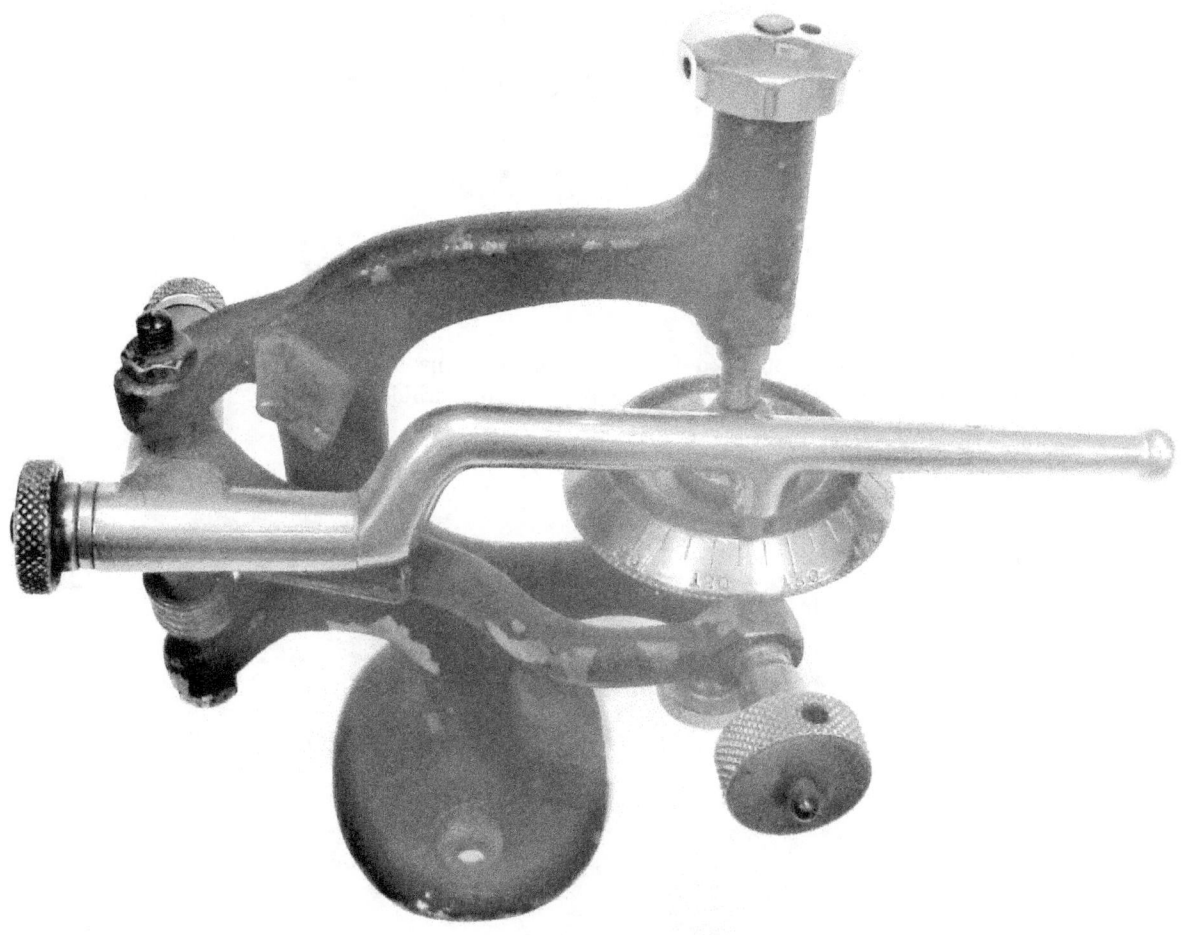

1.   No ID - 76 stamped on bottom of brass base - frame is brass painted with black stipple finish (another on internet stamped 107) - the lever arm is either stainless steel or plated brass - diamond point cutter - 6" high by 5" wide

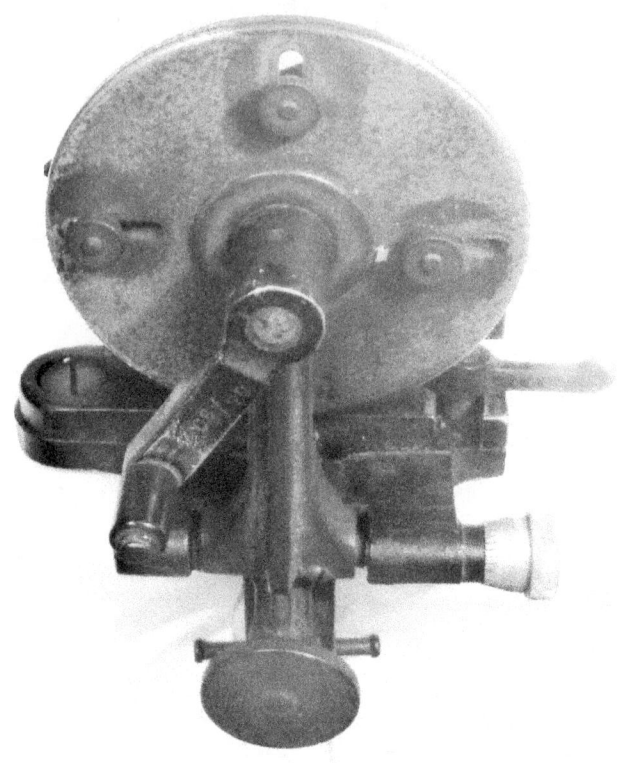

2. No ID except 1008/79 stamped into steel handle - clamps to edge of table or counter top - aluminum and steel construction - 9" high by 6" wide by 4" deep - carbide cutter

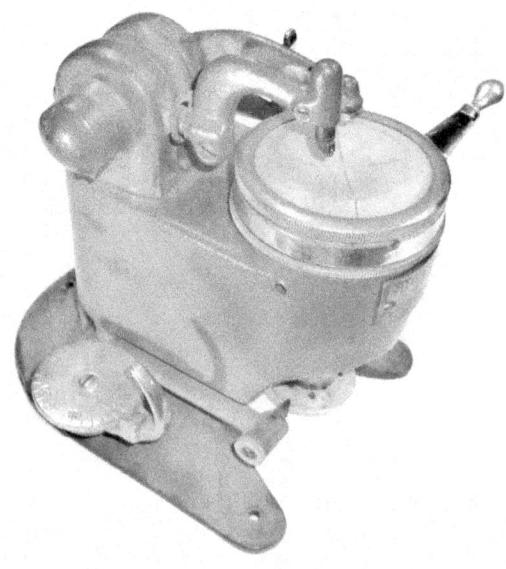

3 SHURON OPTICAL COMPANY, INC., GENEVA, N.Y., U.S.A. - SHURON 82A No. 1765 - PATENT No. 1,997,561 - wheel cutter - all blue painted steel construction except for dial, handle, and lens holding units -   8" high by 7" wide by 7.5" deep. Note: Arm at upper left was broken off before a very nice repaint job. Three holes on base for mounting to table top

CATEGORY XVII   WALL & BOARD

This category is comprised of both wall mounted and table top units. Three known owned by others are listed below.

    A.   C & H - Model 210-48 - 48"

    B.   Keeton; MAT, CARDBOARD, and GLASS CUTTER - 48"

    C.   PHILLIPS, F.C., Stroughton, Mass.. - Pat. # 1,495,523 - base: 25" long by 5" wide – adjustable to 23" - cutter wheels on both top and bottom of glass sheet.

Four wall and table top units in this category are shown following the 68 U.S. Patents pulled for this Category.

33,380	1,115,333	1,720,883	2,534,775	3,253,756	4,187,755	4,709,488
87,626	1,117,736	2,013,216	2,556,757	3,439,426	4,221,150	4,871,104
295,603	1,140,143	2,058,091	2,578,919	3,537,344	4,275,633	4,881,439
453,867	1,167,254	2,058,092	2,591,828	3,787,040	4,277,889	4,890,526
507,395	1,307,844	2,078,386	2,595,862	3,800,639	4,307,643	4,939,968
599,620	1,495,523	2,155,885	2,619,775	3,812,748	4,437,376	5,169,045
635,265	1,504,696	2,174,183	2,750,647	3,903,767	4,446,768	5,535,933
728,417	1,589,910	2,174,469	2,841,163	4,057,184	4,494,444	6,202,530
752,017	1,610,547	2,254,541	3,127,680	4,098,155	4,667,555	
1,100,878	1,649,282	2,361,049	3,227,016	4,120,220	4,679,476	

Price Range: $ 20 - $250

It is interesting that U.S. Patent 1,115,333 (Oct. 27, 1914) shows the same brass slide but different glass cutter attachment means on a wood ruler as Circle Category XV-35 which gave a patent date of Feb. 8, 1898 - of which there is no relative patent subject on glass cutters or cutting board, etc.

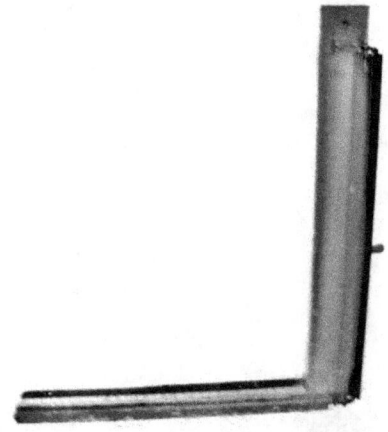

1.   MARVEL RACK MFG. CO., Inc.   MINNEAPOLIS, MINN. U.S.A. - MARVEL GLASS HOLDER Patent No. 2,013,216 printed on the 31" aluminum measuring stick attached to the 36" X 4.5" X 1.6" wood horizontal base which is attached with steel framing by bolts to the vertical arm of same size - according to the patent, a hand held glass cutter is used not like the attached sliding units on newer models like XVII-1 above - 36" X 36"

This item was also sold by FLETCHER during the period prior to 9-3-1935 as referenced by "PAT. Applied For" in FLETCHER Catalog No. 226 page 23 with date of Aug. 12, 1935 stamped inside cover.

2. FLETCHER GLASS CUTTING MACHINE(a FLETCHER innovation in 1949) - MODEL No. 495 48" wide 69 5/8" high 1957 Catalog NO. 957's also shown in 1963 Catalog No. 630 - A label on the triangular masonite support says: THE FLETCHER-TERRY CO. FORESTVILLE CONN., U.S.A. MADE IN U.S.A. PAT. No. 2,591,829 2,619,775 - A brass plaque on front of base says: W 13053 SERIAL NUMBER - IMPORTANT: This base on which the glass rests must be kept free of glass chips and other foreign material. Use only FLETCHER "GOLD TIP" Glass Cutters THE FLETCHER-TERRY COMPANY, FORESTVILLE, CONN. U.S.A.

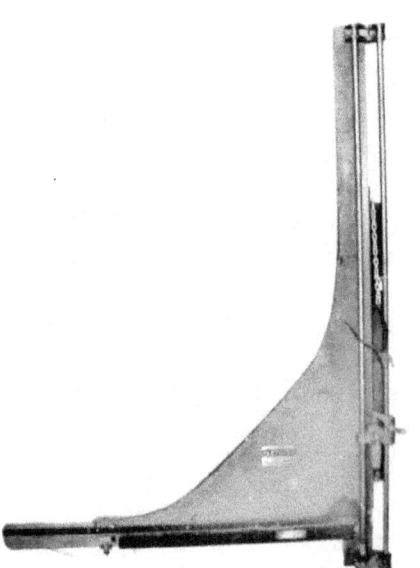

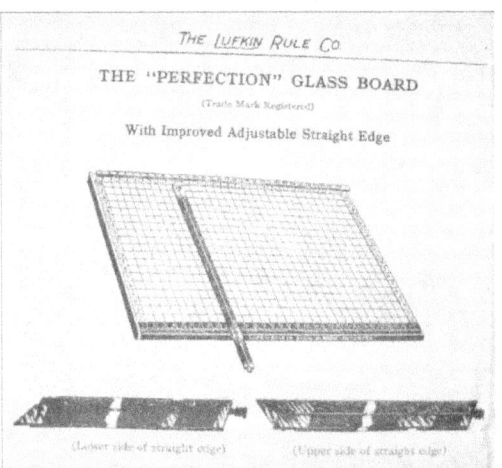

4.

3. ADEPTO TOOL - MULLEN INDUSTRIES 3291 VIVIAN DRIVE, WHEAT RIDGE, COLO. 80033 - Pat. Pending - Wood Grain Formica Working Surface - NO ID on board – info on an accompanying folder - 13" X 20"

THE LUFKIN RULE CO.

THE "PERFECTION" GLASS BOARD
(Trade Mark Registered)

With Improved Adjustable Straight Edge

(Lower side of straight edge)   (Upper side of straight edge)

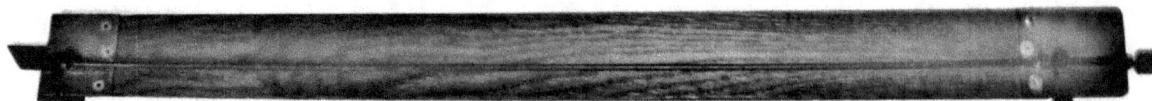

5. "PERFECTION" GLASS BOARD - (I have only the 31" long oak straight edge with brass fittings shown above). Catalog dated circa 1920 - Reprint 2005 by N-WTCA. Inset AD: 1888 Catalog. Horton. Gilmore, McWilliams & Company, Chicago, Illinois

CATEGORY XVIII NOVELTY - KITCHEN - COMBINATION

This Category: NOVELTY - KITCHEN - COMBINATION TOOL glass cutters come in a myriad of shapes, sizes, material, and styles.

There are twelve different glass cutters of this category known in other collections.

Twenty U. S. Patents for this Category are listed below:

515,973	667,914	953,806	2,019,217	4,541,176
546,669	789,103	1,423,127	2,839,110	4,905,335
601,302	858,003	1,749,442	4,161,819	5,070,563
618,426	858,532	1,770,418	4,205,438	5,438,757

The myriad of styles in this Category are divided into eight groups as follows:

A. THICK WOOD HANDLE - DUAL DISC KNIFE SHARPENER - .4" PLATED STEEL FERRULE   PRICE RANGE: $5 - $10

B. LONG WOOD HANDLE - DUAL DISC SHARPENER   PRICE RANGE: $8 - $10

C. DASHHOUND DOG STYLE   PRICE RANGE: $5 - $10

D. WIRE HANDLE - DUAL DISC KNIFE SHARPENER - BOTTLE CAP OPENER   PRICE RANGE: $5 - $12

E. WIRE OR CAST HANDLE PAT. No. 1,749,422 STYLE   PRICE RANGE: $5 - $ 15

F. ROCKET STYLE   PRICE RANGE: $8 - $20

G. DUAL DISC - MISC STYLE   PRICE RANGE: $10 - $50

H. OTHER - MISC STYLE   PRICE RANGE: $10 - $50

A. THICK WOOD HANDLE - DUAL DISC KNIFE SHARPERER - .4" PLATED STEEL FERRULE PRICE RANGE: $5- $10

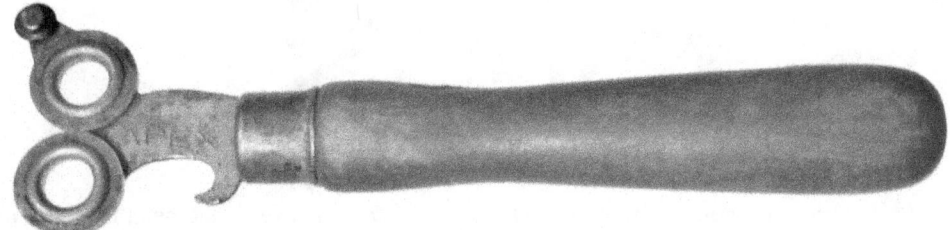

1. APEX on neck of steel head - smooth crimp on discs - red paint - 5 1/8"
2. KRISTEE – KRISTEE PRODUCTS Co. AKRON, OHIO USA on decal on red paint handle - smooth crimp on discs - 5"
3. No ID - serrated crimp on discs - light green paint - 5"
4. No ID - smooth crimp on discs - cutter wheel mounted on reverse side versus above three glass cutters - red paint - 5"
5. No ID - serrated crimp on discs - red paint - 5 1/8"
6. No ID - smooth crimp on discs - red paint - 4 15/16"
7. No ID - smooth crimp on discs - cutter wheel mounted on reverse side like XVIII-4 above - dark mahogany finish on bulbous shaped handle - 5 ½"
8. No ID - smooth crimp on discs - no bottle cap hook - light green paint - 5"

B. LONG WOOD HANDLE - DUAL DISC SHARPENER   **PRICE RANGE: $8 -$10**

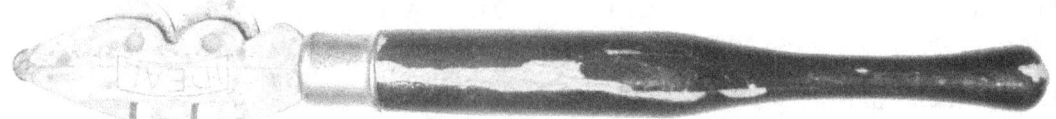

9.   IDEAL - on non-mag. head with 2 breakers on curved top - .45" steel ferrule - black paint - 6"

10. MENTONE - on non-mag. head with no breakers on curved top - .35" steel ferrule - fruitwood finish - 6 3/16"

11. No ID - non-mag. head with no breakers on straight top - .35" steel ferrule - fruitwood finish - 6 3/16"

C. DASHHOUND DOG STYLE   (flat steel)(all smooth crimp on discs except 19 which are serrated)
PRICE RANGE: $5 - $10

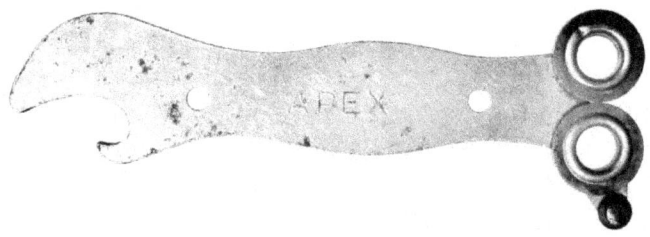

12. APEX stamped at mid-plated handle - a hole at either side of name - 4 ¼"

13. APEX stamped at mid-blued handle - a hole at either side of name - 4 ¼"

14. APEX stamped in broad letters at mid-plated handle - one hole on head side of name - 4 ¼"

15. No ID - 2 holes in same location as XVIII-12 & 13 above - 4 ¼"

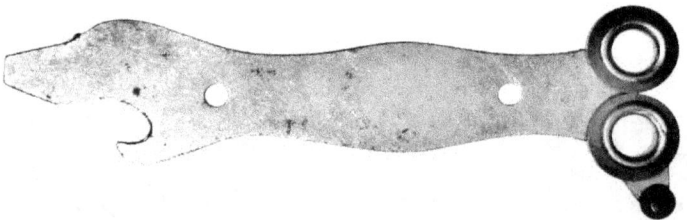

16. No ID - 2 holes in same location as XVIII-12 & 13 & 15 above - the head is a bit longer and flatter with a flat screwdriver nose than the "whale nose" shown in picture above - 4 3/8"

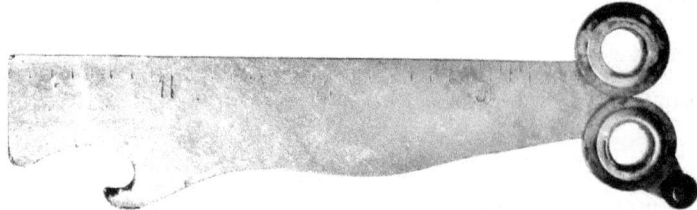

17. No ID - 3 ½" ruler along straight back with full flat square nose - no holes - 4 3/8"

18. No ID - same as XVIII-17 above except this has four holes in body - 4 3/8"

19. No ID - same as XVIII-17 & 18 above except this has two holes in body and serrated crimps on discs - 4 3/8"

D. WIRE HANDLE - DUAL DISC KNIFE SHARPENER - BOTTLE CAP OPENER
PRICE RANGE: $ 5 - $12

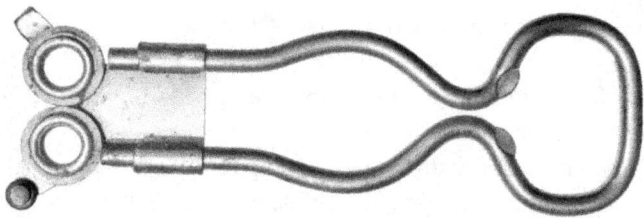

20. No ID - tapered glass cutter wheel holder - 4"
21. No ID - tapered glass cutter wheel holder - red heavy serrated crimp on discs - 4 ¾"
22. No ID - straight folded over glass cutter wheel holder - red lightly serrated crimp on discs - 5
23. No ID - straight folded over glass cutter wheel holder - red heavy serrated crimp on discs - 5"

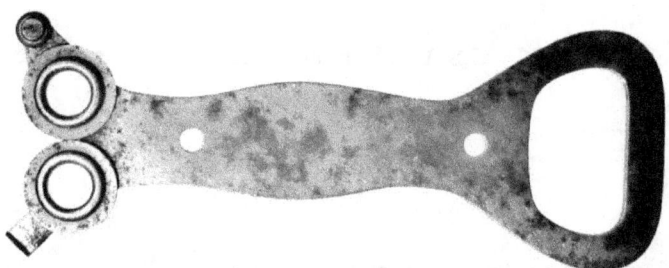

24. No ID - NOTE: not wire but flat steel - two holes - tapered glass cutter wheel holder on opposite side versus XVIII-20 picture above - 4 3/8"

E. WIRE OR CAST LOOP HANDLE - U. S. PAT. No. 1,749,422 style
PRICE RANGE: $5 - $15

Pat. No. 1,749,422 as noted in the text does not include an attached glass cutter wheel. Listed are two(XVIII-25 & 26 below) per the patent that do not have the glass cutter wheel attachment and then many different with wheel attached as shown in picture below with all having non-mag. aluminum alloy heads with knife sharpener slots.

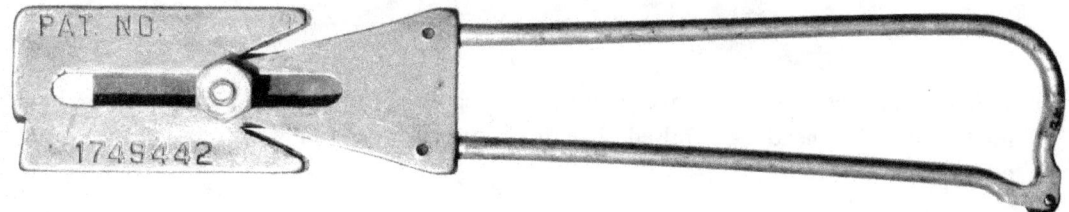

25. PATENTED MARCH 4 1930 large letters stamped or cast on head - no cutter wheel - steel loop handle - 7 1/16"
26. PAT. NO. 1749442 large letters & numbers stamped or cast on head - no cutter wheel - steel loop handle 7 1/8"
27. PAT. NO. 1749422 medium letters and numbers stamped or cast on head - cutter wheel at end of plated steel loop handle - 6 ½"
28. PAT. NO. 1749422 medium letters and numbers stamped or cast on head obverse - 1 cast on base of reverse head - cutter wheel at end of plated steel loop handle - 6 ½"
29. Same as XVIII-28 above except a 3 cast on base of reverse head
30. Same as XVIII-28 & 29 above except a 6 cast on base of reverse head

31. Same as XVIII-28 & 29 & 30 above except three raised dots cast in a recessed circle on reverse

32. APEX PAT. NO. 1749422 cast raised letters & numbers on obverse of head - a cast raised 4 on base of reverse - cutter wheel at end of steel loop handle - 6 9/16"

33. APEX same as XVIII-32 above except a 5 on base of reverse - 6 ½"

34. GRANT SHARPENER large slim letters stamped onto obverse of head - a raised 1 cast on base of reverse - cutter wheel at end of steel handle - 6 ½"

35. SCISSORS cast in raised letters on reverse with arrow pointing to a third sharpening notch near the end of head - cutter wheel at end of cast aluminum loop handle with parallel arms - 6 9/16"

36. SCISSORS cast in raised letters on reverse with arrow pointing to a third sharpening notch near end of head - MOWER cast in raised letters on reverse with arrow pointing to end of head and steel sharpening blade - cutter wheel at end of non-parallel arms cast of aluminum - Bought in a box marked ACME, Raymond Products, Toronto, Canada - 6 3/16"

37. Same as XVIII-36 above except MADE IN U.S.A. cast in raised letters on obverse base

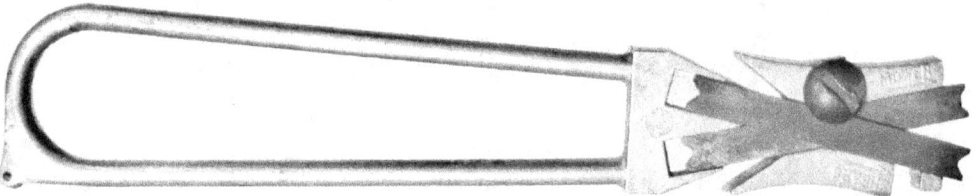

38. SHEARS (raised letters both obverse & reverse with arrow pointing to third notch near head) - MOWER (raised letters both obverse & reverse pointing to end of head) - KNIFE GUIDE (raised letters with arrows pointing to slots) - MADE IN U.S.A.(raised letters near base of head) - cutter wheel at end of non-parallel arms cast of aluminum - 6 1/8"

39. Same as XVIII-38 above except a 3 cast on reverse of head near base - 6 1/8"

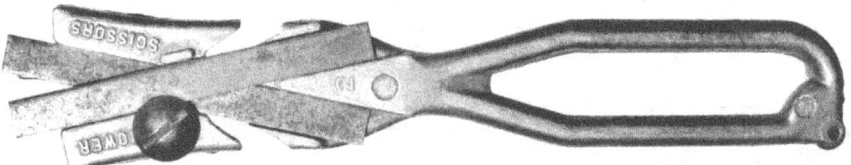

40. U.S.A. raised letters cast on obverse of base of head - SCISSORS MOWER raised letters cast on reverse of end of head - a raised 2 cast near base of head on reverse - all one piece aluminum construction - 4 15/16"

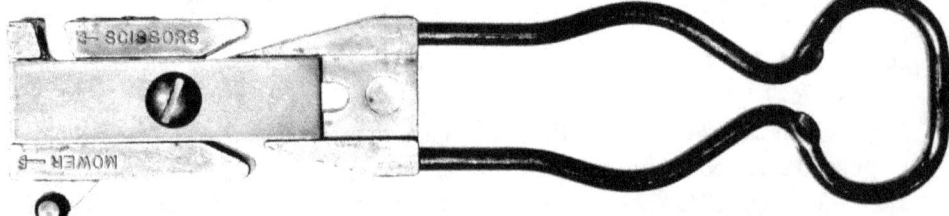

41. SCISSORS raised letters with arrow pointing to third notch near head - MOWER raised letters with arrow pointing to end of head - cutter wheel at head next to MOWER at end of cast aluminum head - shaped steel wire handle with bottle opener - 6 "

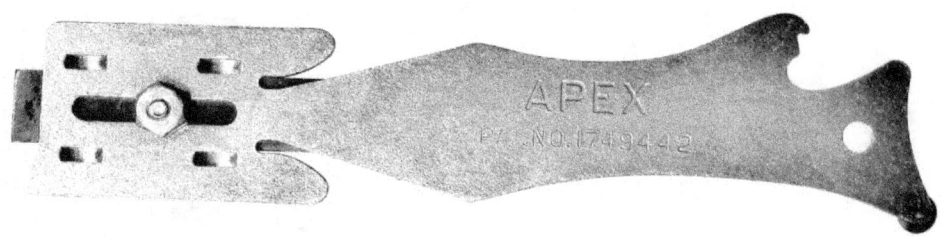

42. APEX stamped in wide letters on obverse of center of flat steel handle - PAT. No. 1749442 stamped in line letters on handle beneath APEX - look at picture upside down and envision a dogs head with cutter wheel at end of ears - the hole being an eye - the bottle cap opener being the open mouth - 5 9/16"

F.   ROCKET STYLE   all have knife sharpener per the rocket motor nozzle area
PRICE RANGE: $8 - $20

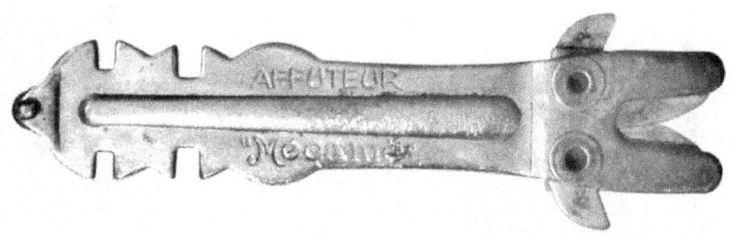

43. AFFUTEUR - "MECANIC" on both obverse and reverse - open rivets on reverse - two ply steel construction - 4"
44. No ID but exactly the same as XVIII-43 above
45. No ID - nose with cutter wheel more pointed - hump down center is wider and higher than XVIII-43 & 44 above - two ply steel construction - solid brass rivets - 4"
46. AFFUTEUR - MECANIC on both obverse & reverse - two ply steel construction - open rivets on one side - 4 3/8"

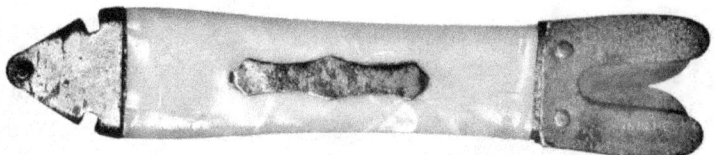

47. GERMANY   stamped on one rocket tail - a pair of small solid rivets holding two ply steel construction - 2 ¼ " plastic cream color marblized body - 4"
48. GERMANY beneath "WHALE" logo on one rocket tail - a pair of small solid rivets near tail & a single rivet on head - breakers on head are more decorative than functional - 1.85" light cream color marbleized body with no medallion - 4"

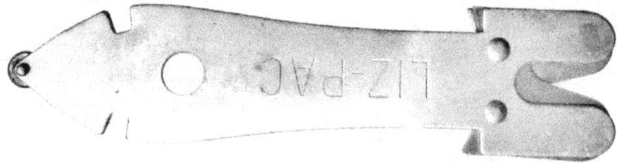

49. LIZ – PAC stamped in large letters both obverse & reverse - a pair of solid rivets at tail holding two ply steel construction - 3 15/16"

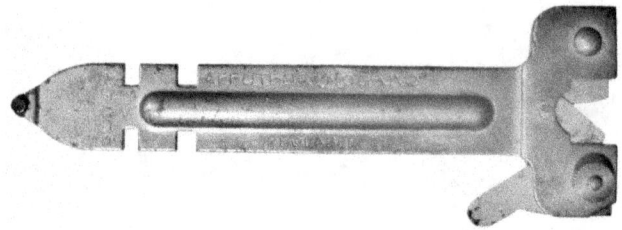

50. AFFUTEUR "MECANIC" REGLABLE BREVETE stamped on both obverse & reverse - brass finish on two ply steel construction - one open rivet on one tail - the other tail has a brass screw & a brass knurled nut to adjust the knife sharpener blade - 4 13/16"

51. No ID - similar to XVIII-50 above - .2" diam. hole & 4 breakers on head - a pair of open rivets on tail holding the two ply steel construction - hump on center is lower & longer than XVIII-50 above - 5 9/16"

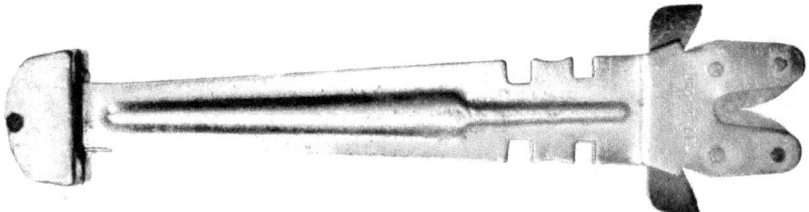

52. EURO-PRADEL DEPOSE stamped on both obverse & reverse of tail - four small closed rivets hold two ply plated steel construction at tail & the solid non-mag. alloy crescent head with cutter wheel secures that end - 5 ½"

53. EURO-PRADEL M –C stamped on obverse of tail - MARQUE ET MODELE DEPOSES stamped on reverse of tail - otherwise the same as XVIII-52 above

G. DUAL DISC - MISC STYLE   **PRICE RANGE: $10 - $50**

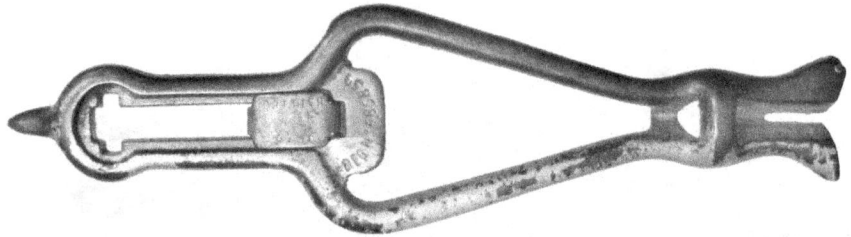

54. THE IDEAL BRITISH MADE stamped on can opener slide - REG. No 685859 recessed on yoke of cast iron tool - triangular sharpener missing near the glass cutter wheel - 6 ¼"

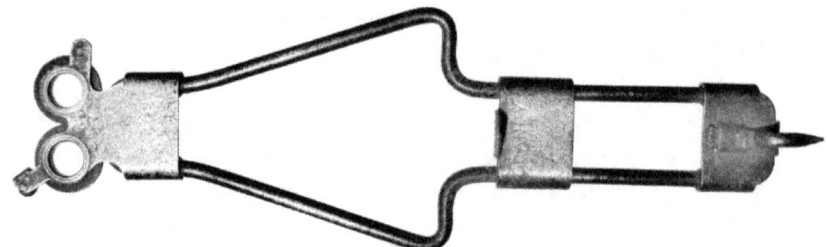

55. DANDY GOLD MEDAL PAT. PEND. stamped on can opener slide - all steel construction except the crimping for the dual discs - 7"

56. No ID - same as XVII-55 above except the glass cutter wheel unit is mounted at the other dual disc and is longer - 7 1/8"

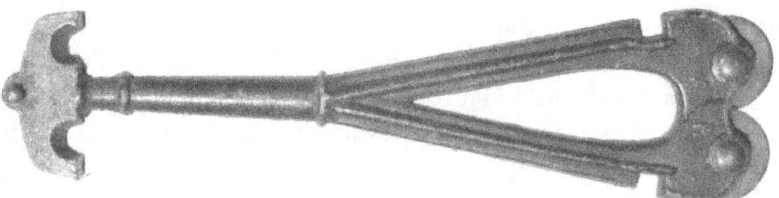

57. DEPOSE cast raised on obverse near discs - A R cast raised on reverse near discs - "French crescent head" all cast in pot metal painted black - 4 1/8"

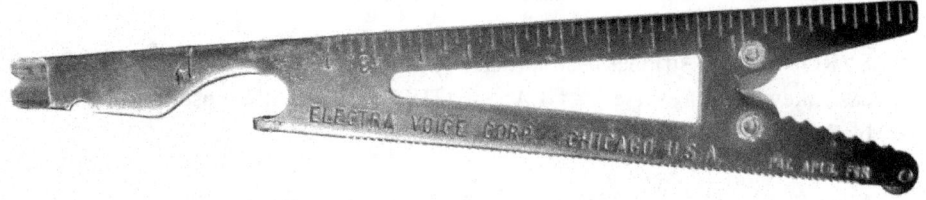

58. ELECTRA VOICE CORP. CHICAGO U.S.A. PAT. APLD. FOR & a 4" rule stamped on obverse - one piece steel tool - bottle cap opener - tack puller - file on edge - wrench - 5 1/16"

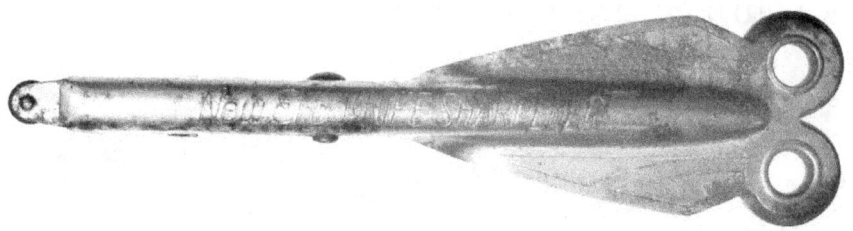

59. NEW ERA KNIFE SHARPENER stamped on rounded top center of plated steel tool - PAT. PEND. stamped on reverse of head next to bottle cap opener - hinged corkscrew on underside - 4 5/8"

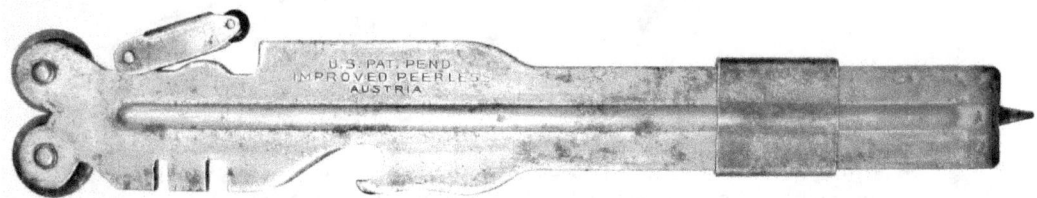

60. IMPROVED PEERLESS - AUSTRIA - U.S. PAT. PEND. stamped on center of flat steel tool - can opener slide - bottle cap opener - two breakers - glass cutter on a hinged arm near dual discs - 6.8"

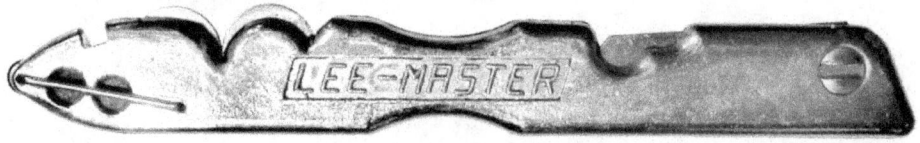

61. LEE-MASTER raised letters cast mid handle on non-mag. alloy - swing out razor blade - glass cutter wheel held in place by bent wire axle that crosses two extra wheel storage holes in side of head - 4 15/16"

62. CLEMAC - PAT. APP. 34228/62 cast in raised letters & numbers in a recessed oval on obverse of a plated non-mag. alloy - R. D. NO. 907942 - MADE IN ENGLAND cast in recessed oval on reverse - swing out razor blade - glass cutter wheel held in place by bent wire that crosses over two extra wheel storage holes in side of head - 4 1/8"

63. GRAFTON cast in raised letters in a recessed oval in middle on obverse of non-mag. alloy tool - MADE IN ENGLAND same on reverse - swing out razor blade - glass cutter wheel held by brass axle - 4 1/8"

64. RENOWN cast in raised letters on obverse of white plastic body - MADE IN ENGLAND WIRE STRIPPER cast in raised letters on reverse - swing out razor blade - a pair of open brass rivets hold the dual discs - a pot metal head holds the glass cutter wheel - 4 3/8"

65. SYRONE wire stripper cast in raised letters on obverse of red plastic body - MADE IN ENGLAND cast likewise on reverse & GLASS CUTTER cast on the nose holding the wheel - swing out razor blade - 4 1/8"

66. MULTI-TOOL 1 2 3 4 cast on obverse of black plastic body where the numbers indicate the multi uses - 1 dual discs - 2 wire stripper - 3 swing out razor blade - 4 the two breakers - glass cutter wheel held by axle in a non-mag. head - Packaging reads: TOMAHAWK BRAND XL323 1997 UNITED CUTLERY CORP. - 5 ½"

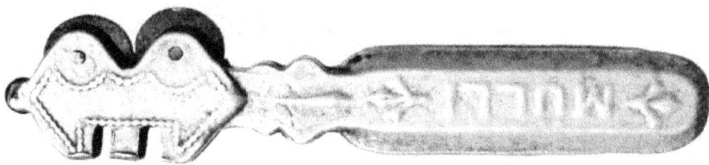

67. MULLI cast on both obverse & reverse of straight handle solid aluminum tool - two breakers & dual discs on head - 4"

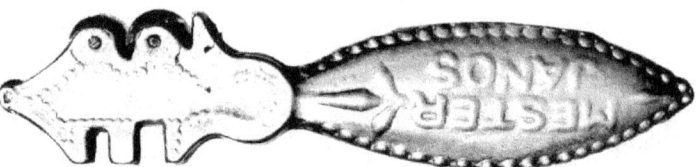

68. MESTER JANAS cast on obverse of "beavertail" handle of solid aluminum – ES TARSA BPEST cast on reverse of handle - two breakers & dual discs on head – 4"

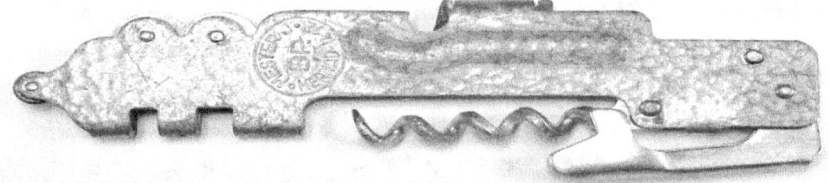

68 – A. MESTER J BP. HERNAD-U 72 (in a circle) - corkscrew – can opener – bottle opener – knife sharpener – blue enamel painted folded over steel body – 4"

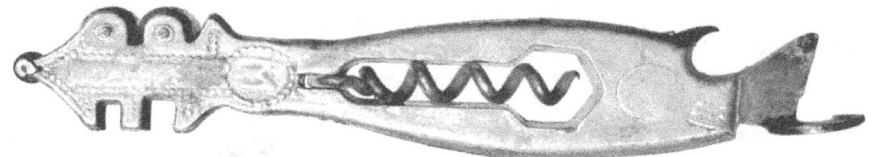

68 – B. J on obverse – M on reverse: corkscrew, can opener, bottle opener, knife sharpener, - aluminum body - 4.9"

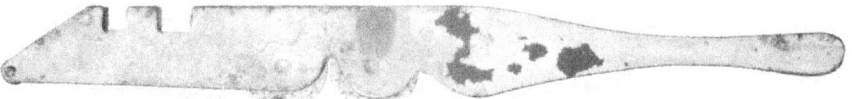

69. No ID - 1/8" thick flat non-mag. alloy - two breakers on head - knife sharpening discs - red paint nearly gone - 4 7/8"

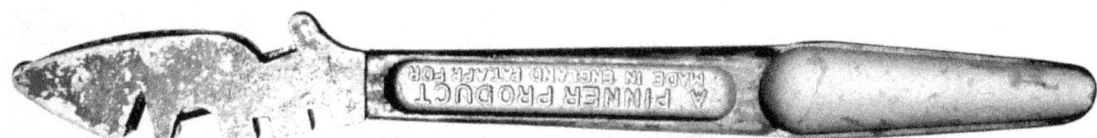

70. A PINNER PRODUCT - MADE IN ENGLAND PAT. APP. FOR cast in raised letters in a recessed center part of aluminum handle - a raised 5 ¾" ruler on reverse from head to end - notch next to glass cutter is a knife sharpener - the second is a razor sharp string cutter - the third & forth are glass breakers - the 1.9" red plate (half of the head) holds the wheel & other blades in place by three rivets seen on the reverse - 5 7/8"

71. No ID - thin sheet steel folded over held be a pair of brass rivets for dual discs & pin axle for glass cutter wheel - 4 1/8"

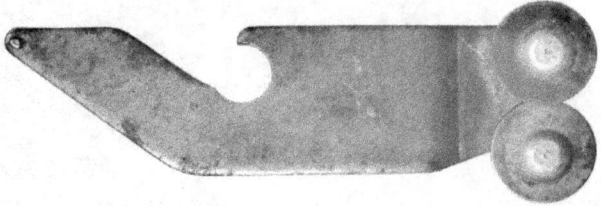

72. No ID - .1" thick flat steel with bottle cap opener - dual discs with solid steel rivets   - glass cutter wheel at the pointed end - 4 ½"

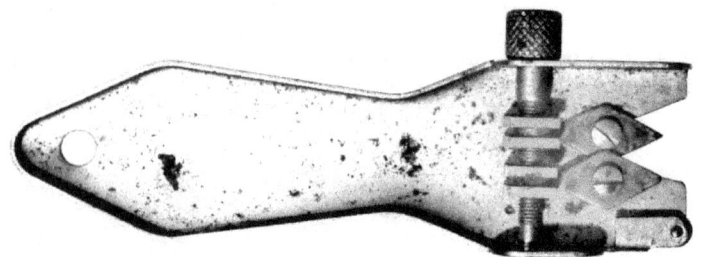

73. MEYER in a diamond - Bte SGDG - FRANCE – ETRANGER   stamped on obverse near pointed end next to hole - knurled knob adjusts the angle of the dual knives - glass cutter wheel on reverse at corner - 4 ½"

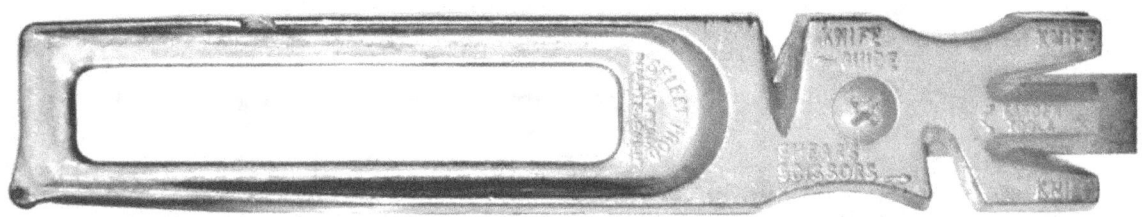

74. SELECT PROD. DURANTE, CALIF. - PAT. PEND. cast in raised letters on obverse of yoke web - MADE IN U.S.A. cast on reverse of curved yoke - KNIFE GUIDE (obverse & reverse) - GARDEN TOOLS - KNIFE(twice) - SHEARS SCISSORS - aluminum alloy with webbing on inside of handle arms - glass cutter at end of handle - 6 3/8" DESIGN PATENT   #199,132 SEPT. 15, 1964

75. Similar to XVIII-74 above - No Name - PAT. PEND. on straight yoke web - same head style and data - aluminum alloy with no webbing on inside of handle arms - 6 3/8"

76. SELECT TOOL SHARPENS EVERYTHING on sticker label on both obverse & reverse of solid web between grey plastic arms - U. S. AND FOREIGN PATENTS also on webbing - head & data design similar to XVIII-74 & 75 above - 6 3/8"

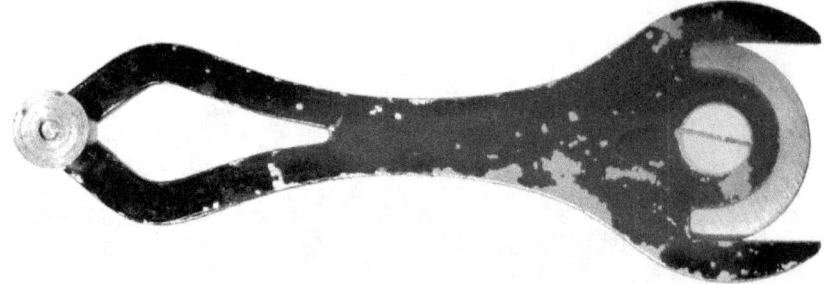

77. No ID - black paint on .6" flat steel tool - knurled brass knob adjust rotation of hardened steel sharpening wheel - glass cutter wheel held in place by screw & round, slotted steel disc -4 ½"

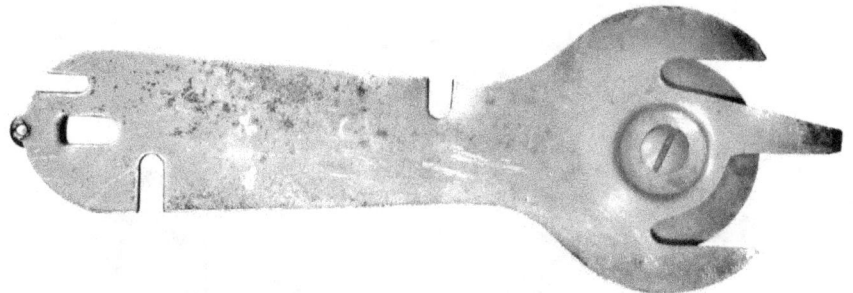

78. RAPID stamped on mid-handle of thin sheet steel - knurled brass knob adjust rotation of hardened steel sharpening wheel - three breakers - glass cutter wheel held in place by bent punch out strip - 5"

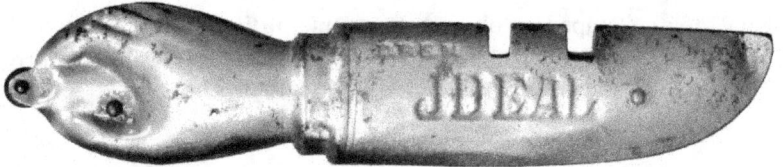

79. JDEAL RPGM stamped into thin sheet steel on both obverse & reverse - note: hand holding the glass cutter wheel - 4 9/16"

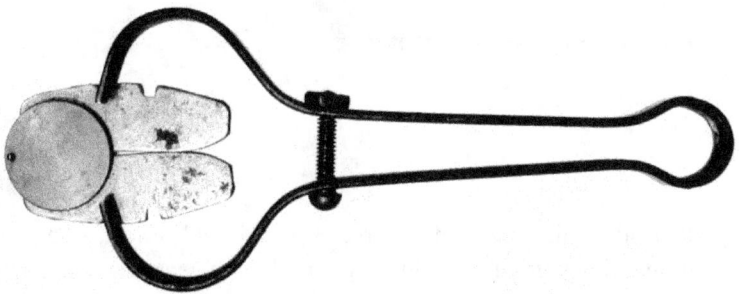

80. No ID - brass nut & bolt hold tension on ¼"deep by 1/20" thick black painted steel loop handle that holds a pair of hardened steel plates secured together by a 5/8" diam. dual brass disc with glass cutter wheel - 4.2"

81. "Belfor" cast on edge of middle of non-mag. alloy - on same edge at ends next to the glass cutter wheels are 1 & 2 in a recessed circle - BRITISH MADE cast on opposite edge - 3 5/8"

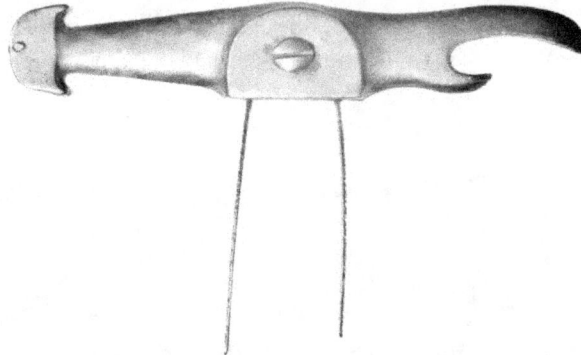

82. No ID - one piece brass body - crescent head with glass cutter - bottle opener - 2 1/8" spring held in place by a brass screw and block - 4"

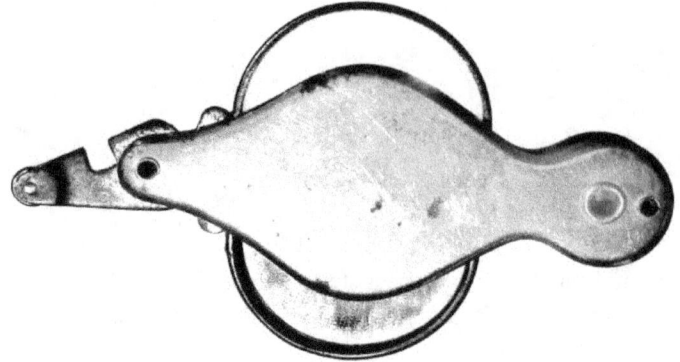

83. REGD. No 715660 stamped on obverse & reverse of thin sheet steel around the open brass rivet at end opposite the glass cutter which is pivoted with magnifying glass and mirror - 3 5/8"

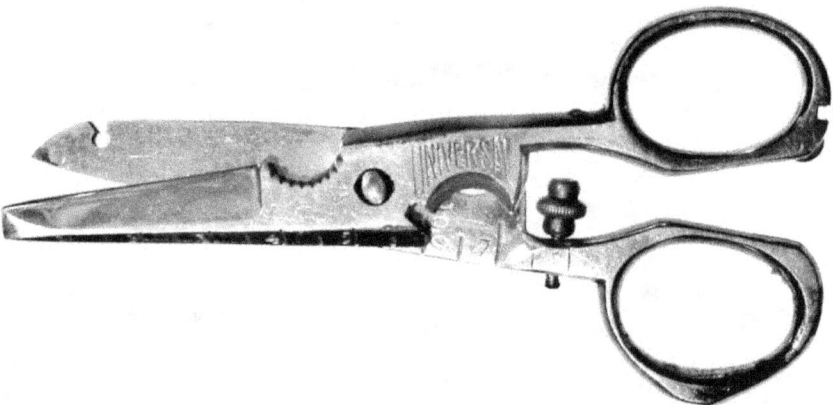

84. UNIVERSAL stamped at mid handle of obverse of plated steel sissors - this blade has an 8cm ruler - a file is the length of outer edge of other blade knurled knob near finger opening adjusts blade closure - glass cutter wheel at outer edge of top loop - a pointed sewing wheel is on other loop - 4 5/8"

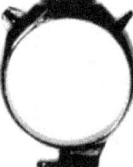

85. THE ULTIMATE GLASS CUTTER PAT. No. 5,070,563 black plastic finish over stainless steel ring with: string cutter, magnet, screwdriver(slot & Phillips), actually no glass cutter on this one (to expensive to produce) - only the five original ones had the glass cutter wheel attached

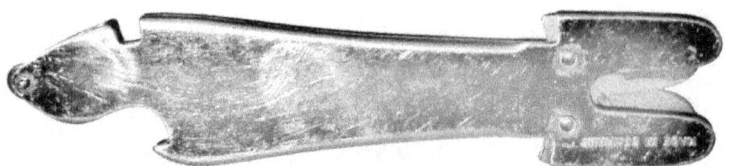

86. MADE IN GERMANY - bottle opener - knife sharpener - riveted two-piece polished steel body - 4"

CATEGORY XIX   JACKKNIFE

This combination tool has been overlooked by many until the advent of the internet auctions. This combination tool with a glass cutter blade is not mentioned by either Fred O'Leary in his book <u>CORKSCREWS</u> published by Schiffer Publishing, 1996, nor by Yvan A. Riaz in his book <u>The Book of KNIVES</u>, published by Crown Publishers, 1981. O'Leary does show examples of early iron combination tools (see Category VI).

Twenty four other different jackknives with glass cutters are known in other collections. Three U.S. Patents were found for this category: 111,269   1,264,430   1,755,946

Price range: $10 - $50 with a few to $100.

Five subsets assist in describing the varieties in this Category:

A. Turtle Shell Celluloid Style	**D. Pearlized Faces**
B. Ripple Metal Faces	**E. Grained Faces**
C. Smooth Metal Faces	**F. Other**

A. Turtle Shell Celluloid Style - length is with the glass cutter blade extended

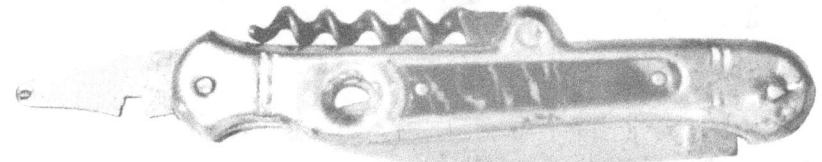

1. CELEBRATE CUTLERY Co. - GERMANY - corkscrew - 4.5"

2. DIXON,J., CUTLERY Co. - GERMANY - corkscrew - 4.5"

3. ELLIOTT CUTL. CORP. - GERMANY - corkscrew - 4.5"

4. GERLING CUTLERY Co. - GERMANY - corkscrew - 4.5"

5. MANOS CUTLERY Co. - GERMANY - corkscrew - 4 5/8"

6. ROYAL BRAND CUTLERY Co. - GERMANY - corkscrew - pick - special small blade - 4 5/8"

7. "RUNNING-MAN WITH STICK" logo - GERMANY - corkscrew- pick- special small blade - 4 5/8"

8. SAXONIA CUTLERY Co. - GERMANY - corkscrew - 4 5/8"

9. WADSWORTH, A. W. & SON (on both large & small blades) - GERMANY - corkscrew - 4 5/8"

10. No ID - otherwise the same as XIV-9 above

11. No ID - corkscrew - pick - second blade is a pipe bowl scraper - 4 5/8"

12. CLARK BROS. (on small blade) - corkscrew - glass cutter blade is a solid piece with slit to hold the wheel and axle: the only one like this - 4.55"

13. SWANWORKS CUTLERY Co. – GERMANY on small blade – no corkscrew - 4.5"

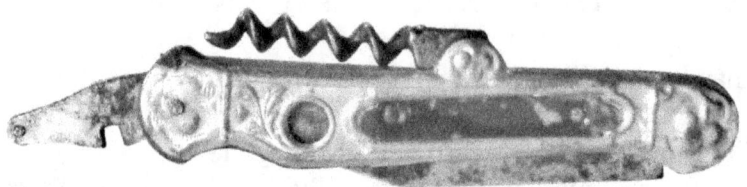

14. MAJESTIC CUTERY Co. - GERMANY - (on both small & large blades) – corkscrew – Ornate faces on both sides - 4.5

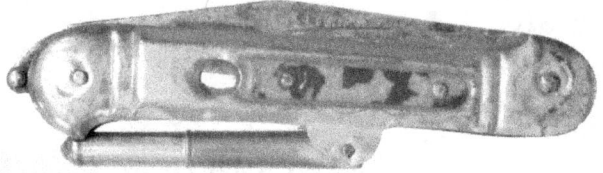

15. SPADICK CHICAGO (on face of large blade) - glass cutter wheel located tight on heel of jackknife - use of tube hinged at usual spot of corkscrew unknown - 3.9"

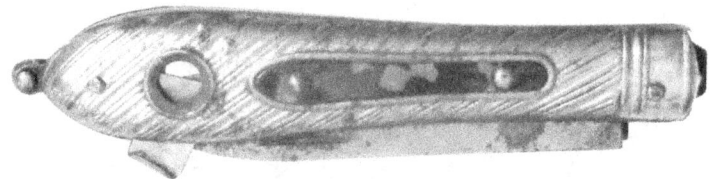

16. BICHON FORGE (on face of large blade) - cigar tip cutter blade - screw driver at hinge end and glass cutter wheel at other end - 4"

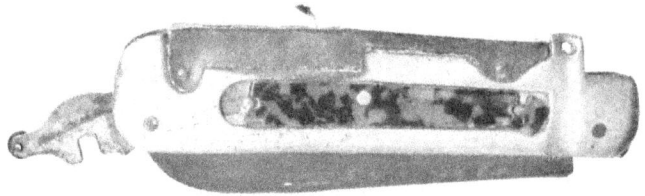

17. No ID - saw blade & small & large blades - spring scale - brass - 4 ½"

B. RIPPLE FACES (metal) with metal medallion on one face

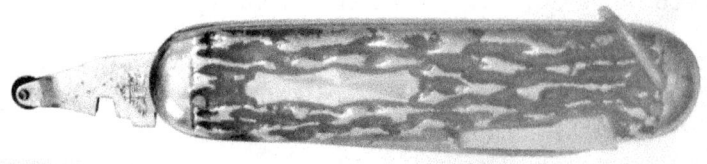

18. A G & J PRODUCT (in diamond) - GERMANY on base of large blade - can opener - "winged crown" logo on base of glass cutter blade - 4.5"

19. BERK CULTERY Co. NEW-YORK - MADE IN GERMANY (on base of large blade) - bottle opener/screw driver blade - "winged crown" logo on base of glass cutter blade - 4.5"

20. COSMO MFG Co. - GERMANY - on base of large blade - "winged crown" logo on glass cutter blade - bottle opener - screw driver - 4.5"

21. GUTALSKY - GERMANY - REGISTERED on base of large blade containing bottle opener & screw driver - can opener blade - SCOUT KNIFE on the outlined medallion the face – 4.5"

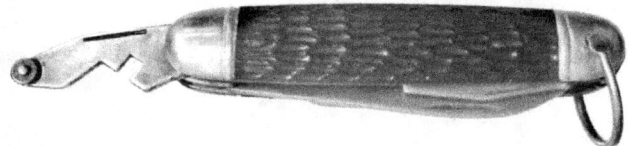

22. IMPERIAL ("crown" over the second I) PROV. R.I. USA on base of large blade - pipe bowl scraper, screw driver & bottle cap opener on small blade - RIPPLE FACE is black plastic - note different style breaker on cutter – 4.5"

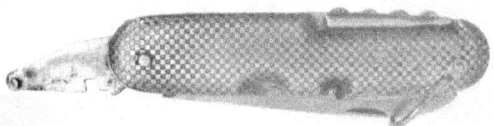

23. FOREIGN on base of large blade - corkscrew - can opener - pick/scraper - note raised & recessed checkerboard pattern on face - 4.6"

C. SMOOTH METAL FACE

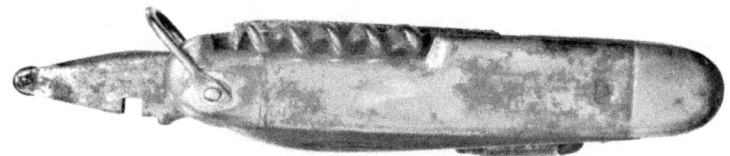

24. SOLINGEN on base of large blade - D.R.G. M. ; D.R.P.A. ; FIXA on base of hinged can opener blade - corkscrew - pick - 4.65"

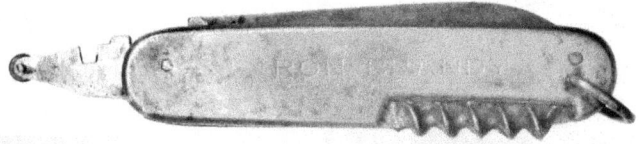

25. SOLINGEN on base of large blade - can opener - corkscrew - RON BRANDY stamped into one face - 4.55"

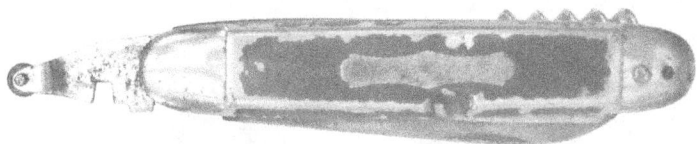

26. SOLINGEN - D.R.P. on base of large blade - can opener - corkscrew - red paint on faces – metal medallion on one face - 4.5"

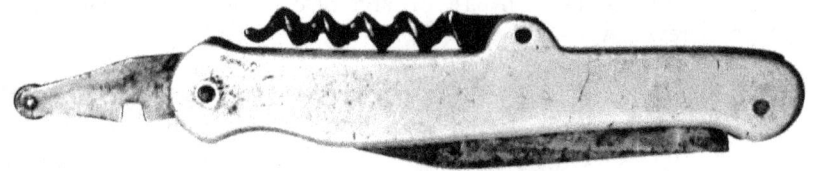

27. SOLINGEN – SWAN WORKS - GERMANY on base of small blade - corkscrew - smooth aluminum faces - 5.6"

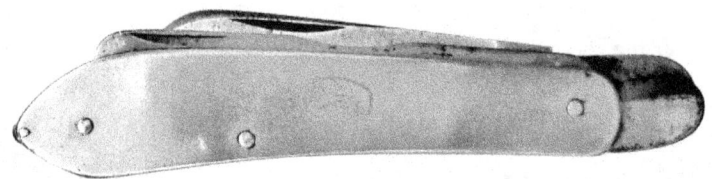

28. STAG BRAND under running "stag" stamped in an oval on one of smooth stainless faces - MADE IN SHEFFIELD ENGLAND on base of large blade - spring loaded cigar cutter - glass cutter tight at other end - 4.3"

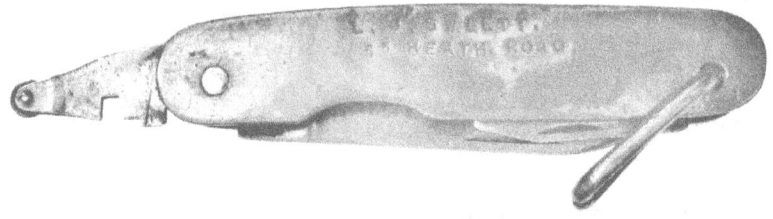

29. L.J. SWEET, 65 HEATH ROAD. Stamped into one of smooth brass faces - MADE IN SHEFFIELD ENGLAND on base of large blade - bottle opener - heavy wire bail - 4.6"

D. PEARLIZED PLASTIC FACES unless otherwise noted

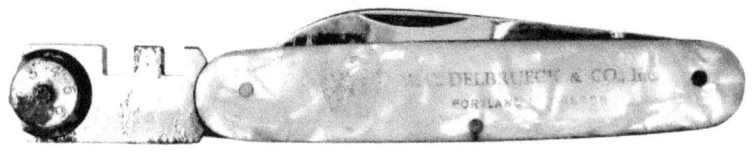

30. W.C. DELBRUECK & Co., INC. PORTLAND, OREGON & "family crest" on one of the pearlized faces - 6-wheel turret with 2 breakers - single blade marked: GERMANY , STAINLESS - 4.85"

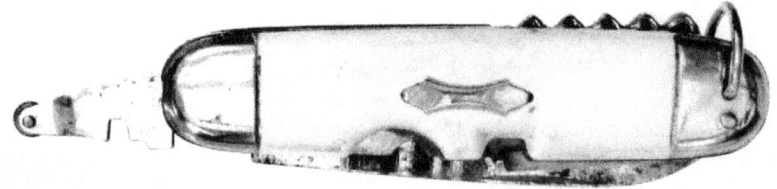

31. FORGED STEEL - FOREIGN (side one) , running man with flag on other base of long blade - can opener - corkscrew - metal medallion on one of the plain cream colored plastic faces - 4.55"

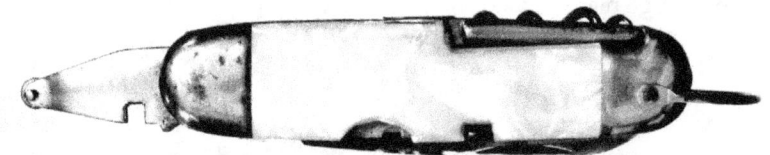

32. GARANTIE STAHL (side one) - MADE IN GERMANY on other base of long blade - can opener - corkscrew - pick - 4.65"

33. GERMANY "whale" logo on base of large blade - can opener - pick - corkscrew - 4.6"

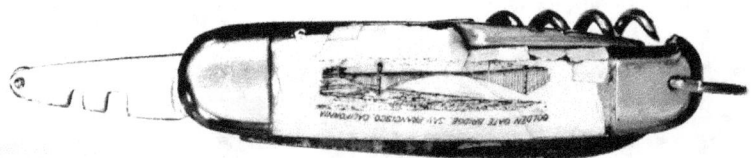

34. GOLDEN GATE BRIDGE SAN FRANCISCO, CALIFORNIA (on pearlized face) - MADE IN GERMANY on base of large blade - bottle opener - corkscrew - 2 breakers – 4.8"

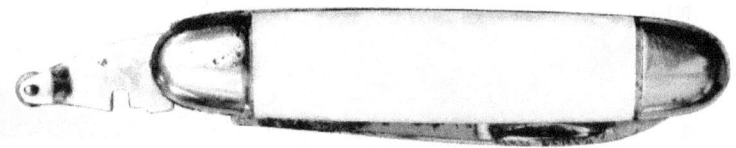

35. MADE IN GERMANY on base of single large blade - 4.5"

36. STAINLESS on base of single large blade - can opener - pick - corkscrew - 4.6"

E. GRAINED FACES - black with creamed lines

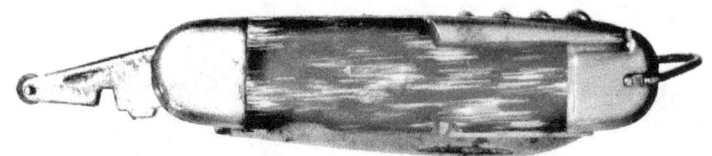

37. MADE IN GERMANY on base of large blade - can opener - pick - corkscrew - 4.6"

37-A. MADE IN GERMANY on base of large blade – INOXYDABLE(stainless in French) on base of large blade – can opener – pick – corkscrew – 4.6"

38. MADE IN GERMANY on base of large blade - can opener - pick - corkscrew - 2 breakers on glass cutter blade - 4.8"

39. GARANTIE STAHL on base of large blade - can opener - pick - corkscrew - small medallion on one face - 4.55"

40. GARANTIE STAHL – IMPORT on base of large blade - can opener - pick - corkscrew - 5.5"

41. SOLINGEN on base of large blade - can opener - pick - corkscrew - brown with cream lines - 4.6"

42. MADE IN SHEFFIELD ENGLAND on base of large blade - bottle opener with screw driver - mottled brown & cream faces - 4.6"

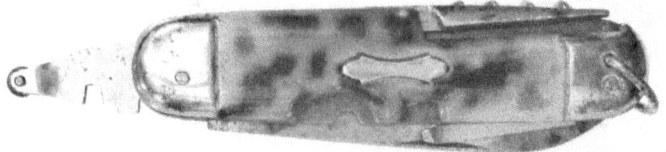

43. OPAKI beneath "animal" logo on base of large blade - can opener - pick - corkscrew - medallion on one face - mottled brown spots on faces - 4.55"

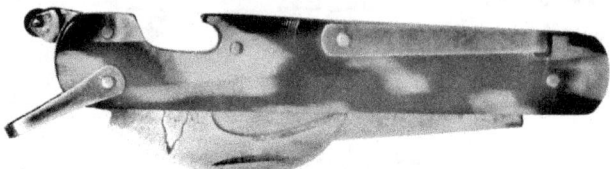

44. TRADE MARK with "flag" logo on smooth flat black & pearlized face - same logo on base of large blade & the bottle/can opener blade - tweezers pivot from mid-point - inside one tweezer blade is a file - note location of cutter wheel next to the flat sheet metal bail - 3.8"

F. OTHER

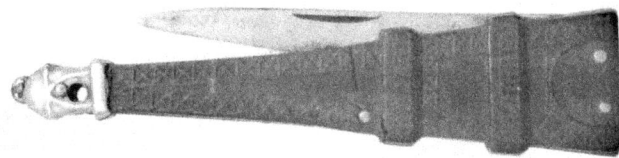

45. TOUR EIFFEL on obverse & reverse at base of tower - the black plastic replica of the EIFFEL TOWER conceals a 2.5" slender knife blade - glass cutter wheel held by the metal tower cap - 3.95"

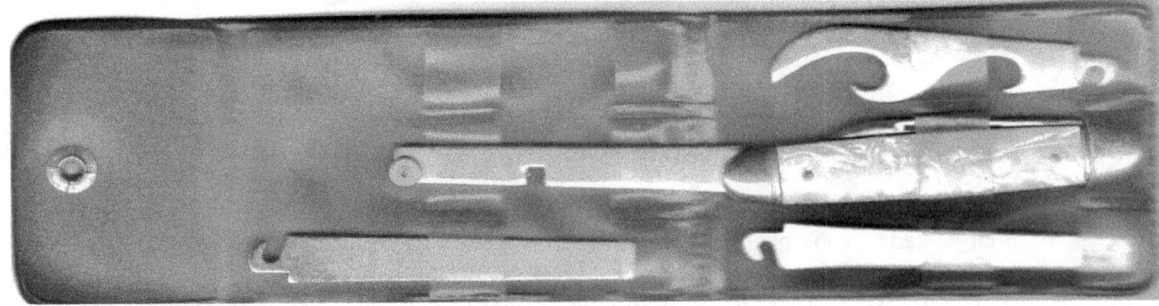

46. IMPERIAL PROV. R. I. USA with crown on base of single blade - blades are attachable with hook: double bottle opener, screwdriver, file, one unknown tool blade missing - glass cutter blade with breaker shown attached to jackknife - knife with glass cutter blade attached is 4.9"

CATEGORY XX   BASIC STANDARD - SINGLE WHEEL
Variety of Designs

After the Early Cast Iron varieties, this style became the norm as evidenced by the number of patents and different manufacturers and/or distributers. There are nineteen different known in other collections and many more from ads and U. S. patents.

Fifty two U.S. Patents and two Design Patents are listed below:

166,684	1,721,361	1,589,536	2,156,249	2,652,659	4,203,209
166,954	1,731,257	1,634,323	2,210,193	2,735,228	4,224,738
231,225	1,750,913	1,697,044	2,260,706	2,892,291	4,327,488
778,023	1,102,843	1,865,242	2,283,134	3,026,153	4,451,981
863,316	1,161,889	1,870,585	2,289,718	3,106,018	4,528,752
915,447	1,201,515	1,884,635	2,312,635	3,138,868	4,672,874
915,818	1,221,076	1,941,221	2,341,030	3,392,445	4,819,535
942,152	1,347,972	1,962,238	2,394,138	3,462,835	D – 93,639
989,603	1,547,451	2,096,284	2,529,735	4,040,182	D -107,180

RED DEVIL & FLETCHER-TERRY glass cutters of this Category style have their own Categories respectively XXI & XXII. They both produced many for other companies.

There are Five Subsets for this Category as follows: Price Range: $5 - $35

> **A. ALPHABETICAL: MANUFACTURERS OR DISTRIBUTORS**
> **B. MODIFIED BALL END**
> **C. NO NAME BUT SOME ID**
> **D. NO IDENTIFICATION AT ALL**
> **E. MODIFICATIONS NOT IN THE MISCELLANEOUS CATEGORY XXIII**

A. ALPHABETICAL: MANUFACTURERS OR DISTRIBUTORS

PICTURES of basic (1) with ball end and (2) straight end

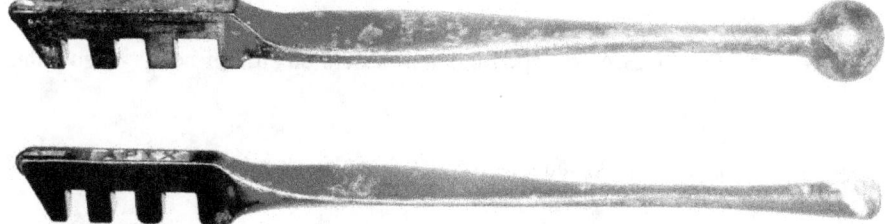

1. APEX in recess on top of cutter head - red paint - 5"
2. BARRETT on handle near ball end - brown paint on heavy iron(see also VI-55) - 5.1"
3. BARRETT cast in recess on bottom of handle - MADE IN U.S.A. just below finger rest - narrow head - red paint - large ball - 5"
4. BARRETT cast in recess on bottom of handle - MADE IN U.S.A. closer to finger rest than XX-3 above - blue paint - medium ball - 5.25"
5. BARRETT same as XX-4 above except: for blue painted sheet steel hinged cap over the cutter wheel with PAT APPLD FOR stamped on it - 5.25"
6. BARRETT same as XX-5 above except: PAT APPLD FOR faces the opposite direction - 5.25"
7. BARRETT same as XX-5 & 6 above except: PAT 2283134 stamped on the hinged wheel cover 5.25"

8. BINSWANGER cast just below finger rest - MADE IN U.S.A. cast in bottom of handle - 2 stamped on side of head - mottled steel finish - no evidence of paint - small ball - 5.1"

9. BLACK PANTHER cast in recessed rectangle on bottom of black paint handle - 100 U.S.A. cast in a recessed rectangle on top of handle - ½" red tip - 4.9"

10. BLACK PANTHER cast in recessed rectangle on bottom of black paint handle -- 101 USA cast on top of handle - small red paint ball - 5"

11. BROWNIE cast in recessed diamond on bottom of brown paint handle - MADE IN U.S.A. cast below finger rest - ½" red tip 5.25"

12. BULL DOG – HI-775 – 152035 – HARDWARE, D.W. of NEWELL RUBBERMAID only ID is on package - MADE IN TAIWAN same as XX-14 except this handle has three oval recesses, one on top & two on bottom - completely red paint - small ball - 5.1"

13. CAL-HAWK - MADE IN TAIWAN for: CTT TOOLS, INC. EL MONTE, CA AZGC - same as XX-12 except this handle does not have any oval recesses - 5.1"

14. CAMP "BELL" logo on side of head - no evidence of paint - very small ball - 5.1"

15. CAMP "BELL" logo on side of head - no evidence of paint on the plated brass tool - very small ball with an 1/8" extension of the handle through it - 5.25"

16. CRL on finger rest - MADE IN U.S.A. cast recessed on top of head - blue paint on non-mag. alloy - medium ball - CAT. No. 202(on box) - 5.15"

17. CRAFTSMAN MADE IN USA stamped in tiny letters on side of head - blue paint - large ball - 5.1"

18. CRAFTSMAN MADE IN U.S.A. stamped in large letters on side of head - blue paint - large ball - 5.05"

19. CRAFTSMAN MADE IN U.S.A. stamped in small letters on side of head - red paint - large ball - 5.1"

20. CRAFTSMAN MADE IN U.S.A. same as XX-19 above except: medium ball - 5.15"

21. CRAFTSMAN NO. 3794 stamped on side of head - MADE IN USA cast in on bottom of red painted handle with medium ball - 5.15"

22. CRAFTSMAN NO. 3794 same as XX-21 above except: black paint - 5.2"

23. DIAMANTOR GERMANY stamped on side of steel head - DIAMANTOR cast in both top & bottom of light green plastic handle at finger rest area - 5.05"

24. DIAMANTOR cast on finger rest - MADE IN GERMANY cast on top of head - EXTRA cast on bottom of handle - evidence of metallic red paint - end of handle has been sawn off - 4.7"

25. ECLIPSE(in script) MADE IN USA cast on bottom of dark green painted handle - 5.1"

26. ECLIPSE same as XX-25 above except red paint - 5.1"

27. EFETCO cast in recessed rectangle MADE IN U.S.A. on bottom of red paint handle 5.2"

28. EMBEE (on package only) - EMBEE CORPORATION SPRINGFIELD, OHIO 45501 U.S.A. - U.S.A. cast in small oval on bottom of red painted non-mag. alloy tool - other ovals on top & bottom of handle - .85" dark blue sock - medium dark blue ball - 5.1"

29. EMPIRE 2749 MADE IN TAIWAN (on package only) LOGO cast in finger rest - non-mag. alloy all painter red - small ball - 5.1"

30. FLASH cast in raised letters on bottom of red painted handle - 5"

31. FOREST CITY 0400327 (on package only) - orange paint on non-mag. alloy tool - .5" black sock & black medium ball - 5.15"

32. F R W stamped on side of head - slender black painted handle - 4.8"

33. F R W 240 stamped on side of head - slender black painted handle - 5.1"

34. G.P. CO. NO. 979 MADE IN USA stamped on side of head - no evidence of paint 5.3"

35. G.P. CO NO. 444 MADE IN USA stamped on side of head - off-set finger rest to the left - blue paint - 5.15"

36. GOODELL-PRATT COMPANY GREENFIELD, MASS. U.S.A. stamped on side of head - orangish/ red paint - medium ball - 5"

37. GOODELL TOOL CO SHELBOURNE FALLS MASS . U.S.A. stamped on side of head - orangish/red paint - medium ball - 5"

38. GREAT NECK USA cast in bottom of orange paint handle - GC – 101 cast in top of handle - black medium ball and 3/8" black sock - 5.2"

39. GREAT NECK & U.S.A. recessed letters in recessed ovals reading toward the head on bottom of orangesh/red non-mag. alloy handle - GC – 101 recessed in a recessed oval on top of handle reading to the black medium ball and 5/8" black sock - 5.2"

40. GREAT NECK & U.S.A. recessed letters in recessed ovals reading toward the head on bottom of orangesh/red non-mag. alloy handle - GC - 101 recessed in a recessed oval on top of handle reading to the head - orange paint with a ½" black sock and a black medium ball - 5.2"

41. GREAT NECK cast in raised letters in a recessed oval on bottom of non-mag. alloy handle - SPAIN cast in raised letters twice, once on mid handle & second next to ball - ribbed finger rest - all red paint with medium ball with a 1/16" diam. hole .3" deep(evidently to hang tool white painting) - 5.2"

42. GREAK NECK GC 101 (only on package) - U.S.A. recessed in a slightly recessed oval reading towards head of non-mag. alloy handle painted red with medium ball - 5.1"

43. HOWARD ENGLAND cast raised letters in a recessed oval on bottom of non-mag. alloy handle painted celery green - ribbed finger rest - 5"

44. HOYNE U.S.A. cast recessed in recessed ovals reading toward the head of brown painted non-mag. handle - 1053 recess cast in recessed oval next to finger rest - ¾" orange sock & orange medium ball - 5.15"

45. HYDE R on diamond shape decal mid top of black painted handle - MADE IN USA cast in top next to the finger rest - 2/3's of medium ball is silver paint - 4.9"

46. HYDE U.S.A. cast in recessed ovals on bottom of black painted non-mag. alloy handle - 45700 cast in oval next to finger rest - black medium ball - 5.2"

47. HYDE cast in raised letters on side of head - 45700 © 1996 on package - MADE IN TAIWAN - blue paint with medium ball - 5.1"

48. IDEAL cast raised letters on bottom of slender red painted handle - 5.05"

49. INDIAN cast raised letters on bottom of slender maroon painted handle - 5

49-A. IVY CLASSIC - 26006 - MADE IN TAIWAN - zinc alloy body - all black paint - 5.1"

50. JENNINGS cast in top next to finger rest & NO-4 cast on bottom of blue painted handle - 1" red sock & red medium ball - 5.15"

51. "J W stamped on side of head - some evidence of black paint on slender handle - 5"

52. J. W. C. stamped on side of thick head - black painted slender handle - 5"

53. KEEN KUTTER cast raised letters facing head - plated handle - 4.7"

54. LENOX cast raised letters in a recessed rectangle on bottom under finger rest - top of head is rounded - dark blue paint on handle with a .6" red tip - 4.95"

55. LENOX same as XX-54 above except: a large red ball - 5.2"

56. MEPHISTO cast raised letters in a recessed rectangle on bottom of red painted handle - cross-hatched finger rest - 5.1"

57. MILLERS FALLS cast raised letters facing head on bottom of maroon painted handle - large ball - 5.05"

58. MILLERS FALLS NO. 66 MADE IN USA stamped on obverse of plated steel tool - PAT. 1956 - U. S. NO. 2735228 stamped on reverse of head - evidence of red paint - 5.15"

59. MILLERS FALLS NO. 66 MADE IN USA on obverse of head of plated steel tool - CARBIDE WHEEL U.S. PAT. 2735228 stamped on reverse of head - ¾" red tip - 5.15"

60. MILLERS FALLS NO. 66 MADE IN USA on obverse of head of plated steel tool - CARBIDE WHEEL printed on top of head - 1.1" red tip - 5.2"

61. M. F. CO. NO. 337 stamped on side of head - MADE IN USA cast in at mid bottom of black painted handle - .15" sock & medium red ball - 5.2"

62. M. F. CO. NO 337 MADE IN USA stamped on side of head - .3" red sock - red medium ball - 5.2"

63. M.F. CO. NO 444 MADE IN USA stamped on side of head - finger rest off-set to the left blur paint - .7" orangesh/red tip - 5.15"

64. M. F. CO. NO 444 MADE IN USA stamped on side of head - finger rest off-set to the left - blue paint - 5.15"

65. M – S MADE IN U.S.A. stamped on side of non-mag. alloy head – orangesh/red paint - 5.2"

66. MONCE on obverse & U S A on reverse of vertically flattened end of plated steel handle - top of head slightly rounded - 5.2"

67. MONCE, S. G. UNIONVILLE, CT. stamped on side of head with slightly rounded top - slender steel handle - 5.1"

68. MONCE, S. G. UNIONVILLE, CT. stamped on side of head with slightly rounded top - large ball - 5.25"

69. N E stamped on side of head - black paint - large ball - 5.2"

70. O F stamped on side of head - black paint - 5.2"

71. ONONDAGA stamped on side of head - dark red paint with .3" dark blue tip - 5.05"

72. ONONDAGA stamped on side of head - three concentric recessed circles on finger rest - MADE IN U S A on bottom of red painted handle - ¾" sky blue tip - 5.05"

73. PIT BULL item no: TAIC720 made in Taiwan on package only - three recessed ovals, one on top & two on bottom of all red painted non-mag. alloy tool - small ball - 5.1"

74. RED BIRD stamped on side of head - red paint on handle - ¼" silver tip - 4.9"

75. REDMAN cast on bottom of handle under finger rest - No 105 cast on finger rest - red paint on slender handle - 5.1"

76. REDMAN cast on bottom of handle under finger rest - No. 105 MADE IN U.S.A. cast on top of red painted handle - 5.1"

77. RELIANT STOCK NO 81601 MADE IN TAIWAN 1989 only ID is on package - all red paint on non-mag. alloy tool - medium ball - 5.05"

78. RICHARD recess cast in finger rest of non-mag. alloy tool - GL -1 cast on bottom beneath finger rest - yellow paint - MADE IN U.S.A. cast in top of head - .85" dark green sock and medium ball - 5.1"

79. RIDGLEY USA stamped on side of head - no apparent paint on plated steel tool with slender handle - large ball - 5.2"

80. ROWLAND, ALEX NEW YORK stamped on side of head - slightly rounded top of head - maroon paint 5.3"

81. RUBY cast in raised letters on bottom of red painted tool - 5.0"

82. RUBY raised letters cast in recessed rectangle on bottom of red painted tool - 4.95"

83. RUBY raised letters cast in recessed rectangle on bottom of red painted tool - MADE IN U.S.A. on bottom of handle - 5.1"

84. RUBY stamped on side of head - maroon paint - 4.6"

85. RUNNING RABBIT GC RRT38 MADE IN CHINA all data on package - all painted black - slightly recessed ovals on both top and bottom of handle - medium ball - 5"

86. SERVISTAR cast in recessed letters in a recessed oval on bottom of non-mag. alloy tool - 1063 cast in recessed numbers in a recessed oval next to finger rest - dark blue paint - .65" red sock red medium ball - 5.2"

87. SHAW ENGLAND cast raised letters in a recessed long oval on bottom of red painted tool -   cast into finger rest - thick head - 5.15"

88. SHAW ENGLAND cast raised letters in a recessed long oval on bottom of black painted tool - 5.25"

89. SHAW ENGLAND cast raised letters in a recessed long oval on bottom of celery green painted tool - bent wire for wheel holder - thick head - TUNGSTON CARBIDE stamped on side of head - center 2 inches of handle is flat with tapering sides - 5"

90. SHAW ENGLAND cast raised letters in a recessed long oval on bottom of red painted 2 inch flat section of handle - thick head - .7" blue tip - 5"

91. SHAW ENGLAND cast recessed letters in a recessed long oval on bottom of red painted 2 ½ " flat rectangular cross-section of mid section of red painted handle - coarse ribbed finger rest - .6" blue tip - 5.05"

92. SHAW ENGLAND raised letters cast in recessed long oval on bottom of a non-mag. alloy tool - only red paint shows on ribbed finger rest and in the recessed long oval - 5.05"

93. SHAW ENGLAND cast raised letters in recessed long oval on bottom of a non-mag. alloy tool - striped finger rest - unique slip-in sheet metal axle holder - red paint with .9" blue tip - 5"

94. SHAW ENGLAND cast raised letters in recessed long oval on bottom of a non-mag. alloy tool - raised dots finger rest - yellow paint - 5.1"

95. SHAW ENGLAND cast in raised letters in recessed long oval on bottom of non-mag. alloy tool - striped finger rest - unique slip-in sheet metal axle holder - light blue paint - small ball - 5.1"

96. S. & H. CO. stamped on side of head - evidence of red paint - 4.9"

97. SINGER cast raised letters in a recess on bottom of red painted handle - MADE IN USA cast in next to finger rest - 5.2"

98. SINGER   Copyright 1940 by Wm. L. Barrett Co., Bristol, Conn., U. S. A. this data is on card only - cream color paint with .2" red sock and red medium ball - 4.8"

99. SIXTY cast raised letters in a rectangular recess on bottom of red painted tool - 4.95"

100. SOMACA cast in finger rest - MADE IN U.S.A. recess cast on top of head of non-mag. alloy tool - black paint with .25" orange sock and orange medium ball - 5.1"

101. STANLEY U.S.A. cast raised letters in two recessed ovals on bottom of black painted non-mag. alloy tool - 14-120 recessed numbers in a recessed oval next to finger rest - small ball - 5.1"

102. STANLEY cast in raised letters in recessed oval on bottom of all black painted non-mag. alloy tool - 14-125 recessed numbers cast in recessed oval next to finger rest - small ball - 5.1"

103. STANLEY cast raised letters in a recessed oval on the finger rest - MADE IN U.S.A. recessed letters cast on top of head of a non-mag. alloy tool - black paint - medium ball - data on card: MONARCH 20-8400 MA26742 - 5"

104. STRONG GUY 001 Taiwan 1993 (data only on package) - all red paint - two recessed ovals on bottom of handle & one recessed oval on top - small ball - 5.1"

105. TROJAN raised cast letters in recessed oval on bottom of handle - NO 41 stamped on side of head - some red paint - 5.2"

106. TROJAN raised cast letters in recessed oval on bottom of handle - NO 50 stamped on side of head - red paint - 5.2"

107. TROJAN raised cast letters in recessed oval on bottom of handle - NO 55 stamped on side of head - red paint - large ball - 5.2"

108. TROJAN raised cast letters in recessed oval on bottom of handle - U.S.A. recess cast on bottom of handle - No. 50 recess cast next to finger rest - red paint with a .7" dark blue tip - 5.2"

109. TROJAN raised cast letters in recessed oval on bottom of handle - MADE IN U.S.A. recess cast on bottom of handle - NO 50 stamped on side of head - red paint with .2" dark blue tip - 5.15"

109-A. TROJAN same as XX-109 above except is shorter and the "MADE IN USA" is larger – 5.05"

110. UTICA raised cast letters in a recessed rectangle on bottom of handle - PAT. JULY 5, 1927 stamped on side of head - Patent concerns the U bent pin as axle - cross-hatch finger rest - red paint threaded end with cap missing - 4.8"

111. UTICA raised letters in a recessed rectangle on bottom of handle - cross-hatch finger rest - red paint - 5"

112. VITREX N° 335 raised cast letters & numbers in a recessed long oval on bottom of a non-mag. alloy tool - MADE IN ENGLAND cast raised letter on top of handle - raised dots finger rest - no paint - small ball - 5.2"

113. WARNER & U.S.A. separate recessed ovals cast on on bottom of red painted non-mag. alloy tool - 1053 cast in recessed oval next to finger rest - .6" dark blue sock & small ball - 5.2"

114. WARNER #138 data on package - MADE IN U.S.A. cast in top of head of non- mag. alloy tool - black paint small ball - 5.1"

115. WIZARD U.S.A. stamped on side of head - red paint - 4.6"

116. WIZARD U.S.A. stamped on side of slightly rounded head - red paint - 5"

117. WIZARD U.S.A. stamped on side of head - red paint - large ball - 5.2"

118. WOOLWORTH U.S.A. recess cast in recessed ovals on bottom of red painted non-mag. alloy tool - No. 1085 data on card - 1" dark blue tip - 5.15"

119. WOOLWORTH, F. W. CO. LIMITED MADE IN TAIWAN TR08398B 292 10/91 data from package - all red paint on non-mag. alloy tool - small ball - 5"

B. MODIFIED BALL END WITH ID flat / tapered end. According to SMITH & HEMENWAY CO., INC. in their Green Book of Red Devil Tools, Irvington, N.J.,(eighth edition)(possibly 1917)
"The advantage of this style cutter is its squared point-driver end" as illustrated on page 4 of the book.

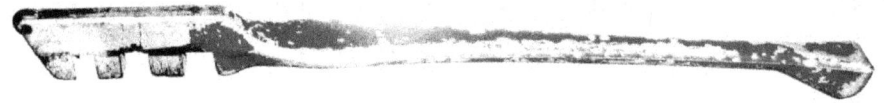

120. BEST MADE IN U.S.A. cast raised letters in recessed oval on bottom of handle under finger rest - non-mag. alloy tool - red paint - modified ball - 4.9"

121. BEST MADE IN U.S.A. cast raised letters in recessed oval on bottom of handle under circular finger rest - non-mag. alloy tool - red paint - modified ball - 4.8"

122. HYCO MADE IN U.S.A. otherwise same as XX-121 above & XX-123 below - 4.8"

123. HYDE MADE IN U.S.A. otherwise same as XX-121 & 122 above - 4.8"

124. PENNVERNON MADE IN U.S.A. green paint - otherwise same as XX-121, 122, 123 above - 4.8"

125. PENNVERNON MADE IN U.S.A. sky blue paint - otherwise same as XX- 121,122,123, 124 above - 4.8"

126. SINGER raised cast letters in recessed rectangle on bottom of handle - MADE IN USA cast in top of handle next to finger rest red paint - modified ball - 4.9"

127. No ID - black paint - modified ball is flat on sides and tapered both on top and bottom with square end - 5.2"

C. NO NAME BUT SOME ID

128. U.S.A. recessed letters in a recessed oval on bottom of non-mag. alloy tool - red paint - small ball - evidence of black sock and black ball - 5.2"

129. U.S.A. cast in bottom of handle with light blue paint - 5.05"

130. U.S.A. cast in bottom of non-mag. alloy tool - black paint - small ball - 5.15"

131. MADE IN USA cast in top of handle next to finger rest - red paint - small ball - 4.9"

132. MADE IN U S A cast lengthwise on bottom of handle - three concentric circles on finger rest dark green paint - 4.9"

133. MADE IN U. S. A. cast lengthwise on bottom of handle - green paint - medium ball - 5.2"

134. MADE IN U. S. A. cast lengthwise on bottom of handle - three concentric circles on finger rest - red paint - small ball - 5.05"

135. MADE IN USA (small letters close) lengthwise on bottom of handle - black paint - medium ball - 5.15"

136. MADE in U.S.A. cast recessed on top of head of non-mag. alloy tool - .6" gold sock with gold medium ball - 5.2"

137. MADE IN ENGLAND raised letters reading toward head in a recessed rectangle on bottom of non-mag. alloy tool - striped finger rest orangesh-red paint - 5.45"

138. Same as XX-137 above except that MADE IN ENGLAND reads toward the end of handle - 5.45"

139. MADE IN ENGLAND cast recessed on top of handle - red paint - 5.25"

140. GERMANY(very small letters) stamped on side of head - red paint covers some data on bottom of handle - large ball - 4.8"

140 – A. GERMANY cast in recessed rectangle on finger rest – red paint – medium ball – 4.95"

141. GERMANY(very small letters) stamped on side of head - red paint - 24 cast in bottom of handle - large ball - 4.8"

142. GERMANY(very small letters) stamped on side of folded over sheet steel head - a rivet serves as axle and holds head together - red paint - medium unpainted aluminum ball holds this end together - 4.8"

143. GERMANY raised letters cast on top mid handle - thin steel head - red plastic handle - 5.15"

144. JAPAN stamped on reverse of steel head - red paint - large ball - 4.8"

145. JAPAN stamped on reverse of steel head - red paint - larger ball than XX-144 above - breakers closer together - nose angle sharper and wheel bigger - 4.9"

146. JAPAN stamped on reverse of steel head - thicker head than XX-145 - red paint - large ball - 4.85"

147. JAPAN just barely stamped on top edge of reverse side of head - red paint - large ball -extreme angle on nose of head - 4.95"

D. NO IDENTIFICATION AT ALL

148. Maroon paint - large ball - blunt angle on nose of .4" high head - 5.15"
149. Red paint large ball - .47" high head - 5.05"
150. Red paint - .46" high head - slender handle - 5"
151. Possibly a RUBY as BY is on side of head - dark red paint on slender handle - 4.6"
152. Red paint - .45" high head - slender handle - 5.5"
153. Black paint - thick head 1.3" long - wide bars between breakers - 5.3"
154. Black paint - slightly rounded top of head - slender handle - 4.9"
155. Black paint - slightly rounded top of head - slender handle - 5.1"
156. Red paint - non-mag. alloy tool - 5.2"

E. MODIFIED HEADS - HANDLES (not in Category XXIII)

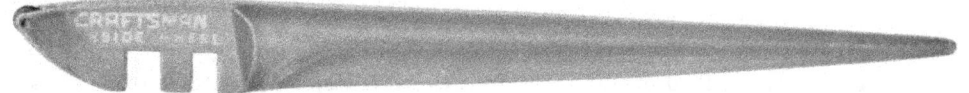

157. CRAFTSMAN - CARBIDE WHEEL on obverse side of head - MADE IN U.S.A. PAT. 1956 U. S. NO. 2,735,228 on reverse side of head - light brown paint - non-mag. alloy tool - 5.5"

158. CRAFTSMAN - CARBIDE WHEEL on obverse side of head - MADE IN U.S.A. NO. 3796 on reverse side of head - light brown paint - non-mag. alloy tool - 5.5"

159. CRAFTSMAN - CARBIDE WHEEL on obverse side of head - 9 3797 MADE IN U.S.A. on reverse side of head - anodized gold - non-mag. alloy tool - 5.5"

160. MILLERS FALLS CARBIDE WHEEL on obverse side of head - MADE IN USA NO 66 on reverse side of head - matte silver finish - non-mag. alloy tool - 5.5"

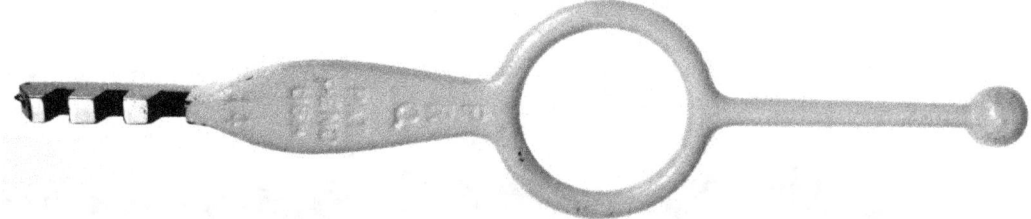

161. PRQ PAT PEND USA 14 cast recessed on bottom under the finger rest - baby blue paint on all except the polished & plated steel head - small ball - 6.35"

162. PAT NO 4224738 cast recessed on bottom under the finger rest - no breakers on plated steel head - baby blue paint on all except the polished & plated steel head - small ball - 6.35"

163. PAT NO 4224738 cast recessed on bottom under the finger rest - no breakers on polished & plated split steel head - MAGEWICK stamped on a plate that makes up the entire obverse side of head, attached with a screw with head on reverse side of head, this anchors the wheel axle - baby blue paint on all except the head - small ball - 6.35"

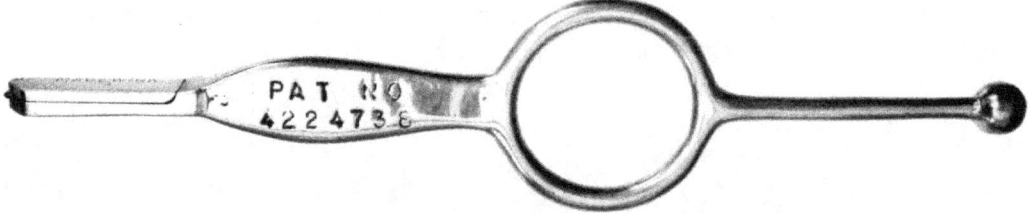

164. Same as XX-163 except all brass construction but the polished & plated steel plate marked MAGEWICK - small ball - 6.25"

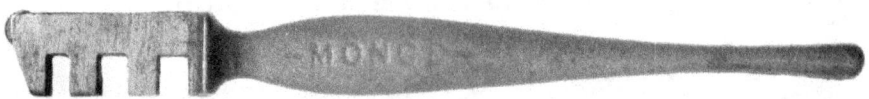

165.   –MONCE- cast recessed on side of handle which is in the vertical plane vs. all others that are in horizontal plane in relation to the head - thick head with a square hilt type base - 5.1"

166.   –MONCE- cast recessed on side of handle which is in the vertical plane vs. all others that are in horizontal plane in relation to the head - thick head with a square hilt type base - MADE IN U.S.A. cast raised letters on reverse side of handle - 5"

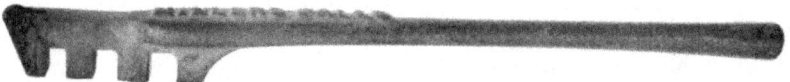

167. MILLERS FALLS cast raised letters starting above the rear breaker on the straight red painted handle - thick head - 4.8"

168.   No ID - picture above tells all - note the position of the cutter wheel which is at right angles to all others - heavy steel construction - flattened ball - 5.2"

169.   DE with arrow through the DE all inside a two line diamond stamped on side of head - note position of the cutter wheel - heavy polished steel construction - 4.95"

170. MILLERS FALLS CO   MILLERS FALLS, MASS - stamped on side of steel head - same construction as XX-169 above - 4.9"

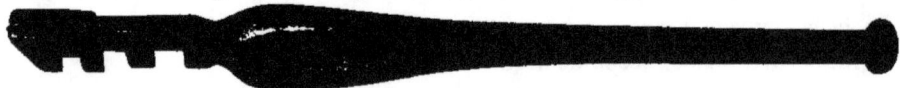

171. No ID - front ½ of head cast and machined thicker than 2nd half - bronze paint starts mid head back to include the flattened ball - note the double side by side finger rests - 5.1"

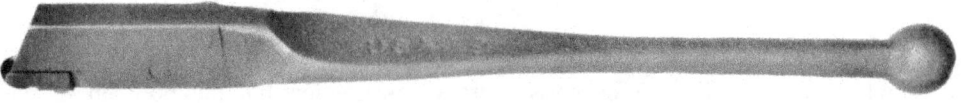

172. MACINNES cast into finger rest - USA 9 cast on bottom below finger rest - handle & small ball are rough finish brass - head is smooth steel with a small brass clip mounted with screw to hold wheel axle in place - A Pro-Score product by MacInnes Tool Corp. - 5.3"

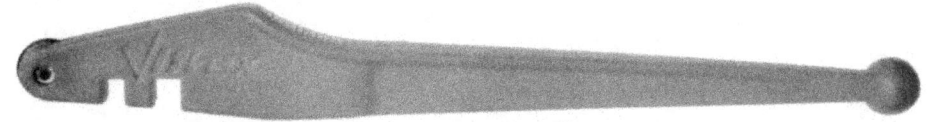

173.   VITREX ®ENGLAND on obverse near head - N° 2234 raised numbers on reverse mid handle - ribbed finger rest - .35" diam. cutter wheel - small ball - all stiff rubberized red material - small ball - 5.15"

174.   PATERSON · NO · 1 stamped into ¼" diam. part of smooth handle - rest of handle is 3/8" diam. knurled surface - all brass construction - 4.8"

175.   1948 stamped facing the head on the ¼" diam. smooth part of handle rest of handle is 3/8" knurled surface - all brass construction - 4.9"

176.   TOYO   TC – 10   JAPAN   cast recessed on .2" X .25' steel head - .6" brass ferrule - 4.6" long X .45" diam. knurled, grey paint , brass, handle with brass plated steel bolt at end with black rubber gasket for oil reservoir - 6.9"

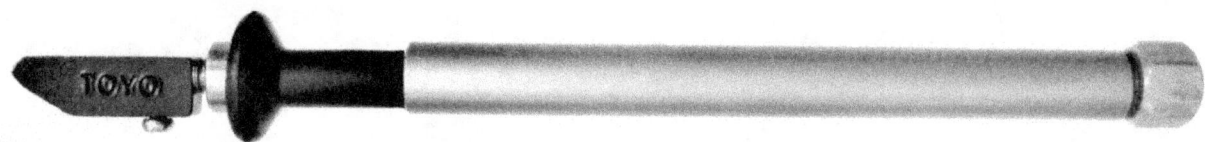

176 – A.   TOYO on head   - black rubber finger rest and ferrule - brass color steel handle with brass hex-ball cap – 6.5"

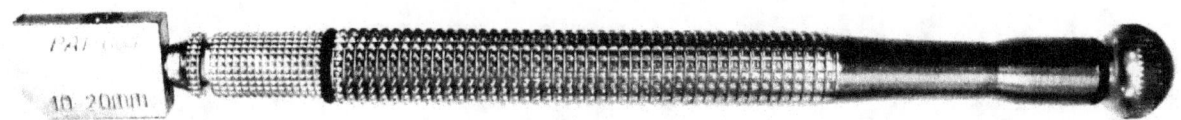

177.   PAT – 051   10-20mm stamped on steel head - .9" brass plated knurled steel ferrule - 2.7" X .4" section of handle is brass plated knurled steel then 2 " smooth handle to the black rubber gasket and knurled brass plated knurled bolt for oil reservoir - 6.6"

178.   GILKIN(sticker on handle) – 3 shallow breakers near head - .8" deep & .7" wide breaker(?) welded at end of orange painted handle - 6.75"

CATEGORY XXI RED DEVIL

There are 71 Red Devil glass cutters in this Category and two known in other collections. The CIRCLE / OVAL(XV) & TUBING(XIII) cutters are shown in those respective Categories.
There is one Design Patent: July 27, 1982, # 265,543 (see # 48 below)

This Category is subdivided into seven subsets.   Price Range: $5 - $30

        A. **THE DEVIL "FACE" SINGLE WHEEL CUTTER**
        B. **SINGLE WHEEL - METAL HANDLE (sans "Face")**
        C. **SINGLE WHEEL - WOOD HANDLE**
        D. **TURRET - WOOD HANDLE**
        E. **TURRET/MULTI WHEEL - METAL HANDLE – some DEVIL "FACE"**
        F. **DEVELOPMENTAL FROM RED DEVIL INC.**

A. THE DEVIL "FACE" SINGLE WHEEL CUTTER

1. RED DEVIL raised letters cast in recessed oval on bottom - MADE IN U.S.A. cast in bottom - No 023 cast in next to finger rest red paint - medium ball - 5.2"

2. RED DEVIL same as XXI-1 above except: small ball - 5.1"

3. RED DEVIL same as XXI-2 above except: MADE IN U.S.A. is cast 1/4 " shorter - 5.1"

4. RED DEVIL raised letters in recessed oval on bottom   - No 024 cast in next to finger rest - slender handle - red paint - 5.1"

5. RED DEVIL raised letters cast in recessed oval on bottom - NO 024 (large O in NO & double space between letters & numbers) cast next to finger rest - red paint - 5.1"

6. RED DEVIL raised letters in recessed oval on bottom - MADE IN U.S.A. cast in bottom - No 024 cast next to finger rest - red paint - 5.05"

7. RED DEVIL raised letters cast in recessed oval on bottom - MADE IN U.S.A. cast in bottom - No 024(larger than XXI-6 above) cast next to finger rest - red paint - 5.2"

8. RED DEVIL raised letters cast in recessed oval on bottom - NO032 (yes, together) cast in next to wider finger rest - red paint - 5.2"

9. RED DEVIL raised letters cast in oval on bottom - MADE IN U.S.A. cast in bottom - 555 PAT. PENDG. cast in on top of thin handle next to finger rest - thick head - thin sheet metal insert to hold wheel axle - red paint - .2" white sock with .65" blue tip - 5.2"

10. RED DEVIL raised letters cast in oval on bottom - MADE IN U.S.A. cast in bottom - N° 888 PAT. 1884685 cast in top of thin handle next to finger rest: (Patent pertains to the retractable thin sheet metal insert to hold wheel axle) - red paint - 5.1"

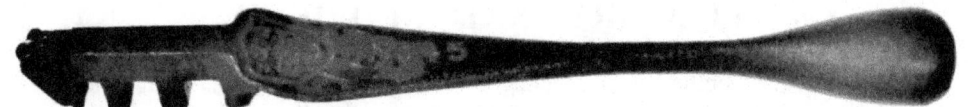

11. RED DEVIL raised letters cast in recessed oval on bottom - MADE IN U.S.A. cast in bottom of bulb end of handle drilled and threaded for extra wheel storage - thick head - No45 cast in top next to wide finger rest - red paint - missing the knurled end bolt - 5.05"

B. SINGLE WHEEL - METAL HANDLE (sans "Face")

12. RED DEVIL raised cast letters on bottom - thick head - bent wire on reverse of head to form axle for wheel - red paint - bulb end drilled and threaded for extra wheel storage with knurled bolt as closure - 5.35"

13. RED DEVIL raised cast letters on bottom - thick head - wide finger rest to the right - retractable thin sheet steel insert that holds axle - red paint - bulb end drilled and threaded for extra wheel storage - missing the knurled end bolt - 5.25"

14. RED DEVIL raised cast letters in recessed oval next to finger rest - 45 USA cast in bottom of handle - retractable sheet metal insert that holds axle - red paint - .2" white sock and dark blue tip including drilled out large ball with knurled bolt as closure - 5.1"

15. RED DEVIL raised cast letters on bottom of handle - slender handle - maroon paint - 5"

16. RED DEVIL raised cast letters on bottom of handle - dark red paint - 4.9"

17. RED DEVIL raised letters on bottom of handle - slightly rounder top of head - reddish-orange paint - 4.75"

18. RED DEVIL raised cast letters on bottom of handle - maroon paint - large ball - 5-1"

19. RED DEVIL raised cast letters in oval next to finger rest - red paint - .3" dark blue sock with small blue ball - 5.2"

20. RED DEVIL raised cast small letters in recessed oval next to finger rest - 023   U.S.A. cast in bottom of handle red paint - .2" dark blue soc and small blue ball - 5.2"

21. RED DEVIL raised cast small letters in recessed oval next to finger rest - 023   USA cast in on bottom of handle - red paint - .18" white sock and .25" dark blue sock and small dark blue ball - 5.2"

22. RED DEVIL raised cast large letters in recessed oval next to finger rest - 023   USA cast in large numbers & letters on bottom of plated handle - red paint - small ball - 5.15"

23. RED DEVIL raised cast letters in recessed oval next to finger rest - 023   U . S . A . cast on bottom of handle - red paint - .2" dark blue sock with small dark blue ball - 5.2"

24. RED DEVIL raised cast large letters in recessed oval next to finger rest - 024   USA cast in bottom of plated handle - red paint in recess and a 1.1" at tip - 5.2"

25. RED DEVIL raised cast small letters in recessed oval next to finger rest - 024   USA cast small in bottom of handle - .4" white sock and .6" dark blue tip - 5.2"

26. RED DEVIL raised cast small letters in recessed oval next to finger rest - 024   USA small numbers and letters cast in bottom of handle - red paint - .5" dark blue tip - 5.2"

27. RED DEVIL raised cast large letters in recessed oval next to finger rest - 024   U S A in large numbers and letters cast in bottom of handle - red paint - .65" dark blue tip - 5.2"

28. RED DEVIL raised cast letters in recessed oval next to finger rest - 032 stamped on obverse side of plated head - USA cast in bottom of handle evidence of red paint - small ball - 5.2"

29. RED DEVIL stamped on obverse side of head - little evidence of red paint - large ball - 5"

30. "RED DEVIL" stamped in logo font on obverse side of head - slightly rounded top of head - reddish-orange paint - large ball - 5.25"

31. RED DEVIL 024 stamped in logo font on obverse side of head - slender handle - dark red paint - 4.85"

32. RED DEVIL 032 stamped in logo font on obverse side of head - reddish-orange paint - 4.85"

33. RED DEVIL   G 1 in script cast in finger rest - USA in three concentric circles cast on bottom under finger rest - non-mag. alloy tool - red paint with .35"dark blue sock and small ball - 5.15"

34. RED DEVIL same as XXI-34 above except: handle is all red paint

35. RED DEVIL same as XXI-35 above except: G2 on finger rest instead of G1

36. RED DEVIL USA cast in bottom of handle - gold paint - .2" celery green sock top with 1.25" silver-grey tip - 5.15"

37. RED DEVIL USA cast in bottom of handle - 063 cast in next to finger rest - red paint - .3" dark blue sock top with .4" silver sock and small ball - 5.15"

38. RED DEVIL cast recessed in a recessed oval with U.S.A. likewise in another oval on bottom of handle reading toward the head - 1063 recessed cast in a recessed oval next to finger rest - non-mag. alloy tool - red paint - .55" dark blue sock and small ball - 5.2"

39. RED DEVIL, INC. USA cast in bottom of handle reading toward small ball end - 1063 cast in recessed oval next to finger rest on non-mag. alloy tool - red paint - 5.15"

40. RED DEVIL U.S.A. cast in a pair of recessed ovals reading toward the head on bottom of non-mag. alloy tool - 1063 large numbers cast in recessed oval next to finger rest reading toward head - red paint - small ball - 5.2"

41. RED DEVIL (in script) U.S.A. cast in bottom of handle of non-mag. alloy tool - 023 cast in top of handle - red paint .3" white sock top with .4" dark blue sock and small ball - 5.15"

42. RED DEVIL USA cast in bottom of handle - 1023 cast in top next to finger rest - red paint - small ball - 5.15"

43. RED DEVIL INC cast in bottom of handle - 1023 cast in top next to finger rest - red paint - .75" dark blue sock and small ball - 5.1"

44. RED DEVIL USA cast in bottom of handle - 1023 cast in top next to finger rest - red paint - .6" dark blue sock with small ball - 5.15"

45. RED DEVIL cast in bottom of handle - 1024 cast in top next to finger rest - red paint with 1" dark blue tip - 5.15"

46. RED DEVIL cast in recessed oval on bottom of non-mag. alloy tool - 1053 cast reading toward head in recessed oval on top - red paint with .55" dark blue sock ans small ball - 5.1"

47. RED DEVIL INC cast in bottom of handle - red paint with .8" silver-grey sock and small ball - 5.1"

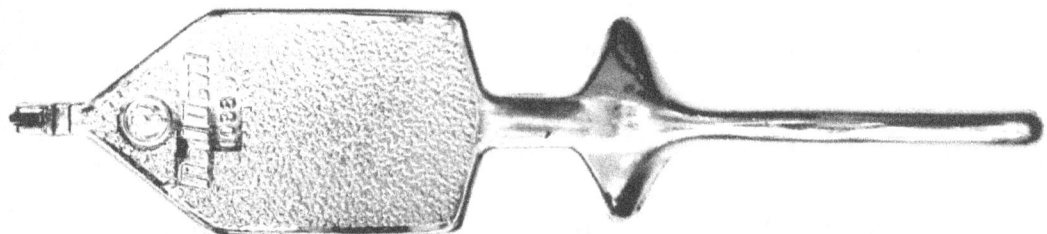

48. RED DEVIL 1038 with "Face" above cast in on top of head near wheel - 1 cast on bottom of handle - chrome plated non-mag. alloy tool - 5.7" (Design Patent # 265,543 dated July 27, 1982) (donation from RED DEVIL, INC.)

C. SINGLE WHEEL - WOOD HANDLE

49. RED DEVIL XXX S. & H. CO. PAT. ALP'D FOR stamped on obverse of elongated two piece steel head - .25" plated brass ferrule - very dark stained handle - 5.6"

50. RED DEVIL(in script) PAT APL'D FOR No 5 S & H CO stamped on obverse side of elongated two piece steel head - bent wire for wheel axle - .25" plated brass ferrule - very dark stain finish - .25" collar and knurled bolt for extra wheel storage area at end of handle - 5.6"

51. RED DEVIL(smaller than XXI-51 above) PAT. APL'D. FOR No5(larger than XXI-51 above) S & H CO. stamped on obverse of elongated head - .25" plated brass ferrule - very dark stain - .25" collar and make-do ball end plug for extra wheel storage area at end of handle - 5.8"

52. RED DEVIL NO 999 MADE IN U. S. A. stamped in obverse of thick steel head - .4" non-mag. alloy ferrule - mahogany stained handle like XXI-54 below - 5.9"

D. TURRET - WOOD HANDLE

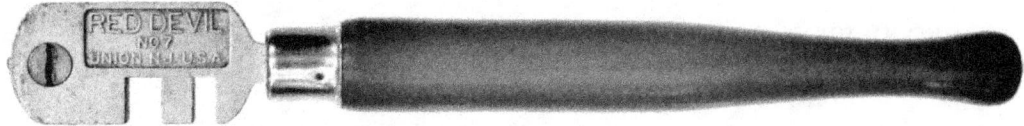

53-A. RED DEVIL same as XXI-54 below except screw head holding turret is larger, different script for raised numbers, and handle is thinner with mahogany stain – 5.45"

53. RED DEVIL NO. 7 UNION N.J. U.S.A. raised letters in recessed rectangle on obverse side of plated steel head -- raised numbers on non-mag. flush turret - .4" plated brass ferrule - dark stain handle - 5.5"

54. RED DEVIL NO. 7 IRV. N.J. U.S.A. raised letters in a recessed rectangle on non-mag. alloy head - recessed numbers on protruding steel turret - .4" non-mag. ferrule - mahogany stain handle - 5.5"

55. RED DEVIL NO. 7 IRV. N. J. U.S.A. raised letters in recessed rectangle with red paint on non-mag. alloy head - raised numbers on non-mag. flush turret - .4" plated steel ferrule - red stain finish - 5.4"

56. RED DEVIL No.7 L.P.SMITH,INC.   MADE IN U.S.A. raised letters in recessed rectangle on plated non-mag. alloy head - raised numbers of non-mag. flush turret - .4" plated brass ferrule - mahogany stain finish - 5.5"

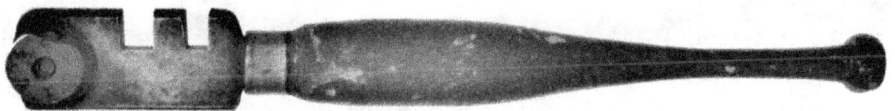

57. RED DEVIL 37 stamped on obverse side of rounded top steel head - recessed numbers on extended brass turret - .25" plated brass ferrule - second half of short dark red stained handle tapers quickly to flattened ball end - 5.05"

58. RED DEVIL stamped in obverse side of plated, rounded top, steel head - recessed numbers on extended steel turret - .25" plated brass ferrule - second half of short red stained handle tapers quickly to flattened ball end - 4.8"

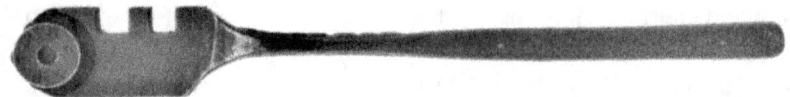

59. RED DEVIL raised cast letters on bottom of handle - recessed numbers on extended steel turret - head is .6" tall X 1.25" long X .18" thick - 5.1"

60. RED DEVIL raised letters cast in recessed oval on bottom of handle - NO 48 cast next to finger rest with "DEVIL FACE" - recessed numbers on extended steel turret - red paint - 5.3"

61. RED DEVIL raised letters cast in recessed oval & MADE IN U.S.A. cast in bottom of handle - NO 48 cast in top next to finger rest with cast in "DEVIL FACE" - large bold recessed numbers on flush steel turret - red paint - 5.2"

62. RED DEVIL same as XXI-62 above except: large thin numbers on turret & red paint extends up to the turret on the head - 5.3

63. RED DEVIL raised letters in recessed oval on bottom of handle - 48 USA cast in top of handle - raised numbers on non-mag. alloy flush turret - red paint - small ball - 5.2"

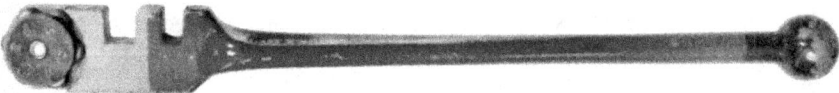

64. RED DEVIL(in script) G5 cast in finger rest - USA in three concentric ovals cast in bottom under the finger rest - non-mag. alloy tool - red paint with .25" dark blue sock and small ball - 5.2

65. RED DEVIL raised letters cast on bottom of handle under finger rest that offsets to the right - recessed numbers on flush brass turret - oversize steel head: .7" high X .3" wide X 1.25" long - orangesh-red paint - 5.35"

66. S & H Co. stamped on obverse side of very slightly rounded top of head - note three fixed position cutter wheels - orangesh-red paint - 4.8"

67. RED DEVIL stamped in obverse side of slightly rounded top of head - note three fixed position cutter wheels - orangesh-red paint - 4.8"

F. DEVELOPMENTAL FROM RED DEVIL INC.

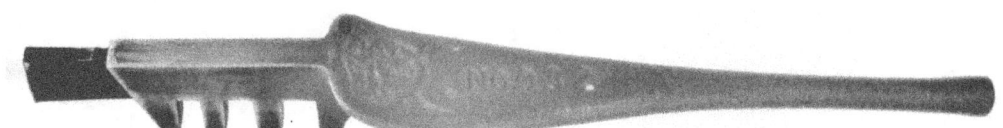

68. RED DEVIL raised letters cast in oval on bottom - N0 023 cast next to wider finger rest - brass head with sprue still attached, soldered to brass plated non-mag. alloy handle - 5.3" Note: this was a donation from; RED DEVIL INC.

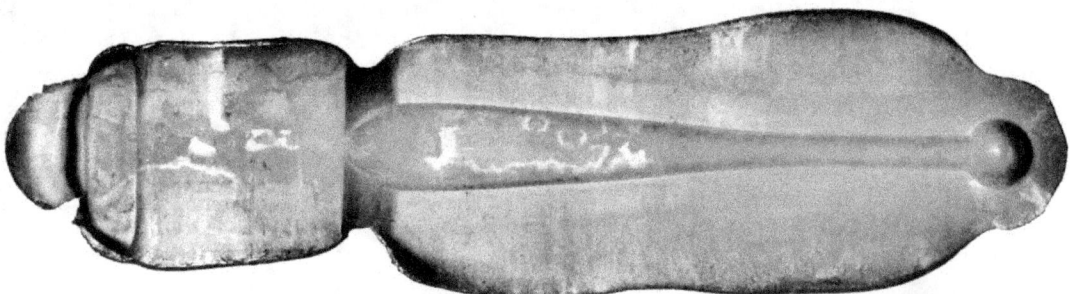

top view above ↑ **and the bottom view below** ↓

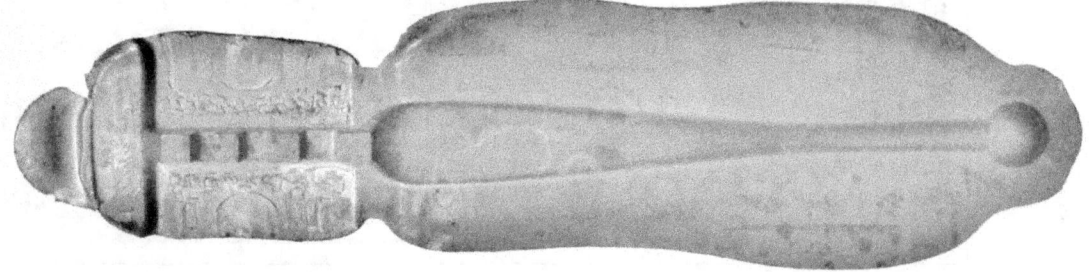

69. No ID (special from Red Devil Inc.) Basic 5.15" glass cutter with lots of "brass" flashing from casting or possibly a drop forge operation.

70. No ID (special from Red Devil Inc.) Basic handle, but two drilled holes in end of head could be for mounting slip-in cutter units. - 5"

71. RED DEVIL raised letters in recessed oval on finger rest - · 888 · USA cast in bottom of grey color, stipple finish, plated steel tool – no slot cut for wheel on thick machined smooth head - 5.2" Donation from Red Devil, Inc. Similar in shape to XXI-10 above

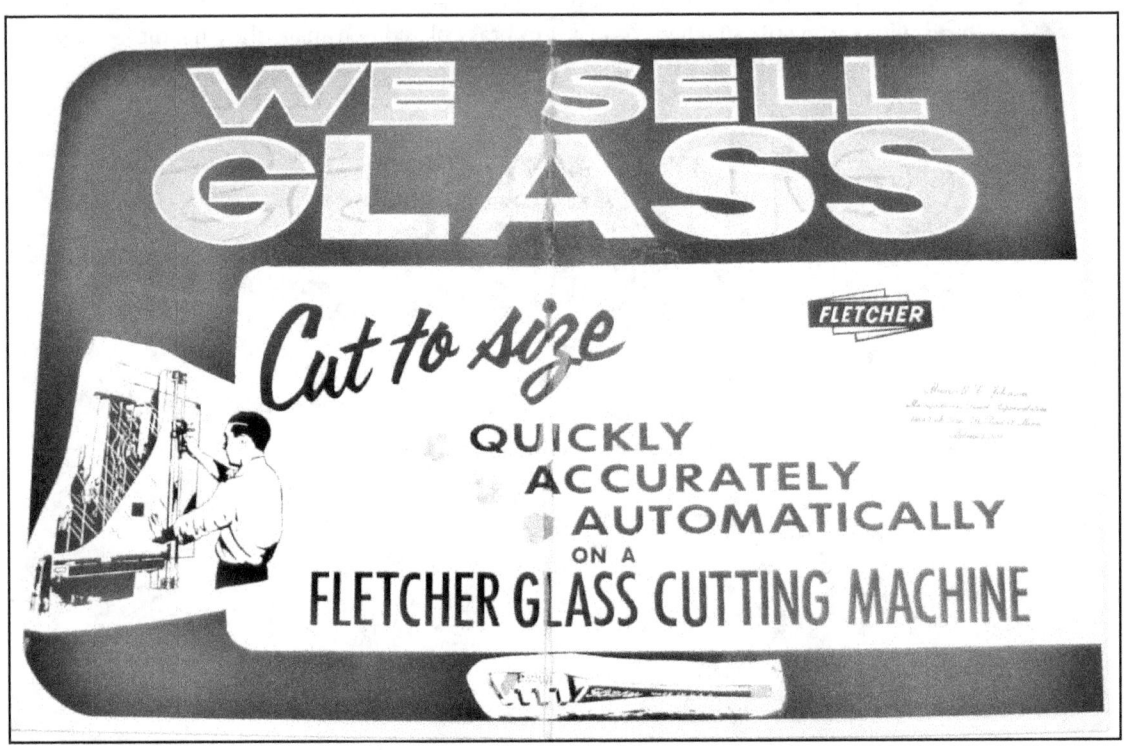

A 14" X 22" poster board countertop or wall advertizing the FLETCHER GLASS CUTTING MACHINE.

The following is stamped in Fletcher green on both front and back:

Maxwell C. Johnson
Manufacturers Direct Representative
1608 Oak Ave. St. Paul 12, Minn.
Melrose 3-5611

CATEGORY XXII   FLETCHER -TERRY CO.

Twenty two of the U. S. Patents listed below are associated with the Fletcher-Terry Co. and some others from the master list in the text may be also.   There is but one known different cutter in another collection.

91,150	*1,028,870 by*	2,341,030	3,550,273	4,030,195	4,201,104
140,426	*E.F. Fletcher, not*	2,576,291	3,682,027	4,083,274	4,203,209
453,867	*family or Co.*	3,373,488	3,850,062	4,098,155	4,226,153
742,179	1,634,323	3,399,586	4,018,372	4,098,156	4,228,711
					4,691,438

Price Range: $5 - $25

The name *Fletcher* is cast into the bottom of most of their cutters under the finger rest. Other font style and/or locations are noted in line items such as **turrets** and oil **reservoir units.**

1.   F. T. CO. stamped on obverse side of head - bent wire anchored in slot atop head is axle for wheel - U.S.A. cast in bottom of handle - red paint - medium ball with knurled brass bolt for extra wheel storage at end - 5.2"

2.   *Fletcher*   MADE IN U.S.A. cast in bottom of handle - wrap around bent wire axle anchored in keyways on sides of thick head - this keyway is U.S. Pat. No. 1,634,323 (July 5, 1927) green paint - 5.1"

3.   *Fletcher* MADE IN U.S.A. cast in bottom of handle - green paint with .4" yellow tip - 5.1"

4.   *Fletcher* cast in bottom of handle - green paint with .7" gold tip - 5.15"

5.   *Fletcher* MADE IN USA cast in bottom of handle - green paint - 5.25"

6.   *Fletcher* MADE IN U.S.A. cast in bottom of handle -- green paint with .25" yellow tip - 4.8"

7.   *Fletcher* MADE IN U.S.A. cast in bottom of handle - black paint with 3/4 yellow medium ball - 5.1"

8.   *Fletcher* MADE IN U.S.A. cast in bottom of handle - dark green paint with .5" baby blue sock and .35" gold sock and small gold ball - 5.2"

9.   *Fletcher* cast in bottom of handle - dark green paint with .2" gold sock and gold small ball - 5.15"

10. *Fletcher* cast in bottom of handle - light green paint with .3" gold sock and gold small ball - 5.2"

11. *Fletcher* MADE IN USA cast in bottom of handle - red paint - ¾" gold medium ball - 5.1"

12. *Fletcher* MADE IN U.S.A. cast in bottom of handle - red paint - ½ yellow medium ball - 5.1"

13. *Fletcher* cast in bottom of handle - N° 01 cast in next to finger rest - green paint - 5.15"

14. *Fletcher* MADE IN USA cast in bottom of handle - BB N° 01 cast in finger rest - green paint 5.2"

15. *Fletcher* MADE IN USA cast in bottom of handle - N° 01 cast in next to finger rest - green paint with .4" gold tip - 5.2"

16. *Fletcher* MADE IN USA cast in bottom of handle - N° 01 cast next to finger rest - green paint with .4" gold tip - 5.2"

17. *Fletcher* MADE IN USA cast in bottom of handle -bold N° 02 cast next to finger rest - green paint w.15" gold sock and small gold ball - 5.2"

18. *Fletcher* MADE IN USA cast in bottom of handle - N° 02 cast in next to finger rest - green paint with ½ gold small ball - 5.2"

19. *Fletcher* MADE IN U S A cast in bottom of handle - N° **02** cast in finger rest - green paint with1/2 gold small ball - 5"

20. *Fletcher* MADE IN USA cast in bottom handle - N° 06 cast next to finger rest - green paint with .55" baby blue sock and .35" gold tip - 5.2"

21. *Fletcher* MADE IN USA cast in bottom of handle - AA N° 06 cast in finger rest - black paint with .4" gold tip - 5.2"

22. *Fletcher* MADE IN USA cast in bottom of handle - N° 08 cast next to finger rest - black paint with .1" baby blue tip - 5.15"

23. *Fletcher* MADE IN USA cast in bottom of handle - V N° 08 cast in finger rest - green paint with .5" gold tip - 5.15"

24. *FLETCHER* cast in finger rest - MADE IN U.S.A. cast in top of head of non-mag. alloy tool - 01-128 (07) data on card - green paint with .5" baby blue sock and .4" gold sock with gold small ball - 5.2"

25. *FLETCHER* cast in finger rest - MADE IN U.S.A. cast on top of head of non-mag. alloy tool - #02A cast in concave area on bottom of handle under finger rest - 01-122 data on card - green paint with .25" gold sock and small gold ball - 5.1"

26. *Fletcher* MADE IN U. S. A. cast in bottom of handle - BRONZE BEARING(small letters) 01 stamped on obverse side of head - green paint - 5"

27. *Fletcher* MADE IN USA cast in bottom of handle - BRONZE BEARING(small letters) 01 stamped in obverse side of head - green paint with .4" gold tip - 5"

28. *Fletcher* MADE IN U. S. A. cast in bottom of handle - BRONZE(large letters) 02(narrow 0) stamped in obverse side of head - green paint with ½ gold medium ball - 5.1"

29. *Fletcher* MADE IN USA cast in bottom of handle - BRONZE BEARING(small letters) 02(wide 0) stamped on obverse of head - green paint with ½ gold medium ball - 5.1"

30. *Fletcher* cast in bottom of handle - BRONZE BEARING(small letters) 04 stamped on obverse of head - red paint with .4" gold tip - 5.05"

31. *Fletcher* MADE IN U.S.A. cast in bottom of handle - BRONZE BEARING 08 stamped on obverse of head - green paint - .3" gold tip - 5.05"

32. No ID - NO. 02 stamped on obverse of head - Fletcher green paint with ½ Fletcher gold paint on large ball - however, mold cast join lines are centered fore to aft on both top & bottom of tool contrary to other Fletcher cutters - 5"

TURRET

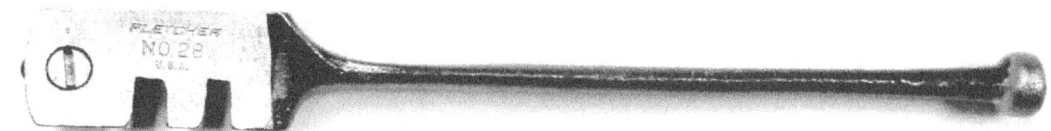

33. *FLETCHER* NO. 28 U.S.A.(very small) stamped on obverse of head - recessed numbers on extended steel turret - cross-hatch pattern in an oval on finger rest - green paint - small flattened gold ball - 5"

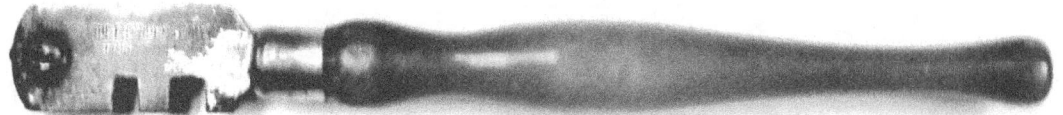

34. THE FLETCHER-TERRY C° FORESTVILLE, CT. U.S.A. stamped on obverse of plated steel head - NO. 29 stamped on reverse of head - recessed numbers on extended steel turret - .4" plated brass ferrule - contoured mahogany finish wood handle - 5.5"

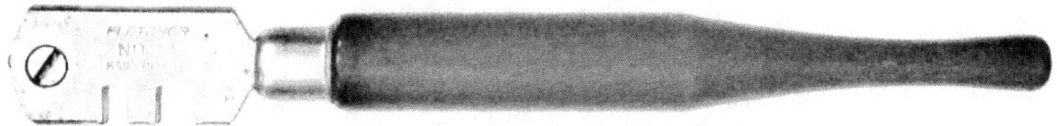

35. *FLETCHER* NO. 29 MADE IN U.S.A.(small letters) stamped on obverse of plated steel head rounded both top & bottom - recessed numbers on extended steel turret - walnut finish on straight wood handle which tapers to .3" diam. at end - 5.7"

36. *FLETCHER* NO. 29 MADE IN U.S.A.(small letters) stamped on obverse of plated steel head rounded both top & bottom - recessed numbers on thin brass extended turret - walnut finish on straight wood handle which tapers less than XXII-35 above to a .4" diam. end - 5.6"

RESERVOIR

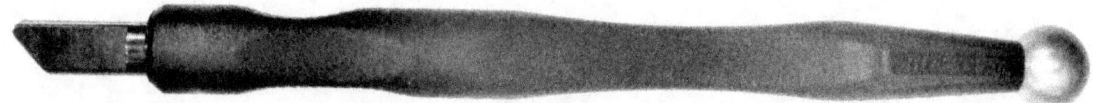

37. *FLETCHER* U.S.A. cast into black plastic "wing" next to the brass plated steel ball end - black painted steel head which is retractable to fill reservoir with cutting oil - 01-701 on package card - 6.5"

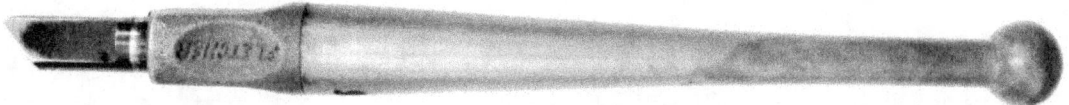

38. *FLETCHER* cast in bottom finger rest - MADE IN U.S.A. cast in top finger rest which is a non-mag. alloy like a ferrule - black paint steel head same as XXII-37 above - .5" diam. (at ferrule) brass handle tapers to .25" diam. at medium size ball end - 6.4"

CATEGORY XXIII   MISCELLANEOUS GLASS CUTTERS

This Category includes the glass cutters that don't easily fall into any of the other twenty two categories.

There are 34 known different ones in other collections.

One hundred sixty two U. S. Patents and one Design Patent selected from the master list are given below:

44,331	921,652	2,184,126	3,122,953	3,600,992	4,098,156	4,451,176*
219,313	922,361	2,219,698	3,126,636	3,682,027	4,137,803	4,495,845
231,225*	997,310	2,243,773	3,130,499	3,703,115	4,155,495	4,576,079
266,193	1,096,782*	2,265,955	3,136,191	3,742,793	4,171,657	4,628,784*
271,868	1,263,129	2,314,327	3,160,043	3,742,794	4,175,684	4,672,874*
376,825	1,301,950	2,375,378	3,165,017	3,756,104	4,183,274	4,726,500
395,704	1,463,374	2,470,444	3,169,683	3,760,997	4,187,755	4,739,555
482,256	1,487,360	2,473,189	3,175,745	3,797,339	4,201,104	4,871,104
494,256	1,495,523	2,504,655	3,198,044	3,797,340	4,209,272	4,987,814
526,444	1,515,129	2,507,779	3,216,635	3,821,910	4,210,052	5,012,393
535,222	1,710,261	2,513,876	3,274,390	3,850,062	4,220,066	5,005,318
539,130	1,753,191	2,539,601	3,276,302	3,850,063	4,222,300*	5,040,445
574,178	1,807,619	2,603,873	3,280,676	3,865,673	4,225,072	5,165,585
601,737	1,904,568	2,612,689	3,373,488	3,880,029	4,226,153	5,168,788
616,825	1,907,297	2,629,173	3,399,586	3,880,029	4,228,711	5,337,483*
630,100	1,932,659	2,685,764	3,461,755	3,908,878	4,275,633	5,381,713
634,336	1,972,210	2,707,849	3,518,907	3,913,812	4,297,059	5,394,505
655,007	1,988,565	2,756,545	3,537,345	3,945,278	4,339,877	5,398,579
674,735	1,996,386	2,763,928	3,550,273	4,018,372	4,372,471	5,480,062
682,966	1,999,594	2,763,929	3,555,944	4,026,262	4,383,460	5,558,565
725,288	2,013,216	2,812,579	3,570,336	4,028,801	4,385,540	5,836,229
781,211	2,091,332	2,964,848	3,577,636	4,030,195	4,392,404	5,924,618
858,003	2,155,802	3,058,220	3,593,899	4,083,274	4,434,582	6,065,215
						6,405,440

Design Patent # 220,745*

*marked numbers refer to glass cutters presented in this category

This Category is subdivided into three sub-sets:

A. **MISCELLANEOUS CUTTERS**
B. **STAIN GLASS CUTTERS**
C. **SHAWL CUTTERS**

PRICE RANGE: $10 - $75

A. MISCELLANEOUS CUTTERS

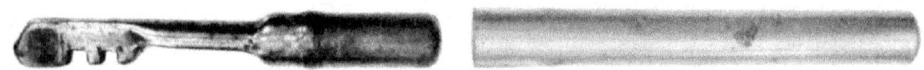

1. VEST POCKET   PAT. AUG. 17, 80 stamped on front end of tin sleeve   -   U. S. Pat. #231,225 by I. W. Heysinger - head and neck are steel - 5"

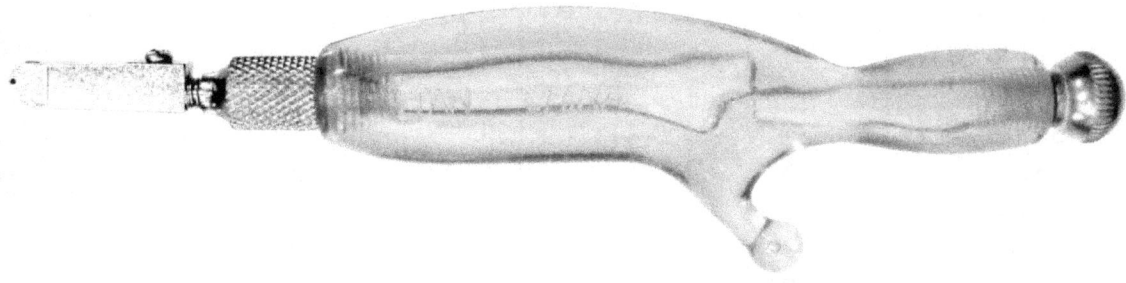

2. TAN   CHINA on orange plastic handle - steel head - knurled brass ferrule and removable ball end for oil reservoir - 6.4"

3. GOODELL TOOL Co. SHELBURNE FALLS MASS.   stamped small letters on obverse of steel head - NO 3 stamped on reverse - 2 glass cutter wheels on end of head - plated brass ferrule - dark mahogany finish on wood handle - 5.55"

4. GOODELL TOOL Co. SHELBURNE FALLS, MASS. stamped medium letters on obverse of steel head - NO 3 stamped on reverse - 2 glass cutter wheels on end of head - plated brass ferrule - dark mahogany finish on wood handle - 5.55"

5. HIBLENTS above a 3 leaf clover stamped on short steel head - 2 glass cutter wheels on end of head - .75" brass ferrule - flat sided walnut handle with flattened ball - 6.45"

6. No ID - steel head with 2 glass cutter wheels and but one breaker - .65"brass ferrule - round walnut handle with flattened ball - 6.7"

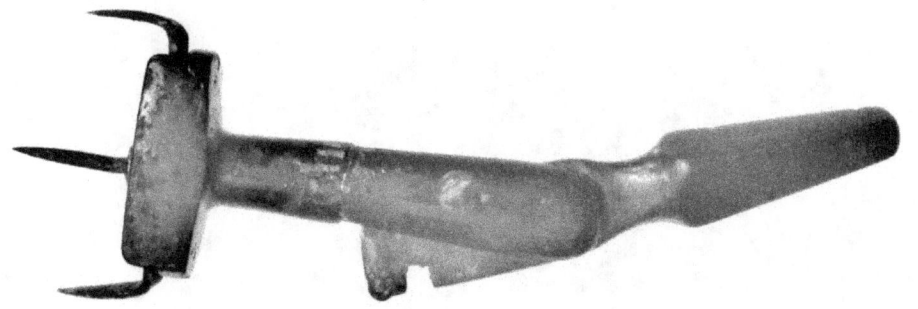

7. WOODWARD'S PAT AUG. 24, '75.stamped on chuck end of all steel gasket cutter tool - deep maroon paint - glass cutter wheel is next to the breaker - 5.1"

8. V with dot inside raised on what could be the ferrule - orange paint on 3 breaker steel head that extends the length of the tool inside the orange rubber handle   - a sharpened tungsten carbide point instead of a wheel - (picked up in Tasmania) - 7"

9. No ID - a home made "make do" - handle is a 6" steel spike - steel hinge holds a .15" X .2" X .12" diamond - 7.4"

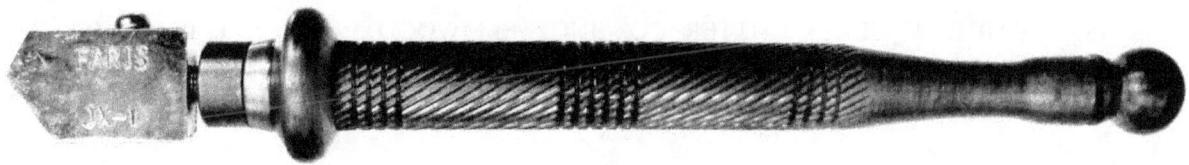

10. FARIS   JX-1 stamped on obverse of plated steel head - .25" brass ferrule unscrews from bronzed knurled steel handle with brass plated steel ball end that unscrews for oil cavity - 6.7"

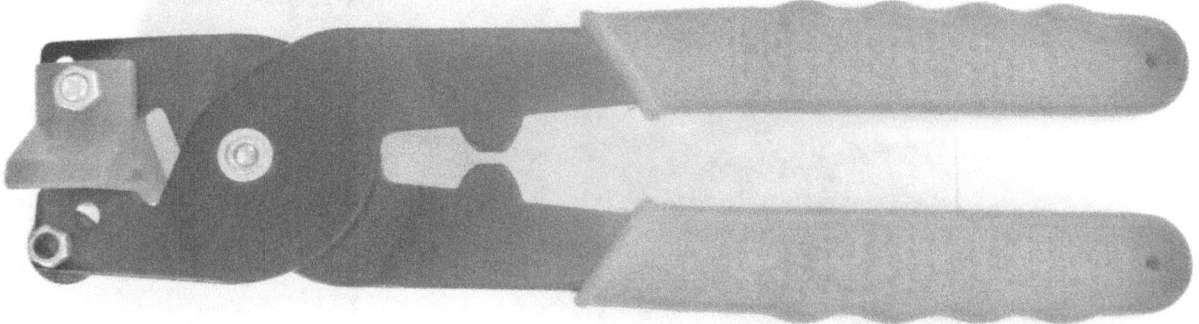

11. No ID - .5" diam. cutting wheel - red plastic snap breaker - black flat steel jaws and handles covered with ribbed red plastic handle grips - 8.25"

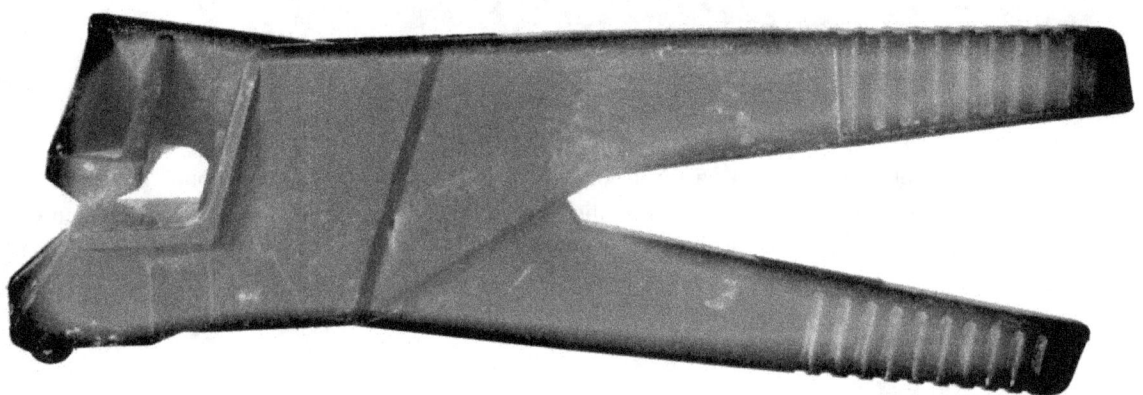

12. No ID - similar but a lot cheaper than XXIII-11 above - .25" diam. cutting wheel mounted loose on axle - all black plastic construction - 6.2"

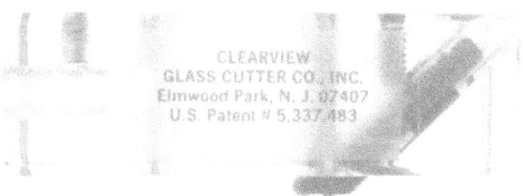

13. CLEARVIEW GLASS CUTTER CO., INC. ELMWOOD PARK, N. J. 07407 U.S. Patent # 5,337,483 on sticker on side of clear Lucite block 3" X 1.25" X .93" - block is drilled(or cast) for two cutter positions

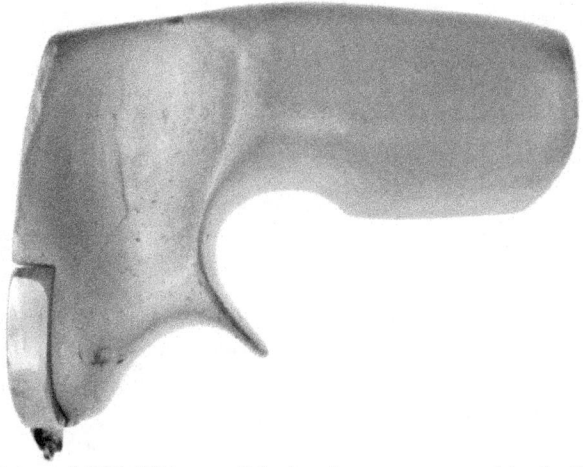

14. No ID - Design Patent # 220,745 - solid aluminum contoured body like a shoe that fits in the hand with a steel plate holding the glass cutter wheel - 3.5" high X 1.7" wide X 2.7" deep at base

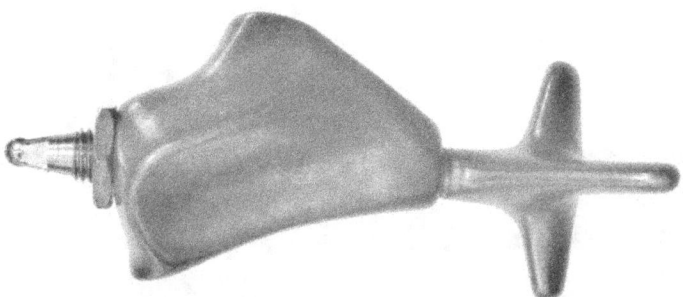

15. *M. R. Raven* vibra-penciled on brass body under the issue number 251 next to brass hex nut holding cutter unit - this is a right hand model, as both left & right were made - this is the first & only one the author has ever seen - solid brass "rudder" is adjustable to fit hand - 3 ½" in closed position

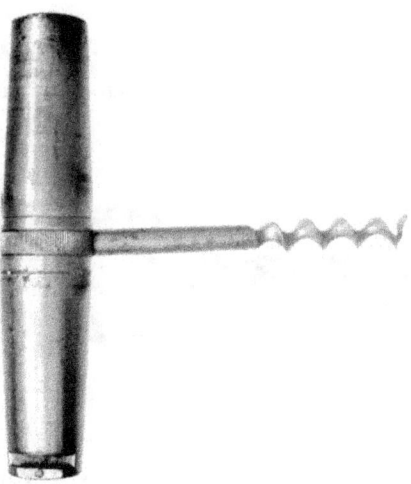

16. No ID - cutter wheel on end of 2 breaker end which unscrews for compartment holding screwdriver and awl which can be exchanged for the corkscrew - plated steel - tube handle is 3.25" wide X .6" diam.

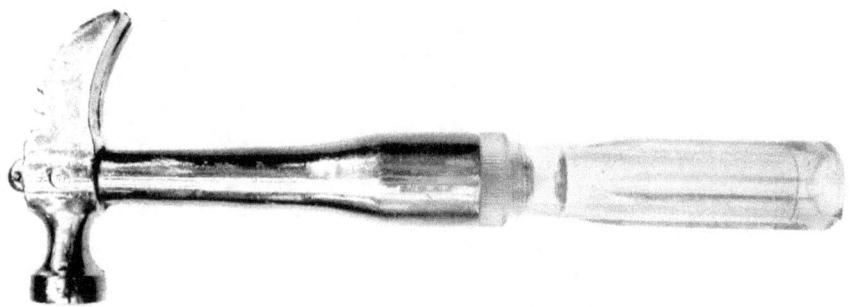

17. DBGM raised letters cast in recessed oval on neck of plated non-mag. alloy   - the only steel is the hammer peen face - clear yellow plastic hollow handle part has: 10000 VOLT GERMANY FOREIGN   cast in a groove - leather case inscribed: GREEN   MOUNTAIN MUTUAL · MONTPIELIER, VT. · - 6.2"

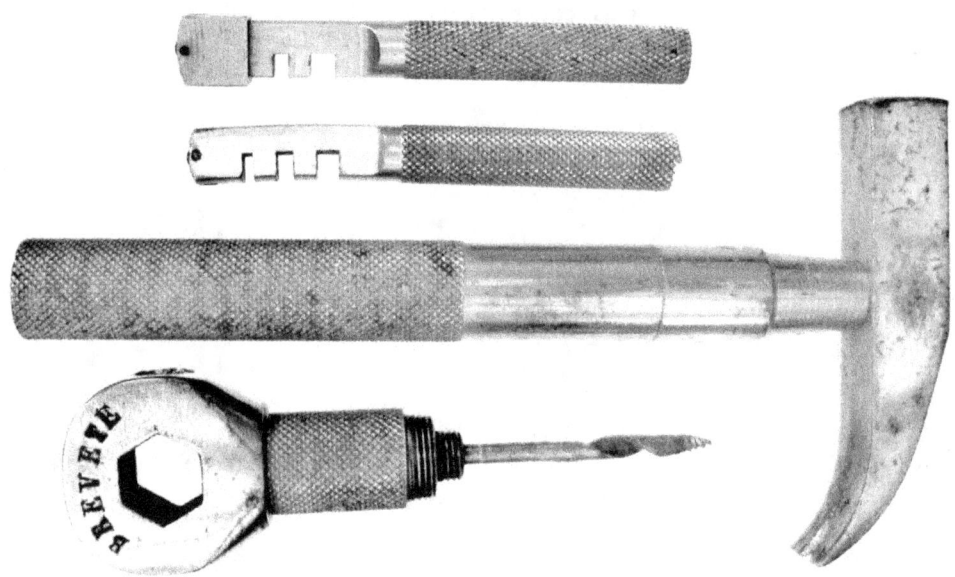

18. BREVETE stamped into 5-wrench end knob which unscrews to expose a 3.25" glass cutter unit that screws onto the penta-wrench unit shown below along beside another cutter design 3.4" long that was obtained separately years apart. Full assembled plated steel tool measures 8.3"

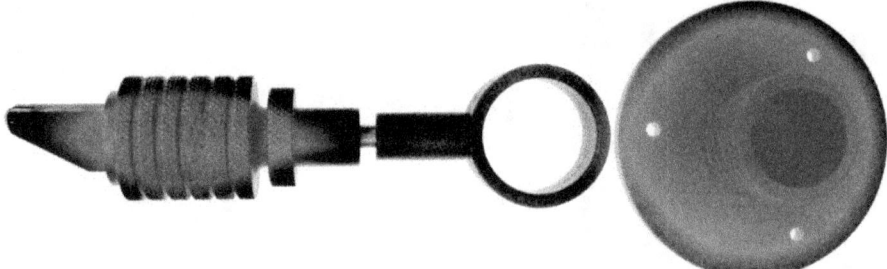

19. PAT. NO. 4,451,176 raised data on recessed 4th & 5th ribs from cutter head - all black plastic except for spring and central steel shaft - Plastic package: THE ULTIMATE GLASS CUTTER - stands upright in base or rests as shown above - 4,75" not including base of 2.35" diam.

19 –A. THE ULTIMATE GLASS CUTTER (XXIII-19) is also made in aluminum

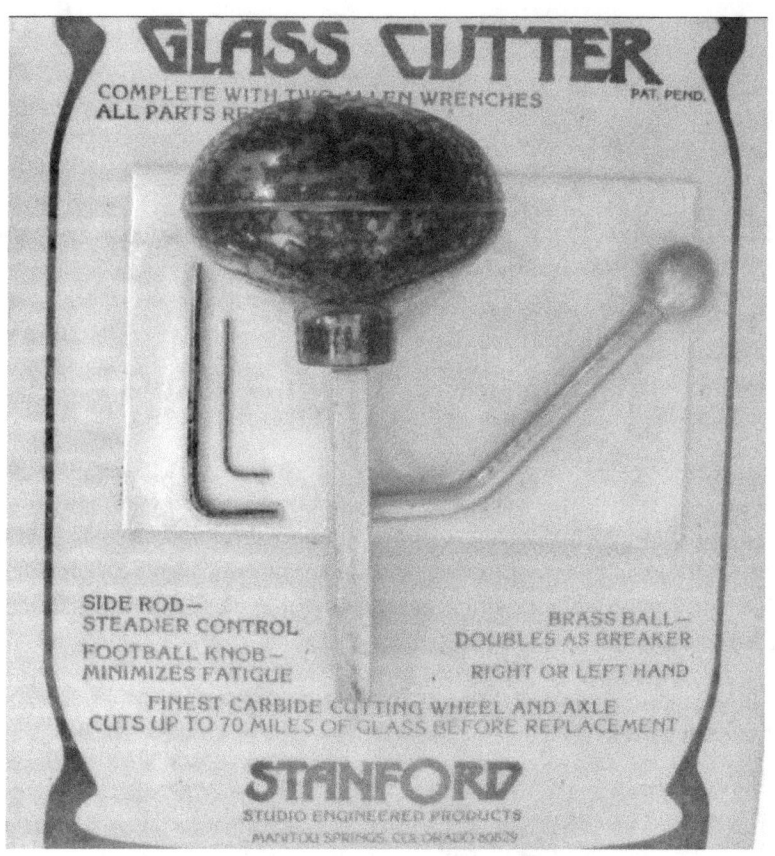

20. No ID on cutter mounted in VAC-PAC on corrugated cardboard - STANFORD - STUDIO ENGINEERED PRODUCTS - MANITOU SPRINGS, COLORADO 80829 -   Black   plastic knob(size of an egg) - steel Cutter shaft and side rod with large brass Ball - 4.3"

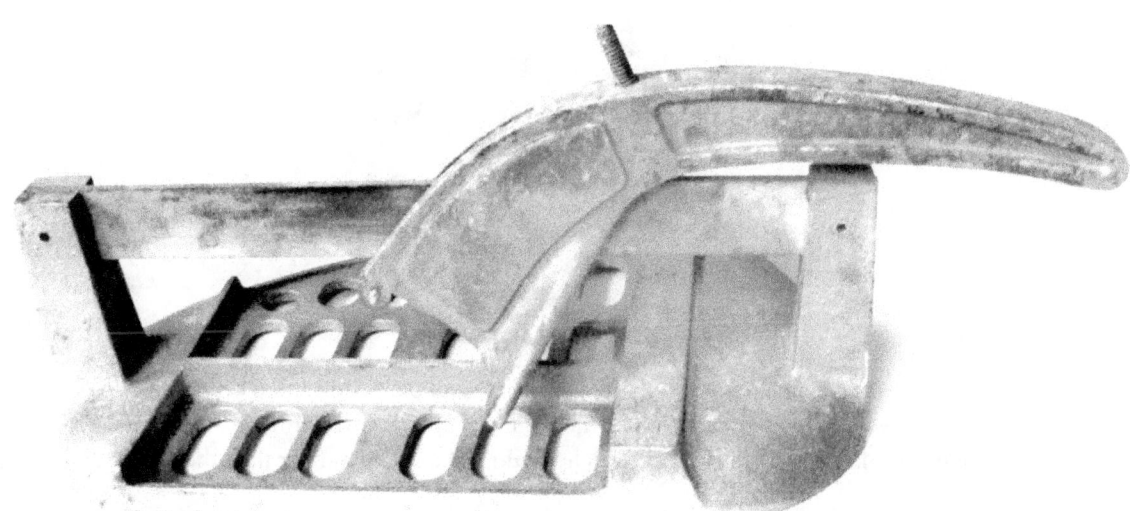

21. No ID - possibly a tile cutter - all cast aluminum except the 1" draw bar which is steel - 6 wheel brass turret with Recessed numbers - base is 10.75" X 6.5"

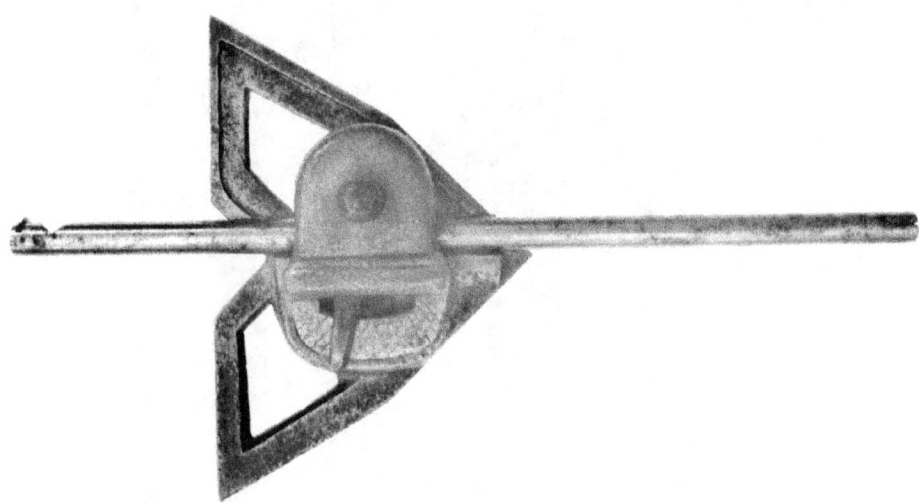

22. PAT 5 12 14 cast into underneath of brass frame with 3.5" base. This is date for U.S. Patent # 1,096,782 by P. F. FREYTAG. Entitled "Combination Tool". When I happened upon it, it had the ¼" diam. by 6.4" long steel rod with a scribe point at one end and the glass cutter wheel at the other secured in the cam clamp.

B. STAIN GLASS CUTTERS

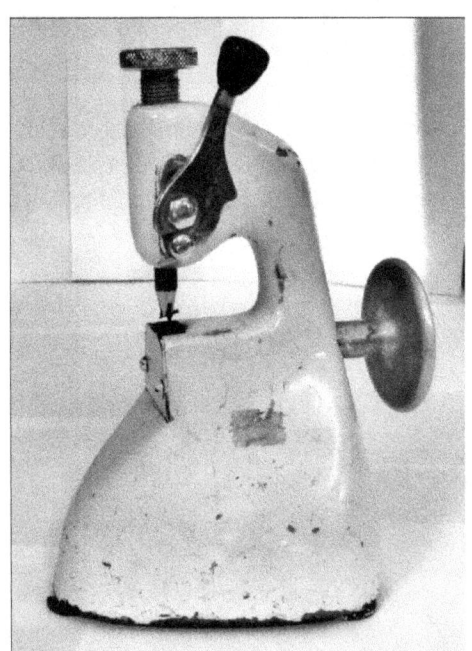

23. No ID - 352 is number stamped into bottom steel plate with three blue rubber feet - upper body and large wheel are aluminum. Single wheel cutter unit and lever arm are steel - 7.4" tall X 4.75" base Does this date from the 1930's , which would place it much older than the patent data listed below?

U.S. Patents of this style glass cutter are:

4,222,300	El-Hbr(1980)	4,628,784	Gach 1 claim(1986)
4,385,540	Dieter(1983)	4,672,874	Gach 7 claims(1987)
4,576,079	Donofrio(1986)	4,726,500	Rock(1988)

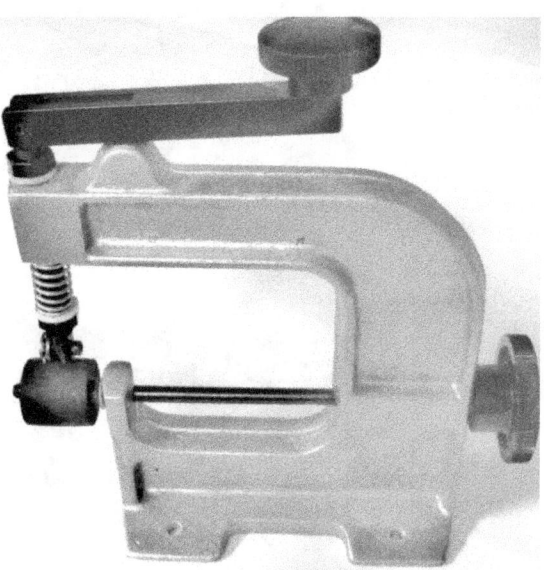

24. No ID - cast aluminum body - black plastic knobs - swing arm at top is black painted aluminum - 6 wheel unnumbered brass turret - this tool was patented in 1980 - U.S. Patent No. 4,222,300 by El-Hbr - 7.5" long X 8" tall X 2.4" wide at base

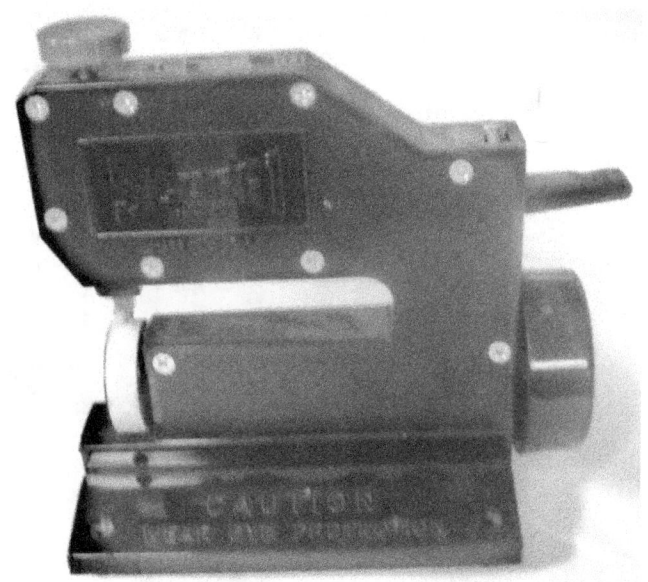

25. SCORE 1 MFG./PAT. NOS. 4,628,784(12-16-86) 4,672,874(6-16-87) MADE IN U.S.A. raised cast data on side of upper body - CAUTION WEAR EYE PROTECTION cast raised letters on both sides of base - all black plastic except red & white plastic knobs on top and the single wheel brass cutter unit - 6.5" high X 6.3" long X 3.5" wide base that has holes holding black rubber feet or to mount on table top. Paul Gach, the inventor, has provided me with a number of pictures of the SCORE 1 in the prototype stages.

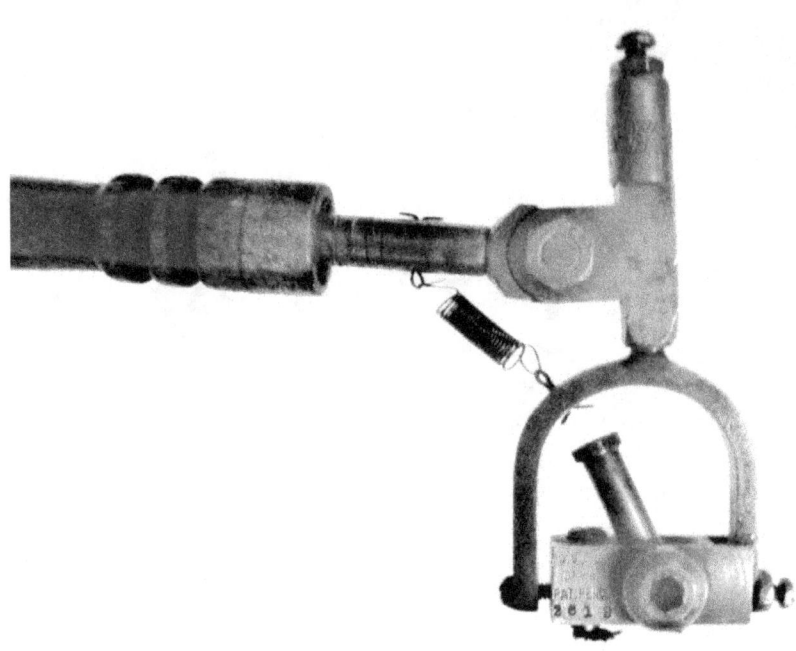

26. W. G. C. L. OF - A. PAT. PEND. 2618 stamped in gimbaled steel block holding the diamond point glass cutter unit - the yoke and linkage are steel and the wood handle 17" long

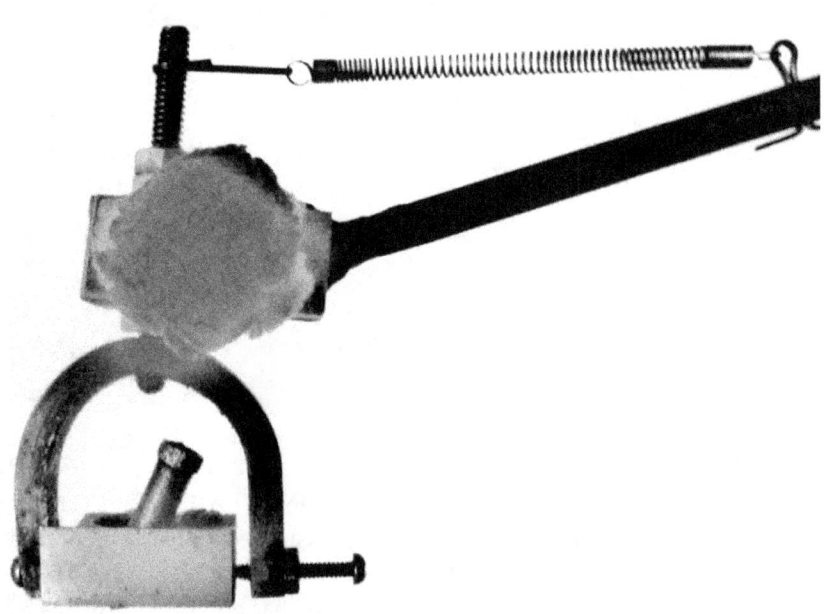

27. No ID except W stamped on the gimbaled steel block holding the diamond point glass cutter unit - the yoke and linkage are steel and this has an obvious replacement - handle not shown - 17" long

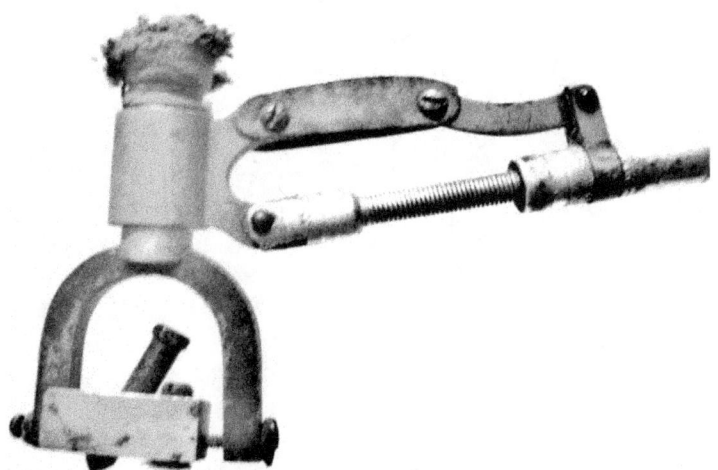

28. W. G. C. L. OF - A. PAT. PEND. 1216 stamped in gimbaled steel block holding the diamond point glass cutter unit - the yoke is steel and linkage is of non-mag. alloy - wood part of handle is 24" with a contoured hand end - overall length is 32"

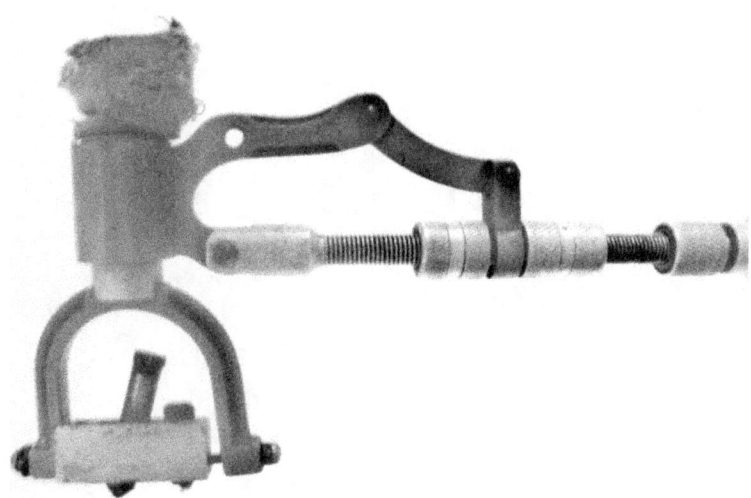

29. W. G. C. L. OF - A. PAT. PEND. 1275 stamped in gimbaled steel block holding the diamond point glass cutter unit - the yoke and linkage are both non-mag. alloy -wood handle part is 35" long - overall length is 44"

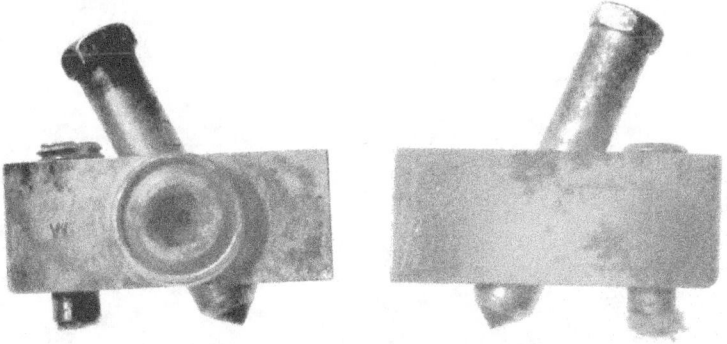

30. Pair of shawl cutter heads showing front and back respectively as in above units.

CATEGORY XXIV ASSOCIATED ITEMS

A broad range of items that a glass cutter and/or glazier would use are shown below.

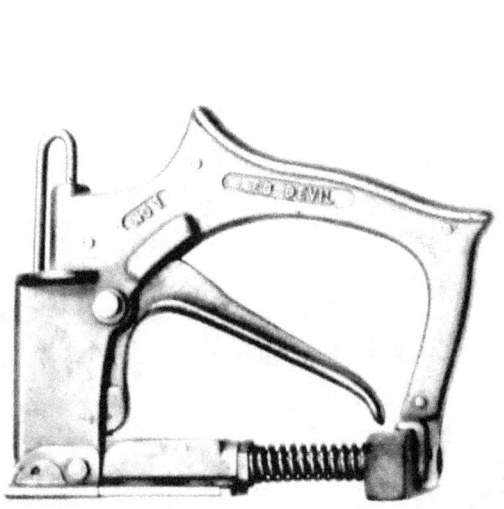 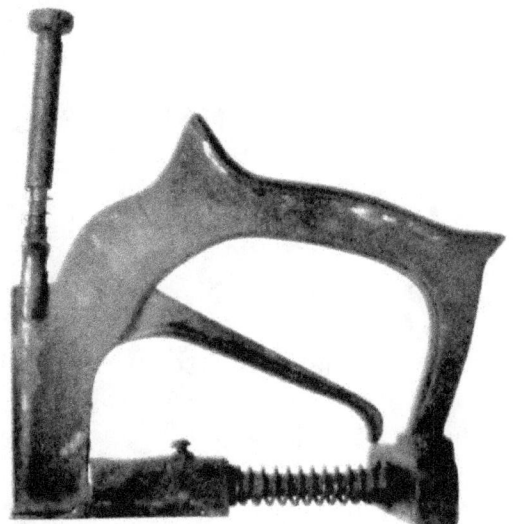

1. Automatic Point Driver - Red Devil - NO 1 - MADE IN U.S.A. - PAT. NOS. 1,134,334 & 1,744,700 - plated steel - uses 3/8" diamond points - 5 ½" base

2. Automatic Point Driver - No ID - green paint on iron - uses 3/8" diamond points Data on JUNE 16, 1958 4-page orange brochure: W.H. MAZE COMPANY, PERU, ILLINOIS – No. 1-G

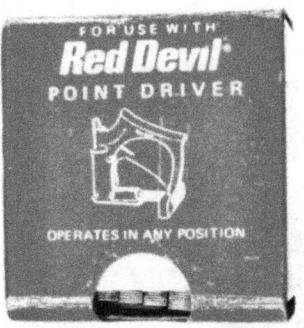 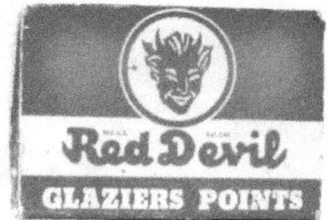

2. GLAZIERS POINTS - RED DEVIL for use with point driver

3. Blow pipe - 4' 10" heavy iron with 2 ¾" diam. at glass end and 1" O.D. main shaft with a 9 ¾" wood hand hold between iron ferrules at mouth end

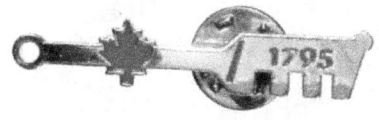 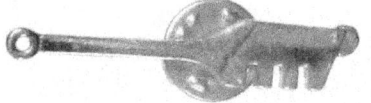 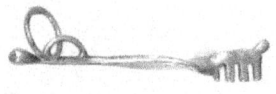

A   B   C

4. A.   Canadian glass cutter lapel pin with red maple leaf logo on handle & 1795 on cutter head - UNION(on back in a circle logo) - brass - 1.6"
    B. Same as 4 – A above but No ID except: CANADA (on back in a circle logo) - brass - 1.6"
    C. No ID - appears to be a silver charm - 1.25"

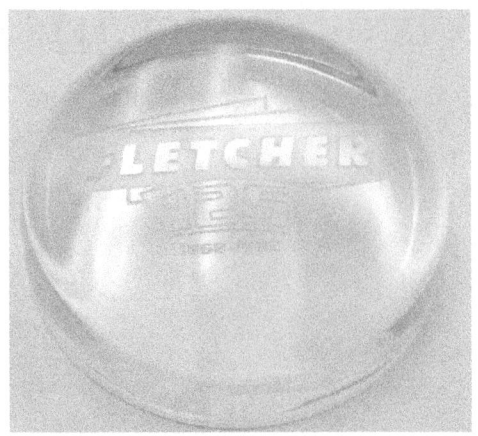

5. FLETCHER 125 1868-1993 etched on top of clear glass paperweight 3.5" diam.

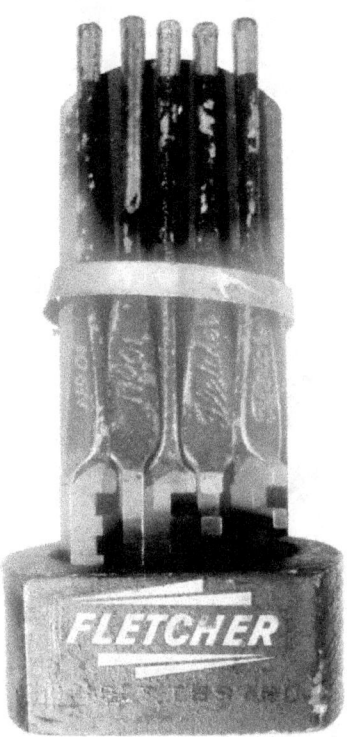

6. FLETCHER TRIPLE TESTED on front panel of counter top wood display holder for about a dozen glass cutters - paper sales label on back - 5 ¼" high X 2" wide

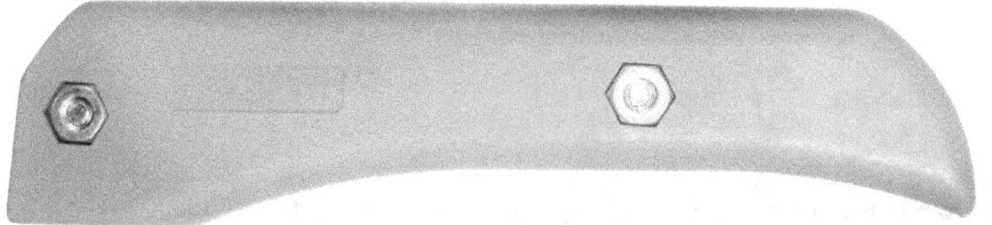

7. Handle - blue plastic CUT – EZE cast on side with PAT D-275260(dated Aug. 28, 1984) cast on the other side - 5.7"

8. Bottom Glass Cutter Stick: KEROYE BRO. MAKERS - SHULTON ST. N.Y. - heavy brass foot at 0" & a brass wrap-around at the 36" end - 36"

9. Top Glass Cutter Stick: LUFKIN NO.7142 MADE IN U.S.A. - heavy brass angled foot at one end & a thin dual plate at other end - 48"

10. Glass Cutter Stick: No. 18 - 3ft(cut off at 12"). - PITTSBURGH PLATE GLASS, PITTSBURGH, PA. - light brass foot at 0"

11. T – Square Glass Cutter Stick: No ID - 48" X 11" base cross - 4 Ft at base next to the square fastened with five 1/10" diam. brass pins - thin brass wrap-around at end & brass plate on "T"

12. The 6" rule: HASKINS GLASS STUDIO Court and Cortland, Rochester, N. Y. - rule by WESCOTT RULE Co., SENECA FALLS, N.Y.

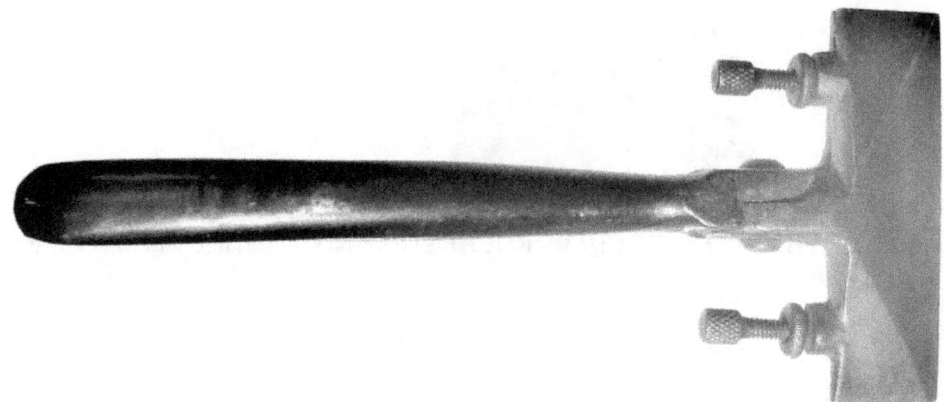

13. Glass pliers No ID - steel jaws are 3 ½" wide with dual knurled screw adjustments for glass depth snap off - 7 ¾"

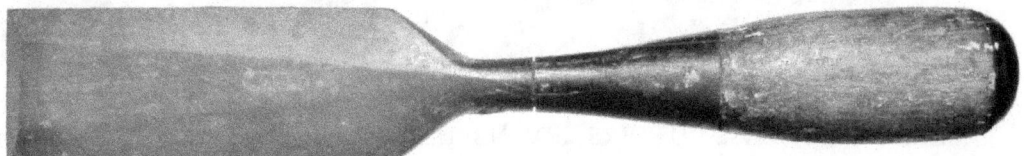

14. Glaziers Chisel - STANLEY cast on mid blade in a recessed rectangle logo - 1.7" steel ferrule - wood handle with leather gasket and an 1" diam. iron cap - 9.5"

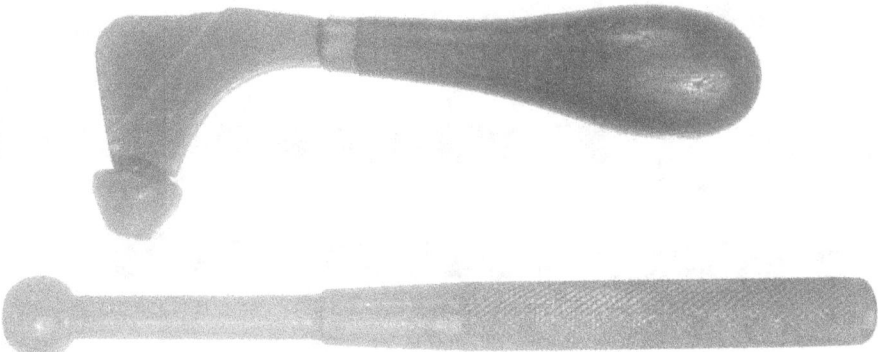

15. Two glass tappers. Top tapper has bulbous wood handle, PAT.APL'D FOR stamped on .1" thick brass head holding hard black rubber tapper. 4.5"   Bottom tapper is one piece heavy steel - knurled handle - 6.05"

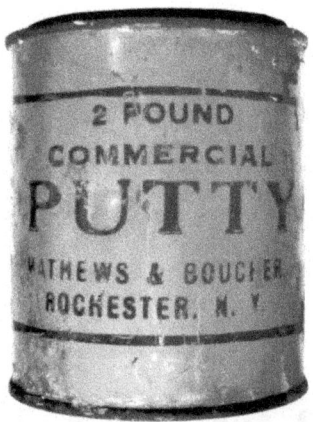

16. PUTTY 2 POUND COMMERCIAL - MATHEWS & BOUCHER ROCHESTER, N. Y. - 3.4" diam.   MATHEWS & BOUCHER ROCHESTER, N.Y. - orange with black print

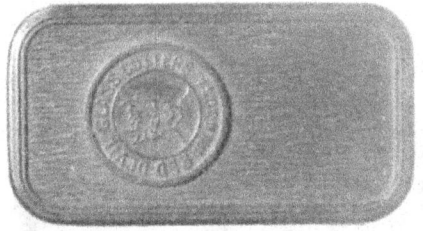 

17. RED DEVIL GLASS CUTTERS IRV. N.J. U.S.A. surrounding "Devil Face" cast in maroon slide top of black plastic box 1.9" X 1" X .9" high - contains spare wheels - second picture is a side view

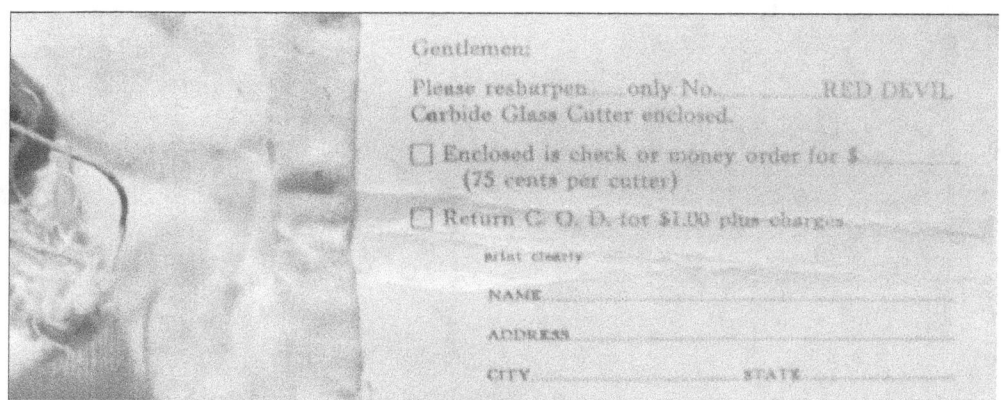

18. Return postcard with attached cloth bag with drawstring closure for returning glass cutters for sharpening to Red Devil Tools 2400 VAUXHALL ROAD UNION, N. J. – red lettering

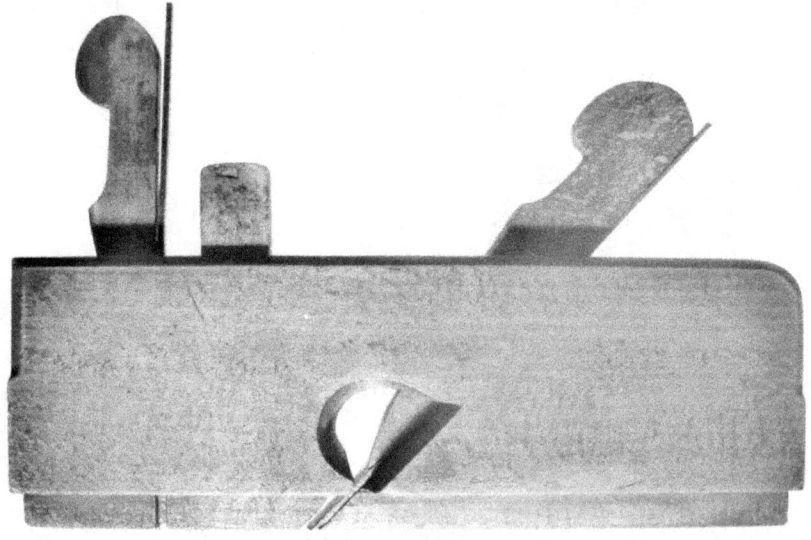

19. Sash Plane: many names stamped into the ends - some overlap - MUTTER - W. SMELLIE - J. DORT - ???YHALL - 9 3/8" X 3 3/8" high (body) X .8" thick

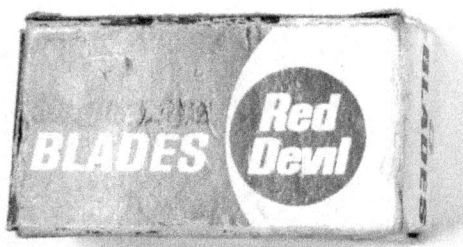
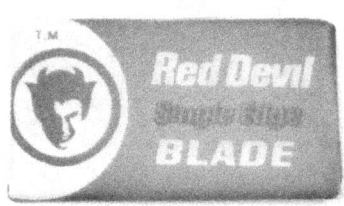

20. Box of Single Edge BLADES Red Devil - 5 BLADES (for scrapers as noted) - single blades were individually wrapped

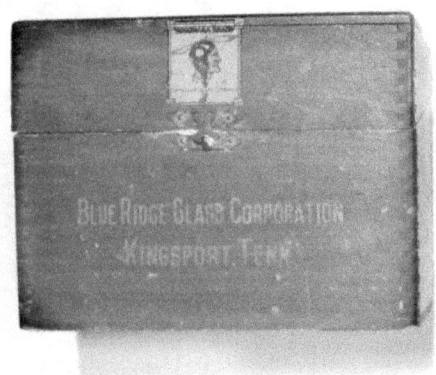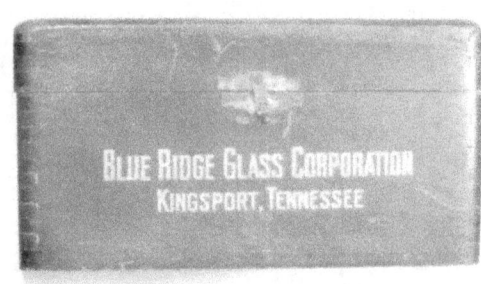

A	B

21. Two Wood Sample Boxes stamped in "gold" letters: Blue Ridge Glass Corporation   Kingsport, Tennessee:

A. ONONDAGA BRAND   SYRACUSE GLASS COMPANY on a gold decal 1.25" X 1.625" on front of hinged cover - 7 ½" X 5 7/8" X 5 7/8" high

B. No other ID - one front to back divider inside -   7 5/8" X 5 7/8" X 4.1/4" high

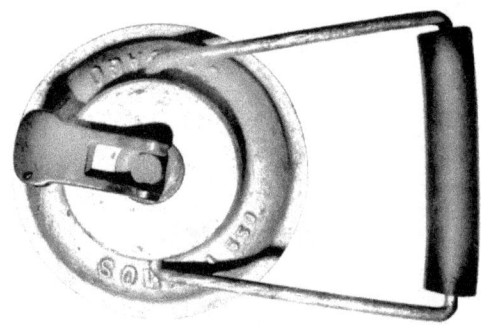

22. Vacuum Cup Plate Glass Holder 6" diam. - SOMACA 550 - CHICAGO cast raised letters   on aluminum dome - brass lever cam - black rubber grip on steel handle loop - bark brown rubber vacuum pad 5/16" thick

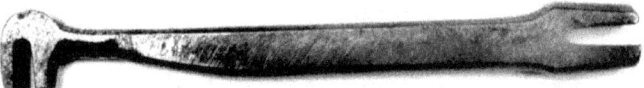

23. Breaker – double ended – steel – 3.6"

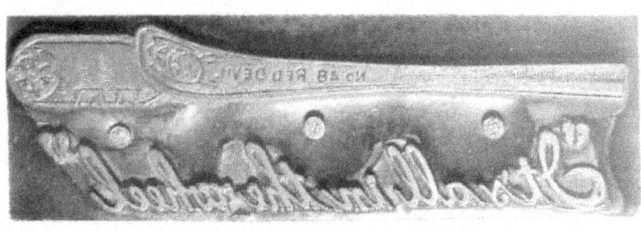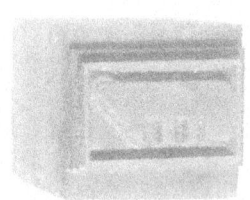

A	B

24. A. "It's all in the wheel" - copper plated lead printer's cut No. 48 Red Devil (face) – 6 wheel turret – 4.5"long X .625" wide

B. Lead letterpress cut of basic glass cutter head .6" X .4"

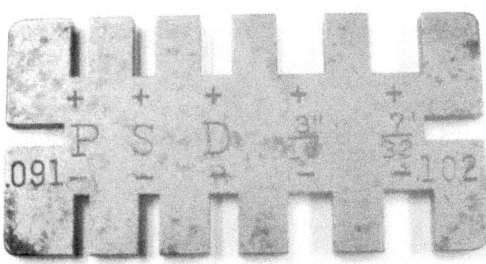

25. Glass Thickness Gauge - steel 2" X 1" X 1/8"

26. SHAW – ENGLAND - B on brass ferrule - slender walnut handle with nine narrow turnings starting about 5/8" from ferrule - (appears to be a "scribe" instead of a glass cutter) - 6.35"

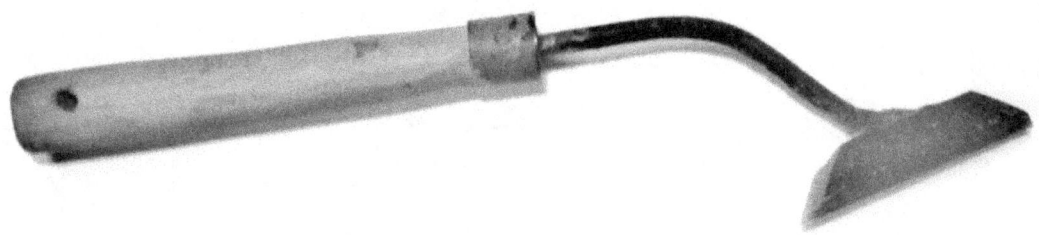

27. Believe this to be a large "soldering" iron to soften old glazing compound(putty) - note hand carved blue painted wood handle - 16.6"

CATEGORY XXV   GUMMED LABELS

In 1961, Mr. Robert J. Traynor wrote to a number of window glass and mirror companies as well as advertized in the October 1961 issue of "GLASS DIGEST" asking for samples of their gummed labels used on glass and mirrors. He received 135 different labels from nine different companies which are listed below followed by a few samples.

American Saint Gobain Corp.   Indiania Glass Co.
American Window Glass Co.   Libby Owens Ford
Carolina Mirror Corp.   Pilkington Bros. Ltd.
Fourco Glass Co.   (Clearlite) Raynor's Glass Works (LOF)
Glaverbel   Virginia Glass Products Corp.

EXAMPLES OF GUMMED LABELS OF ABOVE LISTED COMPANIES ARE REPRODUCED BELOW

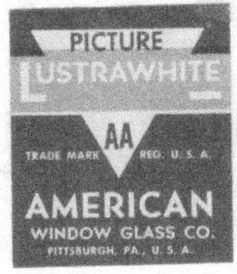 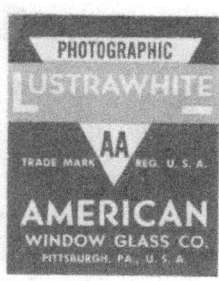 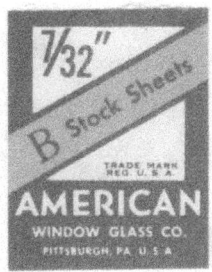 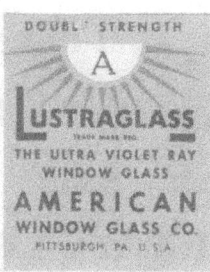 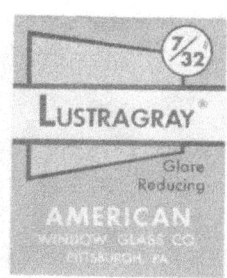

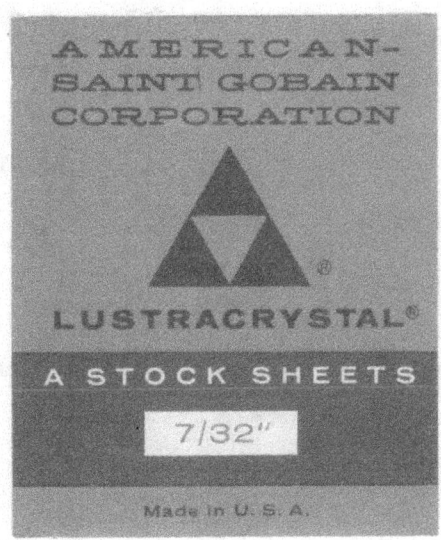  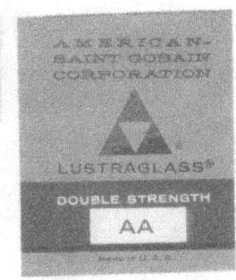 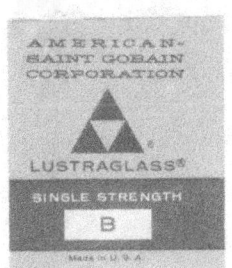

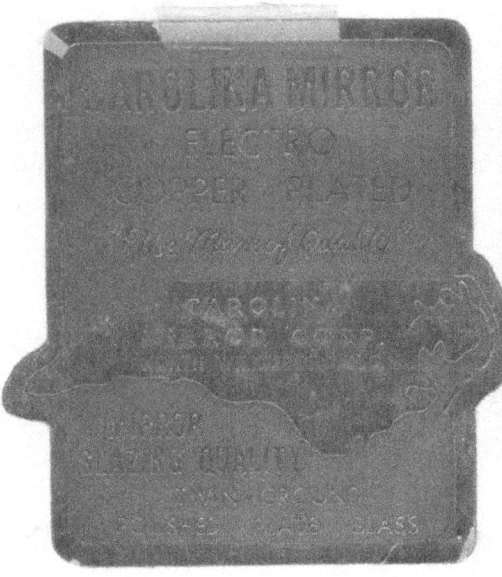

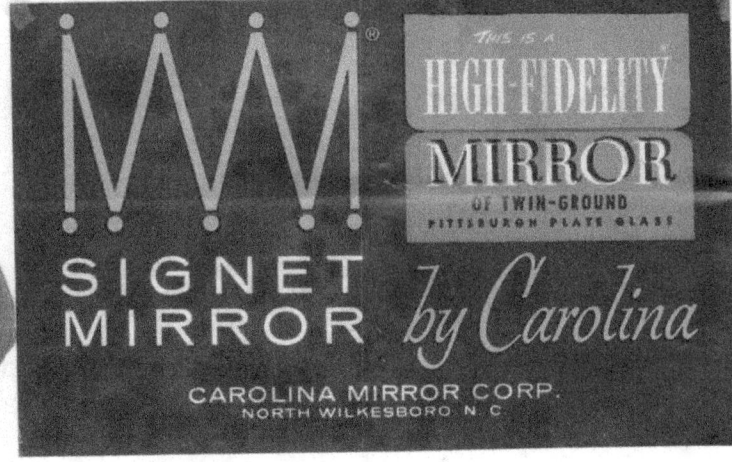

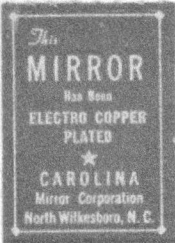

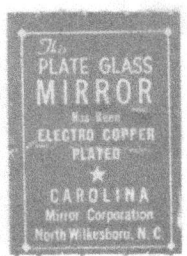

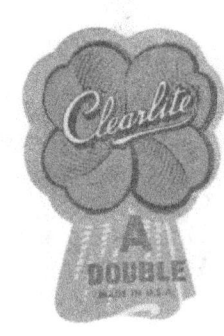

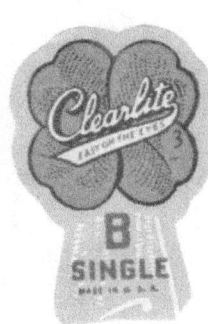

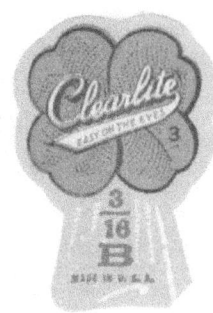

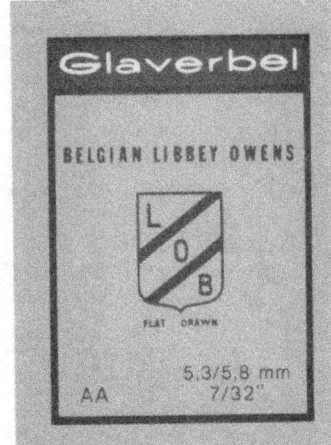

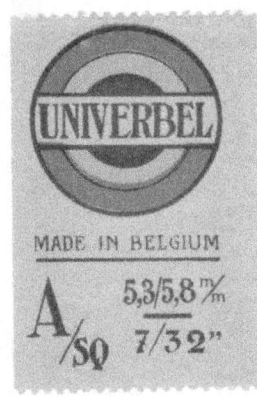

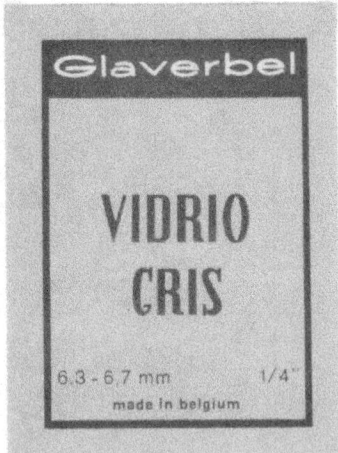

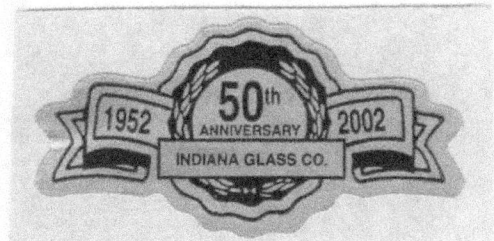

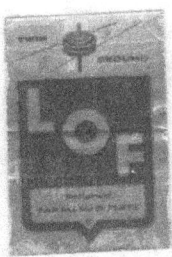

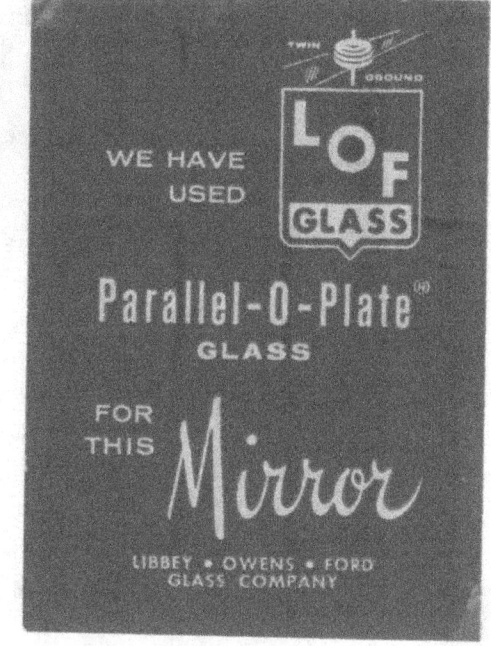

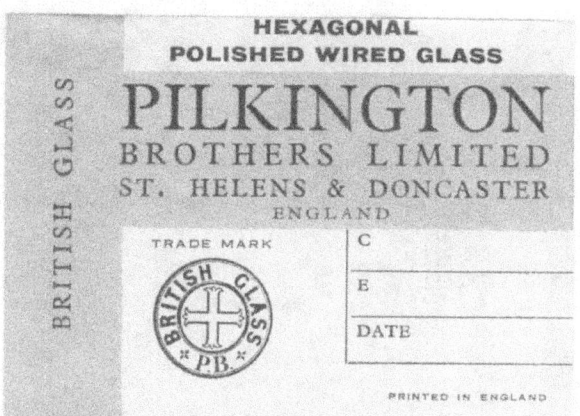

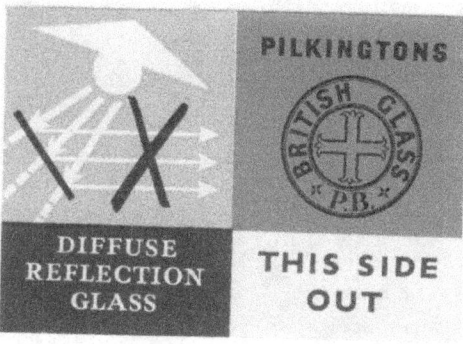

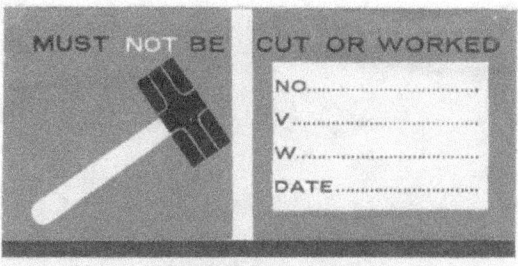

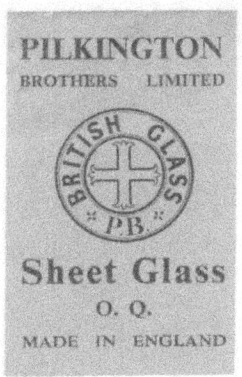

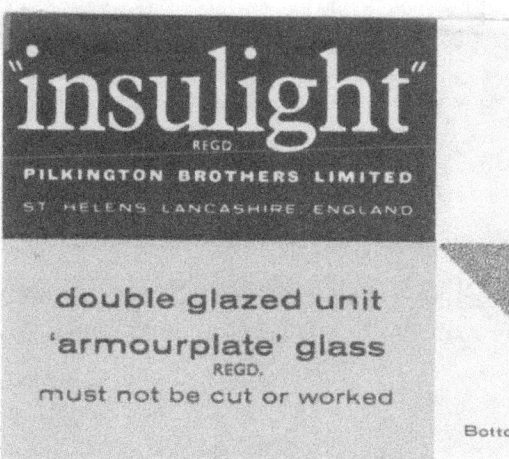

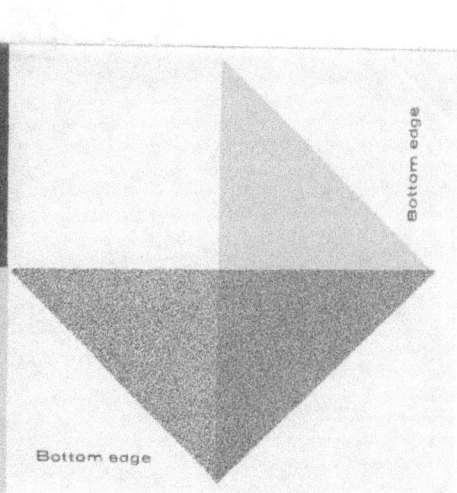

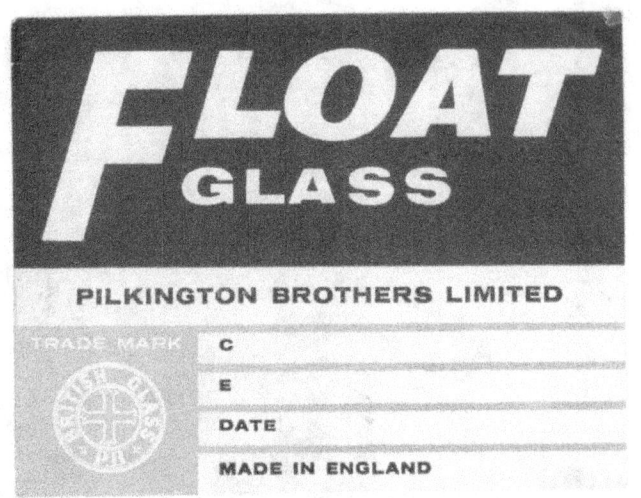

FLOAT GLASS

PILKINGTON BROTHERS LIMITED

TRADE MARK	C
	E
	DATE
	MADE IN ENGLAND

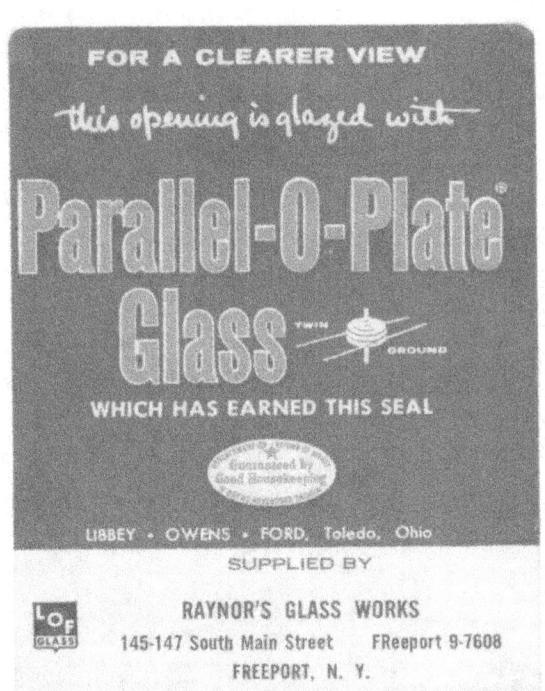

FOR A CLEARER VIEW

this opening is glazed with

Parallel-O-Plate Glass TWIN GROUND

WHICH HAS EARNED THIS SEAL

Guaranteed by Good Housekeeping

LIBBEY • OWENS • FORD, Toledo, Ohio

SUPPLIED BY

RAYNOR'S GLASS WORKS
145-147 South Main Street   FReeport 9-7608
FREEPORT, N. Y.

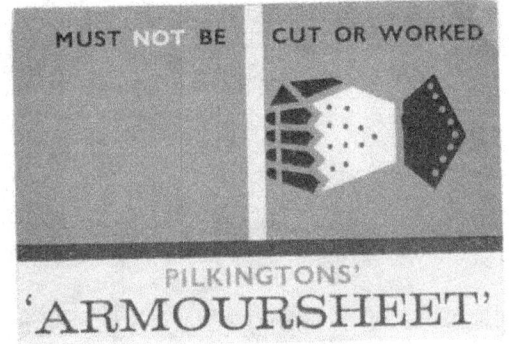

MUST NOT BE   CUT OR WORKED

PILKINGTONS'
'ARMOURSHEET'

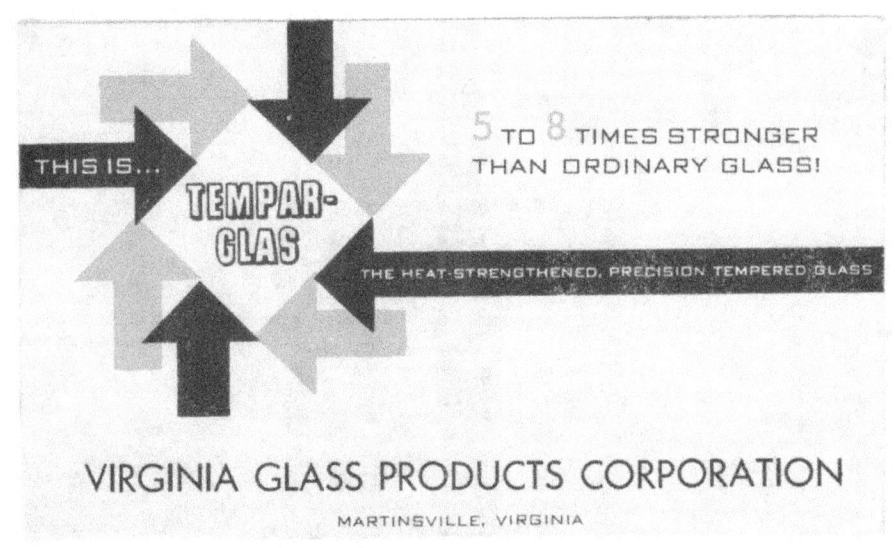

THIS IS...
TEMPAR-GLAS

5 TO 8 TIMES STRONGER
THAN ORDINARY GLASS!

THE HEAT-STRENGTHENED, PRECISION TEMPERED GLASS

VIRGINIA GLASS PRODUCTS CORPORATION
MARTINSVILLE, VIRGINIA

CATEGORY XXVI GLASS & LABEL SCRAPERS

Fourteen different glass & label scrapers are included as a separate associated category. A brief description of each is given. This is a tool not actively searched for but picked up as they were there and inexpensive.

Six U.S. Patents are listed below:

1,708,905	04-09-1929	C. P. Shinn, Jr.	Scraper
1,729,279	09-24-1929	C. P. Shinn, Jr.	Blade holder
2,071,562	02-23-1937	J. Nelson	Scraper
2,141,565	12-27-1838	H. A. Stilson	Blade holder
2,257,314	09-30-1941	C. P. Shinn, Jr.	Scraper
2,787,056	04-02-1957	R.E. Dobratz	Window paint scraper

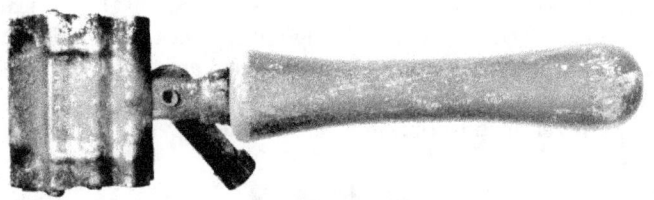

1. A spring actuated steel metal razor blade holder with a blue painted levered cam to tighten is attached to a 1920's or 30's green painted wood handle. The first line of inscription on the rusty sheet metal blade holder reads: W. M ????????. The second line is: ?AM. N. J. PAT. APLD FOR - 5.75"

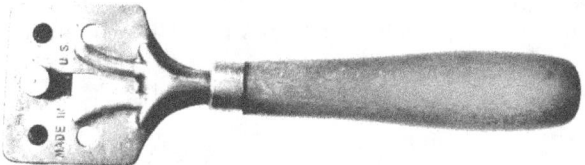

2. A natural wood handled stamped sheet brass, double edge razor blade holder inscribed: PAT. No. 1,708,905 MADE IN U.S.A. - .35" plated steel ferrule - 5.6"

3. Same as No. 2 above except made of sheet steel and is 5.4"

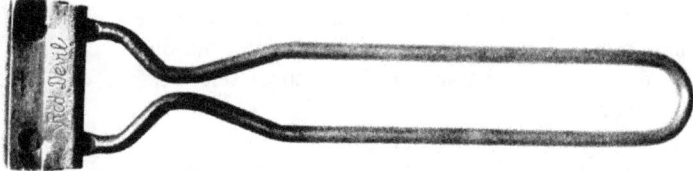

4. Red Devil - IRVINGTON, N. J. NO. 6 - PAT. APD. FOR stamped on flat steel head - 1/8" diameter steel loop handle - 6.1"

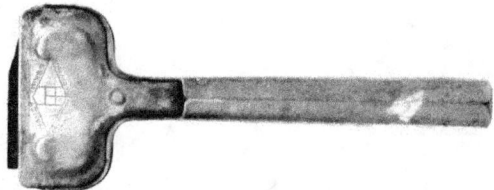

5. HANDY THINGS - LUDINGTON MICHIGAN U.S.A. - Folded over plated sheet steel hollow handle which forms half of the razor blade holder. Knurled brass screw holds back plate - 4.8"

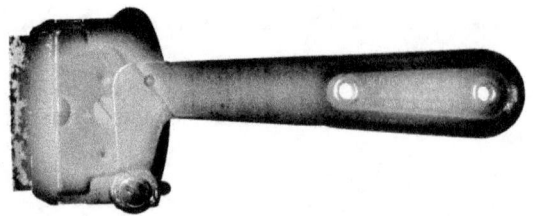

6. RED DEVIL JAk-NIFE NO. 13 – IRV. N.J., U.S.A. PAT. NO. 2,071,562 stamped on recessed area of spot welded, plated, sheet steel handle - knurled nut & screw hold blade holder which pivots into side of handle for safe storage - 5.2"

7. RED DEVIL JAK-NIFE NO. 13 - UNION, N.J. U.S.A. PAT. NO. 2,071,562 stamped in recessed area of open riveted blued sheet steel handle - Wing nut replaces the knurled nut - 5.2"

8. Red Devil UNION, N.J. U.S.A. 3213 stamped in recessed area of open riveted sheet steel handle - wing nut replaces the knurled nut - 5.2"

9. Same as No. 8 above, however, the inscription is larger letters

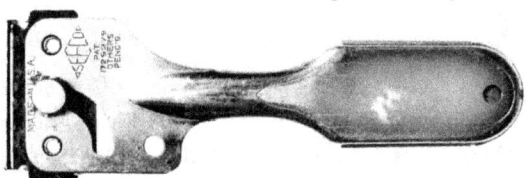

10. SEFCO (forms a diamond logo) PAT. 1,729,279 OTHERS PEND'G. MADE IN U.S.A. stamped on top of blade holder end - OPEN ↓ KEEP EXTRA BLADES HERE stamped on sliding cover on back of plated steel handle - 5"

11. Same as No. 10 above except a second patent is added: 2,257,314

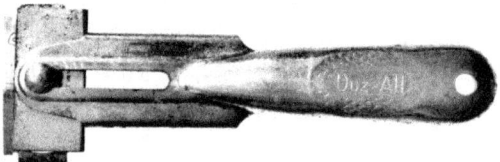

12. Duz – All stamped in oval on plated steel handle - 5"

13. Red Devil stamped on flat area of plated steel handle is the only inscription - blade holder is activated by pressing center button and pushing forward - the two halves of plated sheet steel are attached by three open rivets - 4"

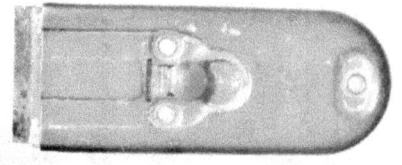

14. Same sheet steel design except three spot welds are used instead of rivets - inscriptions: USE CAUTION WHEN CHANGING BLADES (next to blade opening) - MADE IN U.S.A. WR - 4"

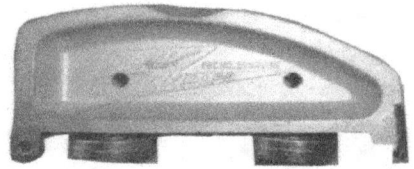

15. KWIK SKRAPE - TRADE MARK – PAT. NO. 2,787,056 – die cast body - 2.8"

CATEGORY XXVII PHOTOGRAPHIC PAPER TRIMMERS

Twelve different photographic paper trimmers are shown on the following two pages. This tool is often described and offered for sale as a glass cutter, which it is not. Excerpts from two pages of an old(supposedly 1884) catalog provided by the Eastman House Museum in Rochester, N. Y. describes this tool as Robinson's New Model Photograph Trimmer. Note that this 1884 catalog calls this a "New Model", yet one of the steel ones like this has cast on it PAT. OCT. 16, 1900. (U.S. Pat. #659,983).

Nine U.S. Patents for various trimmers are listed below:

109,651	117,611	121,198	659,983	685,212	704,352
862,028	949,110				

Five additional different trimmers have shown up on the internet in the past ten years.
A straight "cut" using the large wheel and a "cut" following a pattern from this catalog are shown below.

Robinson's new model photographic trimmer

Robinson's Photograph Trimmer is substituted for the knife for trimming photographs, and does the work much more expeditiously and elegantly. They save time, save prints, and save money.

They do not *cut*, but *pinch off* the waste paper, and leave the print with a neatly bevelled edge which facilitates adherence to the mount. Try one, and you will discard the knife and punch at once. For ovals and rounded corners they are worth their weight in gold.

Robinson's New Model Photograph Trimmers.

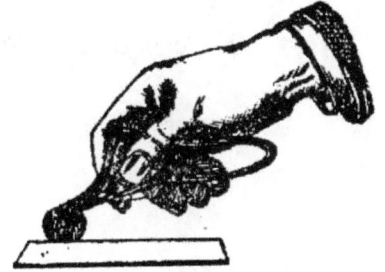

Plan of holding the Straight Cut Trimmer when in use. Price, $0 50.

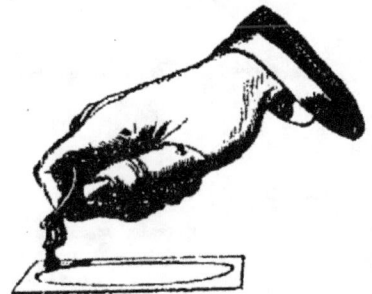

Plan of holding the Revolving Trimmer when in use. Price, $1 00.

Six steel and one brass (French)(the last in this group) photograph paper trimmers are shown below:

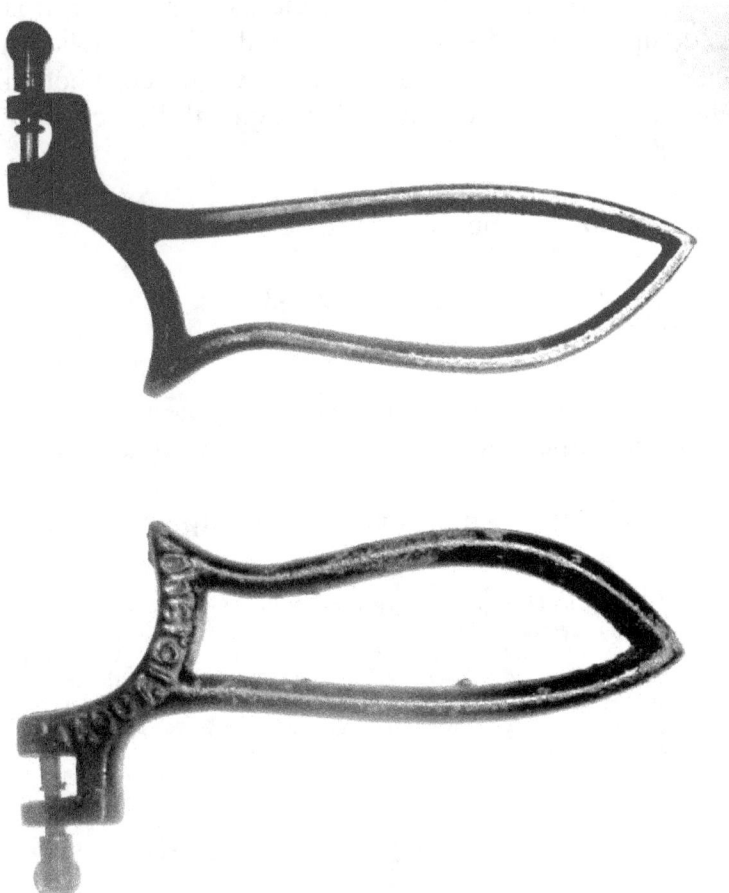

Note: PAT. OCT. 16, 1900 cast on handle of trimmer above.

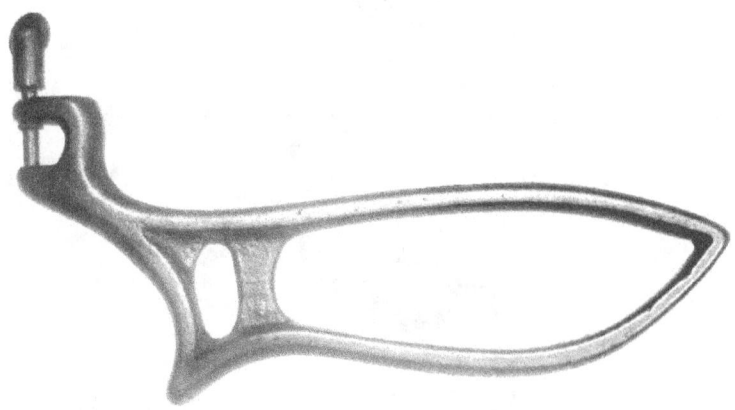

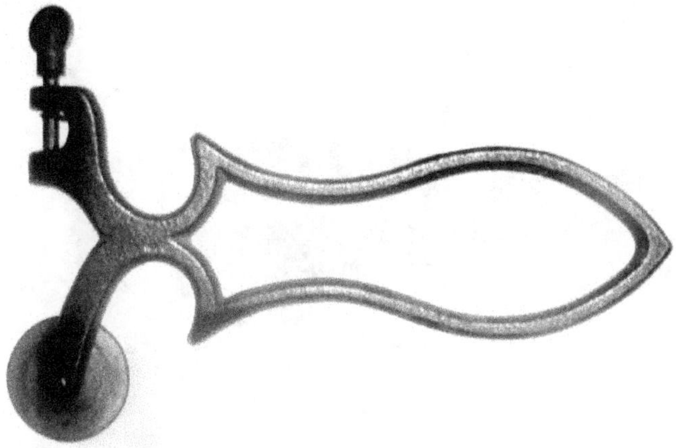

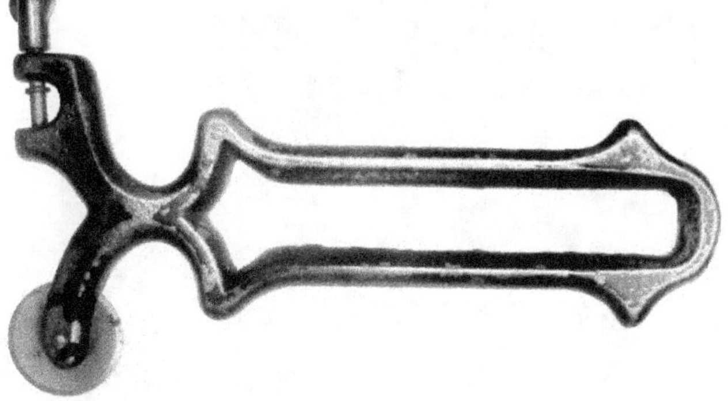

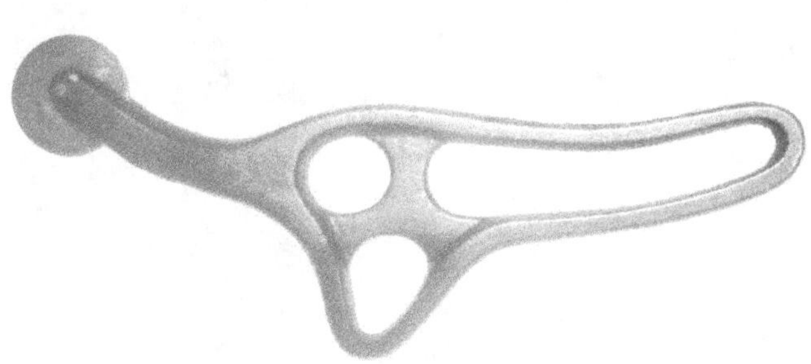

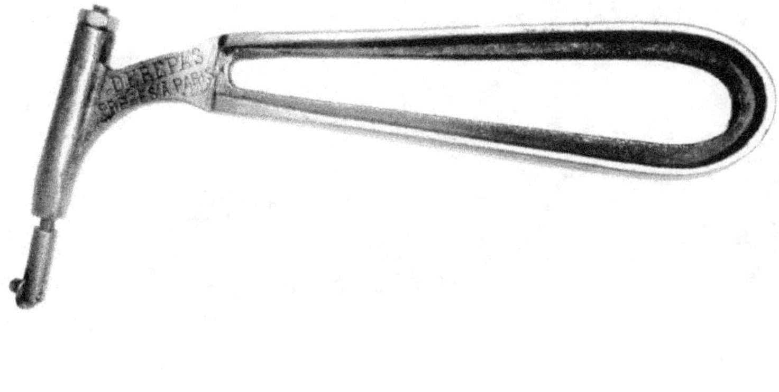

Brass

Five wood handle photograph paper trimmers are shown below:

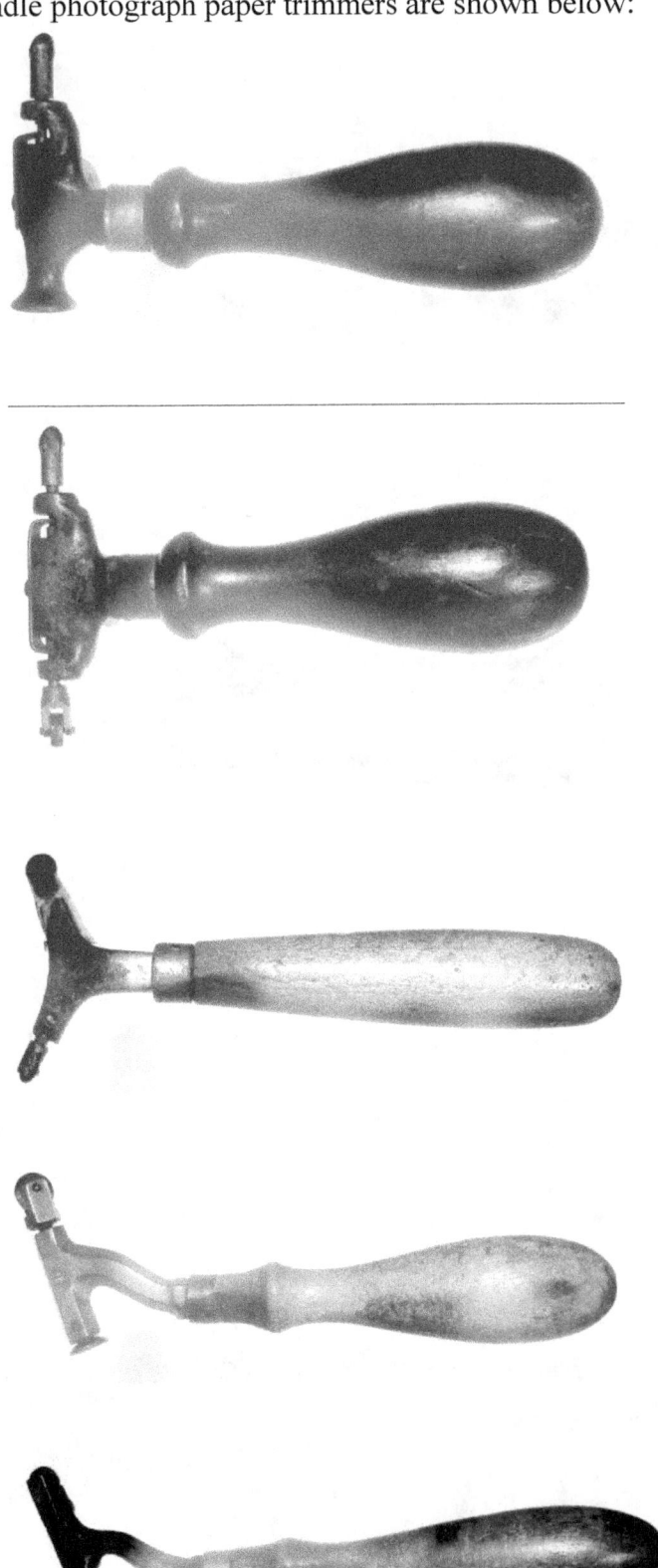

Five additional different photograph paper trimmers now in other collections

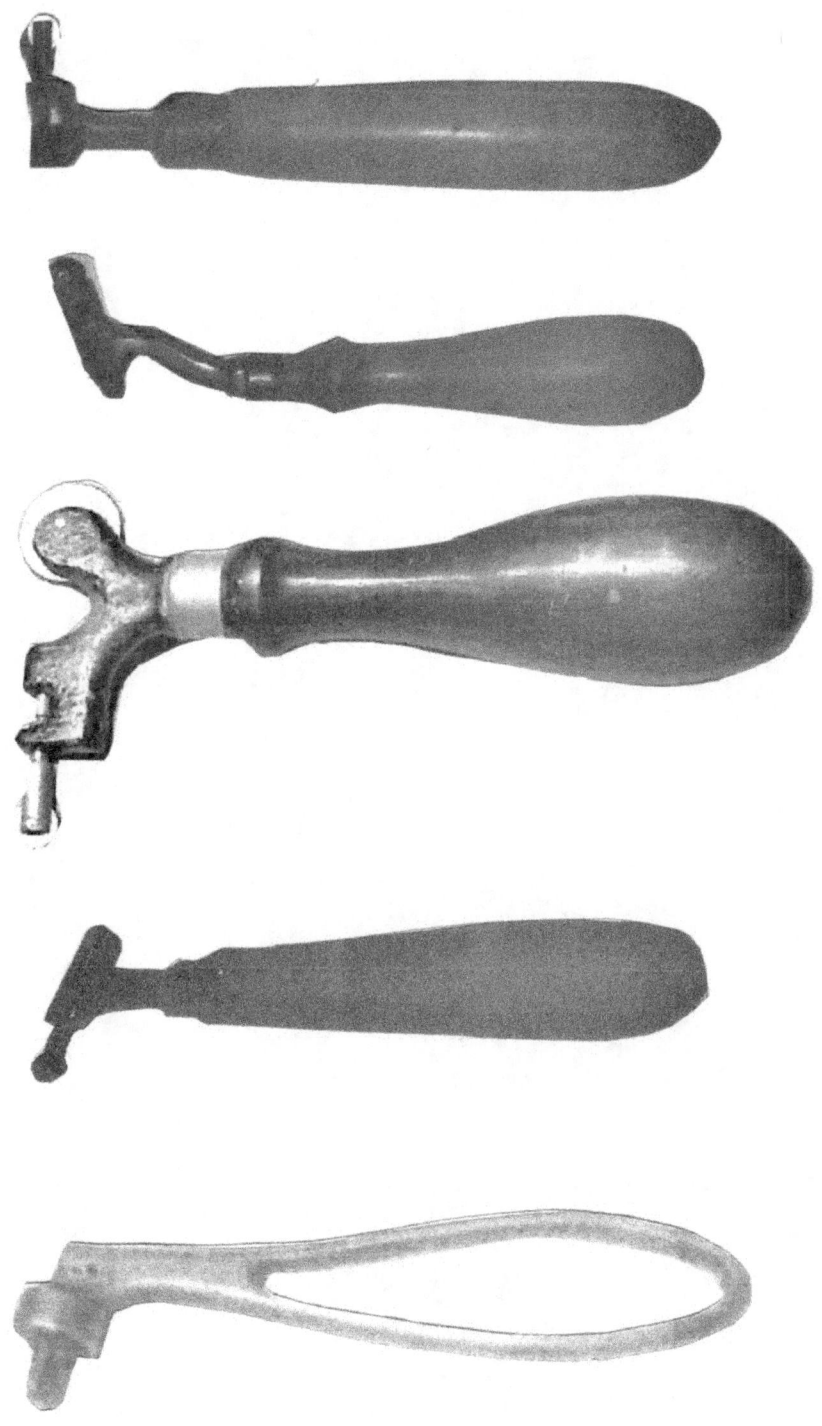

Glossary

Anneal; A slow cooling process that removes stress from glass

Broad Glass; Made by the cylinder process

Bulls Eye; A small thick section of glass from where pontil was attached

Crown; A round platter of glass up to about four feet in diameter made by rotating the pontil and the punty

Crown glass; Composed essentially of soda(wood ashes), lime(shells), and sand

Cullet; Scrap glass used to assist melting of raw glass batch

Cylinder Glass; Also called; rolls, muff, broad: Made by both hand blown and machine blow and draw

Flint Glass; Contains lead oxide and potash for a higher quality glass

Float Glass; A fire polished, on both sides, flat glass made by continuously floating refined molten glass onto a surface of molten tin

Gaffer; One who blows glass using a pontil

Glazier; A construction person that selects, cuts, installs, replaces, and removes residential, commercial and artistic glass.

Grozing; A centuries old term to describe the process and tool used to break off small pieces from the edge of small pieces of glass. A small iron tool with notches at either end, not unlike the notches or breaker slots in modern glass cutters

Lehr; A low temp oven in which glass is cooled slowly to eliminate stresses

Muff; Flat glass made by the cylinder process

Mullion; Flat glass made by the cylinder process

Plate Glass; Usually thicker glass that has been polished on both sides

Pontil; The pipe to which the partially formed glass product is transferred to for final step

Punty; A gathering iron, also a blow pipe

Pot Furnace; Furnace that holds clay pots in which glass batch is melted

Potash; Early on a potassium oxide source mainly from wood ashes to help melt the glass batch

Shawling; The act of "cutting" the cylinder lengthwise on the inside of the cylinder

Shawls; Sections of glass cylinders after they have been divided into lengths and split lengthwise before flattening

Soda; Early on this was a form of sodium oxide obtained from marine plants to help melt the glass batch; later sodium carbonate from the Solvay Process and now from trona ore

Seed; A small bubble in the glass, either round or elongated

Stone; A small piece of unmelted batch or refractory from the melting pot

Striation; Wavy distortions, usually on the surface of the flat glass, as a result of the forming process and/or tools, or by join lines of multiple gatherings from the melting pot

Tank Furnace; A furnace in which glass batch is continuously fed and melted by flame overhead

Bibliography

Angus-Butterworth, L. M. The Manufacture of Glass. New York: Pitman Publishing Corp., 1948.

Aiken, William Earl. Story of Captain Ford – The Roots Grow Deep. Cleveland, Ohio: Lezius-Hiles Co., 1957. (Oversize)

Anon. Discovering Antiques, The Story of World Antiques, Vol. 1, New York: Greystone Press, 1972, (reprint of original published by the British Publishing Corp., 1972.

Anon. *Glass Cutter Tools; NTSA Confiscation 3352.* Boulder City, Nevada, 2004.

Anon. Glass – History, Manufacture and its Universal Application. Pittsburgh: Pittsburgh Plate Glass Co., 1923.

Anon. Glass – The Miracle Worker. Toledo, Ohio: Libbey-Owens-Ford Co., (Public relations Department), n.d.

Anon. "Great American Industries, VIII: A Piece of Glass." *Harper's New Monthly Magazine*, Vol. LXXIX, No. 470, New York, July 1889, pp 245-264.

Anon. History of Window Glass Manufacture; Glass Manufacture in the United Kingdom – Chronology. The London Crown Glass Company website(www.londoncrownglass.co.uk/History.html), April 2001.

Anon. "How To Cut Glass," gardendistrictglass.com/cutglass , January 2000.

Anon. MacBeth-Evans Glass Co. 1869-1919 – 50 Years, Pittsburgh, Pennsylvania, n.d. (Alfred University Library).

Anon. Now Thus, Now Thus 1826-1926. St. Helens, England: Pilkington Bros., Ltd., 1926.

Anon. Pilkington Bros., LTD., Organization – Mfg. Throughout the World, London, 1959, Alfred University Library.

Anon. "The Manufacture of Window Glass With Natural Gas," *Scientific American*, Vol. LVI, No. 12, March 20, 1886. pp 281-284.

Anon. "The Story of Glass," The Fourco Glass Co., Clarksburg, WV, n.d.

Anon. Town of Montague – 200th Anniversary 1754-1954. Millers Falls Tool Co., n.d.

Anon. "Window Glass from Early Times to the Present," New York Museum of Science and Industry (Department of Education), New York, 1934.

Arnold, Hugh. Stained Glass of the Middle Ages in England and France. London: Adam and Charles Black, 1913.

Athineos, Doris. "When Collections Become Obsessions." *Forbes*, December 16, 1996, pp 406-409.

Barlow, Ronald S. The Antique Tool Collectors Guide to Value. El Cajon, California: Windmill Publishing Co., 1985, pg. 69.

Bock, Gordon, "Glass in the Past" *The Old House Journal,* August 1998. pp 54-55.

Bock, Gordon, "Putty and Points," *The Old House Journal,* August 1999, pp 67-70

Boon, George C. "Roman Window Glass from Wales," *Journal of Glass Studies*, Vol. 8, 1966, pp 41-45.

Borel, Edward. "A Drawn Sheet Glass Process of 1871," *Glass Industry,* Vol. 39, No. 9, 1958. pp 482-483, 509-510.

Bridenbaugh, Carl. The Colonial Craftsman. New York: Dover Publications NY, 1990. pp 43-44, 62-63.

Brown, Sarah and O'Connor, David. Glass Painters – Medieval Craftsmen. London: British Museum Press, 1991.

Buckley, Francis, The Glass Trade in England in the Seventeenth Century. London: Stevens and Sons, Ltd., 1914.

Chance, H. "Records and the Nailsea (Somerset) Glassworks, Manufacturers of Crown Glass from 1844 Onwards, and Rolled Plate Glass Beginning in the 1860's," *Connoisseur*, Vol. 165, 1967. pp 168-172.

Charlesworth, Dorothy. "Roman Glass from Chichester, Sussex," *Journal of Glass Studies*, Vol. 19, 1977. pg 182.

Cooper, William. The Crown Glass Cutter and Glazier's Manual. Edinburgh: Oliver & Boyd, London: Simpkin, Marshall & Co., 1835. pgs 84-98, Plate XIX.

Crossley, D. W. "Glassmaking in Bagot's Park, Staffordshire, in the 16th Century, (Manufacture of crown and possibly cylinder glass)," *Post-Medieval Archaeology*, Vol 1, 1967, pp 44-83.

Dell'Acqua, Francesca. "Ninth-Century Window Glass from the Monastery of San Vincenzo al Volturno (Molise, Italy)," *Journal of Glass Studies*, Vol, 39, 1997, pp 33-41.

DeRiaz, Yuan A. The Book of Knives; Anatomy of a Jacknife. New York: Crown Publishers, Inc., 1981.

Diamond, Freda. The Story of Glass. New York: Harcourt, Brace & World, Inc., 1953.

Douglas, R. W., and Frank, Susan. A History of Glassmaking. Henley-on-Thames, Oxfordshire, England: G. T. Foulis & Co., Ltd., 1972.

Duncan, George Sang. "Bibliography of Glass (up to 1940)," (Alfred University Library), n.d.

Eveleigh, David J. Candle Lighting. Haverfordwest, Great Briton: C. L. Thomas & Sons, 1985.

Fairfield, E. William. Fire and Sand – History of LOF, Cleveland, Ohio: Lezius-Hiles Co., 1960. (Alfred University Library).

Fowle, Arthur E. Flat Glass, LOF – Colburn Process, Toledo, Ohio: The Libbey-Owens Sheet Glass Company, 1924.

Garvin, James L. and Belle, Donna. Instruments of Change – New Hampshire Hand Tools and Their Makers 1800-1900, Canaan, New Hampshire: New Hampshire Historical Society (Phoenix Publishing), 1985.

Gillot, E. H. "A History of Trade-Unions in the Window Glass Industry Out of Which Grew the Window Glass Cutters League of America, Columbus Ohio," *Glass Cutter* (serial form), March thru September, 1943.

Godfrey, Eleanor S. The Development of English Glassmaking 1560 – 1640. Chapel Hill, North Carolina: The University of North Carolina Press, 1975.

Halahan, Mrs. "On the Association of Flint Chippings with Fragments of Old Glass Found in Mediaeval Glasshouses at Chiddingfold in Surrey," *The Journal of the British Society of Master Glass-Painters*, No. 1, April 1924, (William Follard & Co. Printers, Exeter, England), pp 11-15.

Halberg, Douglas J. "Waterjet Cutting," an unpublished article from the Internet, January 1997.

Harden, D. B. "Domestic Window Glass: Roman, Saxon, and Medieval," *Studies in Building History*, Odhams Press, London, 1961. pp. 39-63.

Heffron, J. F. "History of Glassmaking: Introduction to Machine Methods, Window Glass," *Glass Container*, Vol 6, 1926. pp 9-30.

Hendrickson, William F. "Complete History of the Manufacture of Window Glass Together with a Review of Labor Organizations, also Many Interesting and Instructive Sketches and Humorous Reminiscences Connected with the Trade," Pittsburgh, Pennsylvania, 1898.

Heuring, Jerry and Heuring, Elaine. Collectors Guide to E. C. Simmons Keen Kutter Cutlery Tools. Paducah KY: Collector Books, Schroeder Publishing Co., Inc., 2000.

Hudson, Paul J. "Glassmaking at Jamestown 1608 – 1609 and 1621 – 1624," *The Iron Worker* (reprint), Lynchburg Foundry Co., Div. of Woodward Iron Co., Jamestown Foundation, Jamestown Virginia, n.d.

Isenberg, Anita and Isenberg, Seymour. <u>How to Work in Stained Glass</u>. Radnor, Pennsylvania: Chilton Book Company, 1983.

Jaskowski, Thomas J., "How to Cut glass Correctly," *Glass Digest*, July 15, 1972.

Johnson, F. Neil. "The Psychology of Collecting." *Christies*, December 1985 - January 1986, p. 4.

Jones, Olive R. and Sullivan, Catherine. "The Parks Canada Glass Glossary for the Description of Containers, Tableware, Flat Glass, and Closurers," National Historic Parks and Sites Branch, Parks Canada, Ottawa, Ontario, 1985.

Keyes, Homer. "Early Window Glass," *Antiques*, Vol. 32, No. 2, 1937. pg 69.

Kimes, Arthur, W. and Kimes, Thomas A. <u>Directory of Glass Factories in the United States and Canada: Embracing Manufacturers of Pressed and Blown Ware, Specialties, Cut Glass and Tubing, Bottles and Hollowware, Window Glass, Polished Plate Glass, Wire, Opalescent, Fancy Figured, Rough and Ribbed, Glass Tile, Laminated, Glass Trade Associations, Workingmen's Associations</u>. Pittsburgh, Pennsylvania: Budget Publishing Co., 1930.

Kohlmaier, George. <u>Houses of Glass: A Nineteenth Century Building Type, A History of Greenhouses</u> (Translated by John C. Harvey). Cambridge Massachusetts: MIT Press, 1986.

Lawro, John K., Jr. "Fourth Time Proves to be a Charm for PPG Industries Founder," *U. S. Glass & Glazing*, Nov/Dec 1983. pp 44-48.

Lillich, Meridith Parsons. "Gothic Glaziers: Monks, Jews, Taxpayers, Bretons, Women," *Journal of Glass Studies*, Vol. 27, 1985. pp 72-92.

Louw, H. J. " The Origin of the Sash Window," *Architectural History*, Vol 26, 1983. pp 49-72.

Lowe, John. The Medieval English Glazier, a Brief Survey of the Origins of Glass-Painting and the Glazier's Craft from 1200 to 1500," Parts I & II, *The British Society of Master Glass Painters*, Vol. XIII, No. 2, 1960-1961. pp 425-432, pp 492-508.

MacLeish, Kenneth. "Legacy From the Age of Faith Chartres," *National Geographic*, Vol. 136, No. 6, December 1969. pp 857-882.

Marinelli, Janet. "Architectural Glass – and The Evolution of the Storefront." *The Old House Journal*, July/August 1988, pp 34-43.

Marks, Richard. <u>Window Glass, Craftsmen, Techniques, Products, English Medieval Industries</u>. London: Hambledon Press, 1991. pp 265-294.

Monro, William L. <u>Window Glass in the Making – Art – Craft – Business</u>. Pittsburgh, Pennsylvania: American Window Glass Co., 1926.

Moyer, David. "Window and Flat Glass for Historical Archaeologists: Bibliography," Iowa City, Iowa: University of Iowa, (Internet, February 2001).

Nugent, Robert. "Monce/Woodward Type Corkscrews," *The Quarterly Worm*, Canadian Corkscrew Collectors Club. n.d.

O'Leary, Fred. <u>Corkscrews</u>. Hong Kong: Schiffer Publishing Ltd, 1996.

Pacey, Anthony. "A History of Window Glass Manufacture in Canada," *Association for Preservation Technology Bulletin*, Vol 13, No. 3, 1981, pp 33-47.

Parkin, R. A. <u>The Window Glass Makers of St. Helens</u>. London: Society for Glass Technology, 2000.

Peddle, C. J. <u>Defects in Glass</u>. London: Glass Publications, Ltd., 1927.

Perry, Josephine. <u>America at Work: The Glass Industry</u>. New York: Longmans, Green & Co., 1945. pp 90-101.

Perry, Robert C. "The Float Process for Manufacturing Flat Glass." Proceedings of the 13th International Congress on Glass, 1983. Hamburg, Germany, July 1983. pp 254 – 259.

Peterson, Charles E (Editor). <u>Building Early America.</u> Mendham, New Jersey: The Astragal Press, 1976.

Pilkington, Alastair. "Flat Glass: Evolution and Revolution over 60 Years," *Glass Technology*, Vol 17, No. 5, 1976.

Pilkington, ACI, Ltd. <u>The Glass Ribbon: Development of the Australian Flat Glass Industry</u>. Melbourne, Australia: Pilkington ACI, Ltd., 1988.

Polak, Ada, <u>Glass – It's Tradition and It's Makers</u>. New York: G. P. Putnam's Sons, 1976.

Powell, Harry J. "Technological Handbooks – The Principles of Glass Making: Crown and Sheet Glass by Henry Chance; Together with Treaties on Plate Glass by H. G. Harris." London, England: George Bell & Sons, 1883. pp 122–131.

Richardson, Philip E. "A Phenomenal Impact." Reprinted from *Glass Digest*, April 1971.

Roger, Robert. "Tool Anatomy," The Gristmill, No. 137, Dec. 2009, a publication of The Mid-West Tool Collectors Assoc., pp 14-16.

Rosenhain, Walter. <u>Glass Manufacture</u>. London: Archibald Constable & Co, Ltd., 1903.

Roth, Ronald. "Windows and Window Glass in the United States before 1860," Unpublished paper, Columbia University, School of Architecture, Technology of Early American Building Course, Columbia University, 1971.

Schiffer, Peter, Schiffer, Nancy, and Schiffer, Herbert. <u>The Brass Book</u>. Exton, Pennsylvania: Schiffer Publishing Co., 1978.

Schofield, Matthew and Youssef, Nancy A. "Museum Looting Likely Well Executed Theft, Officials Say," Knight Ridder Newspapers, April 16, 2003.

Schuler, Fredric and Schuler, Lilli. <u>Glass Forming</u>. Philadelphia: Chilton Book Co., 1970.

Scoville, Warren C. <u>Revolution in Glassmaking – 1880-1920</u>. Cambridge, Massachusetts: Harvard University Press, 1948.
Switosz, Susan. "A Technical History of Late Nineteenth Century Windows in the United States," *Association for the Preservation of Technology Bulletin*, Vol. 17, No. 1 1985. pp 31-37.

Townsend, Ray. "Cow Knob Pincers," *Fine Tool Journal*, Winter 1993.

Turner, Ken., "Questions Recently Raised and Discussed by Three Tool Buffs," *Journal of the Hand Tool Preservation Association Of Australia*, Reprinted in *The Fine Tool Journal*, Vol. 44, No. 2, Summer 1994.

Turner, Ken., "Handy as a Pocket in a Shirt: Glass Cutter Combination Tools," *The Chronical of the Early American Industries Association,* Vol. 57, No. 3, September 2004.

Wilson, Weber H. "Old Glass – New Business, The Mystery of the Steel Wheel Cutter." *Glass Studio*, Portland Oregon, 1982, pp 23-24.

Whittock, et al. <u>The Complete Book of Trades – Glass – Maker.</u> London, 1837. (Reprinted in *Fine Tool Journal*, Vol. 40, No. 3, 1990-9

Catalogs

Arrowhead-Stained Glass – Tool and Supply, San Bernardino, California, 1996. pp 39-41.

Arthur A Crafts & Co. *Diamonds Used in Tools*, No. 22, Boston, Massachusetts: Earnshaw Press Corp., 1921.

Babcock, Hinds & Underwood. *General Catalog # 38*, Binghamton NY: The North American Press, ca 1938. pg 109.

Beals, McCarthy & Rogers, Inc. *Catalogue G*, Buffalo New York, 1940. pp C542, C549.

Belknap, W. B. & Co. *Catalog No. 29,* Louisville Kentucky, 1901. pg. 983.

Buck & Hickman, *Ltd. Illus. & Price List of American Tools*, London, 1902, (Reprint by Mid-West Tool Collectors Association, 1989). pg 499.

Catalogue No. 35, 1915 (Reprinted by The North Village Publishing Co., Lancaster MA, 1981). pp 148-152.

Ducomman Corp. *Catalog G*, Los Angeles California, 1926. pp 296, 439-440.

Edward Joy Co. *Catalog 74*, Syracuse New York, 1949. pg K112.

Establishment Technique Diamantaire. *Le Diamant Industriel*, Anvers, Beique, 1935, p. 12.

Fletcher-Terry Co. *Catalogs #630; #730, #800*, Bristol, Connecticut, n.d.

Fletcher-Terry Co. Catalog No. 226(1935) & No. 957, Forestville, Connecticut

Frothingham & Workman Ltd., Cat. Of General Hardware, pg 32, Montreal, 1907.

Goodell-Pratt Co., *No. 7*, (Reprint by College Press, South Lancaster, Mass.), 1977. p 170.

Goodell-Pratt Co., *No. 14*, 1920. pp 178-182.   No. 16, 1926. pp. 250-253.

Hibbard, Spencer, Bartlett & Co., 16-32 Lake St., Chicago, pg. 921

Lee's Wonderful Catalogue, Chicago, ca 1915.

Marples, William & Sons. Sheffield, England, 1897 (Winterthur Museum). pp 153-154.

Marples, William & Sons. *Tools for All Trades*, Sheffield, England, 1909. (Reprint by Mid-West Tool Collectors Club, 1979). pp 187-188.

Millers Falls Co. *1878 Catalog* (Reprint by Philip J. Whitby, 1992) pg 23.

Millers Falls Co. *1887 Catalog* (Reprint by Ken Roberts Publishing Co., Fitzwilliam New Hampshire). pp 39-40.

Millers Falls Co. *Catalog #35* (Reprint by The North Village Publishing Co., Lancaster Massachusetts, Oct 1981). pp 148-152.

Millers Falls Co. *Catalog #42*, (1938); Reprint by Mid-West Tool Collectors Club, 1999). pp 123-128, 218.

Montgomery Ward. *Catalogue #57, Glass Cutters*, 1895, pg 398.

Red Devil, Inc. *Catalogs #36, #36G*, Union, New Jersey, n.d.

Sears Roebuck & Co. *1902 Catalogue*. pp 530-531.

Silberschnitt 2000 Catalog, Josef Bohle Stiftung & Co., Haan. n.d.

Simmons Hardware Co., St. Louis Missouri, 1881.

Sinsz, Philip. *Glaziers' Diamonds, Price List*, Baltimore Maryland, ca 1876. (Winterthur Museum Library).

Smith & Hemenway Co., Inc. Green Book of "Red Devil" Tools. Irvington, NY (Eighth Edition), n.d. pgs 3-20.

Smith & Hemenway Co., Inc. *Illustrated Net Price List*, New York (Pre WWII).

Southwest Smelting & Refining Co. *Catalog 1065*, 1965. pp 84, 196.

The Diamond Drill Carbon Co. *Industrial Diamonds And Diamond Pointed Tools*, New York, New York, 1922.

Utica Drop Forge & Tool Co. *Catalog No. 28, Utica, Nippers, Pliers, Snips, Wrenches, Glass Cutters*, Utica, New York. pp 30, 31.

Waterman, J. M. *Catalogue No. 25, Tools and Factory Supplies*, (Reprint by Mid-west Tool Collectors Club, 1996). pp 232.

Weed and Company. *1925 Catalog*, Buffalo & Rochester, New York. pp 109-110.

Weed and Company. *Catalog 40*, Buffalo & Rochester, New York, 1939. pp 42, 298.

Weiss, Joh. and Son, Vienna, 1909. (Reprint 1980). pg 99.

Wilson, Hood & Co's., *"Annual Illustrated Catalogue of Photographic Requisites, Frames, Stereoscopes and views,"* Salesroom 822 Arch Street, Philadelphia, PA, October 1873, pg. 77

Wood, Vallance & Co, Hamilton, Ontario, Canada, 1906. pp 32.

INDEX

This is the index for the text pages 11 through 67.

The index for the glass cutters is given on pages 58 through 64.

NOTES

NOTES

NOTES

NOTES

NOTES

NOTES